W9-AEF-294

Latino Language and Literacy in Ethnolinguistic Chicago

Edited by

Marcia Farr

LAWRENCE ERLBAUM ASSOCIATES, PUBLISHERS

2005   Mahwah, New Jersey   London

Lawrence Erlbaum Associates, Inc., Publishers
10 Industrial Avenue
Mahwah, New Jersey 07430

Cover design by Kathryn Houghtaling Lacey
Cover photograph by Michael Maltz

Library of Congress Cataloging-in-Publication Data

Latino language and literacy in ethnolinguistic Chicago / edited by
   Marcia Farr.
          p. cm.
   Includes bibliographical references and index.
ISBN 0-8058-4347-7 (c : alk. paper)
ISBN 0-8058-4348-5 (pbk. : alk. paper)
      1. Anthropological linguistics—Illinois—Chicago. 2. Hispanic
   Americans—Illinois—Chicago—Languages.   I. Farr, Marcia.

P35.5.U6L38 2004
306.44—dc22   2004047232
                                                          CIP

Books published by Lawrence Erlbaum Associates are printed on acid-
free paper, and their bindings are chosen for strength and durability.

Printed in the United States of America
10 9 8 7 6 5 4 3 2 1

Contents

Preface

Marcia Farr

This book, along with its companion, *Ethnolinguistic Chicago: Language and Literacy in the City's Neighborhoods* (Farr, 2004), fills an important gap in research on Chicago and, more generally, on language use in globalized metropolitan areas. Although Chicago has been fairly well studied by scholars interested in ethnicity, including sociologists (Massey & Denton, 1993; Wilson, 1987) and historians (Holli & Jones 1977/1984/1995), few studies have focused on language and ethnicity in Chicago. This is so despite the well-known fact that Chicago, one of the most linguistically and ethnically diverse cities in the United States, often is cited as an archetypical American city. Certainly, Chicago is, and always has been, a city of immigrants (and migrants arriving from other parts of the United States). Moreover, language is unquestionably central to social identity because how we talk constructs for ourselves and others who we are.

The dearth of studies on Spanish-speaking populations in Chicago matches the overall lack of studies focusing on language and ethnicity in this city despite the fact that Chicago is a unique context for Spanish speakers, given its multicultural and multilingual history and the significant numbers of both Mexicans and Puerto Ricans in the city, as well as other Caribbean and Central and South American Spanish-speaking populations. Although Mexicans in the U.S. Southwest (Galindo & Gonzales, 1999;

González, 2001; Schecter & Bayley, 2002; Valdés, 1996) and Puerto Ricans in the Northeast (Urciuoli, 1996; Zentella, 1997) have been studied, neither of these populations has been much studied in the Midwest or Chicago until recently. Recent language-oriented studies of Mexicans and Puerto Ricans in Chicago (Cintron, 1997; Del Valle, 2002; Farr, forthcoming; and Guerra, 1998) grew out of the same overall research project, described in the following discussion.

Arriving in Chicago in August of 1982, I was fascinated by its mosaic of ethnic neighborhoods, although the often neat separation of populations into neighborhoods or community areas illustrated the results of segregation and racism as much as ethnic vitality. Discovering that sociologists in Chicago had provided abundant demographic profiles based on census data for each community area of the city in a periodically published *Local Community Fact Book* (Chicago Fact Book Consortium, 1995), I began to plan a research program investigating language use in local neighborhoods all over the metropolitan area that could rely on these demographic profiles. This program formed an important part of the Language, Literacy, and Rhetoric specialization in the Department of English at the University of Illinois at Chicago, where I taught from 1982 to 2002. My own research on language and literacy practices within transnational Mexican families in several community areas on the south side of the city is one part of this program (Farr, 1993; 1994a, 1994b, 1994c, 1998, 2000a, 2000b, forthcoming). Other contributions to the larger program were made by graduate students whose dissertations I directed. This volume, then, like its companion, contains many chapters by these former graduate students, many of whom have published books based on their dissertations (Cintron, 1997; Del Valle, 2002; Guerra, 1998; Lindquist, 2002; Mahiri, 1998; Moss, 2001; Nardini, 1999). This book, like its companion volume, however, also contains chapters by colleagues carrying out similar studies in Chicago.

Most of the chapters in this book are based on, or are compatible with, ethnographic studies of language as called for by Hymes (1974). Because an ethnographic perspective requires attention to local-level "insider" meanings rather than those imposed from the outside by researchers, the chapters as a whole provide a richly diverse set of portraits whose central themes emerged inductively from the research process and the communities themselves. Despite this diversity of themes, however, all the chapters nevertheless emphasize language use, both oral and written, in specific sociocultural contexts. Language use is explored for the way it constructs ethnic, class, gender, or other (e.g., religious or school) identi-

ties (see Introduction). As such, this volume should be of interest to anthropologists, sociologists, rhetoricians, linguists, historians, educators,
and educational researchers, as well as others whose concerns require an
understanding of "ground-level" phenomena among Spanish-speaking
populations relevant to contemporary social issues.

OVERVIEW

This book is structured into four parts. Part I contains an Introduction to the
volume by myself and Elias Domínguez Barajas. Part II of the book contains
studies carried out Within the Family Circle. These studies, based in home
settings, focus either on ways of speaking (Farr on direct speech among ranchero Mexicans and Domínguez Barajas on Mexican proverb use) or on literacy practices (Del Valle on contrasting literacy practices in two Puerto
Rican families). Part III comprises chapters that explore either oral language
use or literacy practices in school contexts. Two chapters investigate oral
language use in a dual-immersion school (Olmedo on children as language
mediators and Potowski on identity investments in the use of Spanish or
English), and two others investigate literacy, either in Internet chat rooms
(Cohen on identity development among high school girls via the Internet) or
in college composition classes (Spicer-Escalante on rhetoric and identity in
college essays). Part IV of the book includes studies based in Community
Spaces in various neighborhoods. Two chapters in this part of the book focus on adults in community literacy groups (Hurtig on Mexican immigrant
mothers as writers and Colomb on Mexican immigrant mothers reading literature in Spanish). Two other chapters deal with religious literacy (Farr on
a Mexican Charismatic Catholic woman and Gelb on a Puerto Rican
Santería practitioner and store owner). Finally, two chapters are based in
work settings (Gelb again and Herrick on intraethnic communication in a
factory). Finally, an Afterword by Ralph Cintron situates these studies within
the larger context of Latinos in Chicago.

ACKNOWLEDGMENTS

I acknowledge a number of people whose support made this book possible. I thank the Spencer Foundation for providing me with Mentor Network
funds that enabled many graduate students to carry out their dissertation
studies. I especially thank the late Rebecca Barr, who supported my work

over the years not only administratively, but also substantively, and Catherine Lacey, who creatively directed the Mentor Network during the years that I participated. I also thank Robert Bayley for his thoughtful and supportive review of the manuscript.

It seems equally appropriate to thank my wonderful graduate students over the years, from whom I have learned so much. Together we made a reality of research plans hatched in innumerable conversations during graduate seminars and over dissertations and coauthored articles (Farr & Domínguez Barajas, in press; Farr & Guerra, 1995; Farr & Nardini, 1996; Farr & Reynolds, 2004; Guerra & Farr, 2002). I am particularly grateful to Rachel Reynolds, who not only contributed a chapter to the earlier volume and coauthored the Introduction in that volume, but also provided invaluable help as a research assistant for the Ethnolinguistic Chicago Project, which included tirelessly seeking potential contributors to fill in population gaps and communicating with authors during the initial development of the two manuscripts. I am similarly most grateful to JuYoung Song, my graduate assistant at Ohio State University, who speeded both this and the earlier volume to press by spending countless hours on myriad details, including subject and author indices.

I also thank my editor at Erlbaum, Naomi Silverman (who grew up in Chicago), for her vision of the importance of this project. Finally, *mil gracias a mi familia,* especially to my husband Michael Maltz and my daughter Julianna Whiteman, for providing the kind of emotional support that can come only from a loving family.

REFERENCES

Chicago Fact Book Consortium. (1995). *Local Community Fact Book: Chicago Metropolitan Area, 1990.* Chicago: University of Illinois.

Cintron, R. (1997). *Angels' town:* Chero *ways, gang life, and rhetorics of the everyday.* Boston: Beacon Press.

Del Valle, T. (2002). *Written literacy features of three Puerto Rican family networks in Chicago: An ethnographic study.* New York: Edwin Mellen Press.

Farr, M. (1993). Essayist literacy and other verbal performances. *Written Communication, 10*(1), 4–38.

Farr, M. (1994a). *En los dos idiomas*: Literacy practices among *mexicano* families in Chicago. In B. Moss (Ed.), *Literacy across communities* (pp. 1–47). Cresskill, NJ: Hampton Press.

Farr, M. (1994b). Biliteracy in the home: Practices among *mexicano* families in Chicago. In D. Spener (Ed.), *Adult biliteracy in the United States* (pp. 89–110). McHenry, IL, Washington, DC: Delta Systems and Center for Applied Linguistics.

Farr, M. (1994c). *Echando relajo*: Verbal art and gender among *mexicanas* in Chicago. In M. Bucholtz, A. C. Liang, L. A. Sutton, & C. Hines (Eds.), *Cultural performances: Proceedings of the third women and language conference, April 8–10, 1994* (pp. 168–186). Berkeley: University of California Press.

Farr, M. (1998). *El relajo como microfiesta*. In H. Pérez (Ed.), *Mexico en fiesta*. Zamora, Michoacán, Mexico: El Colegio de Michoacán.

Farr, M. (2000a). *¡A mí no me manda nadie!* Individualism and identity in Mexican *ranchero* speech. In V. Pagliai & M. Farr (Eds.), special issue of *Pragmatics* (*10*:1): Language, performance and identity (pp. 61–85).

Farr, M. (2000b). Literacy and religion: Reading, writing, and gender among Mexican women in Chicago. In P. Griffin, J. K. Peyton, W. Wolfram, & R. Fasold (Eds.), *Language in action: New studies of language in society* (pp. 139–154). Cresskill, NJ: Hampton Press.

Farr, M. (Ed.). (2004). *Ethnolinguistic Chicago: Language and literacy in the city's neighborhoods*. Mahwah, NJ: Lawrence Erlbaum Associates.

Farr, M. (forthcoming). *Rancheros* in Chicagoacán: Ways of Speaking and identity in a Mexican transnational community. Austin: University of Texas Press.

Farr, M., & Nardini, G. (1996). Essayist literacy and sociolinguistic difference. In E. White, W. Lutz, & S. Kamusikiri (Eds.), *The politics and policies of assessment in writing* (pp. 108–119). New York: Modern Language Association.

Farr, M., & Domínguez Barajas, E. (in press). Mexicans in Chicago: Language, identity, and education. In A. C. Zentella (Ed.), *Language socialization in Latin@ families, communities, and schools: Anthro-political perspectives*. New York: Teachers College Press.

Farr, M., & Guerra, J. (1995). Literacy in the community: A study of *mexicano* families in Chicago, special issue of *Discourse Processes* (*19*:1): Literacy among Latinos (pp. 7–19).

Farr, M., & Reynolds, R. (2004). Introduction: Language and identity in a global city. In M. Farr (Ed.), *Ethnolinguistic Chicago: Language and literacy in the city's neighborhoods*. Mahwah, NJ: Lawrence Erlbaum Associates.

Galindo, D. L. & Gonzales, M. D. (Eds.). (1999). *Speaking Chicana: Voice, power, and identity*. Tucson: University of Arizona Press.

González, N. (2001). *I am my language: Discourses of women and children in the borderlands*. Tucson: University of Arizona Press.

Guerra, J. (1998). *Close to home: Oral and literate practices in a transnational Mexicano community*. New York: Teachers College Press.

Guerra, J., & Farr, M. (2002). Writing on the margins: Spiritual and autobiographic discourse among *mexicanas* in Chicago. In G. Hull & K. Schultz (Eds.), *School's out! Literacy at work and in the community*. New York: Teachers College Press.

Holli, M. G., & Jones, P. d'A. (Eds.). (1977/1984/1995). *Ethnic Chicago: A multicultural portrait*. Grand Rapids, MI: Eerdman's.

Hymes, D. (1974). *Sociolinguistics: An ethnographic approach*. Philadelphia: University of Pennsylvania Press.

Lindquist, J. (2002). *A place to stand: Politics and persuasion in a working-class bar*. Oxford: Oxford University Press.

Mahiri, J. (1998). *Shooting for excellence: African American and youth culture in new century schools*. New York, Urbana, IL: Teachers College Press and NCTE.

Massey, D. S., & Denton, N. A. (1993). *American apartheid: Segregation and the making of the underclass*. Cambridge: Harvard University Press.

Moss, B. (2001). *A community text arises: Literate texts and literacy traditions in African American churches*. Cresskill, NJ: Hampton Press.

Nardini, G. (1999). Che Bella Figura! *The power of performance in an Italian ladies' club in Chicago*. Albany, NY: SUNY Albany Press.

Schecter, S., & Bayley, R. (2002). *Language as cultural practice:* Mexicanos en el norte. Mahwah, NJ: Lawrence Erlbaum Associates.

Urciuoli, B. (1996). *Exposing prejudice: Puerto Rican experiences of language, race, and class*. Boulder, CO: Westview Press.

Valdés, G. (1996). Con respeto: *Bridging the distances between culturally diverse families and schools: An ethnographic portrait*. New York: Teachers College Press.

Wilson, W. J. (1987). *The truly disadvantaged: The inner city, the underclass, and public policy*. Chicago: University of Chicago Press.

Zentella, A. C. (1997). *Growing up bilingual*. Oxford: Blackwell.

INTRODUCTION

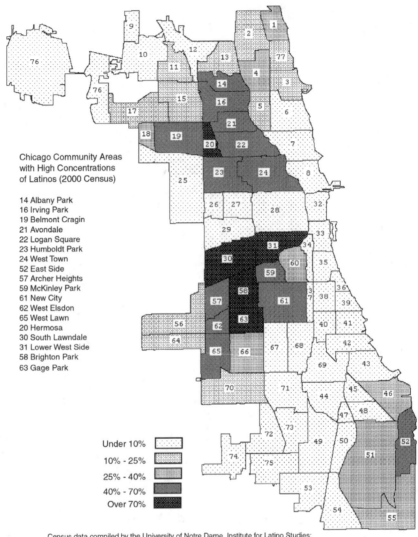

Chicago Community Areas with High Concentrations of Latinos (2000 Census)

14 Albany Park
16 Irving Park
19 Belmont Cragin
21 Avondale
22 Logan Square
23 Humboldt Park
24 West Town
52 East Side
57 Archer Heights
59 McKinley Park
61 New City
62 West Elsdon
65 West Lawn
20 Hermosa
30 South Lawndale
31 Lower West Side
58 Brighton Park
63 Gage Park

Under 10%
10% - 25%
25% - 40%
40% - 70%
Over 70%

Census data compiled by the University of Notre Dame, Institute for Latino Studies; map provided by the University of Illinois at Chicago, Chicago Area Geographic Information Study (CAGIS).

1

Latinos and Diversity in a Global City: Language and Identity at Home, School, Church, and Work[1]

Marcia Farr
Ohio State University

Elías Domínguez Barajas
Texas A & M University

Chicago is a global city. That is, its economy is linked globally to other world cities in an increasingly interconnected, globalized world. Globalization as a process, however, can mean many things: a push for free market economic practice across the globe, the spread of American cultural images through media and products, or a growing sense of Western responsibility for economic and political effects on people and the environment worldwide. Some treat "global" as a sociological term expressing the blended or hybrid nature of people, goods and cultural practices that has resulted from the dissolution of traditional boundaries in terms of gender, nationality, ethnicity, and politics. Yet globalization also appears to be realigning peoples into new ethnic, class, and religious groups. This volume focuses on Spanish-speaking peoples as ethnic groups in the United States, specifically Chicago. The companion volume to this book, *Ethnolinguistic Chicago: Language and Literacy in the City's Neighborhoods* (Farr, 2004), focused on a variety of other populations in this context.

3

This second volume is devoted to questions concerning Latino language use and its interface with identity construction in the context of the global city that Chicago has come to be. Chicago, in fact, now has the third largest Latino population in the country (U.S. Census Bureau, PHC-T-6, Table 4), and within this Latino population, those of Mexican and Puerto Rican descent are the most heavily represented. The prominence of these two groups, however, should not mask the presence of varied other Latino groups in Chicago (listed here according to the size of their population in the city) (2000 U.S. Census, QT-P9, Chicago city): Guatemalan, Ecuadorian, Cuban, Colombian, Spaniard, Salvadoran, Honduran, Peruvian, Dominican, Argentinean, Nicaraguan, Chilean, Panamanian, Costa Rican, Venezuelan, Bolivian, Uruguayan, and Paraguayan.

Despite of the variety of Latino groups in Chicago, little, if any, research has investigated their social, linguistic, and cultural differences. This volume, then, serves as a precursor to the type of research that can be done in relation to other Latino groups not included in this book. Such an effort may very likely expand the scope of what currently is considered the Latino experience in the United States by showing diverse conceptions and perceptions of ethnicity in relation to point of origin, migratory experience and transnational ties, educational attainment, economic class mobility, identity formation and group solidarity, and numerous other domains impacted by the social background of Latinos in the United States. In brief, research investigating the daily activities of the diverse Latino groups in a city such as Chicago may elucidate social practices that can inform a deeper understanding of such complex global phenomena as transnational migration, socioeconomic ties that span generations and national boundaries, and the confluence of systems of meanings some scholars have identified as the formation of hybrid cultures (García Canclini, 1989; Rowe & Schelling, 1991) .

Despite these potential implications for understanding globalization, it is important to emphasize that the chapters in this book, like those in the earlier companion volume, are not specifically about globalization. Yet the worldwide processes that comprise globalization provide a backdrop, a context, within which the people represented in these chapters live their lives. More than globalization, however, much of the work in this book is embedded in transnationalism (see especially the chapters by Farr and Domínguez Barajas). Globalization often is contrasted with transnationalism. For some, the latter is a subordinate term, both chronologically and structurally (Kearney, 1995). That is, nation building is seen as preceding the transfer of goods and people across borders, so transnationalism is presumed to be a historical by-product of globalization. Transnationalism is seen as a small piece of global processes because deterritorialization involves "new kinds of political actors" among whom the econcmic and political intersections between ethnic groups and the state are recast (Kotkin, 1993, p. 5; Sassen, 1998). Thus people become "deterritorialized" as they move and work across nation–state borders. With worldwide air travel, telecommunications, and ever-more-rapid flows of information, the deterritorialization of national and ethnic groups becomes even more intense. That is, the movement of people across the globe increases (Giddens, 2000; Harvey, 1990). These large-scale migrations have been prefigured in Chicago, a city of immigrants (Holli & Jones, 1977/1995), making it a good site for studying the predicaments of deterritorialization (Basch, Glick-Schiller, & Szanton-Bpanc, 1994; Holtzman, 2000).

The chapters in this volume take as their subject of inquiry the ethnolinguistic practices of Spanish-speaking people who experience deterritorialization as ethnic (im)migrant groups. Although theories of globalization assert that the new world order involves the erosion of ethnic group identities, the two population groups represented in this volume (Mexicans and Puerto Ricans) experience deeply felt ethnic affiliations. Those in the older generations struggle less with hybrid identities brought on by the demands of a new cultural context than with adaptive responses to the trials of life as immigrants whose practices and self-perceptions are outside the dominant mainstream (see, for example, Hurtig's chapter on Mexican immigrant women's storytelling practices). For the younger generations, especially those who experience schooling in Chicago, ethnic formation may include hybrid identities and the development of new ones that replace the old (see, for example, Cohen's chapter on Mexican American high school girls). In either case, despite the movement toward a "global monoculture" implied and sometimes seen in studies of free market capital and international media marketing, another frequent response to globalization is the entrenchment of highly marked ethnic, class, and religious identities. The eloquent and complex ways in which people of varying class, ethnic, and racial groups (including "mainstream" groups) express their multiple identities in Chicago is a testament to how much more we need to study class and ethnic formation on the ground.

"Borderlands" studies focusing on the interface between peoples as they move across borders provide another relevant context in which to view the work in this volume. Extrapolating from the 2,000-mile U.S.–Mexican border, scholars now use the term "border" metaphorically: A border exists wherever differing "social practices and cultural beliefs" confront each other "in a contemporary global context" (Alvarez, 1995, p. 448). Staudt and Spener (1998) viewed the border "as an ongoing dialectical process which generates multiple borderland spaces" (p. 2), some of which are quite distant from actual international boundaries. Rouse (1991), studying a transnational community located in Redwood City, California, and Aguililla, Michoacán, Mexico, saw "a proliferation of border zones" and the eruption of "miniature borders" throughout both Mexico and the United States (Rouse, 1991, p. 17).

Chicago evidences these multiple miniature borders both in contemporary and historical terms. It could be argued, in fact, that Chicago has always been a global city with transnational populations (Holli & Jones, 1977/1995) confronting each other, creating "miniature borders" all over the city. Certainly, Chicago is known for its cultural and linguistic diversity, its mosaic of ethnic neighborhoods, but just as clearly, this is a scene that now has become characteristic of many more U.S. regions and cities.

The chapters presented in this volume thus ask and begin to answer the following questions: How did Mexicans and Puerto Ricans come to live in Chicago? Have they maintained their "traditional" identities, the Spanish language (and its varying dialects), and their own ways of speaking? Alternatively, have they recreated or transformed these social and cultural practices, including linguistic ones (see, for example, Potowski, 2004)? How does language use change from one generation to the next? Why does it change across the generations, and what does this mean as the demographic and linguistic face of the United States continues to "Latinize"? How do social, economic, and political relations "back home" appear in Latino discourse in Chicago? How do Latino populations adapt their linguistic practices to aspects of globalization, including the worldwide women's rights movement, the increasing use of English as a global language, and the English-only movement in the United States? Does the increasing compression of space and time through communication and travel technology affect language maintenance and group identity? What impact do different communicative practices have on people in multicultural work spaces, or in our public and private schools, and how can we be more intelligent about the issues that disrupt that communication and cross-cultural understanding?

By looking at the history, linguistic practices, and educational experiences of the Mexican and Puerto Rican populations in Chicago, this volume begins to characterize important details about Latino populations in

Chicago and the social dynamics at play within these groups, between them, and in relation to other non-Latino populations. The predominance of the Mexican-origin population among Latinos in Chicago, for example, does not simply mean that they are more numerous than any other Latino group. The numeric predominance of this group often translates into a default representation of Latinos in Chicago by the media. The local Latino television stations, affiliated with the national Spanish-language networks, and radio stations, for example, often orient their programming (e.g., newscasts, variety shows, telenovelas, weekend sports, commercials) primarily to a Mexican-origin audience. Local Spanish-language newspapers also clearly reflect this orientation by focusing frequently on Mexico when covering international news, sports, and entertainment.

Because the Mexican-origin population constitutes 70% of the Latinos in Chicago, this media orientation may be understandable. Nevertheless, the Puerto Rican–origin population, which constitutes 15% of the overall Latino population, and the variety of Latinos groups already mentioned certainly add another dimension to the general conception of a Latino identity. The two numerically dominant groups, for example, have historically shared essential characteristics of their migratory experience and immigrant orientation (i.e., view of initial migration as temporary), but have faced and continue to face different degrees of resistance to their integration into the mainstream.

MEXICANS IN CHICAGO

The Mexican-origin community has a history in Chicago that dates to the early 1900s. According to Padilla (1985, p. 22), "The Mexican revolution of 1910 accelerated the large-scale immigration of Mexicans to the United States," primarily to the Southwest. A cohort of these immigrants followed the path of employment "to farmwork in the Midwest, or to the packing-houses of Kansas City, or to railroad track labor in various cities, and finally to the industrial areas of Chicago" (Año Nuevo-Kerr, 1976; quoted in Padilla, 1985, p. 22), whereas another cohort consisted of immigrants "directly recruited by employers and shipped to Chicago via railroad cars" (Padilla, 1985, p. 23).

The recruitment of immigrant labor quickly turned to forced repatriation of entire Mexican families—despite the status of many as U.S. citizens and legal immigrants—during the Great Depression (Padilla, 1985, p. 26). This was a severe blow to the coherence of an emerging Mexican American community in Chicago. Nevertheless, the employment pendulum swung again in favor of Mexican laborers as the onset of World War II brought about labor shortages in the agricultural and industrial sectors. To counteract those shortages, the United States and Mexico signed an international labor agreement in 1942. The Bracero Program, as the agreement is commonly known, guaranteed the supply of Mexican laborers until 1964. Thus, sanctioned and unsanctioned migration, coupled with migrant influxes from the southwestern states, increased the numbers of the Mexican-origin population in Chicago for the first half of the 20th century. The dramatic rise of this segment of the population in the past four decades followed a similar pattern despite the demise of the Bracero Program. Chain migration supported by social networks (see Farr's chapters in this volume), the adaptability of Mexican laborers to changing labor demands (e.g., a shift from industrial labor to entry level service and light manufacturing positions), and factors contributing to the potential for upward mobility (e.g., improved educational opportunities, less residential segregation, and evolving perceptions of race and ethnicity) may prove to be a boon for the continued rise of the Mexican-origin population in Chicago.

PUERTO RICANS IN CHICAGO

Like their Mexican counterparts, Puerto Rican immigrants came to Chicago in search of economic betterment. But unlike the preceding Mexican immigration, the Puerto Rican migration was spurred by U.S. transformation of the island's economy. With the end of the Spanish American War, the United States, ignoring the status of independent state granted to the island by Spain in 1897, assumed control over Puerto Rico.

> After the takeover of Puerto Rico, the new "colonial masters" transformed Puerto Rico's multicrop agricultural economy into a technologically based, single cash-crop industry; several decades later it was changed again and built around a factory system which was capital—and not people—oriented. Because of their nature, these economic changes failed to provide jobs for an ever-increasing population, resulting, in turn, in a large-scale uprooting and forced exile of hundreds of thousands of people from their native land because of urgent economic needs. (Padilla, 1987, p. 6)

Three decades after the United States took control of Puerto Rico, large-scale migration to the mainland's Northeast became an established reality, and by the 1940s the migration extended to other parts of the United States. Puerto Rican migration to Chicago began in the late 1940s and reached its peak in the 1960s (Padilla, 1985, p. 38). Unfortunately, this influx of laborers came at a time when manufacturing jobs were waning as the result of technological advances, and for Puerto Rican immigrants this meant being relegated to "nonindustrial, poorly paid, menial, dead-end jobs" (Padilla, 1985, p. 43).

In addition to such low-income employment, the Puerto Rican community faced harsher housing discrimination than other Latino groups after reaching a critical mass in Chicago (i.e., becoming a noticeable presence). Massey and Denton (1989) have traced a pattern of housing discrimination directed at Puerto Ricans that persisted from 1960 to 1980 in many U.S. metropolitan areas. As in many of the major U.S. cities Massey and Denton examined, Puerto Ricans in Chicago were highly segregated from Anglos during this period, whereas Mexicans and Cubans were considerably less so.

Yet, unlike the Puerto Ricans in other cities, those in Chicago also were highly segregated from African Americans and Asians. This suggests that the residential areas of Puerto Ricans in Chicago remained highly insular as late as 20 years ago, which speaks to the persistence of a solidified ethnic identity based on the isolation of the ethnic neighborhood (Padilla, 1985, p. 52). Massey and Denton's (1993) more recent study of Chicago, however, has indicated that although Mexicans are more integrated into White neighborhoods than Puerto Ricans, the higher rates of segregation for the latter are accounted for by the fact that "Black" Puerto Ricans are more segregated than "White" Puerto Ricans and live closer to African Americans.

Such differences in integration into the mainstream are vexing given the similarities in the migration histories of Mexicans and Puerto Ricans in Chicago. The major differences are clearly that the Puerto Rican community started growing after World War II, whereas the Mexican community established itself 40 years earlier, and that Puerto Ricans were free to come and go to the United States as a result of their citizenship status, whereas Mexicans were not. These differences, however, seem to dissipate given the more recent history of the two groups. By the 1970s, for example, the two groups coalesced under the emergence of a Latino ethnic identity in response to discrimination against Spanish-speaking minorities and their marginalization in Chicago (Padilla, 1985). In addition, the *va y ven* (to and fro) pattern of migration noted among Puerto Ricans (Padilla, 1987, pp.

69–70) also is now commonplace for many Mexicans in the United States (Farr, 2000, forthcoming; Rouse, 1991, 1992).

The continuous movement to and from the homeland, however, takes a psychological toll because it involves "repeated ruptures and renewal of ties, dismantlings and reconstructions of familial and communal networks in old and new settings" (Rodriguez, Sánchez-Korrol, & Alers, 1984, p. 2), and this toll presumably intensifies with the length of a sojourn in a given community. Despite this toll, the reluctance to sever ties with the homeland appears to characterize the first generations of Mexican and Puerto Rican migrants to Chicago. The desire to maintain such connections may be renewed continuously by the enduring flow of Mexican immigration to Chicago. The same may not be true for the Puerto Rican community in Chicago, given that its population increments in no way suggest the massive migration influxes that are the hallmark of the Mexican population in the past 40 years. Moreover, the Puerto Rican population in the city actually decreased between 1990 and 2000 according to census figures.

Whether other Latino groups maintain an orientation to transnational ties similar to that of the Mexicans in Chicago is another subject for future research. There may be a variety of reasons why other Latino groups do not have such an orientation. In the Southwest, for example, the lack of transnational ties among some, but not all, people of Mexican origin is the result of their nonmigratory history vis-á-vis the United States. These people of Mexican origin did not come to the United States; rather, the United States came to them via the 1848 Treaty of Hidalgo. The U.S. annexation of their homeland was the direct result of that treaty, and this left them, in effect, without a Mexican homeland to which they could return. Although it could be assumed that Puerto Rico's historical lack of national sovereignty may lead Puerto Ricans to adopt a similar perspective, this does not seem to be the case. Moreover, the distance between the island and mainland as well as the prominence of Spanish in the national and cultural heritage may continue to challenge this assumption.

To address internal differences within what is now the largest minority population in the country, research into the formation of an ethnic identity and the role language plays in it is crucial. The maintenance of Spanish as a primary and as a heritage language (see the chapter by Potowski) reflects more than linguistic ability for the Latino groups included in this volume and those whose voice is yet to be recorded. The complex bond between language and culture and the values that are forged, transmitted, and maintained through culturally embedded language use, directs any research involving Latino groups in general to consider the prominence and the impact of linguistic issues in their communities.

NON-ENGLISH TONGUES AND THE UNITED STATES

Despite a multilingual and multicultural history that dates back to the founding of the country, the United States has had an ambivalent relationship with cultural diversity in general, and with non-English languages (and nonstandard English dialects) in particular. Although nation building has been entwined with insistence on the official status and dominance of English, non-English languages nevertheless have been used regularly throughout U.S. history in government agencies, courts, newspapers, schools, and other public contexts (Ferguson & Heath, 1981). Current national debates over such diversity invoke and repeat earlier debates in the second half of the 19th century over German language and culture, and in the early 20th century over heavy migration from Eastern and Southern Europe. Some claim that the fervor in recent decades against non-English languages and their speakers is intensified by the experience of language loss by earlier generations of European immigrants, especially by the numerous German speakers in this country up until World War I (Baron, 1990; Judd, 2004), after which time German was quickly dropped by its speakers and in school curricula. Yet because of the broad range of ethnic groups and their relative numeric strengths in the history of Chicago, conflict over linguistic and cultural diversity has been more muted there than elsewhere in the United States, at least in recent years. Consequently, Chicago presents an interesting contrast to states such as California, Arizona, or Florida, where such conflict is more publicly salient. The recent debate over bilingual education in Chicago, for example, questioned the length, not the existence, of bilingual programs in the public schools (official policy now limits bilingual education to 3 years). Moreover, as of 1998, Chicago had 10 dual-language schools (see the chapter by Potowski).

Chicago has a long history of economic vitality and diversity, and it remains an attractive destination for people ready to work in a variety of industries. For example, Lithuanians, Poles, and African Americans came to work in the stockyards at the turn of the 20th century, and Mexicans arrived by the thousands in the 1920s to sustain the iron and steelworks located in south Chicago. Today, highly educated Africans, South Asians, and East Asians are vital to the western suburban technology corridor, and other ethnic groups are part of the long trajectory in which Irish, Germans, Greeks, Poles, Italians, and others have contributed to the city built by immigrants.

If the numerous ethnic groups in Chicago's historic neighborhoods have created a somewhat more tolerant ambience toward diversity, or at least a more realistic acceptance of it, they also have anticipated the cultural and linguistic diversity now evident across the entire United States, especially, but not entirely, in urban areas. As noted earlier, an increasingly globalized world economy has fomented migratory streams all over the world (Rosenau, 1997; Sassen, 1998; Wallerstein, 1974). In this hemisphere, the United States is the primary destination for these migrant labor forces, followed by Canada and Argentina (United Nations, 1988). Atlanta and other southern locales, for example, now host a substantial number of Mexicans, disrupting the traditional Black–White racial dichotomy (Murphy, Blanchard, & Hill, 1999). Such populations increase not only because of economic "push–pull" factors (e.g., the wage differential between Mexico and the United States, pressures from U.S. businesses for minimum wage workers), but also through the reconstituting, over time, of virtually entire villages in the United States (Farr, 2000, forthcoming; Rouse, 1992).

A number of the chapters in this volume arose from ground level studies within social networks. Transnational social networks (i.e., groups of family and friends both "back home" and at the destination site) facilitate the communication that feeds transnational movement and growth. Migration to the United States probably has always proceeded through family networks and transnational communication. For example, the massive German migrations throughout the 19th century were stimulated at least in part by family networks, letters, emigration handbooks, and newspapers (Kamhoefner, Helbich, & Sommer, 1991; Trommler & McVeigh, 1985).

Furthermore, once settled in American neighborhoods, families rely on social networks to carry out ethnic socialization of youth born in the United States, with some groups maintaining a sense of heritage and a network of cross-border social ties that last for several generations—a phenomenon that we are only beginning to understand (Constantakos & Spiridakis, 1997; Gans, 1999, p. 1304). Our understanding of ethnic formation or "ethnification" is something that may change as jet travel and telecommunications facilitate constant contact between ethnic groups and their home countries. Indeed, the fact that transnational mechanisms are markedly more extensive now than a century ago may cause significant changes in how ethnic formation comes about in the United States (Friedman, 1999). Even so, the contemporary diversity in the United States has its origins in U.S. history, although apparently unique in pace and heterogeneity, with people now coming from all over the world. The studies in this volume explore this diversity through a focus on language use among ethnic Mexicans and Puerto Ricans in a city that is both diverse and archetypical of the larger United States.

As already noted, this volume is the second of a pair. The first volume (Farr, 2004) focused on ethnolinguistic variation among groups with origins in Europe, the Middle East, Africa, and Asia. Because of the recent intense growth in Spanish-speaking populations, this volume focuses entirely on Mexicans and Puerto Ricans, the two largest Latino groups in Chicago and in the United States. The studies in both volumes together contribute to our understanding of ethnolinguistic diversity by showing how it is woven into the fabric of daily life in Chicago, both historically and currently, and how it is an inevitable aspect of human life. Although important work has documented the history of various ethnic Chicago enclaves (Holli & Jones, 1977/1995), and although sociologists have abundantly studied numerous "community areas" (Chicago Fact Book Consortium, 1995), the role of language, either oral or written, in these diverse communities has not yet received systematic attention. Garcia and Fishman's (1997) *The Multilingual Apple: Languages in New York City* is a notable exception, although it does not address variation within languages, only between them. Although the field of sociolinguistics has long studied regional and social dialect variation (see, for example, recent work on African American Vernacular English in Baugh,1999; Baugh, 2000; Rickford, 1999; Rickford & Rickford, 2000), ethnographic approaches to this kind of variation have been fewer (but see Zentella, 1997). These two volumes begin to address this lacuna by presenting "slices of language life" involving both multilingualism and within-language variation in specific home and community settings.

LANGUAGE AND IDENTITY

González (2001) has eloquently portrayed the intensely felt tie between language, emotion, and identity in her study of Mexican-origin women and children in Arizona's "borderlands." These families were headed by either native-born or immigrant parents, who primarily used English and Spanish, respectively. Although González noted the use of Chicano English, most studies of language and identity do not make such differentiations, but define language as an entire "language" such as Spanish or English (e.g., Fishman, 1997). In this sense, variation in language use refers to bi- or multilingualism, or the use of more than one language in a society or group. Language diversity can be viewed more broadly, however, by attending to variation both across and within languages. Even monolingual Americans routinely use one or more varieties of English. That is, they may speak a more standard variety of American English, acquired perhaps in school, along with a regional, class, or ethnic dialect. For example, many African Americans use African American Vernacular English in intimate contexts and standard English in public (Rickford & Rickford, 2000). Similarly, bilingual Americans may use, for example, Spanish in intimate contexts and English in public, but what kind of Spanish, and what kind of English? Zentella (1997) explored both kinds of linguistic diversity among Puerto Rican children in New York, who to varying degrees speak nonstandard and standard varieties of both Spanish and English across the various contexts of their lives.

In Chicago as well, people may speak both Spanish and English, and in some cases multiple varieties of these languages. Variation in Spanish there includes nationality (e.g., Mexican, Puerto Rican, Cuban), as well as rural and urban varieties within these nationalities. Depending on the extent of cross-national interaction for particular speakers, these varieties are sometimes blended in use. Spanish speakers who also know English may code switch between Spanish and English (common among *tejanos*, Mexican Americans from Texas), or borrow English words and phrases and incorporate them into Spanish sentences (common among Mexicans in Chicago). For example, someone may say *"Estamos watcheando TV"* (We are watching TV), incorporating the English word "watch" into a sentence using Spanish grammar. Although such "Spanglish" often is denigrated by Spanish and English speakers alike, in fact such language mixing is common in multilingual situations. For example, both the Swedes (Isaacson, 2004) and the Greeks (Koliussi, 2004) in Chicago created and used "Swinglish" and "Greeklish," and no doubt many other groups have created other mixed languages that parallel and prefigure contemporary Spanglish.

In addition to language mixing and language or dialect choice, stylistic dimensions of language use, or "ways of speaking" (Hymes, 1974b), along with practices involving written language, or literacy, are important indices of identity. Indeed, more attention is paid in this volume to the uses or functions of language, oral and written, in the daily life of Latinos than to the structural or formal characteristics (e.g., pronunciation or syntactic patterns) of the language varieties that they speak. Shifting between and among these language varieties, whether from Spanish to English or from one dialect of Spanish or English to another, often is about social attachment, signifying group membership and solidarity. As Tabouret-Keller (1997) has pointed out, our language use creates our social identities, whether that language use involves one or more varieties of one language, code switching between two languages, or the creation of new language varieties by combining elements from various languages or dialects.

In many chapters of this volume, the language used by the people under study is a nonstandard variety of Spanish. In fact, standard languages have rarely been used by immigrants in Chicago (Farr, 2004). For example, Lithuanian (Markelis, 2004) and Swedish (Isaacson, 2004) immigrants to Chicago spoke nonstandard dialects of their respective languages at home and learned standard varieties of their home languages in Chicago to communicate with each other and to share standardized ethnic institutions such as newspapers and schools. These processes have implications for the shift toward the codifying of ethnic culture through culturally sensitive school curricula using standardized language varieties. Yet the ways that immigration by Mexicans, Puerto Ricans, and other Spanish-speaking groups have contributed to the formation of a popular Chicago Spanish have not yet been studied, although they certainly suggest an interesting and policy-relevant topic for research.

Upon arrival in Chicago, many immigrants feel pressured to attain competence in new languages or dialects to be accepted amicably by neighbors, employers, or customers. For some, this may mean learning Mexican Spanish or African American English. Immigrant speakers of English are acutely aware that native-born Americans label them by their imperfect use of the standard, and that even if they speak the most "proper" (i.e., grammatically standard) English, English spoken with a nonnative "accent" (i.e., pronunciation) instantly evokes their ethnic difference. Ironically, for many immigrants, the non-English language they speak is similarly denigrated in their "home countries" as nonstandard. For example, immigrants from the Mexican countryside often are derided for their *español rancheriado* (rural ranch Spanish) both by urban elite Mexicans and by Spanish teachers in Chicago. It is not only the surface features of language use, such as nonstandard or nonnative grammar and pronunciation, that mark immigrants as different. Favored genres and other ways of speaking also distinguish culture groups, and many immigrants use culturally specific rhetorical genres such as Mexican *relajo* (Farr, 1994c, 1998), or proverbs (see the chapter by Domínguez Barajas), as a performance of identity and solidarity. That culture-specific literacy and oral traditions often are at odds with dominant standards also is a source of trouble for immigrant children who must adapt to standard English forms and uses in school. For example, the ideology embedded in essayist modes of writing (notably the five-paragraph composition-class essay and other genres promoting an "objective" tone that removes the personal voice of the author) often runs counter to the linguistic expectations of Spanish-speaking students' home cultures (Farr, 1993).

In the same way that we identify ourselves and others by the way we speak, we also use other markers. Language is only one means of identity differentiation in semiotic systems that include neighborhood boundaries, clothing, types of houses, and decor, even the kinesthetics of walking down the street. Given the persistence of identity differentiation, we can assume that semiotic markers "place" people in terms of various identities, and, moreover, that language is a central means of placement, whether that placement is generated from inside the group or imposed from the outside. Certainly, language, in addition to other markers, has delineated White and non-White groups in the United States. African American English, Spanglish, and Spanish-accented English are clear examples of this. Recently developed conceptualizations of language ideology explicitly link beliefs about language, including both vernacular and standard varieties, to broader sociocultural and political processes (Kroskrity, 2000; Philips, 1998; Schieffelin, Woolard, & Kroskrity, 1998). As Woolard (1998) noted, language ideologies are never about language alone, but also about such notions as personhood and group identity vis-á-vis others.

The construction of group identities based on language ideologies has proven to have far-reaching ramifications. In the context of schooling, for example, linguistic prejudice has found its way into institutional and public discourse particularly concerning ethnolinguistic minority students. Terms such as "at risk," "remedial," and "culturally deprived" have been applied disproportionately to minority students and their linguistic backgrounds. Because aspirations toward a monolingual and homogeneous society militate, by definition, against linguistic—and, by extension, cultural—diversity, linguistic minority students, particularly Latino students, continue to suffer the results of English chauvinism by being rushed through bilingual programs that encourage the replacement of the home language (or L1) in favor of the target language (i.e., English). This often is exacerbated by the segregation of students into inferior schools and their erroneous classification as learning disabled (Halcón, 2001).

Such marginalization is based on prejudice toward linguistic diversity and a bias favoring the primacy of English in the classroom and society at large. To counteract such deeply seated biases, however, various scholars (Banks, 1991; Barrera, 1992; Delpit, 1995; Farr, 1993, 1994a, 1994b; Farr & Daniels, 1986; Farr & Guerra, 1995; Gutiérrez, 1992; Reyes, 1992; Valdés, 1996) have proposed that awareness of cultural differences is of the essence in contemporary classrooms. This is particularly crucial for students whose L1 is not English because meaning-making in the classroom almost invariably involves language, and language, in turn, is embedded in particular cultural practices and beliefs.

One example of how an attitudinal change can enhance pedagogical approaches to linguistically diverse student populations is the valuing of these students' "funds of knowledge" (i.e., what is known, learned, and valued at home), with the goal of developing continuity between home and school knowledge bases (Moll & Greenburg, 1990). One important factor in establishing such continuity between home and school is the recognition of students' L1 as an asset rather than a hindrance because the knowledge of more than one linguistic system suggests the potential of expanded linguistic repertoires. This perspective is supported by Jiménez (1996, p. 106), who showed that highly competent bilingual readers are characterized by their cognitive flexibility in managing differing textual cues, and warned that "less successful Latino readers may be closing the door of a vast warehouse of potential knowledge by not accessing information gained via their dominant language." Appreciation of a non-English L1 is by no means automatic (see the chapter by Potowski) because young people grow up in a society that does not appreciate bilingualism, and young people, in particular, must grapple with the social and psychological toll that comes with the forging of a linguistic identity.

The issue goes beyond bilingualism because language differences also emerge within languages. Thus similar language ideologies differentiate speakers of nonstandard dialects such as African American Vernacular English (Rickford & Rickford, 2000), or other varieties of nonstandard English (Wolfram, Adger, & Christian, 1999), and nonstandard varieties of Spanish as well (Zentella, 1997). Beliefs about particular languages, or varieties of these languages, organize relations among groups of people and define "us," as opposed to "them," in terms of specific moral, aesthetic, and other qualities that place people into status hierarchies (see Herrick's chapter on such status differences between standard urban Mexican

Spanish and nonstandard rural Mexican Spanish—the denigrated *español rranchereado,* or "ranch Spanish").

In addition to ethnic identities, language also expresses and constructs class identities. Thus, vernacular varieties of both English and Spanish identify speakers as working class. Class is not as salient in Chicago as ethnicity, but it is omnipresent even when more implicit than explicit (Cho & Miller, 2004; Lindquist, 2004). Gender also is an inextricable part of language use, and, like class and ethnicity, it is not only expressed but also constructed linguistically (Morgan, 2004). Women's favored genres often differ from men's, and for many migrant groups, gender roles change over the generations with the move from, for example, a traditional agrarian context to a modern urban one. Such changes, of course, also involve what is considered appropriate behavior for women, including linguistic behavior. Tensions that arise over such changes, as well as their (sometime) resolution, are evident in the language practices of both women and men (Farr, forthcoming).

When the topics or the contexts of talk are specifically about class or about ethnic or gender identity, these are, according to Susan Philip's (2000) discussion of an idea developed by Stuart Hall (1986), "key sites" for these highly marked linguistic practices. Philips used the notion of "site" to highlight those situations in which ideology is most punctiliously brought up and instantiated, hot spots in which "powerful ideological work" is being performed (Philips, 2000, pp. 232–233). For example, the choice of a language, or a particular dialect of a language, may signify an entirely different ideology and identity in the new immigrant context, as opposed to "back home" (see the chapter by Cohen in this volume). Such key sites are methodologically distinct from the ways in which linguists use the term "context" (i.e., an analytical unit based on real-time speech and real gatherings of people). In the chapters of this volume, the investigators have chosen either contexts of verbal performance (oral or written) or group-specific ways of speaking because they are key sites of identity construction, or reconstruction in terms of class, ethnicity, or gender. These include public spaces and institutions such as school classrooms (Olmedo and Potowski), a university composition course (Spicer-Escalante), Internet chat rooms (Cohen), a religious store (Gelb), and a factory (Herrick), as well as informal, intimate, and private spaces and genres such as kitchens and living rooms (Farr, Domínguez Barajas, & Del Valle), or proverbs (Domínguez Barajas), and religious discourse (Farr).

Sometimes what is meaningful in key sites, then, is signaled by the forms and uses of speech, and not by overt topics of discussion. Language thus expresses and constructs identities either implicitly through the choice of dialects, standards, or culturally marked rhetorical styles and genres, or explicitly through overt ideological talk that groups use to define themselves. Because such issues are best studied ethnographically, the work presented in this volume was undertaken within the framework of the ethnography of communication (Hymes, 1974a). The chapters that are not explicitly ethnographies of communication nevertheless are compatible with this framework. In the next sections, we discuss the characteristics of this framework and its methodology.

METHODOLOGY

Chicago provides an abundance of fertile natural settings in which identities are linguistically constructed. Because so much identity formation emerges in felt contrasts with others (Barth, 1968; Cohen, 1978), the diversity of the city and its multiple "miniature borders" makes it particularly productive for research on this topic. The chapters in this book, and in its companion volume, rely on the assets of the city as well as methodological resources in a variety of ways.

First, because insider or "emic" understandings of various communities are fundamental to valid understandings of the ways identities are constructed in language, most of the chapters rely on ethnographic methods and perspectives in their research. That is, they rely on participant observation, "deep listening," a holistic focus, and (implicitly or explicitly) a comparative sense. Deep familiarity with the communities studied and a careful attention to local, not just researcher-generated, meanings, then, characterize all the work. Moreover, the discourse analysis used in many chapters documents the ways people use language to construct, or to reconstruct, social and cultural realities, including their identities.

Second, because all these chapters are centered on language, either in its spoken or written mode, material samples of language have been gathered for analysis. Oral language has been tape-recorded (with the permission of the speakers), selected, transcribed, and studied in different ways, and written language has been collected and analyzed. Both modes of language have been explored for local meanings through oral interviews. All these instances of language in use, however, even augmented by the understandings generated from interviews, would be incomplete without broader (and deeper) ethnographic understandings of the larger contexts in which they occurred naturally. In what follows, we selectively present key concepts developed within an ethnographic approach to the study of language that contribute to a comprehensive understanding of language, both oral and written, and its constitutive role in social and cultural life. These concepts are used differentially across the chapters.

THE ETHNOGRAPHY OF LANGUAGE

Dell Hymes' call four decades ago for an anthropology of language was intended to fill an important gap: the study of language grounded equally in linguistic and cultural realities. He argued that the study of culturally situated language was falling into a gap between disciplines. On one hand, linguistics focused on cognitive rather than social aspects of language, and, on the other, anthropology, although carried out through language, often through a language nonnative to the researcher, ignored language almost entirely. His original conceptualization of the ethnography of communication (Hymes, 1964) spawned the ethnography of literacy (Street, 1984, 1993; Szwed, 1981). Much work following this latter tradition has been stimulated by social concerns regarding inequities in education and literacy. Important as such studies are, they unfortunately have increasingly ignored the relevance of oral language practices to these concerns, although understandings of literacy are deepened and enriched by attention to oral practices among populations learning or using literacy (Farr, 1993), and despite serious critique of an orality—literacy dichotomy (Collins & Blot, 2003; Street, 1984). Although Heath's (1983) seminal research relied centrally on oral language patterns to illuminate educational and literacy issues, much other work has not been equally grounded in a deep understanding of language as the base from which literacy springs. Notable exceptions in this regard are Boyarin (1992), Besnier (1995), and Finnegan (1988). The studies in this book, and in its companion volume, attempt to redress this imbalance by attending to both modes of language use in the daily life of Chicagoans.

Attention to both oral and written language has flourished in the field that Hymes, Gumperz, and others invigorated, which has become the field of linguistic anthropology (Bauman & Sherzer, 1974/1989; Duranti, 1997, 2001; Gumperz, 1982a, 1982b). This work has demonstrated how language, carefully studied, can illuminate other aspects of social, cultural, and political life. Sherzer, quoting Boas (1911), pointed out that "language patterns are unconscious and provide access to unconscious cultural patterning otherwise inaccessible to researchers" (Sherzer, 1987, p. 295). Some aspects of social and cultural life cannot be understood simply by asking people about them, as Briggs (1986) has shown, although this is how most social science, including much ethnography, proceeds. Briggs argued that we need to treat the interview, instead, as a communicative event, a social practice negotiated by interviewer and informant. This methodological insight has far-reaching implications for researchers concerned with cultural and linguistic variation (e.g., Cho & Miller, 2004).

Sherzer (1987) showed how discourse, which he defined as language use, oral or written, brief (like a greeting) or lengthy (like a novel or oral narrative), is "the nexus, the actual and concrete expression of the language-culture-society relationship" (p. 296). Thus through discourse analysis researchers can illuminate social and cultural patterns. Discourse, then, is constitutive because both culture and language are created, recreated, and changed through it. Furthermore, particular kinds of discourse are especially fertile for this:

> It is especially in verbally artistic discourse such as poetry, magic, verbal dueling, and political rhetoric that the potentials and resources provided by grammar, as well as cultural meanings and symbols, are exploited to the fullest and the essence of language-culture relationships becomes salient. (Sherzer, 1987, p. 296)

Poetics and Performance

The study of verbal art, or ethnopoetics, as developed by Hymes (1975, 1981), Bauman (1977/1984, 1986), Bauman and Briggs (1990), Tedlock (1983), Sherzer (1987, 1990), Tannen (1989), and others has shown how cultural insights can be revealed by close examination of people's verbal performances. Verbal performance can occur in formal, scheduled, public events (e.g., church sermons), or it can emerge spontaneously in informal, everyday conversation (e.g., story and joke telling). Bauman (1977/1984) set out the empirically observable characteristics of verbal performance, which he saw as the thread that ties together various artistic genres in a unified conception of verbal, or spoken, art, as a way of speaking:

1. There is a "focus on the message for its own sake" (Jakobson, 1960, p. 356). That is, the form of the message is important beyond the need for communication (i.e., it has poetic qualities). Various linguistic

devices can be used to accomplish this, a central one being *parallelism*, the "empirical linguistic criterion of the poetic function" (Jakobson, 1960, p. 358). Parallelism involves repetition, sometimes with variation, of semantic, syntactic, or phonological (including intonational) structures, and seems to be a fundamental, possibly universal characteristic of verbal art. More recent work shows how oral narrative can be considered a kind of poetry in that spoken lines from speeches and personal narratives are organized in terms of verses, stanzas, and scenes (Hymes, 2002; Ochs & Capps, 2001).

2. Performance reframes "usual" or ordinary language use that often fulfills a referential function in which words carry "literal" meaning. That is, hearers are signaled that words are to be understood in some special sense. Linguistic devices that signal a performance frame include, but are not limited to, a change in code (language), figurative language (e.g., metaphors), parallelism, and paralinguistic features (e.g., pitch contour, rate of speaking, loudness) (Tedlock, 1983).

3. Performance is the authoritative display of communicative competence by a "performer" that is evaluated by an "audience." That is, there is a shared assumption among participants that hearers will judge those who verbally perform as good (or not-so-good) storytellers, jokers, preachers, and the like.

4. Performance is marked as available for "the enhancement of experience" in the present moment. That is, there is a "special intensity" on the part of the audience (e.g., bodies and faces turn toward the performer and other talking ceases).

Performance, then, makes language highly "noticeable." That is, linguistic devices used to make a particular stretch of language a "performance" (e.g., the telling of a joke or story) also make a "text" stand out from surrounding speech (see Gelb's chapter on a woman's story of her own initiation as a *santera*). Language that "stands out" in this way facilitates its own critical examination (Bauman & Briggs, 1990). Thus, performances of verbal art are not just interesting aesthetically, but are key sites for the creation, recreation, and transformation of culture and society. Farr (1994c, forthcoming), for example, showed how Mexican women, using a way of speaking they call *echando relajo* (joking around), challenge traditional gender roles through performances of verbal art. These verbal poetics, performed in all-female contexts, serve to build support for and affirm the kinds of changes they are making in their now-transnational lives. Such "play frames ... provide settings in which speech and society can be questioned and transformed" (Bauman & Briggs, 1990, p. 63), and thus have ramifications for the reconfiguration of social relations.

Genre

The concept of genre has been central in the consideration of the interrelations between language and culture (Briggs & Bauman, 1992; Hanks, 2000; Philips, 1987) and in studies of verbal art. A persistent aspect of work on genre revolves around the question of how to define the concept itself. The key defining features are characteristics of form (i.e., how the writing or speech is organized in jokes, stories, plays, letters, and the like). Equally important as defining features, however, are shared frameworks for reception and interpretation, as well as the larger sociocultural context in which concrete instances of genres are actualized (Hanks, 2000), as illustrated in Spicer-Escalante's chapter on the essays written in Spanish by Mexicans, Mexican Americans, and non-Mexican Americans. Genre, as used in the studies in this volume, then, involves not only aspects of form, but also the dimensions of function and reception, that is, how audience and performer (whether that performer utters a Mexican proverb, sings a Puerto Rican *rosario,* or writes an essay in college) come together in a specific context to share the meaning of a performance and to accomplish a particular function. Thus, local understandings of concrete instances of genres rely not only on form, but also on the broader context in which they occur and the specific functions these instances serve. A final aspect of work on genre concerns the organization of genres themselves within particular local communities and the ideological implications of this organization. For example, the association of genre and gender, when genres are organized hierarchically (e.g., associating the low-ranked genre of gossip with women), affirms the hierarchy of genders in social relations.

Although, as Briggs and Bauman observe, genre has been associated with order for quite some time in Western thought, in actuality, the organization of genres, and their boundaries in real discourse, are much less ordered and neat. Communities differ in the extent to which their genres are organized, and the "messy underside of people's speech" (Briggs & Bauman, 1992, p. 140) is more the rule than the exception. This "messiness" in people's real speech is attributable to the lack of fixed and discrete (empirical) boundaries of genres. Instead, genres sometimes overlap one another, and often are found in complex shapes in which some genres "absorb and digest" other genres (Bakhtin, 1986; Briggs & Bauman, 1992, p. 145). The novels read by Mexican immigrant mothers in Colomb's chapter illustrate this complexity, as do the letters written to God by the Mexican woman described in Farr's chapter on literacy and religion. Thus, genres do not always occur as discrete texts in daily life. That is, they are not fixed, timeless structures. Rather, they are general frameworks, or sets of expectations, according to which people generate and interpret discourse for specific social, cultural, and political ends (see Domínguez Barajas' chapter on the uses of Mexican proverbs). Speakers and hearers then draw on these general sets of expectations as they organize discursive life. In turn, daily discourse can create, recreate, or change generic expectations. That is, the use of genres is a two-way street: shared understandings of culturally specific genres organize our linguistic and social life, but these same genres change through use and time, just as they are used either to maintain or to change aspects of our social order. When the performance of artful verbal genres, themselves already highly changeable by nature, is conjoined to the ways that immigrants negotiate their way through multiple cultures and culture change across generations, these forms become even richer sites for experimentation with language and identity.

OVERVIEW OF CHAPTERS

This section provides an overview of the chapters in this volume, with a special focus on the ways in which they use the themes, concepts, and issues reviewed in this Introduction. All of the chapters deal with language and identity, whether that identity involves nationality (Domínguez Barajas, Cohen, Spicer-Escalante, and Potowski), status or class (Farr on *rancheros* and Herrick), religion (Farr on religion and Gelb), or gender (Farr on religion and Cohen). In addition to these usual aspects of identity, two chapters focus on literacy-specific identities. Hurtig's chapter shows women developing an identity as writers, and Colomb's chapter shows women becoming readers. Many chapters evoke aspects of transnationalism, globalization, or both (Farr on *rancheros*, Domínguez Barajas, Spicer-Escalante, Hurtig, Colomb, and Herrick). In terms of language itself, some chapters focus on oral genres and the performance of verbal art (Farr on *rancheros*, Domínguez Barajas, Del Valle, and Gelb). Two chapters focus on bilingualism in dual-language classrooms (Olmedo and Potowski), and three focus on the overlapping of orality and literacy (Del Valle, Hurtig, and Gelb).

This volume, then, presents research on language use among a wide variety of Mexicans and Puerto Ricans in Chicago. Most of the chapters (Farr, Domínguez Barajas, Cohen, Spicer-Escalante, Hurtig, Colomb, Farr, and Herrick) focus entirely on Mexicans, perhaps reflecting the demographic dominance of Mexicans in Chicago. Two other chapters focus entirely on Puerto Ricans, however (Del Valle and Gelb), and two more chapters focus on mixed populations of Mexicans and Puerto Ricans (and non-Latino children) in dual language classrooms (Olmedo and Potowski). As a whole, the chapters in this volume span a wide age range and are situated in a variety of public and private settings. The three chapters of part II are situated within families, with two of them (those by Farr and Domínguez Barajas) describing Mexican social networks and one of them (by Del Valle) describing Puerto Rican social networks. These three chapters include entire families and thus all ages.

The four chapters in part III are set in school contexts, the first two (by Olmedo and Potowski) in dual-language elementary classrooms. Olmedo reveals the importance of peer interaction and learning, as children help each other with "bilingual echoes" that translate from one language to another when such translation facilitates understanding and thus language development. Potowski complements this focus by showing how Spanish and English actually are used by the children and for what functions, concluding that Spanish may be serving a more limited range of functions in this setting than teachers assume, especially for boys. Cohen's chapter then moves to a focus on high school girls and their Internet use at home, illustrating how such literacy practices are inextricably a part of identity development. Spicer-Escalante moves on to a college setting, analyzing the writing in Spanish and English of Mexican American college students, whose distinctive rhetoric distinguishes them from both Mexican and non-Latino American writers.

Finally, the chapters in part IV follow Spanish speakers into a variety of other public spaces. Hurtig's chapter explores how a group of adult women in a community writing and publishing workshop use storytelling to construct their immigrant experiences, and Colomb relates the development of similar adult women as readers of literature in a family literacy program. Although both of these literacy programs are physically situated in public schools, they are distinct from the classroom and school-based activities in the rest of their buildings. The remaining chapters in part IV treat religion and work, one of them combining these two contexts. Farr demonstrates the critical literacy abilities of a woman intensely involved in reading and writing activities as a Catholic Charismatic, and Gelb illustrates the verbally artistic narration of a woman's account of her own initiation into *Santería,* the synthetic, originally Cuban religion that combines West African Yoruba saints with Catholic ones. This chapter is situated in both a religious context and a work setting because this woman is the owner of a small shop in which she both sells religious items and provides spiritual counsel. The last chapter of this section, and the book, focuses entirely on a work setting. In this last chapter, Herrick illuminates within-nationality (class) differences in a dispute over the translation of a booklet in a plastics factory with predominantly Mexican labor, cautioning us that as we develop cross-cultural understandings, we must take care not to allow them to harden into monolithic generalizations about particular nationalities or ethnic groups.

A final note is warranted. As with the earlier companion volume, there are important populations in Chicago not covered in this volume. We would have liked to include studies of language use among Cubans, Guatemalans, Dominicans, and other Latin American and/or Spanish-speaking populations, but despite a diligent search, were unable to locate any. Although Mexicans and Puerto Ricans are by far the largest groups of Latinos in the United States and in Chicago, studies on these two populations cannot represent all the Latino or Spanish-speaking groups in Chicago. Moreover, not all Latinos in Chicago can even be presumed to speak (only) Spanish. We have heard of children from Mexico assigned to bilingual education classes in the city although they do not speak Spanish, but rather an indigenous language such as *Purhépecha* (the Tarascan language of Michoacán, Mexico). Despite these gaps, it is our hope that this volume and its companion will stimulate more such work, and that future volumes can broaden our understandings of oral and written language in a wider variety of populations, whatever language(s) or dialects they speak.

REFERENCES

Alvarez, R. (1995). The Mexican–U.S. border: The making of an anthropology of borderlands. *Annual Review of Anthropology, 24,* 447–470.

Año Nuevo-Kerr, L. (1976). *The Chicano experience in Chicago, 1920–1970.* Unpublished Ph.D. dissertation, University of Illinois, Chicago.

Bakhtin, M. M. (1986). *Speech genres and other late essays.* Austin: University of Texas Press.

Banks, J. A. (1991). *Teaching strategies for ethnic studies.* Boston: Allyn & Bacon.

Baron, D. (1990). *The English-only question: An official language for Americans?* New Haven: Yale University Press.

Barrera, R. B. (1992). The cultural gap in literature-based literacy instruction. *Education and Urban Society, 24*(2), 227–243.

Barth, F. (1968). *Ethnic groups and boundaries: The social organization of culture difference.* Boston: Little, Brown and Company.

Basch, L., Glick-Schiller, N., & Szanton-Blanc, C. (1994). *Nations unbound: Transnational projects, postcolonial predicaments, and deterritorialized nation-states.* Langhorne, PA: Gordon & Breach Science Publishers.

Baugh, J. (1999). *Out of the mouths of slaves: African American language and educational malpractice.* Austin: University of Texas Press.

Baugh, J. (2000). *Beyond ebonics: Linguistic pride and racial prejudice.* New York: Oxford.

Bauman, R. (1977/1984). *Verbal art as performance.* Prospect Heights, IL: Waveland.

Bauman, R. (1986). *Story, performance, event: Contextual studies of oral narrative.* Cambridge, England: Cambridge University Press.

Bauman, R., & Briggs, C. (1990). Poetics and performance as critical perspectives on language and social life. *Annual Review of Anthropology, 19,* 59–88.

Bauman, R., & Sherzer, J. (Eds.). (1974/1989). *Explorations in the ethnography of speaking.* Cambridge, England: Cambridge University Press.

Besnier, N. (1995). *Literacy, emotion, and authority: Reading and writing on a Polynesian atoll.* Cambridge, England: Cambridge University Press.

Boas, F. (1911). *Introduction: Handbook of American Indian languages* (BAE-B 40, Part I). Washington, DC: Smithsonian Institution.

Boyarin, J. (Ed.). (1992). *The ethnography of reading.* Berkeley: University of California Press.

Briggs, C. (1986). *Learning how to ask: A sociolinguistic appraisal of the role of the interview in social science research.* Cambridge, England: Cambridge University Press.

Briggs, C., & Bauman, R. (1992). Genre, intertextuality, and social power. *Journal of Linguistic Anthropology, 2*(2), 131–172.

Chicago Fact Book Consortium. (1995). *Local community fact book: Chicago metropolitan area 1990.* Chicago: University of Illinois at Chicago.

Cho, G., & Miller, P. (2004). Personal storytelling: Working-class and middle-class mothers in comparative perspective. In M. Farr (Ed.), *Ethnolinguistic Chicago: Language and literacy in the city's neighborhoods* (pp. 79–102). Mahwah, NJ: Lawrence Erlbaum Associates.

Cohen, R. (1978). Ethnicity: Problem and focus in anthropology. *Annual Review of Anthropology, 7,* 379–403.

Collins, J., & Blot, R. (2003). *Literacy and literacies: Texts, power, and identity.* Cambridge, England: Cambridge University Press.

Constantakos, C., & Spiridakis, J. (1997). Greek in New York. In O. Garcia & J. A. Fishman (Eds.), *The multilingual apple: Languages in New York City* (pp. 143–166). Berlin: Mouton de Gruyter.

Delpit, L. (1995). *Other people's children: Cultural conflict in the classroom.* New York: New Press.

Duranti, A. (1997). *Linguistic anthropology.* Cambridge, England: Cambridge University Press.

Duranti, A. (2001). *Linguistic anthropology: A reader.* Oxford: Blackwell.

Farr, M. (1993). Essayist literacy and other verbal performances. *Written Communication, 10*(1), 4–38.

Farr, M. (1994a). *Language, literacy, and gender: Oral traditions and literacy practices among Mexican immigrant families.* Proposal to the Spencer Foundation.

Farr, M. (1994b). En los dos idiomas: Literacy practices among Chicago mexicanos. In B. J. Moss (Ed.), *Literacy across communities* (pp. 9–47). Cresskill, NJ: Hampton Press.

Farr, M. (1994c). *Echando relajo:* Verbal art and gender among mexicanas in Chicago. In M. Bucholtz, A. C. Liang, L. A. Sutton, & C. Hines (Eds.), *Cultural performances* (pp. 168–186). Proceedings of the third women and language conference, April 8–10, 1994. Berkeley: University of California Press.

Farr, M. (1998). *El relajo como microfiesta.* In H. Pérez (Ed.), *Mexico en fiesta* (pp. 457–470). Zamora, Michoacán, Mexico: El Colegio de Michoacán.

Farr, M. (2000). *¡A mí no me manda nadie!* Individualism and identity in Mexican *ranchero* speech. In V. Pagliai & M. Farr (Eds.), special issue of *Pragmatics, 10*(1), 61–85 on Language, Performance and Identity.

Farr, M. (Ed.). (2004). *Ethnolinguistic Chicago: Language and literacy in the city's neighborhoods.* Mahwah, NJ: Lawrence Erlbaum Associates.

Farr, M. (forthcoming). *Rancheros in Chicagoacán: Ways of speaking and identity in a Mexican transnational community.* Austin: University of Texas Press.

Farr, M., & Daniels, H. (1986). *Language diversity and writing instruction.* Urbana, IL: ERIC Clearinghouse on Reading and Communication Skills.

Farr, M., & Guerra, J. C. (1995). Literacy in the community: A study of *mexicano* families in Chicago. *Discourse Processes, 19*(1), 7–19.

Ferguson, C., & Heath, S. B. (Eds.). (1981). *Language in the USA.* Cambridge, England: Cambridge University Press.

Finnegan, R. (1988). *Literacy and orality: Studies in the technology of communication.* Oxford: Blackwell.

Fishman, J. (1997). Ethnicity and language: The view from within. In F. Coulmas (Ed.), *The handbook of sociolinguistics* (pp. 327–343) Oxford: Blackwell.

Friedman, J. (1999). Indigenous struggles and the discreet charm of the bourgeoisie. *Journal of World Systems Research, 5*(2), 391–411.

Gans, H. (1999). Filling in some holes: Six areas of needed immigrant research. *American Behavioral Scientist, 42*(9), 1302–1313.

García Canclini, N. (1989). *Hybrid cultures: Strategies for entering and leaving modernity.* Minneapolis: University of Minnesota Press.

Garcia, O., & Fishman, J. A. (1997). *The multilingual apple: Languages in New York City.* Berlin: Mouton de Gruyter.

Giddens, A. (2000). *Runaway world: How globalization is reshaping our life.* New York: Routledge.

González, N. (2001). *I am my language: Discourse of women and children in the borderlands.* Tucson: University of Arizona Press.

Guerra, J. (1998). *Close to home: Oral and literate practices in a transnational Mexicano community.* New York: Columbia Teachers College.

Gumperz, J. (Ed.). (1982a). *Language and social identity.* Cambridge, England: Cambridge University Press.

Gumperz, J. (1982b). *Discourse strategies.* Cambridge, England: Cambridge University Press.

Gutiérrez, K. D. (1992). A comparison of instructional contexts in writing process classrooms with Latino children. *Education and Urban Society, 24,* 244–262.

Halcón, J. C. (2001). Mainstream ideology and literacy instruction for Spanish speaking children. In M. L. Reyes & J. C. Halcón (Eds.), *The best for our children: Critical perspectives on literacy for Latino children* (pp. 65–77). New York: Teacher's College Press.

Hall, S. (1981). Cultural studies: Two paradigms. In T. Bennett, G. Martin, C. Mercer, & J. Woollacott (Eds.), *Culture, ideology, and social process.* London: The Open University and BT Baseford Ltd.

Hanks, W. F. (2000). *Intertexts: Writings on language, utterance, and context.* Boulder: Rowman and Littlefield.

Harvey, D. (1990). *The condition of postmodernity.* Oxford: Blackwell.

Heath, S. B. (1983). *Ways with words: Language, life, and work in communities and classrooms.* Cambridge, England: Cambridge University Press.

Holli, M. G., & Jones, P. d'A , J. (Eds.). (1977/1995). *Ethnic Chicago.* Grand Rapids, MI: Eerdmans.

Holtzman, J. (2000). *Nuer journeys, Nuer lives: Sudanese refugees in Minnesota.* Boston: Allyn & Bacon.

Hymes, D. (1964). Introduction: Toward ethnographies of communication. In J. Gumperz & D. Hymes (Eds.), The ethnography of communication (Part 2). *American Anthropologist, 66*(6).

Hymes, D. (1974a). *Foundations in sociolinguistics: An ethnographic approach.* Philadelphia: University of Pennsylvania Press.

Hymes, D. (1974b). Ways of speaking. In R. Bauman & J. Sherzer (Eds), *Explorations in the ethnography of speaking* (pp. 433–451). New York: Cambridge University Press.

Hymes, D. (1975). Breakthrough into performance. In D. Ben Amos & K. Goldstein (Eds.), *Folklore: Performance and communication* (pp. 11–74). The Hague: Mouton.

Hymes, D. (1981). *"In vain I tried to tell you": Essays in native American ethnopoetics.* Philadelphia: University of Pennsylvania Press.

Hymes, D. (2002, May). Problems of translation, *Anthropology News, 43*(5), 23.

Isaacson, C. (2004). They didn't forget their Swedish: Class markers in the Swedish-American community. In M. Farr (Ed.), *Ethnolinguistic Chicago: Language and literacy in the city's neighborhoods* (pp.223–250). Mahwah, NJ: Lawrence Erlbaum Associates.

Jakobson, R. (1960). Closing statement: Linguistics and poetics. In T. Sebeok (Ed.), *Style in language* (pp. 350–377). New York: John Wiley.

Jiménez, R. T. (1996). The reading strategies of bilingual Latino/a students who are successful English readers: Opportunities and obstacles. *Reading Research Quarterly, 31,* 90–112.

Judd, E. (2004). Language policy in Illinois: Past and present. In M. Farr (Ed.), *Ethnolinguistic Chicago: Language and literacy in the city's neighborhoods* (pp. 33–49). Mahwah, NJ: Lawrence Erlbaum Associates.

Kamhoefner, W. D., Helbich, W., & Sommer, U. (1991). *News from the land of freedom: German immigrants write home.* Ithaca, NY: Cornell University Press.

Kearney, M. (1995). The local and the global: The anthropology of globalization and transnationalism. *Annual Review of Anthropology, 24,* 547–565.

Koliussi, L. (2004). Identity construction in discourse: Gender tensions among Greek Americans in Chicago. In M. Farr (Ed.), *Ethnolinguistic Chicago: Language and literacy in the city's neighborhoods* (pp.103–136). Mahwah, NJ: Lawrence Erlbaum Associates.

Kotkin, J. (1993). *Tribes: How race, religion and identity determine success in the new global economy*. New York: Random House.

Kroskrity, P. (Ed.). (2000). *Regimes of language*. Santa Fe, NM: School of American Research Press.

Lindquist, J. (2004). Class identity and the politics of dissent: The culture of argument in a Chicago neighborhood bar. In M. Farr (Ed.), *Ethnolinguistic Chicago: Language and literacy in the city's neighborhoods* (pp. 295–320). Mahwah, NJ: Lawrence Erlbaum Associates.

Markelis, D. (2004). Lithuanian and English language use among early twentieth century Lithuanian immigrants in Chicago. In M. Farr (Ed.), *Ethnolinguistic Chicago: Language and literacy in the city's neighborhoods* (pp. 275–294). Mahwah, NJ: Lawrence Erlbaum Associates.

Massey, D. S., & Denton, N. A. (1989). Residential segregation of Mexicans, Puerto Ricans, and Cubans in selected U.S. metropolitan areas. *Sociology and Social Research, 73*(2), 73–83.

Massey, D. S. & Denton, N. A. (1993). *American apartheid: Segregation and the making of the underclass*. Cambridge, MA: Harvard University Press.

Moll, L. E., & Greenburg, J. B. (1990). Creating zones of possibilities: Combining social contexts for instruction. In L. E. Moll (Ed.), *Vygotsky and education* (pp. 319–348). New York: Cambridge University Press.

Morgan, M. (2004). Signifying laughter and the subtleties of loud talking: Memory and meaning in African American women's discourse. In M. Farr (Ed.), *Ethnolinguistic Chicago: Language and literacy in the city's neighborhoods* (pp. 51–78). Mahwah, NJ: Lawrence Erlbaum Associates.

Murphy, A. D., Blanchard, C., & Hill, J. (Eds.). (1999). *Latino workers in the contemporary south*. Athens: University of Georgia Press.

Ochs, E., & Capps, L. (2001). *Living narrative: Creating lives in everyday storytelling*. Cambridge, MA: Harvard University Press.

Padilla, F. M. (1985). *Latino ethnic consciousness: The case of Mexican Americans and Puerto Ricans in Chicago*. Notre Dame, IN: University of Notre Dame Press.

Padilla, F. M. (1987). *Puerto Rican Chicago*. Notre Dame, IN: University of Notre Dame Press.

Philips, S. (1987). *The concept of speech genre in the study of language and culture*. Working Papers and Proceedings of the Center for Psychosocial Studies no. 11, Center for Psychosocial Studies, Chicago.

Philips, S. U. (1998). *Ideological diversity in judges' courtroom discourses: Due process rights in practice*. Oxford: Oxford University Press.

Philips, S. U. (2000). Constructing a Tongan Nation State through language ideology in the courtroom. In P. V. Kroskrity (Ed.), *Regimes of language* (pp. 229–258). Santa Fe, NM: School of American Research Press.

Potowski, K. (2004). Spanish language shift in Chicago. *Southwest Journal of Linguistics, 23*(1).

Reyes, M. L. (1992). Challenging venerable assumptions: Literacy instruction for linguistically different students. *Harvard Educational Review, 62*, 427–446.

Rickford, J. (1999). *African American Vernacular English*. Oxford: Blackwell.

Rickford, J. R., & Rickford, R. J. (2000). *Spoken soul: The story of Black English*. New York: John Wiley.

Rodríguez, C. E., Sánchez-Korrol, V., & Alers, J. O. (1980). The Puerto Rican struggle to survive in the United States. In C. E. Rodríguez, V. Sánchez-Korrol, & J. O. Alers

(Eds.), *The Puerto Rican struggle: Essays on survival in the U.S.* (pp. 1–10). Maplewood, NJ: Waterfront.

Rosenau, J. (1997). *Along the domestic–foreign frontier: Exploring governance in a turbulent world.* Cambridge, England: Cambridge University Press.

Rouse, R. (1991). Mexican migration and the social space of postmodernism. *Diaspora, 1*(1), 8–23.

Rouse, R. (1992). Making sense of settlement: Class transformation, cultural struggle, and transnationalism among Mexican migrants in the United States: Towards a transnational perspective on migration. *Annuls of the New York Academy of Sciences, 645,* 25–52.

Rowe, W., & Schelling, V. (1991). *Memory and modernity: Popular culture in Latin America.* New York: Verso.

Sassen, S. (1998). *Globalization and its discontents: Essays on the new mobility of people and money.* New York: The New Press.

Saville-Troike, M. (1989). *The ethnography of communication.* London: Basil Blackwell.

Schieffelin, B. B., Woolard, K. A., & Kroskrity, P. V. (Eds). (1998). *Language ideologies: Practice and theory.* New York: Oxford University Press.

Sherzer, J. (1987). A discourse-centered approach to language and culture. *American Anthropologist, 89*(2), 295–309.

Sherzer, J. (1990). *Verbal art in San Blas: Kuna culture through its discourse.* Cambridge: Cambridge University Press.

Staudt, K., & Spener, D. (1998). The view from the frontier: Theoretical perspectives undisciplined. In D. Spener & K. Staudt (Eds.), *The U.S.-Mexico border: Transcending divisions, contesting identities* (pp. 1–44). Boulder, CO: Lynne Riener Publishers.

Street, B. (1984). *Literacy in theory and practice.* Cambridge, England: Cambridge University Press.

Street, B. V. (1993). *Cross-cultural approaches to literacy.* Cambridge, England: Cambridge University Press.

Szwed, J. (1981). The ethnography of literacy. In M. Farr-Whiteman (Ed.), *Writing: Functional and linguistic-cultural variation* (pp. 13–23). Hillsdale, NJ: Lawrence Erlbaum Associates.

Tabouret-Keller, A. (1997). Language and identity. In F. Coulmas (Ed.), *The handbook of sociolinguistics* (pp. 315–326). Oxford: Blackwell.

Tannen, D. (1989). *Talking voices: Repetition, dialogue, and imagery in conversational discourse.* Cambridge, England: Cambridge University Press.

Tedlock, D. (1983). *The spoken word and the work of interpretation.* Philadelphia: University of Pennsylvania Press.

Trommler, F., & McVeigh, J. (Eds.). (1985). *America and the Germans.* Philadelphia: University of Pennsylvania Press.

United Nations. (1988). World population trends and policies. *Monitoring report population studies No. 103.* New York: United Nations.

U.S. Census Bureau. Hispanic origin population in Chicago city. Database C90STF1A. Retrieved June 4, 2003, from http://venus.census.gov/cdrom/lookup

U.S. Census Bureau. Hispanic origin population in Cook county. Database C90STF1A. Retrieved June 4, 2004, from http://venus.census.gov/cdrom/lookup

U.S. Census Bureau. QT-P9: Hispanic or Latino by type: 2000. Data set: Census 2000 summary file 1 (SF 1) 100-percent data, Geographic area: Chicago city, Illinois. Retrieved June 2, 2003, from http://factfinder.census.gov/servlet/QTTable?

ds_name=D&geo_id=16000US1714000&qr_name=DEC_2000_SF1_U_QTP9 &_lang=en

U.S. Census Bureau. QT-P9: Hispanic or Latino by type: 2000. Data set: Census 2000 summary file 1 (SF 1) 100-percent data, Geographic area: Cook county, Illinois. Retrieved June 2, 2003, from http://factfinder.census.gov/servlet/QTTable? ds_name=D&geo_id=05000US17031&qr_name=DEC_2000_SF1_U_QTP9&_l ang=en

U.S. Census Bureau. PHC-T-6, Table 4: Population by race and Hispanic or Latino origin, for States, Puerto Rico, and places of 100,000 or more population: 2000. Internet release date April 2, 2001. Retrieved June 4, 2003, from http://landview. census.gov/population/cen2000/phc-t6/tab04.pdf

Valdés, G. (1996). Con respeto: *Bridging the distance between culturally diverse families and schools: an ethnographic portrait*. New York: Teachers College Press.

Wallerstein, I. (1974). *The modern world system*. New York: Academic Press.

Wolfram, W., Adger, C., & Christian, D. (1999). *Dialects in schools and communities*. Mahwah, NJ: Lawrence Erlbaum Associates.

Woolard, K. A. (1998). Introduction: Language ideology as a field of inquiry. In B. B. Schieffelin, K. A. Woolard, & P. V. Kroskrity (Eds.), *Language ideologies: Practice and theory* (pp. 3–47). New York: Oxford University Press.

Zentella, A. C. (1997). *Growing up bilingual: Puerto Rican children in New York*. Oxford: Blackwell.

ENDNOTE

1. Parts of this Introduction are a revised version of the Introduction by Marcia Farr and Rachel Reynolds for *Ethnolinguistic Chicago: Language and Literacy in the City's Neighborhoods*, the earlier companion volume to this book.

PART

II

WITHIN THE FAMILY CIRCLE

Man strolling through his avocado orchard in Rancho. Photograph by Marcia Farr.

Woman using machete on pine boughs to decorate chapel for annual Saint's Day in Rancho. Photograph by Marcia Farr.

2

¡A Mí No Me Manda Nadie![1]
Individualism and Identity in Mexican
Ranchero Speech[2]

Marcia Farr[3]
Ohio State University

Mexican migration to Chicago has always been predominantly from Western Mexico (Año Nuevo Kerr, 1977), notably including the states of Michoacán, Jalisco, and Guanajuato. These states also are known to be notably *ranchero* in identity, constituting a distinct subgroup among the larger category of rural Mexican *campesinos* (peasants). Because of the importance, and predominance, of this identity in Chicago's Mexican neighborhoods, and because of close transnational ties between Chicago and innumerable *ranchos* (rural hamlets) in western Mexico, understandings of Mexicans in Chicago can be enriched by research that explores this group's origin, not only in terms of geographic space, but also in terms of cultural and ethnic identity as Mexicans. This chapter, then, attempts to delve into *ranchero* identity, focusing in particular on how the cultural attributes of this identity are constructed in speech.

Only recently have a few Mexican researchers (Barragán López, 1990, 1997; González, 1974) begun to distinguish *rancheros* from other Mexican *campesinos*. Most research literature in both the United States and Mexico has long ignored the differences among *campesinos*, either assuming "peasant" to be the significant category or distinguishing only between *indígena* (Indian) and *mestizo* (racially mixed)[4] peasants. All *mestizo* peasants, however, are not alike. *Rancheros* own (or wish to own) their own land individually, even relatively small parcels, and it is the valuing of such private property that is central to their identity. They do not own land communally, as do Indian communities, or as do *ejidatarios* (co-owners of agricultural cooperatives that resulted from land reform after the Mexican Revolution of 1910–1920). *Rancheros,* in fact, disdain both Indians and *ejidatarios,* and the *agraristas* (agrarian reformers) who worked to create the *ejidos,* or communal properties, and have been known to refuse, out of pride, government offers of free land (Gledhill, 1991). Private property is highly valued, but it must be earned through one's own efforts.

A liberal individualist ideology is the central underpinning of *ranchero* identity. This ideology generally is shared by both men and women, although both age and gender affect the cultural practices in which it is embedded. *Rancheros* are "ranch" people, able to control horses, shoot guns, kill chickens, and, in their view, create their own destinies through hard work. In defining themselves this way, *rancheros* distinguish themselves from those identified as *indígenas* (indigenous Indian Mexicans) on the one hand (whom *rancheros* view as communally oriented), and from *catrines* (city people whom *rancheros* see as fancily dressed, and acting, "dandies") on the other. *Rancheros* view Indians as working hard, but not progressing, and they view many city people as not really working because "real" work involves manual labor. In contrast to these other identities, *rancheros* espouse an individualist, upwardly mobile ideology constructed in a verbal style, or "way of speaking" (Hymes, 1974b), characterized by *franqueza* (frankness).

The history of the origins and development of *rancheros* in western Mexico after the Spanish conquest describes the socioeconomic conditions in which this way of life, and its ways of speaking, developed (Farr, forthcoming). Briefly, *rancheros* originated from the lower ranks of Spaniards who mixed with some Indians and Africans, and who handled the cattle, imported from Spain, on large haciendas. They were the original cowboys of the western hemisphere, always on the frontier of the colony, domesticating land (smaller *ranchos* based on less desirable land not part of, but often surrounding, large *haciendas* [plantations]) and dominating indigenous populations. They are known as *hombres de a caballo* (men on horseback), because the land on which they lived (and on which some still live) could be traversed only on horses (González, 1991). This history of isolation and geographic movement made their housing perennially provisional and developed a culture in which mobility, both geographic and socioeconomic, was valued and achieved through hard work, autonomy, and toughness, particularly for men, but also for women. In light of this tradition of mobility, migration to the United States can be seen as only the latest chapter in their history, part of their continuing strategy to progress, or move "up," in the world.

A history of frontier isolation and mobility also facilitated the development of strong ties of reciprocity for mutual support in hostile conditions, and common ways of living, dressing, and speaking. Although self-reliance was, and is, of utmost importance, so were, and are, ties of kinship, both real and fictive (*compadrazgo*). This valuing of both autonomy and affiliation undermines the often-invoked dichotomy between "Mexicans" (characterized as communal, or group-oriented) and "North Americans" (characterized as individualistic, or self-oriented). Instead of being only one or the other, *rancheros* evidence both orientations, as discussed more fully later.

In traditional *ranchero* society, an antigovernment attitude coexisted along with a social system based on honor which depended on one's word (*la palabra*), and the legitimation of violence to settle conflicts. *Franqueza* as a way of speaking is particularly emblematic of the *ranchero* identity that developed under these material conditions. *Franqueza* is direct, straightforward, candid language that goes directly to the point. *Rancheros no se andan con rodeos* (don't beat around the bush), and their language can be blunt and rude (in the sense of uncultured), sometimes peppered with obscenities.

An example of *franqueza* follows, excerpted from a tape-recorded conversation between a mother and her daughter at home when I was not present.[5] This family is headed by the mother, who was widowed when her youngest of six daughters was 1 year old. The family had migrated to Chicago partly because the father wanted a better education and future for his children. Yet at the father's death, the mother was stranded in a new land and devastated that her husband (whom she still talks of as the love of her life) had suddenly developed stomach cancer and died, possibly as a result of his years as a supervisor in industrial agriculture back in Michoacán.

To make a long and painful, yet inspiring, story short, the mother pulled herself together, went to the city of Chicago to obtain a permit to sell food on the street, and found herself being interviewed for a city construction job. Her first paycheck, based of course on male salaries, seemed so large to her that she thought it was a mistake. Eventually, through her hard work and perseverance (and the mentoring of a Puerto Rican man on the job), she bought first one house, then another (located in a better neighborhood farther south in the city), constructed one back in the *rancho* (and is now retired there), and helped to support various of her daughters through high school, college, and even graduate school. The upwardly mobile progress (*el progreso*) of this family illustrates the importance of these values to *rancheros,* both male and female.

In this particular conversation, the mother is criticizing some young Mexican American acquaintances who are not direct and straightforward in their speech, nor candid in how they represent themselves or their relationships with others. Specifically, the mother objects when *novias* (girlfriends, traditionally considered engaged to be married) of many years are introduced as *amigas* (friends), even when the young people in question are presumably (these days in Chicago) intimates. The daughter, born and raised in Chicago, points out that people certainly are not going to introduce their girlfriends as lovers because that is not her mother's business. The mother denies that she is interested in knowing their "business," saying that knowing about her own love life would be sufficient. The daughter quickly picks up on this and says, "What love life?" (the mother is a widow), to which her mother replies, "Well, you beat me to it" (saying it before I could). At this point the mother recycles her claim that it is insincere and false not to be frank about one's relationships and oneself. She criticizes some Mexican Americans, especially those who look very Mexican,[6] for Anglicizing their names (e.g., Chon changed to Shawn). In her view, one should be honest and candid about one's identity, as well as one's relationships in life. (Rural dialect features in the transcript are marked with an asterisk.)

1	Daughter:	*Ma /?/. O eso de que tú*	Ma /?/. Or like when you [say], "Ah, now they
2		*[dices] "Ah ya se le cambia—ya*	change—now they changed the names of the
3		*le cambiaron los nombres a las*	girlfriends /?/."
4		*novias /?/."*	
5	Mother:	*Pos sí*	Well, of course.
6	Daughter:	*Te van a andar diciendo*	They're going to go around saying, "Look,
7		*"Mira, este es mi*	this is my lover" [sarcastic tone].
8		*amante"* [sarcastic tone].	
9	Mother:	*Pos sí ¿qué tenía eso?*	Well, yes, what's wrong with that?
10	Daughter:	[Laughing] *Ay ¿qué te interesa*	[Laughing] Well, what business is that of
11		*a ti eso?*	yours?
12	Mother:	*¿Pa' qué les cambian de*	Why do they change the name?

13		*nombre?*	
14	Daughter:	*La vida amorosa de otra*	The love life of another person /?/.
15		*persona /?/.*	
16	Mother:	*No-o-o, ¿yo para qué qu'ero*	No-o-o, why would I want to know about
17		*saber la vida amorosa de otra*	someone else's love life?
18		*gente?*	
19	Daughter:	*Pero sí, pero está diciendo—*	But yes, buy you're saying—
20	Mother:	*Con que me die—supiera la mía*	As long as—knowing my own [love life]
21		*era lo suficiente.*	would be sufficient.
22	Daughter:	*¿A cuál ya?*	What [love life] now?
23	Mother:	*Pero—me ganates.* Si hubiera*	But—you beat me [to it]. Had this been a
24		*sido una torta te la des—*	sandwich—you would have eaten it, and I
25		*[hubieras] comido tú y yo pura*	would have had pure shit.
26		*chingada.*	
27	Daughter:	[Laugh]	[Laugh]
28	Mother:	*Pos sí. A ver ¿pa' qué andan ahi*	That's right. Well, why do they go around
29		*con medias copas, podiendo ir*	beating around the bush, when they could
			go directly?
30		*directamente? "Ay, su*	"Oh, her friend" ... bah, now
31		*amigo," bah, ya les cambiaron de*	they changed the name. After all these
32		*nombre. Después de tantos*	years ... with the same name and now, now
33		*años con el mismo nombre ya*	they changed them to make them shorter
34		*'ora ya les cambiaron*	and more decent. Wealthy is what they are
35		*pa' hacerlos más cortitos y*	acting like.
36		*más decentes. De centavos 'b'ían*	
37		*de ser.*	
38	Daughter:	*Como ese, ¿cómo se llama?*	Like that guy, what's his name?
39	Mother:	*Pinchi* muchacho indio mocoso*	Damned snotty Indian kid and "Shawn."
40		*y "Shawn."*	

As this excerpt shows, the mother, a woman in her fifties, uses and claims to prefer a direct, "no bull" approach to communication. This style, of course, is not the only style in which *rancheros,* including this woman, speak. But it is a predominant style that evokes a deeply held ideology of *rancheros* tied historically to the ecology of *ranchos,* rural hamlets traditionally isolated from large urban centers of sophistication and schooling. In these rural hamlets, men and women have coped for centuries in Mexico, creating their own housing, growing their own food, raising their own livestock, and making their own cheese, clothing, and many other items of necessity. Now, of course, many *rancheros,* like those in this study, are producing food for commercial purposes (and/or working for wage labor both in the United States and Mexico), and buying their own food at nearby markets. Nevertheless, the deeply ingrained *habitus* (Bourdieu, 1977) of the independent rancher persists, and this *habitus* includes a propensity to use direct, frank language. This style of language, here called *franqueza,* constructs an identity for *rancheros* that contrasts sharply with other identities in their region of Mexico.

Primarily, *ranchero franqueza* contrasts sharply with the stereotyped image of the *humilde peón* (humble peon), standing with head bowed and hat in hand before a powerful landowner/boss, in many popular representations of Mexican peasants. In contrast to this humble image, which is found in both popular fiction and research literature, *rancheros* enact a proud stance, with heads held high and gazes direct, even when interacting with those who are more powerful than they. The directness of this verbal style also serves to contrast *rancheros* with more educated and "cultured" urbanites, who consider people rude if their language does not conform to *cortesía*, an elaborate and often indirect verbal politeness style (Haverkate, 1994). *Cortesía* in polite society requires verbally elaborate greetings and leave-takings, for example, whereas the *franqueza* of *rancheros* usually is much more concise, allowing people to (appropriately) leave with a simple *Ya me voy* (I'm leaving now).

In what follows I explore the construction of *ranchero* identity in informal verbal performances within the homes of the performers. Performances "stand out" in the flow of ordinary conversation because the audience orients attentively to the performer, who often is telling a story or joke (Bauman, 1984; Hymes, 1975, 1981). Such verbal performances are especially important occasions for constructions and interpretations of identity because they are instances of heightened aesthetic experience, and since they are intended for display. Instances of *ranchero* direct verbal style, or *franqueza,* in such performative talk from a large corpus of tape-recorded discourse illustrate how language and ideology are intertwined in the construction of individualist *ranchero* identity.

BACKGROUND OF THE STUDY

The *rancheros* in this study are a transnational network of Mexican families living in both Chicago and their village of origin in Michoacán, Mexico with whom I have become close during a 10-year ethnographic study. The focus of this study has been on culturally embedded ways of using oral and written language (see chapter 11 in this volume, as well as Farr, 1993, 1994a, 1994b, 1994c, 1998, Farr & Guerra, 1995; Guerra, 1998; Guerra & Farr, 2002) within the framework of the ethnography of communication (Bauman & Sherzer, 1989; Hymes, 1974a).

Members of these families first migrated to Chicago in 1964. First, men came, then their wives and children, and, eventually, single women. In Chicago, they work in factories and construction. Most of the women work in food preparation, glass painting, and other factories, and almost all the men work in railroad construction. Chicago is, as one woman put it, *para mejorar* (to improve [our lives]). They are part of a transnational community (Schiller, Basch, & Blanc-Szanton, 1992) because they regularly return to and communicate continuously with people in their village, and because they maintain social, emotional, economic, and political ties with network members on both sides of the U.S.–Mexican border. Many families live for years in Chicago, then move back to Mexico, either to retire or to raise children through their teenage years. Some then move again to Chicago. Especially for the adults in this network, it can be said that they form the fabric of each other's lives. That is, they form a dense and multiplex social network (Milroy, 1980) because not only are they related by kinship and *compadrazgo* (coparenting fictive kinship), but they also work, live, and socialize together. True to their beliefs, most of these families have used the money they have earned in Chicago to buy houses in Chicago, and to buy land (and construct or improve houses) back in Mexico. On the land bought in Mexico, they have planted avocados, selling them commercially.

A note on methodology is in order. I am fortunate to have been accepted and included within this network of families during the past 15 years. Our acquaintance, which began with this ethnographic study, grew into deep friendship, starting in Chicago and soon including their *rancho* in Michoacán, which has become my "home away from home." I am especially close with the women in these families, both those my own age and those with young families, although I also count several men as close friends. My participant-observation with these families has been, then, intense and long term. In Chicago it has of necessity involved more visiting than "living with," but in the *rancho*, I stay with families, sharing bedrooms, and even beds, when space is tight, with other women and children. I spent a year there (1995–1996) as a Fulbright scholar, and I have visited for a few weeks or a month on many other occasions, often during fiestas. I have carried items and papers back and forth for others in the network, like everyone else, and a number of the women have helped me in my research, and have been paid for this through my research grants. Their work has included recording discourse for me, transcribing tapes, making maps, and carrying out interviews. In short, it has been a very collaborative and satisfying endeavor at the human level. It is important to note that this depth and quality of participant-observation is essential for understanding the discourse style I discuss because it occurs in the interstices of everyday life, which I have shared with them.

RANCHERO IDENTITY

Identities are clearest in their contrast with others. In fact, they are constructed against these others: "we" are not "them." The region in which the *rancho* is located, northwest Michoacán, has a large indigenous (Indian) population, and the *rancho* is nestled up against the edge of the *meseta tarasca* (Tarascan tableland). Identity as a *ranchero* is important in these families, and this frequently is expressed as a primarily nonindigenous (non-Indian) ethnic identity. In northwest Michoacán, *rancheros* and *indígenas* (indigenous or Indian Mexicans) distinguish themselves from each other, sometimes fiercely. Although the *rancheros* have some indigenous "blood," they continuously construct a nonindigenous identity, although not without some ambivalence. As Barth (1969) noted, it is "the ethnic *boundary* that defines the group, not the cultural stuff that it encloses" (p. 15). Otherwise, over time, ethnic groups in interaction, as *rancheros* and *indígenas* have been for centuries in Mexico (Barragán, 1997), would tend to exchange "cultural stuff." In fact, such exchange has occurred in both directions, including the movement of individual people, and yet the boundary between these two groups has remained distinct. Thus whereas *rancheros* can be distinguished for their deeply held beliefs in individualism, private property, and progress, it is how these beliefs contrast with their perceptions of their indigenous neighbors that lends them salience.

Talk about such ethnic identity is frequent in these families, in both Mexico and Chicago, and this talk makes it abundantly clear that a primarily nonindigenous identity is central to their self-definition, especially among the older generation. Among the younger, formally schooled, generation, such talk entails more ambivalence and acknowledgment of their own (partial) indigenous heritage because they are taught in school that *todos somos indios* (we are all Indians). Yet in practice, comments about the indigenous, whether positive or negative, always make it clear that they are different, and usually relegate them to lower status. My field notes and tapes are full of comments such as the following, made by different men and women across a range of contexts:

> "You see, I'm so healthy because I have some Indian blood." (The reverse comment is never made, indicating that the assumed "default" mode is Spanish/European.)

> "The indigenous are very intelligent! They can make textiles, pottery, many things!"

> "In our family, two brothers were sent over by the King of Spain to retrieve the bones of a dead priest. They looked around, saw how rich the land was, and decided to stay. Of course, then they mixed the bloods."

> "Yes, there are people with darker skin [*morenos*] here in the *rancho,* but they're not indigenous."

> "With the indigenous, one can't have *confianza* [trust]; they change on you, and they are very closed."

> "The indigenous, they don't progress" [unspoken: as we do, in going to Chicago, making money, buying land, and planting avocados as an entrepreneurial enterprise].

Rancheros, however, not only distinguish themselves from indigenous Mexicans. They also distinguish themselves from other (non-*ranchero*) *mestizos* who are seen as "really" *mestizo*. Comments refer to such *mestizos* as people, basically indigenous, who have acculturated to Spanish ways of living (e.g., by wearing "regular" clothes), in contrast to the indigenous Tarascan or, in their own language, *purhépecha* people in this region. In nearby *purhépecha* villages, many women, and even young girls, still wear distinctive blouses, skirts, belts, and shawls to indicate their ethnic identity, although most men no longer wear the traditional male Indian peasant garb of white pants and shirt. A local joke in the *rancho* tells of people in a nearby, heavily indigenous *mestizo* town who are said to have learned to dance with their arms around each other, European style, and then to have announced, "Okay, now we're Spanish."

The *rancho* from which the *rancheros* in this study originate is situated in a microregion in which there never have been large landowners with *haciendas* (plantations), unlike other regions in the state and nation. In regions where *haciendas* have long existed, relations of domination and subordination are presumably more deeply established, with ruling families expecting and receiving verbal and bodily deference from their workers and other landless peasants dependent on them for material resources. The land in this particular microregion, comprised of rolling hills on a high plateau, apparently was not conducive to the large-scale agriculture of *haciendas,* which were located in flatter, and more easily exploitable, expanses of land. The shape of the land in this microregion, then, may have contributed to the predominance of *ranchos* here. It has always been *ranchero* territory, that is, the province of small landowners rather than *hacendados* (plantation owners). Thus the microregion does not have an entrenched tradition of a *patrón* (boss), usually from a dominant family, to whom workers owe deference. This fact may partly explain why these *rancheros* do not publicly assume a humble, deferential stance toward more powerful others, especially not on their own turf. In contrast, an interview with an older man living one half hour's drive away, over the hills to the west in the flat expanse of land that had been part of an *hacienda,* contains the frequent deferential use of *el patrón* and *la patrona* in reference to male and female family members who owned the hacienda until the revolution.

In the status hierarchy of this region of northwest Michoacán, the indigenous Tarascan or *purhépecha* Indians are at the bottom, the *rancheros* in the middle, and the urban elite at the top. Yet except when doing business (e.g., receiving medical services) in cities that have an urban elite population, *rancheros* can avoid most contacts with those "above them" in the regional status hierarchy with whom they might feel uncomfortable. (Even in interactions with the urban elite, however, I have observed these *rancheros* enacting self-assertion and *franqueza.*) Nevertheless, most of the time, their interactions are with other *rancheros* or *indígenas.* When interacting with other *rancheros,* their demeanor and language is egalitarian. In interactions with the indigenous, in contrast, *rancheros* expect, and often receive, deference, at least publicly. Friedrich (1977) noted the extreme hostility toward these *mestizos* on the part of the indigenous *purhépecha* of this region, suggesting that their public deference to *rancheros* is a form of resistance, a "weapon of the weak" (Scott, 1990). An interview of the indigenous woman who sells bread as well as other corn and wheat products daily in the *rancho,* walking door to door, confirms the resentment of the indigenous toward the *rancheros,* who are seen as "the same" as the indigenous themselves, except for the fact that "they look down on us."

Rancheros, then, distinguish themselves from other rural peasants by the importance they give to private property, especially land ownership, and to an upwardly mobile notion of *progreso* (progress). In the popular imagination in Mexico, they have played an important role in this regard, because *rancheros* were valorized as epitomizing *lo mexicano* (true Mexicanness) in the Golden Age of Mexican cinema during the 1940s and 1950s. Some contemporary scholars view this use of *rancheros* rather critically as a conservative promotion of capitalism and nationalism, but there is no doubt that the film stars who portrayed *rancheros* (e.g., Jorge Negrete in *Allá en el Rancho Grande* (Over on the Big Ranch) still represent the values, demeanor, and status that many contemporary *rancheros* hold dear. For despite the historical (and contemporary) positive image of *rancheros* in both film and music, the term *ranchero* also evokes negative connotations in some parts of contemporary Mexico, as well as among some members of Mexican communities in the United States (Cintron, 1997). As rural Mexicans, *rancheros* are stereotyped as backward (not "modern"), shy, and uneducated. This is epitomized in the expression *no seas ranchera!* (Don't be so backward/ungracious!) used in social situations among the cultured elite in urban areas of Mexico. Moreover, there is a long tradition in Mexico of equating rural with Indian and urban with Spanish (e.g., Bonfil Batalla, 1996), especially because during the colonial period and afterward, many Spanish *hacienda* owners lived in cities while lower status Spanish and *mestizo rancheros* lived on *haciendas* as administrators (Barragán López, 1997). The *rancheros* in this study quickly acknowledge the higher education of people in the cities, and when in a city, are quite aware of their own difference. On their own turf in the *rancho,* however, they do not hesitate to ridicule "citified" people, especially men, who, if they do not work with their hands, do not really work. Clearly, then, these two identities are sharply differentiated by both the urban elite and the *rancheros.* Linguistically, the difference between the two is captured by contrasting *franqueza* and *cortesía* as verbal styles. Whereas *franqueza* is frank and direct, even blunt and rude at times, *cortesía* is cultured, elaborate, and indirect (Haverkate, 1994). In the following discussion, I explain in more detail the ideology that *franqueza* both expresses and constructs.

LIBERAL INDIVIDUALIST IDEOLOGY

Studies of Mexicans in the United States have characterized them as "collectivist" (Delgado-Gaitán, 1993) or "deeply familistic" (Valdés, 1996), and thus more committed to family and other reciprocal relationships than many members of the dominant Anglo "individualist" culture that, according to LeVine and White (1986), has been inculcated by mass schooling. While encapsulating some truth, these contrasting character- izations of "collectivist/familistic" versus "individualist," too often are perceived as a simple dichotomy. In my ethnographic experience with *ranchero* Mexicans, however, such a dichotomy dissolves into a "both," rather than an "either/or." *Ranchero* Mexicans generally evidence a very individualist orientation, although they do so within a context of familism and networks based on reciprocity. That is, although the family and hu- man relationships are of central importance in social life, individuality also is highly valued, both within and beyond the family. It is possible, then, to be both individualistic and collectivist/familistic, to be autono- mous without being isolated. What is significant, then, may be the differ- ences between U.S. Anglo and Mexican *ranchero* individualism, the latter coexisting with an emphasis on familism. *Rancheros* see them- selves as differing from other Mexicans in terms of such individualism, particularly those identified as indigenous or Indian Mexicans.

A variety of recent studies indicate that although *rancheros* across Mex- ico vary in their relative wealth, they share cultural practices, beliefs, and the frequent use of a frank verbal style. They can be rich or poor, dominant or "middle class" (i.e., sandwiched between an elite dominant class and those on the bottom of the status hierarchy; Jacobs, 1982; Lomnitz-Adler, 1992). Yet no matter the size of their land holdings, and thus their relative wealth and influence, they share certain cultural values (Brading, 1994), including the overriding importance of hard work and autonomy, ideally living off their own land on livestock and other food products, and being their own bosses (Barragán López, Hoffman, Linck, & Skerritt, 1994). A popular *ranchero dicho* (saying) expresses this: *¡A mí no me manda nadie!* (No one orders me around!) *Rancheros* historically are frontiersmen and women, the "ranch" men and women of Mexico, although many Mexi- cans who no longer live in isolated *ranchos* in Mexico, and now live in cit- ies either in Mexico or the United States, still retain *ranchero* values. In addition to pride in hard work, individual efforts at entrepreneurship are highly valued and practiced by both men and women (e.g., in Chicago, men fix up and rent apartments in the backs of the houses they own, and women sell Tupperware and other commodities, apart from their regular factory or construction jobs. One teenager recently airbrushed and sold tee shirts while still in high school in Chicago, a fact proudly announced by aunts and other family members, who reported that he was "doing really well" at this endeavor. Another teenager worked part-time in a candy store throughout high school in order to buy a used car so she could drive her mother and siblings around, as well as drive herself to community college.

The social order in the *rancho,* then, is based on a liberal individualist ideology (Cosio Villegas et al., 1995, pp. 114–115) in which people are believed to be equally free and able to work their way up in the world through their own hard labor and enterprise, rather than have their social status determined at birth. Lomnitz-Adler (1992) traced the *ranchero* discourse that constructs this ideology to liberal individualism from late 19th century Mexico. Barragán López (1997), in contrast, claimed that *rancheros* have been socially, economically, and geographically mobile for centuries within Mexico, from soon after the conquest to the contemporary migration to the United States. Whatever its origins, however, upward mobility and a belief in progress are centrally important to these *rancheros,* and Chicago has figured significantly in this drive toward progress.

As indicated earlier, this belief in progress and upward mobility provides the basis upon which the *rancheros* in this study distinguish themselves from others. Many *ranchero* families from this area, in fact, trace their ancestry back to Spain (and one prosperous family in the *rancho,* with professional members in Guadalajara, has a Spanish coat of arms on the wall of their architect-designed house), although most people readily acknowledge that their ancestors (and those only a few generations back, after the Revolution of 1910–1920) "mixed the blood" with indigenous Mexicans. Genetically, although they presumably are *mestizo,* many individuals, and even entire families in this *rancho,* are quite "white." That is, many people have blue or green eyes, blond or light brown hair, and light skin with freckles that turns red, not brown, in the sun. Others look more evidently *mestizo,* with tan skin and some indigenous features. Despite their acknowledgment of *mestizaje* (the mixture of "races"), however, these *rancheros,* especially the older generation, maintain clear distinctions between themselves and the indigenous, whom they say "do not progress." This discourse thus creates clear ethnic boundaries that separate the *rancheros* in the current study from nearby lower-status indigenous Mexicans, with whom, at least in the recent past, they have shared extreme poverty.

A final note on *ranchero* individualist ideology is in order. An important aspect of the social order in *la sociedad ranchera* (*ranchero* society) is that it is patriarchal. De la Peña (1984) described kinship ideology of traditional *ranchero* society in this region of Mexico as extremely patriarchal, with a "bearded patriarch" an unquestioned authority heading a multigenerational cattle-raising and agricultural "organization." Although this ideology is changing because of changing social and economic circumstances, *el hombre ranchero* (a *ranchero* man), as one of the women in these families said to me, still wants a *servienta* (servant) for a wife. Men, as heads of families, see themselves as maintaining order through a code of *respeto*, literally meaning "respect," but connoting more than the English word, as explained in the following discussion. Uses of *tú* (familiar you) and *usted* (formal you) generally reflect this system of *respeto*, which organizes relations by gender and age. Women use *tú* with each other, as do men, but *usted* is used from one gender to another and, in many contexts, from children to parents. Outside the family, *usted* generally is reserved for strangers and respected people such as priests and teachers, but within the egalitarian ethos of the *rancho*, within gender at least, *tú* is frequently used. Valdés (1996, p. 130) defined *respeto* as "a set of attitudes toward individuals and/or the roles they occupy," adding that although important in relations among strangers, it is especially important for guiding relations within the family. For example, children, even adult children, are expected to show respect for their parents by obeying them. Among equal adults within *ranchero* society, the social order and *respeto* are explicitly described as egalitarian: *Todos somos iguales* (We are all equal) and *Respeto es vivir en paz* (Respect is living in peace). The latter saying alludes to the often-quoted words of Benito Juárez, a famous late 19th century President of Mexico, and means that if everyone is treated as an individual with rights, then there will be peace. Within this *rancho*, *respeto* is described by virtually everyone as consisting of two primary aspects: respecting the private property of others (not stealing) and not committing adultery with someone else's wife or husband (perhaps also a kind of property).

Despite all the explicit egalitarian talk, however, several factors differentiate members of this community. Although there are economic differences among various families, these differences are not organized into a rigid status hierarchy. That is, because people deeply believe in an egalitarian ethic, they behave accordingly, at least within same-gender and same-age interactions, and they do not draw attention to economic differences in these interactions. Gender and age, however, do organize relations hierarchically. Women ideally owe public deference to their fathers and then their husbands, and younger men owe deference to older men. Official discourse such as that found in church sermons affirms this gender- and age-based system of *respeto*, but, even so, this ideal is not always enacted in everyday practices, and tensions in this social code allow for variation and hence change. For example, although wives and daughters traditionally serve food to fathers and brothers, in families wherein it is the daughters who are working and thus paying for the *mandado* (weekly groceries), men have been known to heat their own tortillas in the presence of their wives and daughters (and have been teased by other men for allowing this). Chávez (1994) argued that because *ranchera* women traditionally work not only in "female" domains such as the kitchen, but also help out in "male" domains such as the fields, they are "part of everything" and thus have much control over the entire household. Similarly, as Rogers (1975) argued for French peasant women, because the significant economic unit at the level of a village is the household, women in such settings acquire a significant degree of power, and although they publically defer to their men, privately, they often control everything. Moreover, within the transnational community in this study, women work outside the home, in factories in Chicago, and in packing plants near the *rancho*. For all these reasons, then, there is substantial "room" for them to assert themselves, even in a traditionally patriarchal system.

It is important to note in this regard that *franqueza* as a verbal style indexes qualities associated publicly with masculinity. It is, then, primarily a male style of talk. *Ranchera* women, however, far from fitting the public stereotype of (good) Mexican women as self-abnegating, docile, and subservient to men (Melhuus, 1996), appropriate this verbal style to assert their own toughness and individualism, as younger men on occasion assert their own selfhood vis-à-vis older men. Sometimes, such appropriation occurs within the verbal play frame of *relajo* (joking around) (Farr, 1994c, 1998). Usually, however, *respeto* calls for verbal strategies of respect, entailing an egalitarian *franqueza* between men (and between adult women) that is frank and direct, indicating candor and integrity in social relations, and a more formal verbal deference (e.g.,the use of a formal second person singular pronoun, *usted,* rather than the informal *tú*) based on an age and gender hierarchy within both the family and the community. In this article, I focus on the former, an egalitarian *franqueza* used by both men and women.

FRANQUEZA AS A VERBAL STYLE

I have argued that the distinctness of *ranchero* identity rests centrally on the importance attributed to individual land ownership and thus autonomy. As land owners, *rancheros* enact a proud, authoritative stance performed in a predominant verbal style of *franqueza*. Such performative talk constructs a *ranchero* identity that emphasizes independence and self-assertion. As a verbal style, it is direct, powerful, and at times even rude, and as such it invokes an individualist, egalitarian, and often entrepreneurial ideology. Lomnitz-Adler (1992), who studied *rancheros* in another Mexican state (although there they dominated the region politically and economically), described this rough talk as "bold, frank, and open," full of "regional sayings and down-to-earth obscenities" (pp. 199–200). Its very frankness, he argued, created a populist and egalitarian stance for these *rancheros,* who used this verbal style and stance quite effectively in gaining political dominance in their region.

In my own study, unlike that of Lomnitz-Adler (1992), the *rancheros* are not regionally dominant, nor are they rich. Yet they nevertheless evidence the same ideology and verbal style as the more powerful *rancheros* of Lomnitz-Adler's study and other studies of *rancheros* (Barragán López, 1990, 1997; González, 1974). González (1991) traced this stance of authority and pride on the part of *rancheros* to their Spanish heritage:

> They inherited from their Spanish parentage a practice of arrogance. They never owe anything to anyone, and they are very sensitive to humiliation. Being haughty they are individualists and disrespectful of authority. They regard honor highly and look down on the humility of the indigenous, as well as on the shame of the *ejidatarios* (co-owners of communally owned land). (p. 7; my translation)

Thus *rancheros* disdain those who are not autonomous "self-made men (and women)." They look down on both communal Indians and *ejidatarios,* who were given land by the government instead of earning it themselves through their own hard labor. (Of course, from the indigenous point of view, this land was stolen from them when the Spanish arrived.)

The authoritative, even haughty, stance of *rancheros* lends itself to a frank verbal style. It is "bald on record" in the terms of politeness theory (Brown & Levinson, 1987). This theory is based on Goffman's (1967) notion of face, defined by Brown and Levinson as "the public self-image that every member [of a group] wants to claim for himself" (1987, p. 61). Depending on various aspects of the context (such as power relationships, distance or closeness, and cultural values), certain linguistic acts on the part of a speaker are considered "face threats" to a hearer. In Brown and Levinson's (1987, pp. 67–71) scheme,

> Doing an act *baldly, without redress,* involves doing it in the most direct, clear, unambiguous and concise way possible (for example, for a request, saying

"Do X!")…. Normally, an FTA [face threatening act] will be done in this way only if the speaker does not fear retribution from the addressee, for example in circumstances where (a) S and H both tacitly agree that the relevance of face demands may be suspended in the interests of urgency or efficiency, (b) where the danger to H's face is *very* small, as in offers, requests, suggestions that are clearly in H's interest and do not require great sacrifices of S (e.g., "Come in" or "Do sit down"), and (c) where S is vastly superior in power to H, or can enlist audience support to destroy H's face without losing his own….

By going *on record* [baldly], a speaker can potentially get any of the following advantages: he can enlist public pressure against the addressee or in support of himself; he can get credit for honesty, for indicating that he trusts the addressee; [and] he can get credit for outspokenness, avoiding the danger of being seen to be a manipulator.

When these circumstances do not obtain, and when the speaker wishes to avoid threatening the hearer's face, she or he will either speak "off record" (very indirectly) or "on record," and he or she will use "redressive action," which "gives face" to the addressee, through what Brown and Levinson (1987) called "positive" or "negative" politeness. Without going into all the details of this theory and its critiques, Spanish address terms such as *tú* and *usted,* as well as other linguistic devices, can be used strategically to emphasize either positive (solidarity-oriented) or negative (deference-oriented) politeness. Bald on-record communication, in contrast, is communication stripped of conventional linguistic politeness devices that reduce the face threat to the hearer by humbling the speaker. For example, a directive, *¡Venga, apague esa luz!* (Come, turn out that light!) is bald on-record communication. In contrast, a request, *Apaga esa luz, ¿quieres?* (Turn out that light, would you?), with the added "would you?" includes redressive action for the sake of politeness, that is, to reduce the face threat to or to be more respectful of the hearer (Haverkate, 1994, p. 167).

The *rancheros* in this study frequently use direct, bald on-record directives that do not humble the speaker. Such directives support a stance of independence and toughness, indexing their individualist ideology. Men, women, and children all use such directives frequently, but not always (e.g., I have heard daughters use such directives to mothers), to someone lower in the family hierarchy. In one instance of the general pattern, a young girl in the *rancho* who was attending to a cut on her older brother's arm said to him as he grimaced from the pain, "*¡Aguantase, si es hombre!*" (Handle it, if you're a man!).

Theoretically, such bald on-record communication is used in two situations: first, when there is little distance (much intimacy) between speakers, and second, when there is a hierarchical relationship between the interactants in which the speaker has more power than the hearer. In other words, it is used between intimates (in which case, there is, by definition, little distance between speakers), or it is used by a higher status speaker with a lower status speaker. Of course, bald on-record language not only expresses status and power differentials, it also attempts to create them on the spot as this young girl did with her brother. An incident from my field notes provides another example of this pattern.

Early in my fieldwork in the *rancho* I was introduced to a man outside the chapel after the weekly Sunday morning mass. This dialogue is reproduced as follows:

1	Man:	*¿Qué eres?*	What are you?
2	MF:	*Soy Marcia Farr.*	I am Marcia Farr.
3	Man:	*No, ¿QUÉ eres? ¿Inglés, Alemán,*	No, WHAT are you? English, German, what?
4		*qué?*	
5	MF:	*Bueno, pues, Inglés, Alemán, y un*	Well, English, German, and a little French and
6		*poquito de francés e irlandés.*	Irish
7	Man:	[nodding and smiling] *Bueno,*	[nodding and smiling] OK, what religion are
8		*¿cuál religión eres?*	you?
9	MF:	*Fui bautizada católica.*	I was baptized Catholic.
10	Man:	[nodding and smiling] Well, then,	[nodding and smiling] Well, then, you are
11		you are very welcome here in the	very welcome here in the *rancho.*
12		*rancho.*	

As shown in line 1, the very first thing this man said to me was, "What are you?" Thinking I had misheard him as asking me who I was, not what I was, I replied with my name. "No," he said firmly, WHAT are you? English, German, what? Somewhat taken aback, I replied with my ethnic background as I understand it. Nodding approval for my ethnic background, he continued to interrogate me: OK, what religion are you? Thinking quickly, I replied that I was baptized Catholic (which is true, but in saying this I avoided claiming that I was a practicing Catholic). He smiled, slowly nodded, and then said, switching to English, "Well, then, you are very welcome here."

This incident illustrates not only the *franco* (frank) verbal style of bald on-record communication. It also shows how such a verbal style constructs a powerful stance on the part of the speaker toward the hearer. Not knowing anything about me except that I was from the United States, instead of acknowledging distance, and possibly higher status, through various verbal politeness devices, he used direct questioning and a bald on-record verbal style. Moreover, he used *tú* (second person singular, familiar pronoun) rather than *usted* (second person singular, formal pronoun). The use of *tú*, of course, like the use of *franqueza*, indexes either intimacy or higher status on the part of the speaker vis-à-vis the hearer. Because we were virtual strangers, his use of *tú* did not index intimacy. Instead, it indexed a claim of at least equal, if not higher, status on his part vis-à-vis me.

The man's verbal choices must be understood against the widespread awareness in the *rancho* of the power of the United States vis-à-vis Mexico, both historically and currently. Virtually all the families in this *rancho* either have members working in the United States and sending money for daily necessities such as food and clothing, or they have worked there in the past and now live off those earnings. Moreover, the man in whose household I stay when in the *rancho* has pointed out to me explicitly that the United States has exerted much control over affairs in Mexico. His son even told me once that the United States was planning to annex some northern Mexican states. Although this struck me as a wild rumor, it nevertheless vividly evoked the Mexican–American War in the mid-19th century in which the United States took over half of what then was Mexico and incorporated it into the United States. During the interaction in front of the church, then, all of these background understandings came into play. Although I was in some respects of a higher status (more educated, richer, and from a powerful nation), this man chose to use *franqueza* with me to assert himself and claim his own high status, a status at least equal to, if not higher than, my own.

It is interesting to consider whether my interrogation, evaluation, and then (fortunate for me) welcoming in front of the church would have happened in this way had I been male, a *gringo* rather than a *gringa*. Certainly, the fact that I am female facilitated a man's use of a bald-on-record verbal style in this traditional patriarchal *ranchero* society. Viewed this way, I was being incorporated into the local status order. The use of *franqueza* with me communicated that although I may arguably have been of higher status than he, I was, after all, a female, and so could more easily be confronted with such direct questioning than a male of my class and national status. This is not to say that *franqueza* is not used between men (it most certainly is), either as equals or from a higher status speaker to a lower status hearer. Depending on the context, *franqueza* constructs somewhat varying meanings.

In this context, however, the fact that it was a male–female interaction unavoidably invoked gender relations, especially in a society that regards gender as such a fundamental principle for social ordering.

It also is interesting to consider this interaction in the light of critiques of politeness theory. Hernández-Flores (1999) argued that Brown and Levinson's (1987) definitions of positive and negative politeness are grounded in Anglo-Saxon cultural values:

> [Brown and Levinson's] proposal presents some problems of adequacy to cultural values from some communities. In fact, the features ascribed to face wants focuses on the individuality of people, on their right to privacy, by claiming own territories (negative face) and social approbation of own wants (positive face). Wierzbicka points out that the focus on individualism is a characteristic cultural value of Anglo-Saxon communities, but this value is not shared by other communities (Wierzbicka, 1991, ch. 2). (Hernández-Flores, 1999, p. 38)

Following Bravo (1996), Hernández-Flores (1999) argued for autonomy and affiliation to replace the concepts of negative and positive face. Autonomy and affiliation, seen as universal categories, then are "filled" with the cultural content of each case. In Spanish society (the locus of the Hernández-Flores study), autonomy and affiliation are not opposed to each other, but are linked in a common emphasis on group belonging. Autonomy is the wish to be seen as an original individual standing out from his or her group (and therefore worthy of group acceptance), and affiliation is the wish to achieve closeness within a group. Autonomy is expressed as self-affirmation, so that one is seen as having such desirable qualities that the group will extend acceptance. Affiliation is expressed through the search for *confianza* (trust) in a close relationship, such that open, candid communication can occur. To fulfill the face requirement for autonomy, "the individual is expected to display her/his self-confidence by means of assertive behavior" (Hernández-Flores, 1999, p. 40). To fulfill the face requirement for affiliation, the development of *confianza* (which presumably follows from self-affirmation), allows speakers to speak openly and intimately, as though they were in a family context, which is highly valued in Spanish society. Distance, then, and a corresponding lack of *confianza*, is negatively valued.

In the aforementioned interaction, I initially was taken aback by the *franqueza* expressed in direct, blunt interrogation, which I interpreted as a face-threatening (FTA) act. My "interrogator," however, may not have perceived this as an FTA. Rather, his *franqueza* may have been intended as a "natural" expression of self-assertiveness, putting "one's best foot forward," so to speak. Moreover, it may have been thought especially appropriate, given our gender differences. It was my interrogator's strategic choice, of course, to foreground the gender differences and background the class and national differences. In doing so, he was incorporating me into his group, on local terms, laying the groundwork for *confianza*, wherein such candid language is appropriate. At the same time, of course, he was impressing me with his own positively valued *ranchero* qualities of independence and self-sanctioned authority.

In similar interactions between men, *franqueza* can index either an egalitarian relationship or a relationship of unequal status. The latter often occurs in interactions between *rancheros* and the occasional *indígena* who comes to the *rancho* to work for or do business with them, especially if it is clear that the person is *indígena*, but unknown. If the former (within *ranchero* society), this direct unadorned verbal style sets up expectations of a basically egalitarian social order based on *respeto* (respect) between independent, authoritative men (or between self-assertive women as equals). For both men and women, at least when they are communicating among their own gender or with intimates, the ethic invoked is that of a frontier society in which the individual must be strong and independent to survive.

As I described them earlier, *ranchera* women, although publicly subservient to men, are physically and emotionally tough and resilient. They work not only in the kitchen, but also in the fields when necessary, and they take care of the smaller animals, killing chickens and other birds in order to cook them. Some know how to use guns and ride horses. They learn at an early age, like everyone else in the *rancho*, to take care of themselves in the natural and social world wherein they live, defending themselves both verbally and physically when necessary. Thus when these women appropriate this verbal style, it directly indexes strength, whereas when men use it, it also indexes masculinity indirectly (Ochs, 1992).

FRANQUEZA CONSTRUCTED IN NARRATIVE PERFORMANCE

As shown by the interaction in front of the church described earlier, *franqueza* is an emergent quality of discourse constructed by interactants "on the spot." In this sense, it is an emergent quality of performance (Bauman, 1984; Hymes, 1975, 1981), introduced by one speaker and then either accepted or contested by the other speaker or speakers. (In my eagerness not to offend anyone during my early fieldwork, in the aforementioned dialogue that took place in front of the church, I did not contest my interrogator's *franqueza* and implicit status claim.) *Franqueza's* bald-on-record style either indexes an egalitarian ideology among equals (e.g., male to male or female to female, when both are roughly of equal age) or a patriarchal ideology of hierarchy (e.g., older to younger or male to female).

In the following excerpt from a tape made early in the research project, when we were relative strangers to each other, *franqueza* is constructed in a narrative recounted by a very senior male of the extended family to Juan Guerra, my then doctoral student and co-ethnographer in the first phase of the study. At the time, this man, the eldest brother in this extended family, was visiting from the *rancho*, where he had retired after many years working in Chicago, and where he managed the family avocado business.

The interaction took place in the kitchen of a home in Pilsen, the most well-known Mexican neighborhood in Chicago and the traditional "port of entry" for Mexican immigrants in recent decades. The kitchen was filled with people because this house and family served as a center for the entire extended family in the early years of the study. We had finished eating and were about to teach a class that would help family members prepare for examinations and interviews in the amnesty process that would make them legal residents of the United States. Don Jaime (a pseudonym), unlike most other family members, already had a green card that granted him residency in the United States, although in this excerpt, he tells Juan about his interactions with the immigration authorities when he was still working without legal papers.

Juan began the interaction by asking, *"Bueno Don Jaime, me dicen que usted, cuando primero vino a los Estados Unidos, fue a Harlingen."* (Well, sir, they tell me that you, when you first came to the United States, went to Harlingen.) After some back and forth discussion about where Harlingen, Texas was located near the Texas–Mexican border, Juan tells Don Jaime that he was born there. Don Jaime agrees that, yes, he is familiar with the town, but that he does not like it, because he was incarcerated twice there by the immigration authorities before he was legally sanctioned to work in the United States. Then he tells Juan that he was the first to come here illegally from his *rancho*, and that eventually about 100 people followed him to Chicago. He continues to explain that with money earned in Chicago, many of them bought land back in the *rancho* and planted avocado orchards, so that *rancho* today is vastly different from the pre-Chicago days when only a few people had money and most of the *rancho* was very poor. (The few people who had some money had migrated to Kansas in the previous generation.) After two interruptions from others in the kitchen, and in the midst of multiple conversations being carried on by others, Juan and Don Jaime continue their conversation, and Don Jaime launches into his story.

1	Jaime:	*Este, a mí la ley americana*	Well, to me, the American law [man] NEVER
2		*NUNCA me dobló la vista. O sea*	made me look down in fear. That is, they
3		*nunca le tuve su puro miedo. Me*	never made me really scared. He would tell
4		*decía mira que esto y que l' otro,*	me, look, this and that. [I would say] "OK,
5		*"Está bien, tú estás en tu derecho.*	you're within your rights. I am going to assert
6		*Yo voy hacer el mío. Cometí un*	mine. I made a mistake, I'm going to pay for
7		*error, lo voy a pagar, nomás que*	it, only over there in Mexico."
8		*allá en México."*	
9	Juan:	*Sí, sí.*	Yes, uh huh.
10	Jaime:	*Dice—ya después me encontré con*	He says—then after that I encountered an
11		*un emigrante de, en /?/, Detroit,*	immigration officer of, in /?/, Detroit,
12		*Michigan. Y me agarró allá /?/*	Michigan. And he grabbed me over there /?/
13		*entonces había un muchacho qu'*	so there was a young boy who began to tell
14		*empezó a decirle, "Que mira" /?/ le*	him, "Hey look" /?/ I told him, "Look, tell him,
15		*digo, "Mira, dile, dile nada más*	tell him nothing more than that you are from
16		*que eres de México, y, este, no*	Mexico, and, well, you don't have to tell him
17		*tienes que decirle cómo llegaron."*	how you got here."
18	Juan:	*Sí.*	Yeah.
19	Jaime:	*'Tonces m' empezó a hablar el, el*	So the immigration official began to speak
20		*emigrante, "Sabes qué, me da pena*	with me, "You know what [I told him], I
21		*con él. Apenas es un muchacho y*	feel sorry for him [the young boy]. He is
22		*siento feo que lo, este, que lo estés*	just a boy and I feel bad that, well, that you
23		*investigando así." Dice, "Oye me*	are investigating him this way." He says,
24		*gustas como pa' emigrante," y me*	Listen, I'd like you as an immigration
25		*rogó tanto que me quedara en, en*	official," and he begged me so much to stay
26		*Michigan para donde la frontera*	in, in Michigan for, at the Canadian border,
27		*de de Canadá pero, "Pero yo, ¿qué*	but [I said] "But what am I going to do
28		*voy a hacer aquí? Todo está*	here? Everything is strange and I don't
29		*afuera y yo no sé hablar inglés."*	know how to speak English." He says, "No,
30		*Dice "No, tienes un sentido /?/"*	you have a feel /for it/.
31	Juan:	*Sí.*	Yeah.
32	Jaime:	*"Vete a la frontera. [slight pause]*	"Get yourself to the border [slight pause]
33		*y vas a—" "¿Y voy a denunciar a*	and you're going to—" "And I'm going to

34		*la gente?" le digo. Dice, "Sí."*	denounce my people?" I say to him. He
35		*"/Pos/ no-o-o!"* [marked rising	says, "Yes." "Oh-h-h no!" [marked rising
36		intonation] *Al poquito ya me volví*	intonation] After a little while I returned
37		*a venir aquí, fui a traer a mi*	here, I went to bring my wife, two children
38		*esposa, nacieron dos niños.*	were born. [pause] The—they admitted us
39		[pause] *La—nos admitieron aquí*	here in this country because of those two
40		*en este país por medio de esos*	children; now they are grown; that one is
41		*dos niños, ya 'tán grandecitos,*	my daughter; she is my sister and, and,
42		*aquella es m' hija, ella es mi*	that's how it is.
43		*hermana y, y así.*	
44	Juan:	*Sí.*	Yes.
45	Jaime:	*De veras fue reduro.*	Really, it was very hard.
46	Juan:	*Es muy difícil al principio, ¿verdá?*	It's very hard at the beginning, right?
47	Jaime:	*Sí.* [pause] *Muy difícil.*	Yes. [pause] Very hard.

In this brief excerpt, Don Jaime tells a story within a story. While telling Juan the story of his migration to the United States, he recounts the story of his capture, along with a younger male migrant, by the immigration authorities in Michigan. This capture occurred during the period in which he was a migrant without legal papers, after he had been a legal *bracero* (manual laborer recruited by a U.S. program that ended in 1964) and before he became legalized through the birth of his two youngest children in Chicago. In this story, he stands up to the immigration officer (referred to colloquially as *el emigrante*), saying that American lawmen NEVER caused him to *dobló la vista*, literally to "look down at the ground," meaning in fear. I have described *rancheros* as particularly proud people with erect posture and direct eye gaze, so for them, this colloquial phrase is particularly apt. To be strong (NOT afraid) is to maintain direct eye gaze, literally to "stand up to" another person.

In this story, Don Jaime not only stands up for himself in front of *el emigrante*. He also stands up for the younger male who is captured with him, and who, possibly out of fear, begins to tell *el emigrante* everything. Don Jaime stops him, saying, all you need to say is that you are from Mexico, not how you got here. Don Jaime is aware of his rights under American law and points this out to the representative of this law who is arresting him: "You are within your rights to arrest me; now I am going to assert my rights." Although this storytelling could be perceived as masculine "bragging" about toughness and strength in the face of authority, this particular performance is not unusually highlighted. That is, although fleeting, it is a performance in the sense that Don Jaime is aware of his attentive audience (Juan) and crafts his language in aesthetically pleasing and persuasive ways (Bauman, 1977; Hymes, 1975, 1981; Tannen, 1989). But it is not as highly performative as Don Jaime's storytelling language is on other occasions. Masculine "bragging" within this network generally coincides with a more highlighted or intense verbal performance, often involving humor and coarse language.

How is this performance, then? In other words, how does it differ from Don Jaime's ordinary conversational language? The primary device that Don Jaime uses to make this story performative is reported speech, or what Tannen (1989) more accurately calls "constructed dialogue." He quickly shifts back and forth between his own voice and that of *el emigrante* in the recounted episode. By doing so, he embellishes a simple narrative with artfulness, constructing a dramatic dialogue between himself and the immigration officer in which he is placed in a position to decide whether he would denounce his people by becoming an immigration official himself. As he shifts between these two voices, he sometimes includes and sometimes omits *digo* (I say) and *dice* (he says), but the speakers are clear to Juan, the listener, through marked changes in pitch level, pronominal reference (through verb endings in Spanish), and semantic context.

Displaying these various voices within his story allows Don Jaime to construct his own identity in contrast to the others. First, he contrasts himself with the boy, who is frightened and talking too much. In recounting this episode, Don Jaime calmly stops the boy in midsentence and then speaks on his behalf to the Immigration and Naturalization Service (INS) officer. Second, he contrasts himself with the INS officer, whom Don Jaime represents as trying to get him to switch allegiances. Here Don Jaime constructs himself as a self-assertive individual who is sophisticated enough to know his rights and insist on them in the face of authority, and as someone who is responsible and loyal to his people. Note here the construction of an identity that evidences both autonomy (i.e., standing out from one's group) and affiliation. Because identity construction relies on the creation of salient contrasts with other identities, the constructed dialogue here is crucial to Don Jaime's representation of himself through *franqueza*.

In the following section, I extract the constructed dialogue from the story within the story told to Juan in Chicago to clarify this artfulness and identity construction (I include here only the English translation. The original Spanish is provided in the full story earlier, lines 1–47).

Constructed Dialogue Within the Story

J (to official):	OK, you're within your rights. I am going to assert mine. I made a mistake; I'm going to pay for it, only over there in Mexico. (original Spanish lines 5–8)
J (to boy):	Look, tell him, tell him nothing more than that you are from Mexico, and, well, you don't have to tell him how you got here. (original Spanish lines 15–17)
J (to official):	You know what [I told him], I feel sorry for him [the young boy]. He is just a boy and I feel bad that, well, that you are investigating him this way. (original Spanish lines 20–23)
Official:	Listen, I'd like you as an immigration official. (Original Spanish line 23–24)
J:	But what am I going to do here? Everything is strange and I don't know how to speak English. (original Spanish lines 27–29)
Official:	No, you have a feel /for it/. Get yourself to the border [slight pause] and you're going to— (original Spanish on line 30 and lines 32–33)
J:	And I'm going to denounce my people? (original Spanish line 33–34)
Official:	Yes. (original Spanish line 34)
J:	Oh-h-h no! [marked rising intonation] (original Spanish line 35)

In lines 34 and 35, Don Jaime enunciates /*Pos*/ *no-o-o!* (Oh-h-h no!) with a marked rising intonation pattern, marking this particular speech as especially performative. These words also serve as the resolution to the climax of the story-within-a-story. When urged by the immigration official to become an *emigrante* himself because he has "a feel" for the work, Don Jaime refuses so that he will not have to denounce his own people.

Don Jaime's own voice in the story clearly shows the self-assertive verbal style of *franqueza,* which constructs him as independent, strong, and in control in the face of authority. His first words to the official in lines 5 to 8,

Está bien, tú estás en tu derecho. Yo voy a hacer el mío. Cometí un error, lo voy a pagar, nomás que allá en México.	OK, you're within your rights. I am going to assert mine. I made a mistake, I'm going to pay for it, only over there in Mexico,

are direct and unadorned, and they all are in the active voice. With their uniformly pronominal *tú* (you) and *yo* (I) subjects, they develop both a grammatical and a semantic parallelism that aligns the equally short independent clauses into a staccato-like rhythmic pattern, which signals performance. The first two lines parallel each other, one focusing on *tú* or "your" rights (the rights of the officer to arrest him), and the other focusing on *yo* or "my" rights under your law. The staccato-like rhythm is especially notable in the last three lines, which begin with *Cometí un error* (I made a mistake):

Está bien, tú estás en tu derecho	OK, you're within your rights.
Yo voy a hacer el mío.	I am going to assert mine.
Cometí un error,	I made a mistake,
lo voy a pagar	I'm going to pay for it,
nomás que allá en México	only over there in Mexico.

These poetic qualities affirm Don Jaime's authoritative stance. Moreover, he uses *tú* with the official rather than the more self-humbling and respectful *usted*, and in his account, the official accepts Don Jaime's claim of equality between them with his own use of *tú* (here in second person singular Spanish verb endings). Thus, their words immediately construct an egalitarian relationship between the two men, although one is an immigration official arresting the other, a migrant without legal papers. In Don Jaime's account, his self-assertive claim to rights is not contested. In fact, it is admired so that the official begs him to consider becoming an INS official himself. These two are the two equals. The younger man, whom Don Jaime also addresses with *tú* (see *es* verb endings in lines 16–17), indexing his lower status because of age, is under the protection of Don Jaime.

What is important in this story is not its truth value, although it may well be factual. Of more interest is the frank verbal style used in the story and its construction of *ranchero* identity. Don Jaime recounts that he did not *dobló la vista* before the immigration official, but instead addressed him directly, with a bald-on-record verbal style. This is the rhetoric of the self-made man, an independent individualist whom nobody orders around. He is, after all, in a foreign country to work, and thus to improve the social and economic well-being of himself and his family, and, in his view, deserves respect for doing this.

CONCLUSION

The analysis of discourse in this chapter shows how *franqueza* works to construct *ranchero* identity. The bald-on-record verbal style of *franqueza* indexes an egalitarian, individualist ideology, and it is a predominant verbal style among the *rancheros* I have known for more than 15 years now. It is perhaps the most salient characteristic of this group, creating a sense of personhood that is straightforward, candid, and honest on the one hand, and self-assertive, tough, and proud on the other. Qualities of sincerity and honesty are thought to support an egalitarian and stable social order, whereas self-assertiveness protects that order and ensures one's (family's) own progress.

While evoking all these qualities of personhood, this verbal style often indirectly indexes masculinity. Women, however, also use *franqueza,* and thus also frequently, in specific contexts, construct themselves as tough and independent individuals. Even children use this style of speaking. Thus it is an ideology generally shared throughout the community that thus underlies cultural, not just individual, practices, although some individuals are known to be *más franco/a* (more frank) than others. Yet virtually all participate in and generate cultural and linguistic practices that evidence self-assertion and a belief in their own abilities to progress through hard work and effort.

Such examples of a belief in and commitment toward upward mobility through hard work, independence, and interdependence abound in these families, as does discourse that uses such constructs to distinguish themselves explicitly from other groups of Mexicans, primarily indigenous Indians, who are perceived as hard working, but not as valuing private property nor upward mobility. In verbal style, they also distinguish themselves from "citified" people, who, some say, do not really work because they do not work with their hands on their own land. That is, they do not create things and their own material well-being with their own hands and effort. *Rancheros,* in contrast, are proud of doing and making things themselves, including their own houses, and some, their own businesses. They take raw land and other resources, and with their own labor convert them into something profitable that benefits themselves and their families. Migrating to Chicago, then, can be seen as one important manifestation of an ideology fundamental to their identities that permeates their discourse. As Don Jaime once said to me, referring to Chicago, *"Es una herencia"* (It's an inheritance) for his children, giving them a base from which to *mejorar* (improve themselves).

REFERENCES

Año Nuevo Kerr, L. (1977). Mexican Chicago: Chicano assimilation aborted, 1939–1954. In M. G. Holli & P. d'A. Jones (Eds.), Ethnic Chicago (pp. 269–298). Grand Rapids, MI: William B. Erdmans.

Barragán López, E. (1990). *Más allá de los caminos*. Zamora, Mexico: El Colegio de Michoacán.

Barragán López, E. (1997). *Con un pie en el estribo: Formacíon y deslizamientos de las sociedades rancheras en la construccíon del méxico moderno*. Zamora, Michoacán, Mexico: El Colegio de Michoacán.

Barragán López, E., Hoffmann, O., Linck, T., & Skerritt, D. (Eds.). (1994). *Rancheros y sociedades rancheras*. Zamora, Mexico: El Colegio de Michoacán.

Barth, F. (1969). *Ethnic groups and boundaries: The social organization of culture difference*. Boston: Little, Brown.

Bauman, R. (1984). *Verbal art as performance*. Prospect Heights, IL: Waveland Press.

Bauman, R., & Sherzer, J. (1989). Introduction to the second edition. In R. Bauman & J. Sherzer (Eds.), *Explorations in the ethnography of speaking* (pp. ix–xxvii). Cambridge, England: Cambridge University Press.

Bonfil Batalla, G. (1996). México profundo: *Reclaiming a civilization*. Austin: University of Texas Press.

Bourdieu, P. (1977). *Outline of a theory of practice*. Cambridge: Cambridge University Press.

Brading, D. (1994). *Epilogue, A 25 años del encuentro con "Rancheros."* In E. Barragán López, O. Hoffmann, T. Linck, & D. Skerritt (Eds.), *Rancheros y sociedades rancheras* (pp. 329–334). Zamora, Mexico: El Colegio de Michoacán.

Bravo, D. (1996). *La risa en el regateo: Estudio sobre el estilo comunicativo de negociadores epañoles y suecos*. Stockholm: Institutionen för spanska och portugisiska.

Brown, P., & Levinson, S. (1987). *Politeness: Some universals in language usage*. Cambridge, England: Cambridge University Press.

Chávez, M. (1994). *Una es la de todo*. In E. Barragán López, O. Hoffman, T. Linck, & D. Skerritt (Eds.), *Rancheros y sociedades rancheras* (pp. 109–124). Zamora, Mexico: El Colegio de Michoacán.

Chávez Carbajal, M. G. (1995). *El rostro colectivo de la nación mexicana*. Morelia, Michoacán: Universidad Michoacana de San Nicolas de Hidalgo.

Cintron, R. (1997). *Angel's town: Chero ways, gang life, and rhetorics of the everyday*. Boston: Beacon Press.

Cosio Villegas, D., Bernal, I., Moreno Toscano, A., González, L., Blanquel, E., & Meyer, L. (1995). *A compact history of Mexico*. Mexico, DF: Colegio de Mexico.

De la Peña, G. (1984). Ideology and practice in Southern Jalisco: Peasants, rancheros, and urban entrepreneurs. In R. Smith (Ed.), *Kinship ideology and practice in Latin America* (pp. 204–234). Chapel Hill: University of North Carolina Press.

Delgado-Gaitán, C. (1993). Parenting in two generations of Mexican American families. *International Journal of Behavioral Development, 16*(3), 409–427.

Farr, M. (1993). Essayist literacy and other verbal performances. *Written Communication, 10*(1), 4–38.

Farr, M. (1994a). Biliteracy in the home: Practices among *mexicano* families in Chicago. In D. Spener (Ed.), *Adult biliteracy in the United States* (pp. 89–110). McHenry, IL and Washington, DC: Delta Systems and Center for Applied Linguistics.

Farr, M. (1994b). *En los dos idiomas*: Literacy practices among *mexicano* families in Chicago. In B. Moss (Ed.), *Literacy across communities* (pp. 9–47). Cresskill, NJ: Hampton Press.

Farr, M. (1994c). *Echando relajo*: Verbal art and gender among *mexicanas* in Chicago. In M. Bucholtz, A. C. Liang, L. A. Sutton, & C. Hines (Eds.), *Cultural performances: Proceedings of the third Berkeley women and language conference* (pp. 168–186). Berkeley: University of California Press.

Farr, M. (1998). *El relajo como microfiesta*. In H. Pérez (Ed.), *Mexico en fiesta* (pp. 457–470). Zamora, Michoacán, Mexico: El Colegio de Michoacán.

Farr, M. (forthcoming). *Rancheros* in Chicagoacán: Ways of speaking and identity in a transnacional Mexican community. Austin: University of Texas Press.

Farr, M., & Guerra, J. (1995). Literacy in the community: A study of *mexicano* families in Chicago. *Discourse Processes Special Issue, Literacy Among Latinos, 19*(1), 7–19.

Friedrich, P. (1977). *Agrarian revolt in a Mexican village*. Chicago: University of Chicago Press.

Gledhill, J. (1991). *Casi nada: A study of agrarian reform in the home of Cardenismo*. Austin: University of Texas Press.

Goffman, E. (1967). *Interaction ritual: Essays on face to face behavior*. Garden City, NY: Anchor Books.

González, L. (1974). *San José de Gracia: Mexican village in transition*. Austin: University of Texas Press.

González, L. (1991). *Del hombre a caballo y la cultura ranchera. Tierra Adentro, 52,* 3–7.

Guerra, J. (1998). *Close to home: Oral and literate practices in a transnational* mexicano *community*. New York: Teachers College Press.

Guerra, J., & Farr, M. (2002). Writing on the margins: Spiritual and autobiographical discourse among *mexicanas* in Chicago. In G. Hull & K. Schultz (Eds.), *School's out! Literacy at work and in the community* (pp. 96–123). New York: Teachers College Press.

Haverkate, H. (1994). *La cortesía verbal: Estudio pragmalingüístico*. Madrid: Editorial Gredos.

Hernández-Flores, N. (1999). Politeness ideology in Spanish colloquial conversations: The case of advice. *Pragmatics, 9*(1), 37–49.

Hymes, D. (1974a). *Foundations in sociolinguistics: An ethnographic approach*. Philadelphia: University of Pennsylvania Press.

Hymes, D. (1974b). Ways of speaking. In R. Bauman & J. Sherzer (Eds.), *Explorations in the ethnography of speaking* (1st ed., pp.433–451). Cambridge, England: Cambridge University Press.

Hymes, D. (1975). Breakthrough into performance. In D. Ben-Amos & K. S. Goldstein (Eds.), *Folklore: Performance and communication* (pp. 11–74). The Hague: Mouton.

Hymes, D. (1981). *In vain I tried to tell you: Essays in Native American ethnopoetics*. Philadelphia: University of Pennsylvania Press.

Jacobs, I. (1982). *Ranchero revolt: The Mexican revolution in Guerrero*. Austin: University of Texas Press.

LeVine, R. A., & White, M. I. (1986). *Human conditions: The cultural basis of educational development*. New York: Routledge.

Lomnitz-Adler, C. (1992). *Exits from the labyrinth: Culture and ideology in the Mexican national space*. Berkeley: University of California Press.

Melhuus, M. (1996). Power, value, and the ambiguous meanings of gender. In M. Melhuus & K. A. Stolen (Eds.), *Machos, mistresses, Madonnas: Contesting the power of Latin American gender imagery* (pp. 230–259). London: Verso.

Milroy, L. (1980). *Language and social networks*. Oxford: Blackwell.
Ochs, E. (1992). Indexing gender. In A. Duranti & C. Goodwin (Eds.), *Rethinking context: Language as an interactive phenomenon* (pp. 335–358). New York: Cambridge University Press.
Rogers, S. C. (1975). Female forms of power and the myth of male dominance: A model of female/male interaction in peasant society. *American Ethnologist, 22*, 727–756.
Schiller, N. G., Basch, L., & Blanc-Szanton, C. (1992). Transnationalism: A new analytic framework for understanding migration. *Annals of the New York Academy of Sciences, 645*, 1–24.
Scott, J. (1990). *Domination and the arts of resistance: Hidden transcripts*. New Haven: Yale University Press.
Tannen, D. (1989). *Talking voices: Repetition, dialogue, and imagery in conversational discourse*. Cambridge, England: Cambridge University Press.
Valdés, G. (1996). Con respeto: *Bridging the distances between culturally diverse families and schools*. New York: Teachers College Press.
Wierzbicka, A. (1991). *Cross-cultural pragmatics: The semantics of human interaction*. Berlin: Mouton de Gruyter.

ENDNOTES

1. A *dicho* (saying) that means "No one orders me around!"
2. This chapter is a revised version of Farr, M. 2000. *¡A mí no me manda nadie!* Individualism and identity in Mexican *ranchero* speech, in V. Pagliai and M. Farr (Eds.), special issue of *Pragmatics* (10:1) on Language, Performance and Identity, pp. 61–85.
3. I thank Elias Dominguez Barajas for his helpful comments and the addition of accent marks to my colloquial, oral Spanish (in fact, my *español ranchereado* "ranch Spanish").
4. Usually *mestizo* refers to mixed Native American and European ancestry, although in recent years scholars have identified African ancestry as the "third root" of Mexico (Chávez Carbajal, 1995). Indeed, this region of Michoacán did have Africans working on sugar plantations and elsewhere several centuries ago. Now, however, African ancestry is not generally acknowledged, and this "third root" has blended in with the general *mestizo* population.
5. The original Spanish is in italics, followed by an English translation (my own). Unclear segments that were not transcribed are indicated by a question mark placed within slanted lines. Reported speech, or constructed dialogue, is enclosed within quotation marks. Words in all capital letters indicate increased stress. Square brackets are used for nonverbal cues such as pauses and marked intonation patterns, and for comments intended to clarify meaning for the reader. An asterisk after a word indicates a Mexican Spanish rural dialect feature.
6. A popular expression, *con el nopal en la frente* (with a nopal, a Mexican cactus, on the forehead) means looking very Mexican, presumably with Indian features.

Photograph by Yulia Domínguez Barajas.

3

Sociocognitive Aspects of Proverb Use in a Mexican Transnational Social Network

Elías Domínguez Barajas
Texas A&M University

INTRODUCTION: PROVERBS IN ACTION

On a mid-November evening, the López[1] family hears the swift winds shaking the windowpanes of its Chicago home. The winds announce the arrival of an early winter, but inside the house the change of weather is not the talk of the evening. The focus of the conversation is the food, and eight people enjoy a lively chat as they get ready for supper. Mrs. López, the matriarch of this family, has a rich chicken soup brewing on the stove, and she wipes her hands on her apron as she turns from the pot to the *comal* on which she warms the tortillas that are to accompany the meal. In the meantime, her children set the table. One gathers and sets the glasses, another pours water into them, and another takes care of setting the plates and utensils. The boiling soup fills the home with its aroma and its steam glazes the windows of the now cramped kitchen.

As is common for them, some of the López siblings who no longer live with their parents have found their way to their parents' house after work. On this day, Aristeo and María López will have six of their ten children arriving in time for dinner. The kitchen is filled with the smell of freshly cooked chicken soup and the sounds of animated conversation in Spanish and English—and sometimes a mixture of both languages.

The siblings come into the house one after the other, "like sheep," says Mrs. López. When almost everyone expected is present, and the place settings have been laid on the table, Tita, one of the younger López siblings, straggles into the kitchen via the back door. The aroma of soup and the sounds of chatter and laughter welcome her. Upon noticing the place settings and that several of her siblings are sitting at the table, she remarks, "*¡Ay, pero sí ya están listos para comer!*" (Oh, but you're ready to eat!). Ana, one of her older sisters, replies: "*Como dice el dicho, el que tiene hambre, le atiza a la olla*" (As the saying goes, he who is hungry stokes [the fire for] the pot). General echoes of agreement follow the utterance of the proverb, and Tita accepts the reply with a smile.

* * *

Socially and linguistically speaking, something remarkable has happened in the brief verbal exchange of the preceding scene. The interlocutors have acknowledged, in a rather subtle way, the existence of a problematic situation where, at first glance, there might appear to be none. In addition, there has been a resolution of that situation without explicit mention of either the potential conflict or the means for its resolution. This lack of referential explicitness begins to illustrate the complexity of proverb use. To understand the function of proverbs in a conversation, we must not only be familiar with the underlying rules that govern linguistic communication in a particular group, but we must also understand the analogic nature of the proverbs themselves.

For example, in the introductory situation, Ana's proverb alludes to an action (i.e., the stoking of a fire) that, literally speaking, is irrelevant to Tita's apparently declarative statement (i.e., that the people sitting at the table are ready to eat). Yet, Tita appears to be satisfied with the reply, and the rest of the participants, in voicing assent, confirm that the reply has been appropriate. The apparently cryptic exchange begins with Tita's pointed observation of her siblings' clear intention to start having dinner without her. Tita's exclamatory tone communicates something to Ana that prompts her to reply with the proverb. The proverb itself alludes to the justification of an action (i.e., expediting the cooking of a meal) in light of a motivating circumstance (i.e., being hungry). Ana's implicit defense of this family's diligence in the preparation of the meal to satisfy its hunger suggests that she has understood Tita's exclamatory utterance as an accusation. That is, it would appear that Tita's comment is understood to be the equivalent of saying, "Aha! Caught you in the act!" Thus, the implication is that the rest of the family is doing something wrong, and because Tita makes reference to their readiness to have the meal, her objection is perceived to be that they are being rude by not waiting for her. This implicit accusation is acknowledged by Ana's voicing of a proverb. Because the accusation is indirectly communicated through a declarative statement, the use of the proverb helps the respondent (i.e., Ana) reply in kind (i.e., indirectly). The accusation is thus not considered openly, but it is considered nevertheless.

The proverb, in presenting an analogy, communicates a socially sanctioned action—one must be diligent to satisfy one's hunger—and that is what the siblings preparing the dinner table are exhibiting. The setting of the table parallels the act of stoking a fire because they both are acts of diligence that lead to the desired goal (i.e., consumption of the meal). The analogy is not voiced explicitly, but it is evidently implicit because the participants do not question the relevance of the proverb and, what is more, express agreement with Ana's use of it as a reply to Tita. It is in the participants' expression of agreement, and in Tita's acceptance of the proverb as a reply, that we see how the use of the proverb defuses the potential point of discord (i.e., an accusation)—and this is done without the participants ever directly mentioning the problem itself.

I point out the chain of details involved in understanding Ana's utterance of a proverb to emphasize that even the most common linguistic exchanges require our use of complex mental resources. Moreover, if we add to the linguistic subtleties of intention (what a speaker meant to do by uttering something), allusion (implicit topical references), and convention (socially sanctioned patterns of expression), the equally subtle distinctions of cultural practices and culture-specific referents, the ability to understand messages fraught with these latter elements seems even more remote for the uninitiated, or the outsider.

In this chapter, I examine these linguistic concerns with regard to proverb use among a *Mexicano*[2] social network.[3] This research is an offshoot of the Mexican-origin Language and Literacy Project headed by Professor Marcia Farr at the University of Illinois at Chicago (UIC). Under the auspices of the Spencer Foundation, Farr, et al. (1994a) researched the oral and literate practices of a transnational *Mexicano* social network based in Chicago, Illinois, and a rural town in the northwest corner of Mexico's state of Michoacán. Similarly, my research focuses on a transnational *Mexicano* social network based in Chicago, Illinois, and Michoacán. However, the town of origin for the social network considered here is Janácuaro, a rural farming town in the northeast corner of Michoacán. This research thus seeks to contribute to the Mexican-origin Language and Literacy Project at UIC by extending its regional scope.

With regard to focus, however, my research seeks to narrow the linguistic object of study to one oral genre: proverbs. I argue that proverbs are amazingly complex linguistic and cognitive constructs, demonstrating this by analyzing how the participants of the social network who provided the data for my research strategically use proverbs to serve some of their complex communicative needs. Because I begin with the consideration that many oral traditions may not be shared across cultures, it is important to point out for the sake of the relevance of this research that many, if not all, cultures appear to have linguistic expressions that act as proverbs. In addition, proverbs are known to be part of the most ancient texts in the history of the world. Paremiologist (proverb scholar) Herón Pérez Martínez (1993), supported by the information collected in an edited volume by James B. Pritchard (1950) on ancient Near Eastern texts, suggested that in ancient Egyptian texts (circa 2450 B.C.E.), we can begin to see "the germ" of some proverbs: "Hold on to the truth and never let go"; "Good words are better hidden than the emerald"; "Bad deeds never took their fruit to good port" (pp. 31–34). Pérez Martínez (1993) further underscored the historical presence of proverbial expressions by citing the work of Samuel Noah Kramer (1985), who documented that Sumerian clay tablets dating back to the third millennium B.C.E. contain some lists of proverbs (Honeck, 1997, p. 4).

The ancient history of this particular type of oral tradition should alone compel us to recognize its value among the many linguistic forms of expression that mark human creativity and reflect mental agility and sophistication, but furthering the interest in paremiology is the idea that proverbs allude to values and lessons that often serve to reinforce cultural bonds. It seems likely that proverbs continue to survive the tests of time and space because they serve this primary function. The evidence of their resilience may easily by seen in the fact that most people have no difficulty identifying proverbs, or even recalling some. But just as proverbs can be considered popular and easily identifiable, they harbor a complexity made evident by scholarly failure to reach a conclusive definition of what a proverb is.[4] I address this issue more fully in this chapter's section on the nature of proverbs.

Notwithstanding the lack of a conclusive definition for those linguistic expressions we call proverbs, the members of the *Mexicano* social network on which this chapter focuses used proverbs freely and regularly in their conversations. The ease and speed with which they interjected, understood, and evaluated proverbs seemed to belie the proverbs' complexity and the numerous mental connections required for the successful manipulation of each one of these linguistic expressions. Here, I analyze the complexity of some proverbs used by the members of the social network, outlining some of the cognitive processes involved in the comprehension of the proverbs. In addition, I argue that the use to which proverbs are put in this social network correspond to four general social purposes: (a) to censure, (b) to teach, (c) to establish rapport, and (d) to entertain. These functions serve to promote intragroup solidarity through the affirmation and reaffirmation of cultural and interpersonal bonds.

THE SOCIAL NETWORK

Despite 25 years of living in Chicago, the López family remains psychologically, socially, and economically bound to their country of origin: Mexico. The extended López family makes up a social network consisting of two cohorts: one based in Chicago and the other in Janácuaro. Many of the network members in Chicago maintain active ties to their country of origin at several levels: the social level (e.g., maintaining continuous contact with relatives and friends via telephone, letters, and physical visits of acquaintances or kin to the region, the latter occurring on the average at least once per year), the cultural level (e.g., celebrating Mexican national holidays, maintaining religious practices, sharing a mental landscape—memories, places, people, activities, and language), and the economic level (e.g., submitting remittances, engaging in investments, buying real estate property, and enacting transnational or local commercial ventures).

The network members' active participation in their community of origin characterizes them as part of a transnational community (Schiller, Basch, & Blanc-Szanton, 1992, p. ix), which speaks to the persistence of ethnic–cultural identity in contexts far removed from what can be thought of as the homeland. In this case, the members of the López social network who reside in the United States, and who are primarily the members of one nuclear family of 12 adult members (2 parents, 5 daughters, and 5 sons), recreate psychological and cultural ties to their country of origin on a daily basis. By maintaining and expanding the oral traditions of its home community, the social network transforms its immediate social and psychological surroundings in the host community.

The parents, Aristeo and María López, were born and raised in Janácuaro. Given the rural characteristics of the town and the recognition of agriculture as the common means of earning a living, it is not surprising to find that the network members use figurative expressions that often allude to this type of environment. Although all of Mr. and Mrs. López's children grew up in an urban setting (Mexico City and Chicago), they are rather familiar with the rural setting in which their parents were brought up. Because the family did not migrate to the United States before all of the children were born, the López children all experienced the life and surroundings of their parents' hometown by virtue of frequent visits there during their upbringing in Mexico City and yearly visits there as adults living in Chicago. It is important to point this out because it highlights the familiarity with the rural environment to which they often refer in their conversations and comments. That is, the social network often refers to salient ecologic features of this familiar environment to index a characterization of a given referent, and in doing so, the network reaffirms and, in fact, recreates for itself the home community at the psychological and cultural level. My argument here is that this is often done with many of the oral traditions shared within the network (e.g., stories, legends, anecdotes, jokes, riddles, songs, and *plática*[5]), and in this essay I focus on the proverb as one such oral tradition, explaining how this creation and re-creation of cultural common ground occurs.

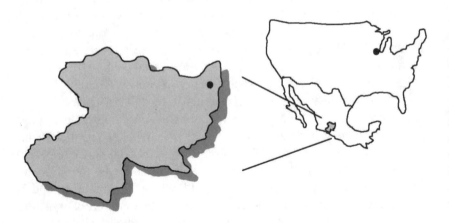

FIG. 3.1.   The López social network's transnational poles: Janácuaro, in Mexico's state of Michoacán, and Chicago, Illinois.[6]

THE NATURE OF PROVERBS

Before addressing the López social network's use of proverbs, a word about the nature of these expressions is in order. Regardless how familiar proverbs may seem to be, scholars have found it difficult to formulate a universal definition of proverbs. Although in terms of structure, proverbs can be said to be very similar to riddles (Dundes, 1981), the form of proverbs can vary enough to create numerous exceptions to just about any definition that seeks to encapsulate them. Dundes (1981) and Ohtsuki (1989) observed that all proverbs require a minimum of two words (e.g., "money talks"), but the same cannot be said about a maximum number of words, although the collective understanding is that proverbs are to be brief, sententious phrases. This leaves plenty of room for considerable variation in syntagmatic, semantic, and poetic aspects of proverbs. The potential for variation multiplies in relation to the number of languages taken into account in any definition of the proverb.

Dundes (1981), for example, admitted that his structural definition of the proverb is tentative because it relies only on Anglo-American proverb data. He is aware that the structural variation of proverbs across languages can affect his definition. That is, what may serve as a proverb in one language may be unrecognizable as such in another simply because the structural parameters differ. For example, the phrase "live and learn" may be seen as a proverb in English-speaking cultures because an implied actor or subject is tacitly attached to the phrase, but minimal pairs may not be recognized as complete proverbial expressions in other languages.

Dundes (1981) defined proverbs as "a traditional propositional statement consisting of at least one descriptive element, a descriptive element consisting of a topic and a comment. This means that proverbs must have at least two words" (p. 60). Dundes then elaborated on the nature of the relation between the components of the "descriptive element": the topic and the comment. But when he asserted that proverbs with a single descriptive element are nonoppositional, and that proverbs with more than one descriptive element may or may not be oppositional, we understand that his definition is going too far afield to express something that is practically self-evident: Expressions with only one referent will not communicate a contrast because there is only one element to consider, and expressions with more than one referent will identify a relation—oppositional or nonoppositional—between those referents. This definition is consequently not very useful in helping us identify proverbs from nonproverbs because it can lead us to countless expressions made up of at least two words, the one identifying a topic and the other commenting on it, but which are not proverbs. For example, using Dundes (1981)' criteria for the identification of a proverb, we can say that the phrase "Life is complicated" is an example of a descriptive element consisting of a topic (i.e., living) and a comment (i.e., its degree of simplicity), and that because no two things are being contrasted in the expression, it is nonoppositional in nature. But having identified this, the question remains whether the phrase is a proverb or not, and if we reply in the negative, a related question is why a structurally similar phrase, such as "Life is short," can be understood as a proverb.

The key might be that for an utterance to be considered a proverb, it must be meant metaphorically instead of literally. We find this aspect included in Ohtsuki's (1989) definition of proverbs. For Ohtsuki, proverbs are expressions that consist of more than one word and whose meaning is not the semantic total of these words, that cannot be modified by addition or subtraction of lexemes or word order, and whose authorship is anonymous. With this definition, Ohtsuki covers the major aspects of proverbial expressions. They must be figurative phrases fixed in form and the product of a social group's collective sensibilities.

Another structural aspect of proverbial expressions is their accompanying communicative features. Briggs (1985) pointed out that certain communicative features regularly accompany proverb use in the community of New Mexico *Mexicanos* he researched. He identified eight factors that characterized proverb use among that community:

1. Tying phrase (utterance that links the preceding utterances to the proverbial text to follow)
2. Identity of "owner" (the person, if any, to whom the proverb uttered is to be attributed)
3. Quotative aspect (used if the proverb is attributed to a particular person or group of people)
4. Proverb text (the proverb itself)
5. Special association (statement of the provenance of the proverb, if known)
6. General meaning and/or hypothetical situation (overt explanation and/or application of the proverb)
7. Relevance to context (overt connection to the context in which the proverb is uttered)
8. Validation (affirmation for the validity of the proverb by the speaker or audience saying something such as "it's true")

Briggs (1985) considered these features part of the proverb performance even though they might not always be used. He said that the presence of any feature aside from the proverb text is part of the negotiation process involved in communication. The speaker makes use of a specific feature if it is required for his or her purposes or by the audience. Thus, Briggs' method takes into account cultural particularities, which is to say that he documented specific ways that a community generates proverbs, the meanings attributed to them, and the social functions they serve. This contrasts with the presentation of proverbs out of context (as in proverb dictionaries) in that the evidence for proverb meaning and use is anchored in actual empirical data rather than generalizations based on structural features or the a priori criteria of the researcher.

The focus on shared social behavior (the setting of proverb performance and the participants within it), background knowledge (the references to particular people, places, and historical events), and linguistic features that accompany a verbal genre such as the proverb allow us to see how particular communities use language, and how this use of language varies cross-culturally. In recognizing that the form of the genre may vary across communities, we are led to consider how meaning is assigned to a proverb—or how a proverb comes to be understood—in different communities.

The works of Seitel (1981) and Kirshenblatt-Gimblett (1981) speak to the issue of a "deep structure" to proverb meaning, proposing that proverbs function in one basic way: as analogies. That deep structure, however, can take on different meanings once it is combined with sociolinguistic features, such as those that Briggs (1985) mentioned, and culture-specific metaphoric associations.

Seitel (1981) proposed that we come to understand proverbs by engaging in analogic reasoning and by recognizing symbolic associations. According to Seitel, the quoting of a proverb is basically the presentation of an analogy. Therefore, when speaker X says to listener Y, "A stitch in time saves nine," in reference to minor automobile repair before a long trip, X is in fact saying, "A [a stitch in time] is to B [saving nine] as C [making a minor car repair] is to D [preventing a major one]" (or A : B :: C : D). To understand the comparison, the addresser and addressee must attend to two mental domains, the particular and the general, to which Seitel referred, respectively, as the "proverb situation" and the "social situation" (pp. 126–128). By "social situation" however, Seitel did not mean the actual social context in which the proverb is uttered, but the abstract domain of social norms and situations that parallel the particular imaginary referents mentioned in the proverb text.

In contrast, Seitel (1981) used the term "social context" to denote the social factors (e.g., age, sex, social status, intention) surrounding and characterizing the interlocutors and their use of proverbs (p. 126). Given these distinctions, Seitel (1981) further observed that the referents of the proverb text are ascribed "culturally defined features," which inform the relation between the "proverb situation" and the "social situation" (i.e., the relation between the concrete proverb referents and the abstract situational referents) (pp. 135–136). That is to say, the referents in a proverb are invested with culturally specific associations, and these associations are the foundation of the meaning embedded in the proverbial analogy. Similarly, the "social context" is informed by the "culturally defined features," which characterize the participants and their interaction (p. 136).

Finally, concerning the potential for the varied uses and understandings of a given proverb, Seitel (1981) considered that the explicit and implicit pronouns used in the casting of the proverb clarify how the proverb is meant to be understood. For example, if a person in need runs to a benefactor and begins by saying, "A toad does not run in the daytime unless something is after its life," the proverb is understood as self-disparaging because the speaker is identified as the one with the urgent need, and the proverb is thus implicitly cast in the first person. However, if the speaker of the proverb is the benefactor seeing the person in need arrive, then the proverb is understood as an invective because the visitor is understood to be the object of the proverb, which implicitly casts it in the second person (p. 129).

Although Seitel's (1981) observations appear to be on target, he did not really explore the impact of the factors surrounding the utterance of the proverb (i.e., the interlocutors' social context), and this probably is why he did not address the issue of multiple understandings for the same proverb in the same conversation (e.g., the proverb "a rolling stone gathers no moss" is understood in Scotland as an exhortation toward activity, whereas in England it is an affirmation for the rewards of stability). This is the point at which Kirshenblatt-Gimblett's (1981) approach offers another view of proverbs that, in turn, demonstrates the complexity of interpersonal communication.

Kirshenblatt-Gimblett (1981) proposed that proverbs have no "base meaning." That is, proverbs do not have one meaning in and of themselves, but are, instead, assigned a meaning in conversation by virtue of the exigencies of the interlocutors and their conversational situations. To put it another way, in addition to its potential analogic meaning or meanings, the understanding of a proverb is conditioned by the social context of the interlocutors. What this does for our understanding of proverb use is to acknowledge, rather than ignore, that proverb use has a driving social force behind it. That is to say that the social agency behind these linguistic expressions is, in part, what gives them meaning. Combining the idea that "proverbs express relative rather than absolute truth" (i.e., there is no "base meaning") with the observation that situations can be evaluated in more than one way, Kirshenblatt-Gimblett (1981) has found a way to account for the multiplicity of meanings, and hence functions, assigned to proverbs.

PROVERBS AND THEIR USE

Because proverbs are analogies that encapsulate general observations, socially sanctioned evaluations of behavior, or a pattern of reasoning, they can be applied to a myriad of situations over time and space. This means that the drawing of a particular meaning from such a wide-encompassing statement is highly dependent on context. For this reason, I recognize a collective effort in the understanding and application of proverbs in social contexts. This, in turn, leads me to consider proverbs as examples of a socially sanctioned—rather than an idiosyncratic—communicative strategy.

The people in Janácuaro (and the López family is no exception) make this evident by using proverbs often in their conversations. This practice has been well established in Mexico, as knowledge and use of proverbs have traditionally been seen as evidence of sharp wit, facility of expression, and adherence to traditional values. Kazan's (1952) film *Viva Zapata!*, although not an original product of Mexican cinema, captures the practice of proverb exchange in what could have been a common situation in early 20th century Mexico. A scene in the film shows the revolutionary hero, Emiliano Zapata, as a gentleman caller paying a visit to the parents of his would-be fiancée. With the aim of testing and proving to her parents her suitor's wit and moral character, Zapata's sweetheart quotes proverbs to him. He replies with proverbs of his own that support and embellish the values expressed in the proverbs uttered by his sweetheart. The relevance and harmony of his proverbs in relation to those of his sweetheart win him the approval of his would-be in-laws. The film thus depicts how proverbs are used to communicate and make manifest points of solidarity for the interlocutors.

In a similar exchange of proverb repertoires, four members of the López social network engaged in an exchange of proverbs that clearly evidenced the use of proverbs to create a sense of rapport and solidarity. The participants were Ana, her husband Gabriel, her aunt Carmela, and her uncle Hector. Ana and Gabriel, who live in Chicago, were at that time visiting Carmela and Hector in Janácuaro. It so happened that all four of them were elementary school teachers, and as they discussed the various issues concerning their profession, they talked about the importance of sustained professional development for teachers.

Carmela complained that two older teachers who had been hired recently at a local school were clearly not interested in updating their teaching approaches, and she punctuated this opinion with the proverb *"pero como dicen, camarón que se duerme se lo lleva la corriente"* (but as they say, the shrimp that falls asleep gets dragged away by the current). Ana replied, *"Pues sí, el que adelante no mira, atrás se queda"* (well yes, he who does not look forward, behind remains). Gabriel asked the others to help him recollect a proverb that said something to the effect of *"el que no oye consejos—"* (he who does not listen to advice—), and the others almost in unison finished it for him: *"El que no oye consejo, no llega a viejo"* (He who does not listen to advice, doesn't make it to old age).

Their conversation was unique in that after the uttering of each proverb, the customary pause intended for reflection did not follow. Instead, other proverbs that shared the same general idea (i.e., it behooves one to continue learning by attending to new information and anticipating change) and social values (e.g., diligence, responsibility, self-reflection) quickly ensued. The resulting chain of proverbs extended, rather than truncated, the conversation, and this is a use of proverbs that is uncommon because proverbs often are used to present generalizable conclusions about a topic and thus draw discussions to a close. In contrast, the neat dovetailing of proverbs in the conversation of these four network members, and the shared values expressed in them, suggests that the exchange of proverbs functioned as a tool for solidarity formation instead of a tool for status differentiation.

Establishing solidarity and rapport was important in this case because Ana and Gabriel, who resided in the United States, were visiting the extended family in Janácuaro. By uttering proverbs that implicitly communicated particular social values and manifested a valued oral genre, these members of the social network reaffirmed their shared background in an efficient and highly marked way. This reaffirmation was particularly important for Ana and Gabriel because they had the added burden of communicating to their older interlocutors that, despite their sojourn in the

United States, a land whose values and ways could stand in direct contrast to those of the people of Janácuaro, they remained culturally and socially wedded to their country and culture of origin. The conversation demonstrates that proverbs are invoked not only to express a given idea in a sanctioned and creative way, but also, and perhaps more importantly, to refer to—and thus generally create or recreate—the network's place of origin, its social values, and the personal traits of the network members and their interpersonal relations.

I call attention to this type of discursive interaction to introduce the idea that network participants seek to carry out a social action with their utterance of proverbs. The use of proverbs is a dynamic element in conversations and social interactions. The proverbs that the network members use can thus be said to carry meanings beyond the purely referential because they in fact affect social status and, correspondingly, effect social change. In the following analysis, I explain how proverbs are used to carry out social objectives. I also examine the cognitive skills and sociocultural knowledge necessary for the successful manipulation and processing of some proverbs used by the members of the social network.

PROVERBS AND THEIR SOCIAL FUNCTIONS

The following analysis of proverbial expressions is by no means meant to be exhaustive or complete, but it is meant to present the general functions of proverbs among the López social network, and to highlight some of the salient aspects of proverb processing (i.e., the understanding of proverbs) that very often go unnoticed in regard to proverbs in general. I present here examples of proverbs used by this social network to illustrate common situations in which proverbs were called upon to meet a social need. Proverbs were commonly used as sociocommunicative tools because they were used to (a) censure or justify individual behavior or comment on a social situation or event; (b) to teach or promote reflection (as they were used much in the way of advice); (c) to establish interpersonal rapport; and (d) to add variety to the conversation and thus entertain or engage the listeners by virtue of the verbal creativity manifested in the proverbs themselves.

Although I present these four functions of proverbial utterances, I do not consider the proverbs I present in this discussion to be intrinsically suited to their use in these instances. That is, any given proverb could conceivably be used with regard to any one or all four of these categories. For this reason, I consider that the aim of this research is not the categorization of particular proverbs, but an examination of the use to which they were put and how they came to be understood by the network members.

The functions of this particular oral genre that I observe within the López network resonate with Roman Jakobson's (1960) identification of the phatic function involved in linguistic communication. Jakobson considered that there are six components involved in linguistic communication: an addresser (who serves an emotive function), a context (which serves a referential function), a message (which serves a poetic function), a contact (which serves a phatic function), a code (which serves a metalingual function), and an addressee (who serves a conative function). However, with regard to these components, Jakobson (1960) observed that "although we distinguish six basic aspects of language, we could, however, hardly find verbal messages that would fulfill only one function" (p. 353). Similarly, I too consider that any given proverb may fulfill more than one function at any given time. However, and once again in agreement with Jakobson's theoretical positioning, I suggest that a proverb's acute dependence on context for its meaning renders a "hierarchical order of functions," to use Jakobson's words, that leads to the consideration of one salient function with regard to a given proverb in a particular context.

To illustrate this point, I examine a proverb for each of the first three categories outlined earlier in an effort to give a sense of the type and variety of proverbs encountered among the network. I also make passing reference to the poetic qualities of each in order to address the fourth category (i.e., the creative or entertaining aspect of proverb use). The reason for not addressing the poetic aspect of proverbs on its own is that the poetic quality of all proverbs keeps us from describing this as their primary function. That is, all the proverbs I examine here serve a poetic function in addition to the other function or functions that they may serve. For this reason, singling out proverb use as exclusively emotive, expressive, or creative and devoid of other functions seems to be misleading because proverbs, in my estimation, do not do this exclusively, but are always used to execute another function in addition to that one.

Another theoretical tool I use to shed light on the phenomenon of proverb processing is that of schema. This concept was initially conceived by Frederic C. Bartlett (1932), who talked about it as

> an active organisation of past reactions, or of past experiences, which must always be supposed to be operating in any well-adapted organic response.

That is, whenever there is any order or regularity of behaviour, a particular response is possible only because it is related to other similar responses which have been serially organised, yet which operate, not simply as individual members coming one after another, but as a unitary mass. (p. 201)

Understandably, researchers have reduced Bartlett's (1932) vague notion of "schema" to background knowledge with regard to any given domain and its impact on memory recall (Caroll, 1999; Rayner & Pollatsek, 1989). The idea is that background knowledge is used as a basic cognitive matrix for organizing incoming information (something akin to an arrangement of compartments that serve to organize and arrange incoming stimuli in a familiar and predictable pattern), and that this enhances memory recall and comprehension. It is for this reason that the experience of dining at a restaurant is one popular example of schemata in action. The activity develops in a very predictable way: one is seated, presented with the menu, asked what is desired, brought the food, and asked to pay. Once a person has had the experience of going to a restaurant, the restaurant-visit schema is fixed because the events that go on in subsequent restaurant visits seem relatively invariable. The few differences that do surface on subsequent visits can be assimilated easily into the existing experiential–conceptual matrix.

Although I agree with the idea that background knowledge is a major component of schema theories about cognitive processing, there is an equally important aspect in Bartlett's (1932) conception of schema that often is ignored: the notion that mental connections leading to understanding are dynamic rather than static. Hence, mere previous knowledge in the guise of discrete facts is not what Bartlett intended by this term, but rather that a schema involves active mental effort to ascribe meaning to a series of concurrent stimuli (or events) by virtue of past experience with similar stimuli or referents. Thus, schema theory informs a theory of proverb processing in this way: To understand a proverb, listeners must not only have background information with regard to the discrete items alluded to in the proverb's content (the literal items), but they also must be able mentally to manipulate the interrelations among those items to reach an understanding that is suitable for the context.

This means that proverb processing involves the reconciliation of concrete referents with general abstract meanings. The reconciliation involves the recognition that the deceptively declarative statement (i.e., the proverb) is a figurative one (which necessarily involves a comparison) and that the goal of the proverbial utterance is to focus on the abstract relationship between the items mentioned in it and those of the immediate context in which the proverb is uttered.

Given this consideration of the cognitive skills involved in the processing of proverbs, the linguistic and intellectual sophistication of those who use and understand proverbs as well as the dangers of dismissing oral traditions as unsophisticated exercises based simply on rote memorization become apparent. In the following analysis of proverbs, I illustrate how complex these figurative expressions are, and I identify some of the mental and cultural resources on which the network members drew as they made use of proverbs in their conversations.

THE NETWORK AND ITS PROVERBS

As previously mentioned, I argue that the use to which proverbs are put in this social network correspond to four general social purposes: (a) to censure, (b) to teach, (c) to establish rapport, and (d) to entertain. In this section I analyze how proverbs are used to carry out these social aims and, in the process, promote intragroup solidarity through the affirmation and reaffirmation of cultural values and interpersonal bonds.

Censuring

Cuando el santo necesita la vela, hay que prendérsela
(When the saint needs the candle, one must light it).

On a late afternoon, after most of the daily chores had been completed, I sat with Martha and Tere, Mrs. López's two sisters, on the porch of Martha's house in Janácuaro. We began the customary *plática,* or chat, about the family. The conversation turned to two of Martha's daughters, Veronica and Irene, whose personalities changed drastically after they were married. We talked about the trials and tribulations of married life, and this prompted Martha to recall a confrontation she had had with Pedro, Veronica's husband. She talked about the mistreatment to which Pedro subjected Veronica, and about being unable to contain herself when Pedro imputed the infidelity of which he was guilty to her daughter. In the heat of argument, Martha revealed to Pedro that she was aware of his extramarital affair and gave voice to it in the presence of her husband and one of her daughters-in-law. After she had rebuked Pedro and he had departed, her husband told her that although she had been right to rebuke him, she should not have exposed him in front of others because "those things are not said [publicly]." Martha responded to her husband with the proverb, *"cuando el santo necesita la vela, hay que prendérsela"* (When the saint needs the candle, one must light it).

It is clear that Martha had used the proverb to justify and support her actions because her husband had questioned whether she should publicly have revealed Pedro's extramarital affair. In voicing his opinion, Martha's husband used a prescriptive key,[7] which effectively communicated that his challenge was based on an established sense of etiquette or normative behavior. Martha deftly, although perhaps unconsciously, replied in kind. By using the proverb, she too made an allusion to a collective and traditional sense of proper behavior because a proverb itself usually cannot be traced to a particular person, but to the wisdom and time-honored experience of the many. Thus, the use of the proverb allowed Martha to deflect personal fault in her handling of the situation by disavowing personal authorship and judgment and attributing them to the social collective.

In the exchange described, Martha's use of the proverb is a deft rhetorical maneuver because it works on more than one sociocommunicative level. Although Martha implicitly claims to be merely a conduit of traditional wisdom by making use of a traditional expression, she, in effect, makes manifest a reconfiguration of social values, gender roles, and normative behavior.[8] Ironically, by using a "traditional" (i.e., a socially sanctioned) form of expression to counteract her husband's equally "traditional" argument, Martha effects a reconfiguration of what is considered proper or traditional behavior (which in this particular case would have led her to stifle her voice and opinion). That is, where her husband calls for discretion and propriety, Martha calls for clarity and accountability. Martha's claim to her right to point out injustice (e.g., the slandering of her daughter) and call for restitution challenges her husband's notion of what should take precedence (i.e., social decorum), and this, in effect, suggests a shift in the weight of competing values. What is more, Martha also claims a stronger role for women by virtue of her rhetorical victory over her husband, and by serving as a spokesperson against gender-based abuse. Martha's defense of her daughter against gender-based abuse is anchored in her deft use of a proverbial expression that shifts authorship and authority from her to her society's traditions. This rhetorical move allows Martha to present her argument as embedded in traditional continuity, when it is in fact an appeal to the reconfiguration of existing social behavior and roles. Martha's argumentative strategy may even be seen as the foundation for future normative behavior. That is, Martha's successful argument may influence her family, friends, and neighbors (i.e., her community) to the extent that they will respond similarly if and when they are confronted with similar situations.

However, the social function of the proverb is predicated on its understanding, so we must turn to its ideational components. The first mental task involved in processing the proverb is the recognition of its referents. There are three major items in the proverb: saint [icon], candle, and light. Martha's proverb relies on conventional metaphoric associations such as those relating light(ing) with action, votive candle with offering, and saints with divine intercession. These three components take on a second degree of signification when their figurative relation to the context the proverb is called on to address becomes apparent (i.e., when the proverb is processed mentally). That is, when the proverb is entextualized—seen only as a text with no bearing on a particular social context—only its literal meaning is apparent, but when it is used in an immediate social context, it is contextualized and assumes a figurative meaning (Bauman & Briggs, 1990). The proverb used in context cannot be understood as anything other than a figurative expression because its referents are not reconcilable with those of the immediate context. In this case, for example, the listener who tries to reconcile the proverb literally with the immediate context very likely will be confused and ask, "What do saints and candles have to do with rebuking your son-in-law?" The answer is, "Nothing." It is only in the recognition of the former items as symbolic or figurative representations of something that does relate to rebuking someone that the use of the proverb makes sense.

In making use of the proverb, Martha succinctly communicated the defense of her actions and justified them by appealing to the social values encapsulated in the proverb's symbolic foundation. Therefore, once the proverb is contextualized, the second degree of meaning the proverb's components take is in relating the lighting of a candle with the telling of the truth, the presentation of the votive candle with the carrying out of one's duty, and the adoration of the saint with the promoting of a desired resolution. To understand this contextualization of the proverb, the listener must reconfigure the elements of the proverb in terms relevant to the context. To manage this, the listener must recognize the implicit cultural information communicated by the particular items mentioned in the proverb.

The proverb is centered on a practice inextricably bound to morality, piety, and duty in the collective Mexican psyche: the adoration of saints.

In terms of religious practice, Catholicism saturates most of the social and physical landscape of the country, particularly in the countryside. For this reason, Martha's allusion to the traditional practice of lighting votive candles before religious icons is easily recognizable to Mexicans in general. This ritual seeks to effect divine intercession. To effect the intercession, however, the particular saint the devotee wishes to implore must be presented an offering, or at least be prayed to. The votive candle comes to be the symbol of that devotion by standing as the offering paid in homage to the deity. It is the devotee's duty to present such an offering to receive the favor sought.

When these particulars are known, it becomes clear that the exposing of a slanderer and the honoring of a saint are incongruous contexts that can be reconciled only via a comparison. The proverb presents the basis of that comparison on the grounds of a metaphor for action and duty: in this case, the lighting of a candle, which clearly is a metaphoric representation of discovery (i.e., light enables scrutiny). Having made that connection, the listener can correlate the particulars of the apparently incongruous contexts—that of the proverb (the literal) and that of the proverb's use (the figurative)—as follows:

Figure 3.2 illustrates the parallel items guiding the listener to the conclusion that just as a devotee is moved to action to receive divine intervention, so must someone who wants to correct a wrong be moved to action. To make the correlation of these abstract ideas, the listener must recognize the metaphoric base of the proverb (i.e., the listener not only must recognize that the proverb is intended as a analogy instead of a literal comment, but also must recognize what elements constitute the metaphor). The metaphoric base activates the schema pertinent to the referents mentioned in the proverb. In this case, that would be knowledge of the ritual of

	Exigency	Actor	Action/Response
Proverbial context (literal meaning)	Adore Saint	Devotee	Light a candle
Social context (figurative meaning)	Rebuke Pedro	Martha	Reveal information

FIG. 3.2.   Corresponding contextual components for Martha's proverb.

worshiping saints. This schema then is related to the actual context of the conversation, so that the referents of the proverbial text and those of the actual context are examined for similarities. In this case, the similarities are mapped according the items in Fig. 3.2. There is an exigency, an action that meets that exigency, and an actor who carries out the action. The similarity between the two contexts is addressed implicitly. It is the listeners who must do the mental work to see the correlation and make it explicit to themselves. That is why the proverb is so efficient in terms of communicating complex relationships: Most of the communicative task is carried out mentally instead of orally. Once the listeners are mentally led to the referents that instantiate an appeal, the task of persuading becomes much easier because less energy is spent on explanation.

Paradoxically, the same frugality that makes the proverbial expression communicatively efficient also poses the greatest risk of miscommunication because the whole message depends on the recognition of the appropriate metaphoric base and corresponding schema. This observation, however, begins to demonstrate how proverbs may illustrate the nexus of the cognitive processes involved in analogic thinking and the awareness of the cultural particulars that, generally speaking, govern social interaction. This example of contextualized proverb use, in effect, can be seen not only as an exercise in social commentary, but also as a reflection of potential socialization processes, which leads to another common function of proverb use in this social network: proverbs as tools of socialization.

Teaching

Esas mansitas no me las des por buenas
(Don't take the tame ones for good ones).

The same day that Martha, Tere, and I discussed the trials of married life, we talked about Martha's daughters, Irene and Veronica. Martha mentioned that their personalities had changed dramatically after they had married. Irene and Veronica were known for their pleasant demeanor as adolescents. Irene was known to be so shy as a child that she would hide beneath the kitchen table when out-of-town relatives came to visit, and Veronica was of a jolly nature and rarely seen without a smile on her face. For this reason it seemed unusual that they had become stern and vociferous women. Irene, in particular, had been characterized as confrontational and assertive in her marriage. The following transcription captures part of our conversation, with nonlinguistic sounds specified within brackets and muffled responses between slashes:

1 E: *Irene se escondía debajo de la mesa, ¿y ahora? ¡Qué carácter!*
(Irene used to hide under the table, and now? What a temper!).

2 T: *Por eso te digo, que este, esas este—¿cómo se dice?—mensitas, o mansitas, no me las des por buenas*
(That's why I tell you, that uh, those uh—how is it said?—goofy ones, or tame ones, don't give to me for good ones).

3 E: *¿Las mansitas?* (The tame ones?).

4 T: *Ajá. Pues fíjate, ahí tienes a Irene. [Risita]*
(Aha. Well, look, there you have Irene) [Chuckle]

5 M: *Pues dice, "Me hicieron sacar las uñas. Pues yo no tengo la culpa," dijo ella.*
(Well, she says, "They made me bare my fingernails. So it's not my fault," she said).

6 E: *Como dijo mi mamá, "La mula no era arisca—"*
(As my mother said, "The mule wasn't bad-tempered—").

7 M&T: *"—los palos la hicieron." [Risita]*
("—the beatings made it so") [Chuckle]

8 T: *Sí, es cierto*
(Yes, it's true).

9 M: *No, deveras, ellas no eran así. ¿Verdad 'mana?*
(No, really, they weren't like that. Right, sis'?).

10 T: */Pues no./*
(/Well, no./).

11 M: *Lo que es ella y Veronica, se hicieron bien—*
(When it comes to her and Veronica, they became really—).

12 T: *Por lo mismo, porque son canijos. [Pausa] Yo también.*
(For the same reason, because they [men] are mean. [Pause] Me too).

In line 1, I emphasize the dramatic change in Irene's personality. To this, Tere replies in line 2: "*Por eso te digo … esas … mansitas no me las des por buenas*" (That's why I tell you … those … tame ones, don't give to me for good ones). Tere's introduction of the proverb with the phrase "*Por eso te digo*" (That's why I tell you) is particularly important in terms of identifying it as advice because Martha was there also, but she seemed to be ignored in this respect. That is, Tere's use of "*te*" (singular familiar "you" instead of the plural "*ustedes*"), and the fact that she was facing me when she uttered the proverb, begins to indicate that she identified me as her audience.

Nevertheless, although the proverb was, on the surface, directed at me, Tere could also have meant it as *sub rosa* criticism of her nieces. This alternate intention is supported by what may be seen as Martha's defense of her daughter (line 5) after the proverb was uttered: "'They made me bare my nails' is what Irene says." Martha clarifies thus that her daughter was forced to become something she was not (i.e., fierce), and the use of an animalistic trait (i.e., baring her fingernails/baring her claws) to convey this idea is of cognitive significance, as I explain in the following discussion.

For now, however, I concentrate on the ambiguity of the intention behind the utterance of the proverb. It seems that Martha aims to dispel that ambiguity by seeking her sister's agreement on her assessment of her daughters' personalities (line 9): "They weren't like that before [they were married]. Right sis'?" Tere's agreement appears halfhearted, because her initial reply is a muttered "Well, no" (line 10), but it then is followed by a clear statement faulting the abusive men for their wives' change in personalities, in which case she includes herself (line 12).

In addition, the conversation after this excerpt continued without a change in tone and demeanor, suggesting to me that Martha, at least, considered that the proverb was intended for me—a relatively young man who could benefit from the proverb's advice—and not simply as criticism for Irene and Veronica. My gender (heterosexual male), age (late twenties), and casual disposition (which might have seemed to be inexperience regarding human behavior) may have served as the salient factors making the proverb suitable for me in Martha's estimation. Combining these characteristics with the fact that the proverb refers to females (the pronouns and adjectives are inflected to refer to the female gender) and cautions against relying on appearances for judgment, Martha presumably considered that I was the one who clearly stood to gain from this advice. Moreover, Martha's insistence on her daughter's lack of fault reconfigured the object of the advice to be a caution against bringing about unwanted changes in someone as a result of abuse.

With regard to the cognitive aspects of this proverb, it is interesting to note that the use of the term "*mansitas*" (tame female ones) evidently activated a mental schema that readily corresponded to the setting and participants with which I was involved. We sat on the porch of a humble house in a rural town where familiarity with livestock, beasts of burden, and predators is the norm. The use of the term "*manso*" (tame), by virtue of its common usage and reference in this type of setting, calls to mind the submissive nature of farm animals labeled as such, and by extension, the word also calls to mind its opposite: "wild" or "untamed." I do not mean to say that the object of the expression was to associate women with animalistic traits, but rather, that the use of particular terms shows how common terms used to describe the surrounding environment are used to describe—and influence the perception of—human nature and behavior. In this case, the women who are considered "tame" by appearance, I am cautioned, could harbor an inner "wild" nature that is yet to emerge or become evident.

This observation was not lost on Martha, who was quick to point out that her daughters were not duplicitous, but had been forced to change their quiet demeanor for outright assertiveness in response to the abusive treatment they had suffered at the hands of their husbands. I assented with a proverb of my own: "*La mula no era arisca; los palos la hicieron*" (The mule wasn't bad-tempered; the beatings made it so). Unconsciously, I also used a proverb that referred to a farm animal and presented it as a metaphoric equivalent for the idea of transformation in personality that we were addressing. The animal-based schema had been activated by Tere's proverb, and in my proverb repository, I had found a comparable phrase to respond to her observation. But with regard to the message of the proverb I selected, I made it clear—although unconsciously at the time—that I sided with Martha in observing that it was not a deceitful nature against which I should guard myself—the core of Tere's advice—but being oppressive and thus bringing about unwanted changes in my mate.

This example of proverb use in particular clearly makes evident the equally complex mental and linguistic resources needed to untangle the multiplicity of meanings that can be derived from a proverbial expression. The complexity of use (i.e., sociolinguistic aspects) and mental connections (i.e., cognitive aspects) is highly dependent on the social context in which the proverb is uttered and the mental acumen of the participants who perceive both the context and the utterance. This consideration of context takes us to the next and final classification of proverb use among this network: the use of proverbs to establish rapport.

Uniting

Más vale solo que mal acompañado
(Better to be alone than in bad company).

Tomás, son of Mr. and Mrs. López and nephew of Martha and Tere, is one of the Chicago-based network members who made the most trips to Mexico during the data collection period of my research. On one of his visits, he sat with his aunts to learn of the events that had taken place during his absence from the *rancho*. Martha began to tell him of the recent fate a mutual acquaintance had suffered as a result of a romantic relationship that had gone sour. They talked about an "older gentleman" who had been lured by the promise of a quiet life in Janácuaro with a local woman. Martha, Tere, and Tomás knew the woman in question, and Martha proceeded to narrate that after having his savings squandered and being generally disrespected by his common-law wife, the older gentleman decided to leave and take with him the few possessions he still had. To his chagrin, the older gentleman was accused of stealing by his spurned lover, and what was more, he had to testify before a magistrate that the items in his possession belonged to him, as well as many of the furnishings that he had left at the woman's house. It was at this point that Tomás, on the verge of expressing outrage, commented that the older gentleman had done nothing but serve the woman and her family during the time he had lived with her, punctuating this comment with the proverb, *"Por eso dicen que más vale solo que mal acompañado"* (That is why they say that it is better to be alone than in bad company).

Thematically speaking, the proverb is appropriate in this situation because it addresses the issue at hand: It is better to suffer a lesser evil (i.e., being alone) than risk a greater one (i.e., keeping undesirable company). What is interesting here is that its intention does not seem to fit the categories mentioned earlier. That is, it seems highly unlikely that Tomás's intention was a didactic one because his interlocutors were much older than he, and by extension were considered to be more experienced and knowledgeable about life and human behavior. It is even more unlikely that he intended to censure the wrongdoer in question or to give advice to the victim because neither was present. The proverb's transparent comparison and evaluation of the situation did little to further the discussion. Indeed, proverbs usually bring conversations to a halt because they present a concluding observation. But because Tomás was emotionally invested in this conversation, and because he was not the teller of the anecdote (which would have given him the prerogative of offering the "moral" or what he perceived as the lesson to be gleaned from the account), it seems unlikely that his intention was to end the discussion.

I thus consider that the interlocutors were a determining factor in what could be seen as the object of uttering the proverb. Although the proverb commented on the situation discussed, it did not do so for the moral edification of the interlocutors, but it did serve as an identification marker with them. That is, Tomás's use of a proverb communicated to his interlocutors that he agreed with the wisdom of the many and tradition, for that is the nature of the proverb. It is a collective repository of experience and a code of evaluation. In addition, Tomás prefaced the value judgment with the phrase *"por eso dicen"* ("that is why they say"), which reaffirmed that this was not his evaluation, but that of "experience" (i.e., that of the ancestors or society in general). This paid homage to his interlocutors because they were, in relation to Tomás, part of the older generation. This leads me to conclude that Tomás—whether consciously or unconsciously—used the proverb in this situation to establish rapport with his interlocutors by communicating to them that he was familiar with, and subscribed to, the moral lessons taught to him by the elders of the community of which the interlocutors were a part.

This use of proverbs reflects what Roman Jakobson (1960) identified as the contact element in linguistic communication. Jakobson writes that a *contact* "[is] a physical channel and psychological connection between the addresser and the addressee, enabling both of them to enter and stay in communication" (p. 353). Tomás's use of the proverb illustrates that the object of its utterance is to maintain such a psychological connection, one that keeps all the interlocutors on the same page, so to speak, by making patent the interlocutors' investment in the values and traditions that are part and parcel of the proverb itself. The practically exclusive use of the proverb to establish rapport among the interlocutors shows, then, that the proverb's function is a phatic one because we see that the utterance is not meant to convince the listeners of something they do not already know, or need to be reminded of, but to maintain their engagement in social contact via this discursive practice. One's place in a social circle and the continuous creation and recreation of that place and the elements that give it significance are central to understanding the use of proverbs as tools for establishing rapport.

CONCLUSION

The complexity of proverb use can be matched only by the complexity of the social, cultural, and cognitive structures involved in the act of uttering and understanding proverbs themselves. Proverbs hold the paradoxical quality of using the concrete and particular to express the general and abstract, and this shows that oral traditions, instead of being simple formulas committed to rote memorization, involve complex higher order cognitive skills fundamental to many human endeavors. One ubiquitous human endeavor is the maintenance and creation of shared social values and behaviors. The examination of proverb use among this *Mexicano* social network shows how this endeavor is met in part, but usually on a daily basis, through the use of this oral tradition.

The use of proverbs to censure, to teach, to unite, and to entertain shows that proverbs can be considered a socializing tool among this social network. In fact, the choice to communicate social values by virtue of such indirect expressions as proverbs reveals the valuing of one social value in itself: discretion. That is, proverbs often function as an indirect way of criticizing something or someone who is not adhering to prescribed social mores or values. The fact that it is indirect, by virtue of attributing authority to a collective or absent entity (e.g., "people say," "as the elders said," "as someone said") who cannot be challenged immediately, allows the speaker of the proverb to waive responsibility for the criticism, which helps her or him to guard against any ill feelings that the criticism may generate. In this way, the speaker of the criticism is protected individually for the sake of the collective good. If the receivers of the proverb are to understand its intended meaning, then they must go through the process of decoding its analogic structure as it relates to their context. This participation in the criticism reinforces the message that the criticism is founded on shared social expectations and not exclusively on the personal judgment of the speaker.

Discretion is furthered by giving those who are the intended targets of a proverb the opportunity to save face by allowing the proverb to remain a general lesson intended for everyone, if they so choose to interpret it that way instead of seeing it as a particular lesson aimed only at one person, namely, themselves. Thus, the prominence of a single person's flaw is reduced, and the receiver is given the option of interpreting the use of a given proverb as less of an open attack on his or her character and more of a general opportunity to share in the values of the community.

As can be seen from the uses to which the proverbs were put in the López social network, the relationships between interlocutors and the aims of communication determine in great part why and how an oral tradition is actualized. By using proverbs that made reference to desired social values and behavior, interpersonal relations, and the participants' place of origin, the members of the López social network created and recreated a culturally specific social environment for themselves in their town of origin and abroad.

In addition, this particular case shows how figurative statements, such as proverbs rooted in everyday conversations, manifest the nexus of the cognitive and the social. That is, the understanding of the metaphoric base of proverbs involves higher order cognitive skills whose task is the integration of particular conceptual items with abstract social behaviors, and this is mediated via discursive practices.

It is through proverbs, along with many other forms of socialization not covered in this chapter because of its scope, that these network members acquire an awareness of the cultural particulars governing their social behavior. With regard to the data considered in this discussion, it is fair to say that the use of proverbs is one of many ways that the members of the López social network make manifest the particulars that guide their social behavior and shape their values, and this demonstrates how solidarity foundations are commonly laid via the use of a particular oral tradition.

REFERENCES

Bartlett, F. C. (1932). *Remembering: A study in experimental and social psychology.* Cambridge, England: Cambridge University Press.

Bauman, R., & Briggs, C. L. (1990). Poetics and performance as critical perspectives on language and social life. *Annual Review of Anthropology, 19,* 59–88.

Briggs, C. L. (1985). The pragmatics of proverb performances in New Mexican Spanish. *American Anthropologist, 87,* 793–810.

Caroll, D. W. (1999). *Psychology of language.* Pacific Grove, CA: Brooks/Cole.

Dundes, A. (1981). On the structure of the proverb. In W. Mieder & A. Dundes (Eds.), *The wisdom of many: Essays on the proverb* (pp. 43–64). New York: Garland. (Reprinted from *Proverbium, 25* (1975), 961–973.)

Farr, M. (1994a). *Language, literacy, and gender: Oral traditions and literacy practices among Mexican immigrant families.* Proposal to the Spencer Foundation, Chicago.

Farr, M. (1994b). *En los dos idiomas*: Literacy practices among Chicago *Mexicanos.* In B. J. Moss (Ed.), *Literacy across communities* (pp. 9–47). Cresskill, NJ: Hampton Press.

Farr, M., & Guerra, J. C. (1995). Literacy and the community: A study of Mexicano families in Chicago. *Discourse Processes, 19*(1), 7–19.

Guerra, J. C. (1998). *Close to home: Oral and literate practices in a transnational Mexicano community.* New York: Teachers College Press.

Honeck, R. P. (1997). *A proverb in mind: The cognitive science of proverbial wit and wisdom.* Mahwah, NJ: Lawrence Erlbaum Associates.

Hymes, D. (1974). *Foundations in sociolinguistics.* Philadelphia: Pennsylvania University Press.

Jakobson, R. (1960). Closing statement: Linguistics and poetics. In T. A. Sebeok (Ed.), *Style in language* (pp. 350–377). Cambridge, MA: MIT Press.

Kazan, E. (Director). (1952). *Viva Zapata!* [Videotape]. D. F. Zanuck (Producer). 20th Century Fox Home Video (Distributor).

Kirshenblatt-Gimblett, B. (1981). Toward a theory of proverb meaning. In W. Mieder & A. Dundes (Eds.), *The wisdom of many: Essays on the proverb* (pp. 111–121). New York: Garland. (Reprinted from *Proverbium, 22* (1973), 821–827.)

Kramer, S. N. (1985). *La historia empieza en Sumer.* Barcelona: Ediciones Orbis.

Milroy, L. (1987). *Observing and analysing natural language.* New York: Basil Blackwell.

Ohtsuki, M. (1989). *Forme et sens dans les proverbes conjoctifs. Sophia Linguistica, 27,* 173–179.

Pérez Martínez, H. (1993). *Refrán viejo nunca miente.* Zamora, Michoacán, México: El Colegio de Michoacán.

Pritchard, J. B. (Ed.). (1950). *Ancient Near Eastern texts relating to the Old Testament (ANET).* Princeton, NJ: Princeton University Press.

Rayner, K., & Pollatsek, A. (1989). *The psychology of reading.* Hillsdale, NJ: Lawrence Erlbaum Associates.

Schiller, N. G., Basch, L., & Blanc-Szanton, C. (1992). Transnationalism: A new analytic framework for understanding migration. In N. G. Schiller, L. Basch, & C. Blanc-Szanton (Eds.), *Annals of the New York Academy of Sciences* (vol. 645, pp. ix–xiv). New York: New York Academy of Sciences.

Seitel, P. (1981). Proverbs: A social use of metaphor. In W. Mieder & A. Dundes (Eds.), *The wisdom of many: Essays on the proverb* (pp. 122–139). New York: Garland. (Reprinted from *Genre, 2* (1969), 143–161.)

ENDNOTES

1. All the names of the social network members referred to in this essay are pseudonyms, as is the name of their hometown in Mexico.

2. I extend Farr's (1994b, p. 10) definition of *Mexicanos* ("immigrants born and/or raised in Mexico") to include people of Mexican origin who primarily identify with Mexican culture regardless of nationality because the term "Mexican American" and/or "Chicano" was not used in the social network with which I worked—or by many people of Mexican origin in the Chicago area, for that matter—although the children of some of the network members could indeed be identified using the latter ethnic identifiers (Guerra, 1998, p. 9).

3. A social network is characterized by the presence of a primary party (be it a person or family) who serves as the hub from which any number of social contacts radiate, and who are, in turn, related to each other by kinship or acquaintance (Farr & Guerra, 1995; Milroy, 1987).

4. There have been notable attempts at giving a generalizable definition of proverbs (Briggs, 1985, pp. 793–794; Dundes, 1981; Honeck, 1997, p. 18; Ohtsuki, 1989), but these invariably get more unwieldy as more aspects of proverbs and their uses are considered.

5. *Plática* is a generic term for any type of conversation.

6. Map illustration by Vianey Domínguez Barajas.

7. I rely on Hymes' (1974) use of this term to signal "the tone, manner, or spirit in which [a speech] act is done" (p. 57).

8. I am indebted to Dr. Beth A. Buggenhagen for her observation on the reconfiguration of sociocultural values brought about by the utterance of the proverb, and to Dr. Rachel Reynolds for her observation on the paradoxical nature of proverbs as simultaneously being implements of sociocultural continuity and reconfiguration.

Photograph by Aldo Blanco from Luna Man in Space Photography.

4

"Successful" and "Unsuccessful" Literacies of Two Puerto Rican Families in Chicago

Tony Del Valle
Columbia College Chicago

This chapter is drawn from a larger ethnographic study (Del Valle, 2002) investigating language and literacy practices in the home and school experiences of three Puerto Rican families living in two Chicago neighborhoods: Humboldt Park and Logan Square. The larger project was a topic-focused ethnography following Hymes' (1974) hierarchical model for types of ethnographic research. I observed, took field notes, and audiotaped literacy events as a participant observer in different settings for 4 years, focusing especially on the high school and the home. My fieldwork was triangulated with native informants, and I relied additionally on my own experience as a Chicago Puerto Rican to check the validity and reliability of my observations.

In this chapter, I focus on the contrast between patterns of language, literacy, and learning in the homes of Ana and Sandy, two of my informants. (All the names of people, institutions, and other places are pseudonyms.) These two young women provide a significant contrast based both on their differing experiences of academic success and on the literacy practices in their homes. Specifically, I contend that Ana's home literacy practices prepared her for academic success, whereas the literacy practices in Sandy's home did not lead her to academic success. Such differences in outcome challenge the commonly held assumption that the presence of literacy in the home always leads to academic success. I explore schooling attitudes, work, oral cultural traditions, and religious literacy for a better understanding of the differences between these two contexts for literacy.

I acknowledge at the outset that my observations of these two Puerto Rican households reflect momentary extancies. I also point out my belief that much of the behavior I observed is deeply rooted in the history of Puerto Rico's relation to the United States. I concur with Heath (1983) that the history of a community is critical to an understanding of the "ethnographic present." The ethnographic present is a window into the social history of a community, but it never remains as it is described. In addition, the ethnographic present does not fully reflect the historical forces influencing the present (Heath, 1983). In the case of the Chicago Puerto Rican community in my study, the influence of conquest, colonization, disruption of means to earn a living, political status vis-à-vis the United States, and subsequent migration to the mainland are powerful factors affecting every facet of life including literacy.

HISTORY OF PUERTO RICANS

Both Padilla (1987) and Rodriguez (1991) have stressed that the genesis of any study of Puerto Ricans in the United States lies in the history of Puerto Rico. Padilla (1987) defined colonialism as classical, internal, and individual, using Blauner's definition of classical colonialism as domination by an external "race" and culture. This domination is political and economic, and colonized peoples are subservient to and dependent on the "mother country" (Padilla, 1987). Internal colonialism refers to the dominant group's socioeconomic "exploitation, subordination, and inequality within the borders of the imperialistic power" (Padilla, 1987, p. 4). Colonialism at the individual level involves "dehumanization." As an illustration, Padilla cited the example of how Puerto Rican children in school are "reminded daily of the inferiority of their culture," "scorned for speaking Spanish in school," "placed in bilingual classes to learn the language and values of the dominant American society," and "made to feel ashamed of their Puerto Rican cultural traditions" (Padilla, 1987, p. 4). According to Padilla (1987), they are "consistently belittled, diminishing their sense of personal worth and dignity" (p. 4). Dehumanization involves the attempt to erase the dominated group's historical and cultural evolution.

Padilla (1987) acknowledged that this definition may not be accepted by mainstream social scientists in the United States. The internal colonial model is limited because the internal colonials vary in aspects such as "land economy, population composition, and power relations" (Padilla, 1987, p. 64). However, Rodriguez (1991) pointed out that social scientists have not been able to answer questions about why Puerto Ricans have or have not been incorporated into mainstream American society, or why they remain at the bottom of the socioeconomic scale in America 70 years after entering American society.

The prevalent reason given why Puerto Ricans have not been incorporated and why they have remained at the bottom of the socioeconomic scale relies on a notion of economic determinism predicated according to a theory of cultural determinism. The notion of cultural determinism is based on the culture of poverty thesis, which cites disordered or "pathological" Puerto Rican behavior as evidence of a flaw in Puerto Rican cultural tradition. According to this theory, the pathological element of Puerto Rican cultural tradition precludes the ability of Puerto Ricans to take advantage of those structures that would enable them to use opportunities in the areas of education and electoral empowerment (Padilla, 1987).

Padilla (1987) offered the internal colonial model theory as an alternative explanatory tool. Although he cautioned that it should be viewed as part of an amalgam of theoretical approaches, Padilla (1987) nevertheless argued that the internal colonial model illuminates the "institutional and structural dimension of Puerto Rican subordination and inequality" (p. 4). As such, it is a conceptual tool that helps to explain the details of everyday life for Puerto Ricans in cities such as Chicago.

Padilla (1987) also contended that it is essential for Puerto Ricans to be viewed as a working class group whose travel to the mainland was occasioned by necessity. The crisis that created this necessity was American colonialism and capitalism at the end of the 19th century and beyond, which rendered Puerto Ricans a displaced and mobile labor force for whom colonialism became a way of life. The internal colonial way of life for Puerto Ricans is a compendium of strategies very different from those used by European immigrants. Despite these circumstances, however, Puerto Ricans have sought liberation, in contrast to the European strategy of assimilation. As a consequence of their status as internal colonials, then, Chicago Puerto Ricans have developed an ethnic consciousness whereby they have responded to attacks upon their ethnic and cultural personality and integrity by affirming the legitimacy of their culture as an ethos and as a means of resistance (Padilla, 1987).

Rodriguez (1991) compared the changes that followed U.S. colonization of Puerto Rico and the experiences of colonized Puerto Ricans on the mainland to established international patterns. Colonization, Rodriguez argued, follows typical worldwide patterns that involve limited autonomy and a subsequent lack of political and economic preparation for participation in the colonizers' economy, which in turn operates on a global scale. Part of the pattern of conquest and colonization also is the creation of migration and, in addition, a colonized consciousness in those who migrate. As Rodriguez explained, conquest establishes power relations very clearly. The conquered can resist dominance, support it, or ignore it. Generally, in colonial situations all these reactions occur. The degree of consciousness may make those emigrants with a colonial past quite different from those without such a relationship to the host country (Rodriguez, 1991). Rodriguez added that there exist myriad relations between the colonized and the colonizer. The colonizer may view the colonized as subjects. The colonized in turn have "historically evolved defenses against encroachments on [their] culture" (Rodriguez, 1991, p.14).

Rodriguez argued that like other colonized peoples, once Puerto Ricans are on the mainland, they generally do not succeed. Rodriguez (1991) noted that "in general 'dominated minorities' do not seem to prosper in their dominant countries" (p. 16). As examples of how migrants from countries not dominated by the host country do well, Rodriguez pointed to Cummins (1986), who offered the examples of Finns in Australia compared with the Finns in Sweden, and the Burakumin in Japan compared with the Burakumin in the United States. Rodriguez (1991) offered the additional examples of West Indians in England compared with West Indians in New York, and Puerto Ricans in St. Croix compared with Puerto Ricans in New York City. Rodriguez (1991) wondered whether "there is at work a colonial holdover that impedes the success of immigrants with a colonial history" (p. 16). She made it clear, however, that the "colonial holdover" of subjugation does not mean Puerto Ricans do not continue to resist domination. Rodriguez agreed with Padilla, who argued that Puerto Ricans not only are continuing their struggle to retain their culture, language, and identity while in the United States, but that they also are continuing their struggle toward liberation within the mainland. I must clarify at this point that the "struggle for liberation" represents a political point of view shared by a small portion of the general Chicago Puerto Rican population. In recent referendums in Chicago, fewer than 20% of Puerto Ricans have favored the political independence of Puerto Rico from the United States.

HISTORY AND THE ETHNOGRAPHIC PRESENT

This ethnography of two Chicago Puerto Rican high school students and their families is a series of descriptions and analyses of the "ethnographic present," a culmination of historical forces that have shaped the lives of Puerto Ricans in Chicago. The struggle to make ends meet, the gang affiliations, the drugs, welfare, patriotism, and school failure and success could be characterized, according to Padilla (1991), as ways of coping in an internal colonial setting.

From this perspective, then, an event as inscrutable to some Chicago residents as the Puerto Rican Parade celebration, beyond an assertion of ethnic pride, is better understood. What many members of the dominant society consider annoying screams of "Viva Puerto Rico!" on Parade Day coming from floats, car windows, motorcycles, the backs of trucks, sidewalks, and apartment windows in Humboldt Park are sometimes an in-your-face assertion of ethnic solidarity, and an assertion of difference and resistance to assimilation.

For some time I believed that such patriotic behavior was meaningless if most of those participating in it did not have a historical sense of what they were celebrating or a clear sense of their cultural heritage. My perspective changed when I realized that even if the people screaming on Puerto Rican Parade day do not fully understand the historical context of colonialism, they do experience the need for solidarity. They experience a sense of "ethnic consciousness" as they fall back upon it every time they encounter a racist event in their jobs, with the police, in school, in the community, or in the media. They also fall back on Puerto Rican ethnic consciousness when dealing with other minority ethnic groups such as African Americans or Mexicans living in the same neighborhood or working in the same place.

It must be emphasized that as internal colonials, U.S. Puerto Ricans are not simply trying to cope. They are trying to succeed, but not at the expense of their identity. As Padilla (1991) put it, "The Puerto Rican of today wishes to 'make it' in America, but to retain the dignity and pride of Puerto Rican cultural life" (p. 15). Like African American people, with whom many Puerto Ricans identify closely, Puerto Ricans have "converted their cultural traditions into weapons, however impractical, of social change" (Padilla, 1987, p.16).

Besides Padilla's seminal work, scholars among Puerto Ricans in Chicago have done much research. The *Centro Journal* (2001) issue on Chicago features articles by Nilda Flores-Gonzalez, Maura Toro-Morn, Gina Perez, Ana Yolanda Ramos-Zayas, Irma Olmedo, Merida Rua, and Marixsa Alicea about Chicago Puerto Ricans. Additionally Ana Yolanda Ramos-Zayas (2003), Gina Perez (2000), Merida Rua (2001), and Merida Rua and Lorena Garcia (2001) also have written about Chicago Puerto Ricans.

Yet no studies have focused on the Puerto Rican family as the nexus for the youngster's literacy and its key role in their socioeconomic mobility and sociopolitical empowerment. Puerto Ricans are the second largest Latino group in Chicago. Two thirds of them have not finished high school. They are at the bottom of the socioeconomic scale (one third of the families live below the poverty level), and more than one fourth of them receive welfare assistance. The lack of knowledge about the patterns of language, literacy, and learning in Puerto Rican families explains in part why the critical problem of Puerto Rican school dropouts has not been solved. To assist the Puerto Rican community in dealing with its myriad social and educational problems, this study provides a basis for understanding the unique ways in which Puerto Ricans use language and literacy in the home.

The descriptions in this study are not based on a representative sample of the Puerto Rican community in Chicago. They rely on my observations of Sandy and Ana, my two adolescent informants, and their families. The purpose of the preceding observations and those that follow is not to provide a definitive portrait of Humboldt Park and Logan Square Puerto Rican families in general. My observations and analysis aim to shed light on the language and literacy practices of the two adolescents and their families who accepted my presence in their lives.

Ultimately, as Geertz (1988) pointed out, "all ethnographical descriptions are homemade; ... they are the describer's descriptions, not those of the described" (p. 145). This is so because "field notes, interviews, life histories, or historical documents do not contain the "reality of the informants' lives. They must be interpreted by the ethnographer whose understandings are often shared with the informants" (Chiseri-Strater, 1991, p. xxii). I present my observations in this study trusting what Chiseri-Strater (1991) called "the reader's acceptance of the ethnographer's ability to depict having been there, having captured the drama of the participants' everyday lives" (1991, p. xxii).

In this study, I use Heath's (1982a, 1983) definition of a literacy event. According to Heath, reading and writing are events surrounded by oral communication. She uses Anderson, Teale, and Estrada's (1980) definition of literacy event as "any action sequence involving one or more persons in which the production and/or comprehension of print plays a role" (p. 93). The phrase "any action sequence" includes not only "obvious" literacy acts such as someone reading a book or newspaper, or someone writing a letter, but also the reading of the TV guide, a letter from the welfare office, a telephone bill, a recipe, junk mail, and so on.

Shuman (1986) broadened the definition of literacy to include a wide variety of mundane interactions with texts such as telephone messages, grocery lists, and numeric graphs. Observation of the use of such texts balances information obtained from informants through questions about their reading and writing. According to Shuman (1986), information provided by informants about reading and writing is filtered through "what they consider reading and writing, not what they actually do" (p. 79). Direct observation of interactions with texts not considered literacy events by informants provides a more accurate ethnographic picture by including important information informants might unknowingly exclude.

I did not have access to that kind of observation until, in the eyes of my informants, I had become more than a researcher from the university. I had to be at least an acquaintance, a friend of the family, or better, "part of the family." (The latter was a title Jackie, one of the mothers, later bestowed upon me.)

Before I present my observations and findings regarding Ana's family, I wish to point out that I have chosen her home in order to present a successful example of mainstream literacy practices in a Puerto Rican household. Ana's family was successful in all areas of the framework used by Goody (1986) and Farr (1994) to analyze the use of written language in human society. Goody examined literacy within a framework involving the institutional categories of religion, economy, the state, and the law. Farr collapsed and expanded Goody's categories to a set of five: the church, the state and law, commerce, the family and home, and education.

As we shall see, Ana's family was successfully involved in literacy activities in all five domains. The Perez family attended church and interacted in Bible study groups. Ana was taking a law-related class in high school because of her interest in law as a career. In addition to Ana's interest in the law, the family showed interest in politics related to Chicago Puerto Ricans and a consciousness about the positive and negative aspects of a Puerto Rican identity in the city. Mrs. Perez and Ana worked in a currency exchange, where the duties included dealing with commercial transactions as well as the writing of reports. Ana's family and home life thus included interactions with recreational, private, educational, and religious texts. Moreover, in the Perez household attaining an education was a highly regarded process and goal.

In the descriptions that follow I intend to take you, the familiar and unfamiliar reader, by the hand and have you walk with me down the streets where my informants lived and into their homes so that you may see the settings of my observations as I saw them. I wish to involve the reader in this way because I believe the experiential contexts of informants provide, consciously or unconsciously, information that makes possible a more accurate way of perceiving and interpreting literacy events. Taylor and Dorsey-Gaines (1988), Heath (1983), and Zentella (1997) have made similar observations in connection with their studies.

ANA PEREZ

When I met Ana she was 16 years old. Born in Chicago, Ana had two brothers: James and Juno. James was no longer living at home. He had completed college and was pursuing a managerial career in industry. Juno was grade school age. Like Jackie, Sandy's mother, Ana's mother was the head of the household. She had divorced and remarried, but her new husband was mostly absent. During the 3 years I knew Ana, I spoke to him on the phone twice, but never met him. Ana's biologic father lived in Miami and Puerto Rico. Ana lived in Puerto Rico for part of her childhood and returned to the United States when she was still in grade school. The fact that most of the time Ana's family owned their home while they were living in the United States places them in an economic bracket above the other family described in this chapter.

Ana's House

When I first visited Ana she was living in a third floor flat near Kimball and Fullerton in Logan Square. The next time I visited Ana and her mother to continue our conversation, they were living on McLean, nearly a mile west of their previous apartment. I point this out because the move represented a conscious choice by Ana's mother to move out of Logan Square and into what she considered a better home and a better neighborhood.

The buildings on McLean Street were single-family homes. It was winter, and the lack of leaves on the trees provided an unobstructed view of the street all the way to where it ended, at the ballast of some railroad tracks. The street was usually all parked up, and the houses—mostly bungalows—all looked alike. Ana lived in one of these bungalows. In fact, when I returned for subsequent visits, I had to be very careful to check on the exact address so I would not open the wrong chain-link gate and ring the wrong doorbell. Ana's Mom had moved from the danger and variety of the old Humboldt Park neighborhood to the noisy business strip of the less dangerous Fullerton and Central Park intersection, and then into the quiet uniformity of McLean.

The first time I entered Ana's house on McLean, I could see, beginning with the modest foyer, that the house had been newly decorated. The colors on the walls and trim were fresh and bright. During my first visits at the third floor apartment on Fullerton, Ana's mother had complained that the rehab and decoration of the new place were taking too long, and that she was anxious to move. The McLean house had a recreational basement, reached through stairs that led from the kitchen to a downstairs dining area with a table and chairs. Next to it was a second full kitchen. The other rooms provided full living quarters for Ana's grandparents, Mr. and Mrs. Perez. I felt secure and sensed that their security extended into the homes and the people living on McLean. After all, that security is the reason they moved here.

Schooling

Ana's family was similar to other Puerto Rican families in the number of different schools the children attended. Ana attended seven different grade schools in Chicago: Brentano, Irving Park, Prescot, Cameron, Picolo, Funston, and Pablo Cassals, graduating from the latter. Because part of this study focuses on school literacy, I asked Ana to assess the schools she attended on the basis of effectiveness. The question I posed was, which was the best school? She felt Pablo Cassals was the best. I asked her to explain why. Ana responded with a general comment on relationships and personalities. Some of her comments were as follows: "The teachers were nice," "The principal was a great person," "Everybody was friendly." She responded in a way similar to Sandy's response. However, in Sandy's case, the outlook was defensive: "Nobody really messed with me because I didn't really mess with anybody...."

When I asked Ana about the learning at Pablo Cassals, she said, "We learned everything. They were there with you and if you wouldn't understand it, they wouldn't just keep on with the other students who were ahead. They would go and help you out till you get it." She also liked the cleanliness of the environment and the discipline of the students. At the other schools, she did not like the way the teachers talked to students. On this particular point, her assessment of what makes a school a poor learning environment is similar to Sandy's. Ana also had difficulties at the poor school with students who were not involved in learning and who started trouble with other students.

Ana's Mother: Cristina Perez

Cristina Perez was born in Santurce, Puerto Rico. When asked about her place of birth, she was eager to make clear that hers had not been one of the poor Puerto Rican families who migrated to the United States. She was quick to point out, "We were not really poor." Her clarification is significant because it may account at least partially for her family's success. She also added, "Ever since I can remember we had a television, a radio. We had everything." Her parents could be described as urban working class. Her father was a long-term employee in the kitchen of the town hospital in Puerto Rico, and her mother was employed in the cafeteria and in the garden. Cristina said their house was made of wood, but they always had everything and always lived in the capital. The latter detail also is significant because usually urban migrants do better than rural migrants to the United States.

I categorize the Perez family as lower middle class and part of the rural Puerto Rican Island mainstream. When they came to Chicago, they maintained mainstream ways. Ana's mother owned her own home, sent her youngest son to private school, sent Ana to college, and had already sent the oldest son through graduate business school. According to Heath (1983), mainstreamers are "school-oriented, aspiring to upward mobility through success in formal institutions, and looking beyond the primary networks of family and community for behavioral models and value orientations" (p. 392). The pattern of literate behaviors in Ana's home would partially fit Heath's description of language in mainstream families. Namely, they are patterns in which "children and adults ... are intensely and consistently involved in literacy events involving oral language in connection with learning from and about written texts" (Heath, 1983, p. 256).

Reading Aversion

During another one of our conversations about school and school assignments, Ana also expressed outright hatred for reading. She stated,

I hate it so much. I don't know. It's like it could be the most interesting book and I would try to read it and my eyes would get watery, I'll start yawning. I could be on the first page only and I would just put it to the side and forget it. I can't. Then we had to go and answer the questions then go back 'cause when I read, since I don't get into it, I don't remember what's going on. So then we had to go back and answer the questions and I used to hate it.

A generally accepted tenet of popular and academic literature on reading advocates that if parents read to their children when they are young, they will develop an affinity for reading that will serve them well later when they reach school age. As mentioned earlier, Heath (1982b) observed a direct relation between home literacy practices and success in school. Specifically, she described the ways in which the bedtime story serves as "preparation for the kinds of learning and displays of knowledge expected in school" (p. 99).

Ana stated that her mother frequently used to sit down with her and read to her both school and non–school-related material such as the Bible. Yet Ana made it clear that she did not develop an affinity or a proficiency in reading. She pointed out, however, that although completion of her school assignments required some time because of her difficulty with reading and writing, she completed them.

It must be mentioned at this point that although Ana felt none of her schooling at Campos High School was particularly engaging, she was an honor student, she participated in extracurricular activities in the ROTC program, and she was involved in student government. Her teacher did not regard her as a poor student. In fact, he selected her to present an award of appreciation at a banquet attended by former Governor Thompson and pointed out in class how proud he was of her demeanor at the presentation.

CRISTINA PEREZ

Schooling

Ana's mother Cristina attended a Catholic school in Puerto Rico. Her school experience involved active participation in such literacy practices as reading publicly and teaching fellow students about religion. She said she was the kind of student who always helped the nuns and other teachers. She was, by her own admission, a teacher's pet. She pointed out that her daughter Ana learned that trait from her. Later in this chapter, I discuss my observation of her daughter Ana's participation in school and some parallels to her mother's experiences.

Cristina had participated in the same way in church, helping the priest during mass, reading the missal on a microphone for the parishioners. She also helped the nuns teach catechism classes. Literacy practices related to religion were also part of Cristina's life outside school. I venture to say that the abundance of literate behaviors and their attendant skills, whether connected with religion or otherwise, is what made the Perez parents and children share characteristics of a mainstream family. Arnove and Graff (1987) documented the importance of campaigns launched by church leaders to raise the level of literacy in different countries throughout history and the transformational power of religious and political literacy for the individual. The intense and consistent involvement in literacy events involving oral language by children and adults in connection with written texts, which according to Heath (1983) characterizes a mainstream family, occurred in the Perez household in the form of school and religious-oriented literate behaviors.

Ana's experience in school stands in sharp contrast to her mother's experience. She did not participate consistently or with much intensity in literacy events in school or outside school. During initial interviews, she described her experience at Campos as good, but later proceeded to contradict her original assessment. In her estimation the learning environment at Campos was no different from the one in the grammar schools in that there was violence inside and outside the school. She assessed the learning aspect of high school as similar to that of the poor grammar schools she attended. That is, the teachers did not treat students well, and they did not help her if she did not understand something. Rather, they ignored her need to have something re-explained. She could not think of a teacher whom she remembered positively.

The number of absences she had at school during my observations made it clear that neither the content nor the teacher engaged her. My ethnographic observations of her class were particularly important because of Ana's stated goal to pursue a legal career as her older brother did. When I asked her specifically about her class, she said:

> Don't talk about Mr. Johnson. He was so boring, my God. And then the way he talks. He has the same tone of voice, and its like, we're there, this is us. [At this point she pushed her head forward and blinked her eyes sleepily.] We're like trying to stay awake—What happened? What's going on?

Attitudes Toward Education

Cristina's father completed fourth grade, and her mother completed eighth grade. According to the 1960 Census, the median of school years completed by new Puerto Rican arrivals to Chicago was 7.9 for men and 7.2 for women (Padilla, 1987). Cristina herself completed 2 years of college in Puerto Rico specializing in commercial administration. Her brother and three sisters also went further in school than their parents. One sister has an MBA, and the other sister attended high school in the United States, then went to Mexico, where, according to Cristina, she took a university course and is now teaching English classes in Acapulco. According to Cristina, her sister was able to advance at a rapid rate in her studies because she took a 1-year course in Mexico allowing her to finish 4 years of college work in a single year.

Cristina's eldest sibling is a half sister from her father's side. During our conversations about family, Cristina emphasized the differences between herself and the older sister in connection with such things as child rearing, attitudes toward school, work, and educational accomplishment. Her comments revealed a well-developed sense that individuals and families achieve upward mobility through education. She summarized her feelings regarding schooling and subsequent personal accomplishment as follows: "We did good for ourselves, yet she didn't finish school." In the following stretch of conversation, translated from the original Spanish, she referred to her sister's case as an example of how parental attitudes toward schooling have an effect on their children:

> And just as she didn't finish, almost none of her children did either. You know, it's like a … her mother didn't push her, and they didn't make her nor did she make my nephews either. The difference is that it is like a tradition. It is as though they don't care about bettering themselves; they don't care. And you know, as I told you recently, that the majority of people who receive public aid teach their kids to live on public aid all their lives. You know, and they don't care if their girls get married at 14 or 15 years old. They don't care at all. What matters to them is to live and eat and raise children, and that's it. You know. The person who studies, likes her children to study to improve themselves and to move ahead. The difference between a family that goes to school and one that doesn't is the parents, how they raise you, how they support you since childhood. It's like in my house, even though Dad and Mom didn't finish school because of the resources available before, or because they had to go to work when they were small, they always told us, you have to go to school.

On the basis of our conversations and my observations at Cristina's house i was able to recognize that she has the same expectations regarding school learning as her parents had for her. When her oldest son completed his fourth year of college she encouraged him to continue, because as she put it, "The person with the most education will get a better position."

Cristina felt that children go to school to learn and to have a future. Her son, whom she calls *el nene* (the baby), had just graduated from fourth grade when I began my visits. Cristina said she had told him, "Don't get stuck there, because when you go to look for a job, the person with the most education will get a better position." She believed education was the basis for everything, and she explained to him that if he wanted to be in a factory getting $5 or $6 an hour, he could stay where he was (as far as education he had completed). Christina had high expectations regarding educational achievement for herself, most likely based on her parents expectations, and she had high expectations for her own children.

Christina offered her children a twofold way of achieving academic success and a better life. She modeled behavior that would help them succeed in school, such as what she had done in connection with the church in Puerto Rico when she was growing up, backing up her talk about the importance of attaining the skills and behaviors purportedly offered by schooling.

Ana seemed to share her mother's beliefs about the great value of attaining an education and the consequent upward mobility, yet there seemed to be a discrepancy between her stated goals to become a lawyer and her classroom behavior. During a high school class oriented to legal careers, Ana did not assume a highly participatory role. When she did participate, she did not seem to be appropriating the legal language the way other students were. Ana seemed content to contribute from the sidelines, although she had been assigned the role of prosecuting attorney. This role required the ability to demonstrate publicly her understanding of the text upon which the mock trial was based, and the ability to manipulate the information in that text for an express purpose—to persuade an imaginary jury. In the context of this class, comprehension and communication of print was a literate act connected in an important way to a goal Ana sought to achieve through schooling: to become a lawyer.

Elsewhere, I explore questions related to Ana's concern about a lack of proficiency in English and its effect on her participation. What Ana did was to meet her mother's expectation about participating in the educational process, not so much by engaging in the cognitive aspects of the curriculum, but instead by responding to the component that invited her participation in the community. That is, she showed up at out-of-school events related to the law class. Her law teacher pointed out that she "took a leadership role in that. She helped with the police training of eighth graders at the police training center. She did the adult thing in the evening where she helped with the social functions there." The factor the teacher considered most important when gauging Ana's success in the law class was what she accomplished, as he put it, "with her feet."

Writing at Work

Cristina's job at the currency exchange required that she write a daily report of two to three pages in English on a computer. The reports were very important to the business, especially when there were financial discrepancies. Cristina would not provide me with a copy of one of her reports, but did give a description of what was involved in producing what she called "a narrative."

The type of work she did at the currency exchange required, among other things, that she balance the books and write reports. In the case of a deficit, she was required to analyze videotape and write a synthesis of the factors that caused the shortage. It is clear that literacy behaviors of higher order complexity also permeated her family history, personal schooling, work, church, and home life. I use literate behaviors in the same sense that Heath (1982a) defined them: as proficiency in analyzing, discussing, interpreting, and so on.

Ana had worked with her mother at the currency exchange since early in her teenage years. The literacy skills and behaviors modeled in her mother's job served her well later when she rose to the level of store manager in her after-school job at a clothing store. Before that job, Ana worked at a law office downtown, where her job consisted of filing hospital-related bills from the clients, filing stenographic documents sent by the court clerks, and docketing court documents. She had hoped the law office job would provide her with a valuable learning experience in the world of law practice. However, she was disappointed because of the hostile atmosphere bordering on bigotry.

Ana experienced greater success at her second job during high school as a store clerk at a clothing store. Her work there overlapped her job at the law office and is worth mentioning at this point because it involved literacy skills of a type not related to what her educational ambition was, but rather to what her mother's educational training was. As mentioned earlier, Cristina completed 2 years of college, specializing in commercial administration.

Ana maintained that she did not use anything she was taught in school on the job, but rather that she learned what she needed to know on the job. Of course, the filing she did for the law office was based on the school-taught skills of knowing the alphabet and alphabetizing, but the skills required at the clothing store she had learned at her mother's job.

Literacy as Pastime: Cristina and Her Family at Home

Outside of work in Christina's personal life, her literacy primarily involved a change from the production of English print to the comprehension of Spanish print. Cristina's literate activities at home involved some writing, but they primarily involved listening to oral reading. Both occurred in Spanish. She taught her children to read Spanish so that when they received letters from Puerto Rico, she would not have to read them for the children. She taught them Spanish by having them read the Bible together, although they now read an English Bible. The writing she did outside of work was in Spanish and was done mostly as part of church activities. She wrote during her Bible study classes one evening during the week, and on Sundays listened to and read Bible excerpts.

At home, Cristina and her family read together sporadically, such as looking something up in a dictionary or other written sources that they wanted to know. One such occasion was the time they were sitting around the dining room table talking about something and the subject of the Seven Wonders of the World came up. At that time, according to Cristina, they pulled a book from one of their encyclopedias (they own three, including a child's version) and started looking carefully to see where the seven wonders were. The children used the encyclopedias mostly in connection with school. Aside from such occasions of reading together, the family members read individually. The children read mostly for school, but also for other interests. Cristina read magazines and a daily newspaper. In Spanish she read *Extra*, a bilingual community newspaper and some magazines such as *Vanidades* in Spanish and *Cosmopolitan* in English.

At this point I describe a literacy event in which I participated with Ana's younger brother, 8-year-old Junito. My purpose is to present an example of how literacy is encouraged and maintained. The following literacy event is different because it involves not only the comprehension of print, but also meticulous categorizing, organizing, and memorizing of printed information. Junito's ability to organize, use classification, order, and commit information to memory indicated literacy skills of the most basic type described by Heath (1982a). The manner in which he used these skills, however, indicated that he had attained what Goody (1987) called "higher order skills," and Heath (1982a) called literate behaviors. Junito's adeptness, to the point of fastidiousness, at baseball card collection, and his ability to explain the system to me and his mother, to the point of overwhelming us with details of the criteria involved, demonstrated he had attained the levels of literacy Goody attributed to school literacy. Junito's use of classification demonstrated the ability to abstract, which Goody categorized as a "higher order" literate behavior. Thus Junito's hobby of card collecting was an important reinforcement for the practice of the literacy skills and literate behaviors necessary to succeed in school and perhaps beyond. In contrast to the literacy practices in Jackie's household, as I explain later in this chapter, in Cristina's home, this kind of activity was encouraged and indulged.

Earlier, I mentioned that Ana regarded her high school learning as an unremarkable experience. I also pointed out Ana's dislike for reading school material. The following two cases of Ana's literacy activities at home and in church, a public place, offer a contrast to earlier descriptions of Ana's experiences with school literacy.

At home, Ana helped her grandfather, who could not see, by reading aloud for him letters in Spanish that he had received from Puerto Rico. She also read and translated letters in English sent to him from agencies in the United States. Besides reading and writing to help her grandfather, Ana practiced literacy behaviors for her own recreation. She wrote letters to maintain contact with others, and she wrote for herself in her journal and on pieces of paper in a process of inner dialogue. She felt no animosity toward these texts. At home, Ana also read *Seventeen* magazine in English and occasionally her mother's subscription of *Cosmopolitan* in Spanish. Other texts around the house, such as books and the encyclopedias, she generally read only when she had to for school.

Shuman (1986) observed a similar pattern within the Puerto Rican families she studied. In her study, adolescents wrote letters in Spanish to relatives in Puerto Rico (p. 102), and reading and writing were often collaborative events that dealt with private matters. These events gave adolescents adult status and allowed them to enter the adult world (Shuman, 1986, pp. 104–106).

My main contention in this chapter is that Ana's home literacy practices prepared her for academic success, whereas Sandy's home literacy practices did not. So far, I have discussed schooling attitudes, work, and religious literacy in the Perez family. The area I explore last, oral traditions and their relation to the attainment of academic literacy, embraces all the areas previously discussed. I believe oral traditions, where they exist in Puerto Rican families, play an extremely important role in the home because they lay the foundation for a text-oriented mind-set. As such, they help develop the bridge between home literacy practices and schooling, work, and other areas of mainstream society by allowing family members to move from the familiar to the unfamiliar without forcing them to relinquish cultural ties. Furthermore, oral traditions in the homes of people living on the socioeconomic periphery exert a powerful influence on both young people and adults by creating a space for creative expression and political and social consciousness.

Oral Traditions: Cristina's Home

When Cristina was growing up, her parents did not read to her brothers and sisters. Her father (who completed fourth grade) and her mother (who completed eighth grade) told Cristina and her siblings true stories, mainly recounting the travails of having to work since they were children. The stories told to Cristina were similar to those told in Heath's (1983) Roadville (rural low-income white) households. Like the stories told in Roadville homes, the stories narrated in Cristina's home were factual, not exaggerated. Her parents used these stories to reinforce rules of behavior and to exert social control (Heath, 1983). According to Cristina, her parents "talked about what had happened." As she explained it, "You know, in the old times it was about experiences and how they had to work since they were children and things like that." Such stories with the subtext "you don't know how good you have it" usually are didactic. They are told to make a point in the same manner that didactic stories in Roadville were about what Heath (1983) called "conventions of behavior." The morals of these stories are "count your blessings," or they offer encouragement of the type that says "it could be worse," trying to change views of current difficulties to an optimistic outlook.

Aside from factual stories, Cristina's father recited *trabalenguas* (tongue twisters). He had memorized them and then had the children try to repeat them. He also told riddles or sang them in the form of *aguinaldos*, a Puerto Rican folk song genre.

Another oral tradition in the Perez family was *rosarios cantados* (sung rosaries), also known as *velorios cantados* (sung wakes). The interchangeability of the term for the Perez family is related to the similarities between a sung rosary and an actual wake. Rosaries literally are a prescribed text memorized and then recited in dedication to the Virgin Mary.

For Ana, such church-related literacy was another aspect of her at-home literacy practices that provided a contrast to her lack of involvement in school literacy. Ana attended church with her mother and grandmother regularly until the third year of my study. After that, only Ana continued attending. However, the at-home reading of church-related text, in this case the Bible, continued on an occasional basis after the mother and grandmother stopped attending. The reading usually began with the grandmother talking about it. According to Ana, they chose a passage randomly, read it, and then continued with what Ana called a "talk," as opposed to a discussion. Sometimes, Ana said, she asked her grandmother what a particular passage meant, and they proceeded to talk about it.

In the church itself, reading was done by a member of the church such as the pastor, with congregation members reading along silently. Individual reading, writing, and participation in the discussion of text was conducted in smaller group gatherings at the homes of members in the case of adults and, in the case of teenagers such as Ana, during Sunday mornings and Thursday evenings when the pastor's wife held youth meetings. Ana expressed an intense pleasure in attending these meetings. During the youth meetings, the teenagers sang, read the Bible, and discussed it. The pastor's wife presented Bible material with the help of pictures, drawings, and transparencies. She used both drawing and writing to teach. Ana expressed great fondness for the way she taught, saying she "explain[ed] everything."

Ana's intense involvement in church literacy practices provides a stark contrast to her level of involvement in the literacy practices found in her high school classrooms. In reference to that contrast, she said, "If there had been someone like [the Pastor's wife] in school it may have been more interesting."

The larger contrast upon which this chapter is based, between the patterns of language, literacy, and learning in Ana's home as opposed to Sandy's, underscores the negative effect of school literacy practices that do not engage students such as Ana or Sandy. In Ana's case, this lack of engagement was offset by home literacy practices that did engage her, in fact passionately. Unfortunately, this was not the case for Sandy, to whose home and family I now turn.

SANDY

Sandy was born in Newark, New Jersey, but she was raised in Chicago. When I met her as a sophomore at Campos High school she was 15 years old. During the first 4 years of my study, she was living at home with her mother, Jackie, and her stepfather, Silo. Her mother and father had been divorced for a few years, but he still lived in the community. I met her father twice during my study, once during Christmas and once during the summer. Sandy had three brothers: Carlos, Tito, and Jumbo. Carlos, the oldest, who experienced many problems as a gang member, lived in Ohio. Tito, the second oldest brother, was a prominent leader in a major Chicago gang and was working on his retirement from that organization. Jumbo, the youngest brother, also had been involved in gangs and was currently working in youth guidance at Campos. Sandy, the youngest in the family, was the only one living at home at the time of my study.

Sandy's Home

My experience of Ana's new neighborhood and her home contrasted sharply with my experience in Sandy's Humboldt Park neighborhood. Having lived in the area of Humboldt Park and Wicker Park for 20 years, I knew that the general area of Division and Western was dangerous in terms of gang activity and violence. My perception is borne out by Chicago police records, which show that during the month I started visits, August 1993, there were one homicide, two sexual assaults, 35 serious assaults, 31 robberies, and 36 auto thefts in the three police beats surrounding the local high school and Sandy's home.

Sandy's building was entered through a first floor hallway cluttered with bicycle and car parts as well as other sundry objects that smelled of old carpeting, rotting wood, and dry dog and cat urine. Such a setting no doubt has a profound effect on anyone living there. Such material living conditions should be understood as part of the context for coping mechanisms related to the colonial status of Chicago Puerto Ricans.

Sandy's Mother: Jackie Rivera

Born in Yabucoa, Puerto Rico, Jackie came to live in Chicago in 1949 at the age of 2 years. She and her mother, sister, and two brothers came to live with her father. Her arrival was during what Rodriguez (1991) called "the great migration," which occurred from 1946 to 1964. According to Padilla (1987), the major factors influencing the location of the first Puerto Rican communities were proximity to the workplace, housing discrimination, and cheap housing. In the 1950s the first Puerto Rican communities settled near the center of the city on streets such as La Salle in the Near North area.

Primary Puerto Rican migrants also settled in Uptown, Lakeview, Lincoln Park, NearNorth Side, and Woodlawn on the South Side.

The trajectory of the Rivera family's moves proceeded as follows. When Jackie was a child, she lived on Morgan Street, near 26th Street, now known as *La Villita*, or Little Village, a Mexican neighborhood (this part of *La Villita* has traditionally been Puerto Rican). When she was 7 years old, she lived in the Cabrini Green Housing Projects. Later, she lived on Division Street and Clark Street, Division Street and Milwaukee Avenue, and then on Jackson Boulevard and Albany Avenue.

Jackie's family lived on Morgan Street near 26th street until her brother got into "some trouble." That is when her father decided to buy a house in a Polish Humboldt Park neighborhood near Division and Campbell. Jackie has lived in that neighborhood through her adult life. When Jackie first came to live in this neighborhood, there were only about three Puerto Rican families living in a mostly Polish neighborhood. At the time of my study, there were only a few Polish people left, many having moved out to the suburbs or to Milwaukee and Pulaski further west in the city.

Such frequent moves have a detrimental effect on the education and consequently the literacy level of U.S. Puerto Rican children. Frequent moves entail "disruption" and "fragmentation of routines, of relationships, and of expectations" (Padilla, 1987, p. 217). They also fragmented group identity as represented by membership in organizations and social relationships. I would add that continuous moves by Puerto Rican families have the effect of disrupting and fragmenting their children's relationships to schooling. Furthermore, if the move involves living in Puerto Rico for a time, a common occurrence, the consequences can be extremely negative. Typically, students involved in such moves are held back one or two grades in Chicago, often leading them to drop out (Fernandez & Velez, 1989). This disruption in Puerto Rican youngsters' lives in school and outside school caused by their parents' frequent moves and the subsequent dropping out of school are part of a larger picture that frequently is not understood. Typically, dropping out of school is mistakenly attributed to language difficulties. Zentella (1997) explained it as follows:

> It is assumed that Puerto Rican children drop out because they do not know English, because they know the wrong kind of English, or because their bilingualism is cognitively confusing. (p. 4)

Zentella (1997), Padilla (1987), Rodriguez (1991), and Walsh (1991) argued that an explanation of the reason why U.S. Puerto Rican children drop out of school must take into account the history and politics influencing their lives. Zentella (1997) called for an "anthropolitical" approach, which she described as follows:

> Because of the harsh reality in which NYPRs [New York Puerto Ricans] raise their children, I argue ... for an anthropolitical linguistics that never loses sight of that reality and struggles to change it. (p. 4)

Jackie's experiences in school leading to her drop-out reflect the "harsh reality" that Zentella argued must be understood and taken into account.

I argue, in addition, that the experiences of the parents in school also have an important effect on their attitudes toward schooling and the attitudes they instill in their children. Ultimately, the children's attitudes toward schooling cannot but affect their academic performance. In Ana's case, for example, there was a strong continuity of literate behaviors in the home despite the moves. In addition, there was the financial wherewithal and a commitment on the part of her mother to ensure that Ana received a good education. Although Sandy and her mother Jackie shared an awareness of the connection between schooling habits and life goals, Jackie was similar to the parents in the Trackton and Roadville communities studied by Heath (1983). Few of those parents "moved beyond believing that schooling ought to make a difference in their children's futures to specifying how that difference can be made" (Heath, 1983, p. 364). Clearly, parents, and especially their children, need to move beyond parroting commonplaces about the value of learning and literacy to a deeper understanding of the why and how of learning and literacy.

JACKIE

Schooling

The first school Jackie attended was Calhoun Grammar School near Madison Street. There because of problems with teachers and students, she was expelled from grammar school many times. She described herself as a troublemaker and as someone who always fought back and never let anybody push her around. In addition to her usual difficulties getting along with other students, she had problems with gangs. She stated that there were a lot of girls in gangs, and that they used to pick on the ones that were not. A "troublemaker," as Jackie called herself, poses problems for teachers indirectly if the conflicts are with other students. However, in Jackie's case, the conflicts were with teachers as well. In the following passage from a tape-recorded conversation about school, she described a conflict with one of her grammar school teachers, a conflict that coincidentally led to her permanently leaving school:

> I never had any problems with the teachers when I used to go to school on the south side [in Little Village]. But when I moved over here to the north side, my teacher was Russian, and I think she didn't like Puerto Ricans. She used to treat me worse than anybody. She used to tell me I was in her school now that she wasn't going to tolerate the things I used to do in the other school. I used to live on Clark and Division. I went to Ogden School. One day the teacher, instead of calling me to go and pick up the book at her desk, she just called out my name and threw the book at me. And when I turned around it hit me in the face. But since I got my father's temper, I turned around and I told her that's not the way to do it. I picked up the book and I slapped her with it. She suspended me and told me I had to bring my mother to school. But since my mother didn't know that much English at the time, my mother's friend went with me, and when my teachers saw her and she saw me, she said, this can't be your daughter. And she said, why? And she said because she's black and you're white. Right there you could tell the woman was prejudiced. Well, why don't you ask her whether she's Puerto Rican, black, white, or what? And then she [Jackie's mother's friend] said, you know something, you should be glad that I don't beat your brains out. After that they told her that I had to transfer to another school and after that I said, forget it, I'm not going to school anymore.

Jackie had three brothers and one sister in school, but said of herself, "I was the dumb one in school anyway. My grades were terrible." Because of her poor performance in school, her problems with other students, and her problems with her teachers, Jackie dropped out of school and went to work at the age of 10 years.

When her own daughter Sandy was of school age, she regretted that she could not help her with her school work and could not participate in her education. This perceived deficiency on her part also caused her to experience low self-esteem and probably affected the degree of authority she could exercise when encouraging Sandy to do well in school. Her encouragement was counterbalanced with the history of her own educational experience including recounted stories of conflicts in school such as the incident with her Russian elementary school teacher. Curiously, Sandy narrated an experience in school with her math teacher similar to her mother's experience:

> We told her we didn't understand it and she started giving us bad inputs ... started saying bad remarks and stuff like that. She told me that—it was before Christmas last year, and we were going on Christmas break, you know, and I was having a lot of problems with my mom. She [Mom] wanted me to leave my boyfriend and everything, you know. And, like she didn't know I was having problems at home, fine but she wasn't helping them then because I didn't understand. I was lost. She was too fast. 'Cause everybody said that she was too fast. And it's like whenever we told her we didn't understand something she wouldn't explain it differently. She would explain it the same way [her voice trails off]. And she told me before Christmas break, she told me that I wasn't gonna make it, that I should just try getting a bachelor's degree in housewife.... She got me mad. My friend grabbed me and she is looking at me, she's like, calm down. She is lucky my mother taught me respect.

Attitudes Toward Education

Despite Jackie's considerable success at a self-education that allowed her to acquire literacy skills in a wide range of domains, including those needed for work and those useful for recreational reading, she felt great regret because she did not finish her grade school education and did not graduate from high school. Her feeling was exacerbated by the fact that all her brothers, her sister, and all her children, with the exception of Sandy, completed a high school education. In a few years, Sandy too would be graduating. Jackie's feelings of regret were coupled with a feeling of being "left out":

> I feel like I haven't accomplished anything, really. I wish I had my diploma. I wish I could get my education where my kids could feel proud of me like I feel proud of them.... And all this time I see my daughter sitting down and doing her homework, and I wish I could go sit down with her and help her, but I can't 'cause I don't even understand half the stuff she's doing.

Jackie expressed a vehement desire to go back to school to get her GED (General Equivalency Diploma), but was fearful of doing so:

> I think very lowly of myself that I think I won't pass those tests that they give you. And that's why I'm scared to go back.

On a subsequent visit, I brought some GED books and explained their contents to Jackie. I also told her I had called some places offering GED classes, but had come up with only one that I thought was close to where she lived. Then her daughter Sandy surprised me by listing two or three others that were even closer to their house. Apparently she had been looking into places offering GED classes after we had talked about them during my previous visit. When I tried to persuade Jackie the first time that she should pursue her GED, and she talked about her misgivings, I acknowledged her reasons but still insisted that she look into it. The second time we talked about her completing a GED, when Sandy contributed the research she had done, Jackie did not say much. She seemed indifferent, almost to the point of making any further pursuit of the topic awkward.

After reviewing the tape-recording of that second conversation several times, I realized that this conversation had included Jackie's husband, a wiry, gray-haired man about my height (5 feet 4 inches). He usually did not say much and seemed to feel awkward during the common formality of greetings, especially when I shook his hand. The only time he seemed at ease conversing with me was the time when he told me about the use of snake oil in the place where he grew up in Puerto Rico. During Sandy's comments about GED classes on this occasion, he did not say much beyond a few unintelligible grunts, but the clear impression was that he was presenting obstacles. I also had the impression that he was inebriated. In one of his intelligible assertions, he said, "Yeah but ...," to which Jackie responded, "That is where this girl goes ...," referring to someone they know who was attending GED classes at that location as a way to counter his objection. Both Sandy and Jackie seemed to feel awkward, perhaps because Tico was not sober or because Jackie's ambitions regarding a GED were a sore subject with Tico. After that conversation, the subject of Jackie completing her GED was never mentioned again in my presence.

Jackie seemed to have accepted that, at least for the time being, she was not going to go back to the type of schooling required to complete her high school degree. As a consequence of her realization that she would not be able to complete her educational ambition and her concurrent belief that education was terribly important, she took on the role of someone who encouraged others, especially young people, to finish their studies in order to secure a job in the future. She expressed her beliefs regarding education as follows:

> Without a good education you don't get far. Because now, everywhere you go, even in Puerto Rico you gotta have a college degree. If you don't have a

college degree, you don't have a job. And in a lot of places here they are asking for it. All I can tell the kids is, stick it out. If you're in school stay in there, it's the best thing you can do.

Despite her stated beliefs about the importance of education, however, Jackie was unable to model them in her own life, undoubtedly affecting her daughter Sandy's educational progress.

Jackie at Work

When Jackie was 10 years old, she persuaded her parents that her time would be better spent helping out with household chores and working to help pay the bills. Her father was under great financial stress because he had just bought a house and was the only one in the family working for pay. Someone falsified her birth certificate to show that she was 18 years old. She put on high heels and makeup and went to work for the Daily Pay Manpower Company, which placed her at a domestic products manufacturer. They asked no questions.

Jackie insisted, however, that dropping out of school did not stop her from learning. She conceded that when she was in school she did not know how to read or spell, and that she did not know any math. After Jackie started working, she realized she needed these school-taught skills. She described her realization: "That's when I said to myself, 'No, I gotta learn how to read and write English, and I need to know how to do it the right way,'" that is, according to mainstream norms expected in the workplace. Subsequently, she started reading and writing on her own.

Jackie's self-education is reminiscent of a pattern Farr noticed in her studies of Mexicans in Chicago. Some men within the family network she was studying had not been able to attend school when they were children in Mexico because they had to go to work. They learned how to read and write *lirico*, or informally, outside of school, with the help of someone who had gone to school and knew his or her "letters" (Farr, 1994). In Jackie's case, she learned the basics, such as the alphabet, from teachers during her first few years in school, and then she continued her education on her own.

At the time of her realization that she needed to learn how to read and write English "the right way," Jackie was working nights. During the day she cleaned the house, cooked, and when she was finished, she had an hour or two before she had to go to work. In that time, she sat down at her table with a magazine, a book, or a spelling primer and studied. She even assigned herself homework and learning activities. The spelling books she used were those she had brought home from school when she was attending and those occasionally left at home by her sister's children. Because of her efforts once outside of school, her reading and her spelling eventually improved, and she was able to work at a clearinghouse for mail order crafts, a job requiring constant use of literacy skills.

Jackie compared her work at the clearinghouse to a post office job. Her duties included processing order lists with product names and customer names and addresses. This included filling out an in-house order form describing what the customers wanted and the specifics of their requests. She said the job required her to be writing constantly, filling out forms, making out lists, and ordering inventory. In this regard, Jackie's literacy demands on the job were similar to those described by Farr (1994) for some Chicago Mexican women who worked in a warehouse shipping catalogue orders.

It is possible to conclude that Sandy and her mom Jackie, like Ana and her mother Christina, looked at schooling from a utilitarian point of view. That is, she kept herself motivated by practical, materialistic considerations. Sandy evidenced a utilitarian view often reinforced by her mother, by some of her teachers, and by society at large. Frequently, U.S. schools have been urged to look to the world of business for "practical" models of pedagogy that will produce a useful labor force. Kyle and Sufritz (1989), for example, investigated how Chicago high schools had adjusted to "the increased need for a more skilled labor force" (p. 3), concurring with the view of the Committee for Economic Development that schools could learn from the best-run corporations in America. As with 19th century corporate interests, the goal of modern corporate interests and those who cater to them is "to produce a managerial class that would ultimately gain power and privilege" over the class of workers also produced by the schools (Greene, 1990, p.160).

Literacy as Pastime: Jackie at Home

Jackie's reading at home—an extension of her self-education—continued. She began to accumulate a collection of books, which she put on a shelf in the living room. She said they were books of poems, fairy tales, stories, and medical stories. When Jackie started to work in the daytime, she came home in the evenings, lay down on the sofa, and read her books. However, one day, Sandy and her brothers decided that the house had to be cleaned up and, as Jackie laughingly put it, "They couldn't stand to see my books anymore." During one of our conversations about this, Sandy happened to be in the room and Jackie asked her about the fate of her books. Sandy told us that all the books were in a box on the back porch. According to Jackie, if Sandy had no use for something, she did not want to see it around the house so she got rid of it. No one knew the whereabouts of the shelf that had held the books.

Later, during one of my visits, I asked Jackie whether I could see the books she had kept on the bookshelf and she graciously indulged me. She sent her husband to get them from the back porch, and he agreed although the temperature outside was below zero. I offered to help, and before Sandy or her mother could refuse my offer, I followed him. We went to the back porch. It was enclosed, but it was bitterly cold on that below-zero night in Chicago. He started pulling out mountains of junk— discarded car parts, old clothes, old household objects—and at the bottom he found an old cardboard box. He pulled the box out into the dim yellow light of the back porch. He opened it for me, and in it I saw that the books were yellow and fragile. They were covered with spider webs, and there were cockroaches scurrying around among their eggs and excrement. I helped him bring them into the kitchen, where I took out the books and noted the titles.

The box included *The Lamb's War*, a novel; *Treasure Island;* cookbooks; *How to Become a Successful Model; The Legacy; How to Get More Out of Sex; Fortress;* the Bible; *Better Homes and Gardens;* and *Children.* As I looked through the books, Sandy pointed out that there were books in the box belonging to everyone. After I finished looking at the books, I suggested that we put the box away and helped to place it back on the frigid porch. Jackie's husband began to drag it back to the porch complaining, *"Esta caja de muerto ..."* [his voice trailed off] (this coffin, literally, 'this dead-man's-box').

It is important to emphasize that it was Sandy who, as mentioned earlier, discarded the books because she had no use for them. The notion prevalent among many educators is that the presence of books in the house is an important indicator of the likelihood that a student will succeed academically and stay in school. Psychologically, their presence may be an indication of attachment to objects that are in some way meaningful, but the widespread assumption that the presence of materials associated with literacy necessarily leads to literacy behaviors and skills is unwarranted, as this example demonstrates. What is needed, then, are ethnographic studies that examine not the presence of literacy materials, but patterns of interaction with them.

Oral Traditions: Jackie's Home

During my observations in Jackie's household and my interviews, I did not witness or see much evidence of extended conversation between Jackie and her daughter Sandy. Once I participated as observer in a discussion between Jackie and her husband about an incident at work. Elsewhere (Del Valle, 2002), I present the conversation as an example of literate behaviors exhibiting complex cognitive skills on Jackie's part. On another occasion, Jackie provided a narrative of an incident (presented earlier) that occurred when she was attending grammar school. However, neither oral communicative event qualifies as a traditional culturally embedded activity (i.e., a Puerto Rican oral tradition). Moreover, neither event involved her daughter. The only story I documented was the one Jackie told me about slamming the Russian teacher in the face with a book. There also was no evidence of stories or *cuentos* told to Jackie when she was growing up, nor were they evident in her home with her own children.

CONCLUSIONS

The literacy patterns in the homes of the two informants I describe stand in contrast to each other. In some fundamental ways, these contrasts are rooted in their different socioeconomic levels and their attendant relations—or lack of them—to mainstream literacy practices. At the same time, the two families' practices share some similarities. The literacy practices in Jackie's childhood home in Chicago contrasted with the literacy practices in Cristina's home in Puerto Rico. Communication in Cristina's "first world" in Puerto Rico was mostly oral, and literacy in her childhood there was related to school. Reading was done by candlelight or kerosene lamp through the greater part of grade school. Jackie, in contrast, came to Chicago at the age of 2 years and left school during the fourth grade. Her reading involved the daily interpretation of street signs, store signs, and other common public texts encountered in urban life, but no literacy activities at home.

Both families were similar in their frequent migration patterns within Chicago. When they arrived in Chicago, they migrated through several communities, and hence their children attended many different schools. The moves had a disruptive effect on their social lives and on their school literacy, but in the one family, the disruption was greatly overcome by consistent and dedicated involvement in literacy events inside and outside school.

The schooling of the adults was linked to work for both mothers, but it followed different patterns. Ana's mother, Cristina, used her 2-year college education to obtain jobs with a salary that allowed her to buy a building with apartments to rent. Sandy's mother, Jackie, dropped out of school early, but returned to school as an adult, and, moreover, taught herself to read and write with the help of grade school primers. She continued working at a low wage and receiving welfare.

The two mothers' "literacy repertoires" (Shuman, 1986) included a wide range of texts. The texts and the literacy events associated with them ranged from temporary to permanent. Both mothers read what Shuman called "ephemeral" texts, such as major city newspapers, community newspapers, magazines, tabloids, and utility bills. Yet Cristina's literacy repertoire also included texts and literacy practices that were established habits (e.g., Cristina and her family consistently read and discussed the Bible). Furthermore those habitual literacy events in Cristina's house were either a combination of English text surrounded by talk in Spanish, or Spanish text surrounded by Spanish talk. Cristina kept Ana in bilingual education classes until seventh grade.

Jackie, in contrast, spoke English to her daughter most of the time. It could be argued that by not speaking Spanish, Jackie did not create the space for Puerto Rican oral traditions that could support a sense of ethnic identity, solidarity, and respect.

Both mothers provided their children with a vision for the future, which included attending college after high school, and yet, for Sandy, this was not sufficient for its realization. Jackie was disappointed that Sandy made decisions before she graduated from high school that precluded going to medical school. Ana's mother saw her daughter begin attending college-level criminal justice courses shortly after graduating from high school. Like the parents in the Roadville families studied by Heath (1983), Sandy "came to school imbued with oral testimonies about the values of reading, but with few models of reading and writing behavior" (p. 348). She experienced success in grade school (Sandy attended a magnet school), but her interest and success in school waned by high school. Like the Roadville children, she waited out high school, and did not pursue further schooling after graduation.

The consistent presence of recreational, personal, and religious literacy in Cristina's house contrasted with the ephemeral nature of literacy in the house of Jackie's mother and later in her own. In fact, the pattern of literate behaviors in Cristina's home partially fit Heath's (1983) description of language in mainstream families. That is, they are patterns in which "children and adults ... are intensely and consistently involved in literacy events involving oral language in connection with learning from and about written texts" (p. 256). Ana's family was mainstream by socioeconomic standards and in orientation. Ana's mother owned her own home, sent her youngest son to private school, sent Ana to college, and had already sent the oldest son through graduate business school. The key difference between Ana on the one hand and Sandy on the other is described in the first part of the Heath definition of mainstreamers I use in this study. According to Heath (1983), mainstreamers are "school-oriented, aspiring to upward mobility through success in formal institutions, and looking beyond the primary networks of family and community for behavioral models and value orientations" (p. 392).

In Ana's family, value orientation came first from the Catholic Church when Ana's mother was growing up, and then from "born again" Protestant churches they joined in Chicago. The influence of religions in Mrs. Perez's literacy development parallels that of Doña C., one woman in the Chicago Mexican-origin community described by Farr (this volume). Like Doña C., Mrs. Perez was a practicing Catholic in her country of origin, in this case, Puerto Rico. Also like Doña C., Mrs. Perez joined a religious group in Chicago that was more book-oriented than her previous church. As Farr points out, "Conversion to and membership in these religions [Judaism, Christianity, and Islam] involves literacy abilities" and "practicing the religions of the book also frequently involves literacy abilities" (pp. 307–308). One purpose of this chapter is to illustrate how religious literacy plays an important role in the lives of practitioners beyond matters of faith.

In addition to the strong value orientation in Ana's home, strong behavioral modeling was also evident. Behavioral models in Ana's family came first, from Ana's grandfather, who performed a literacy service for the community through *rosarios cantados* (sung rosaries), and second, from Ana's aunts, who completed college degrees, and her mother, who completed 2 years of college. Ana's brother also served as a model. He completed a graduate business degree. In addition, Ana had worked with her mother at the currency exchange since early in her teenage years. The literacy skills and behaviors modeled in her mother's job served her well later when she rose to the level of store manager in her after-school job.

The value orientation and modeling for Sandy, in contrast, came not from her relatives' completion of college, but from her older brothers who were heavily involved in gangs and criminal activity. She did, however, have an uncle who had joined a "born again" church and lived in the suburbs. Whenever he came to visit he denounced the neighborhood in which his sister lived, and tried to convince her to move with him to the suburbs. However, his views and manner of speech were dismissed as "uppity" and constantly ridiculed by Jackie and Sandy. They saw nothing terribly wrong with their neighborhood.

My main informants' "literacy repertoires" (Shuman, 1986) were different from those of their mothers. Sandy and Ana participated to different degrees in school literacy events. For obvious reasons, the mothers did not participate in the classroom literacy events in which their children were required to participate. In addition, neither mother participated in the reading and writing assignments her daughter brought home. Aside from school literacy, my informants participated in literacy of their own interests at home. Ana read letters that her grandfather received from Puerto Rico, and she read and translated letters in English sent to him from different government agencies in the United States. Ana also read the magazine *Seventeen,* and unlike Sandy, she also read some of the same texts her mother read. She read the Bible, a text shared by all her family members, and occasionally she read her mother's *Cosmopolitan* in Spanish. I did not see much evidence of Sandy's participation in such communal or solitary literacy events.

The solitary pursuit of personal literacy interests in the home was another area of both contrast and similarity between Ana and Sandy. Their literacy interests differed from and partially duplicated mainstream literacy practices. When Ana retreated to her room to read her magazines, or when she or her grandparents sat quietly reading the Bible, they were respectfully allowed their time and space. This courtesy is similar to one granted to family members in the mainstream Townspeople community described by Heath (1983). In Sandy's case, however, there did not seem to be any personal reading or writing.

Ethnographic studies of communication are extremely useful resources for anyone engaged in education or other settings that involve cross-cultural communication. This study of language and literacy use among Puerto Rican families in Humboldt Park and Logan Square investigated the role that the home plays in Puerto Rican literacy development. The findings help to explain the differences and similarities between home language use and culture and that of mainstream schooling and society. As many scholars have pointed out, there are differences between the literacy practices of non–mainstream and mainstream homes. Ana's home, which by many demographic markers would be included in a generalized category of non–mainstream households, repudiates facile generalization because her household mirrored the behaviors, values, and literacy practices of mainstreamers described in Heath's (1983) ethnographic research.

I hope this ethnographic study will enhance future studies of Puerto Rican adolescents and their families by providing a definition for the nature and extent of linguistic practices in some U.S. Puerto Rican homes. I hope it will help teachers, educational administrators, and social workers understand the unique ways in which Puerto Ricans learn and use language as a fundamental part of their social development. I also hope that it will help them understand how they can work with the skills and knowledge the student brings into the classroom to help transform the U.S. Puerto Rican population group now near the bottom of the socioeconomic and educational scale into a bicultural and viable part of the larger society.

The way to transformation is demonstrated in Heath's (1983) work with children and their communities in North Carolina. It requires teachers to become involved as participant observers, moving with the children "from the familiar to the unfamiliar" to help them improve not only test scores, but also attitudes toward schools. It also involves understanding the developmental patterns of linguistic and cognitive growth as different, in Sandy's case, from those reported in the research literature for mainstream children. It involves expanding cultural patterns as well as knowledge. It involves breaking the boundaries between the community and the classroom and facilitating the two-way flow of cultural patterns between them. Finally, it involves making a beginning toward larger changes in the structures of society and education by developing "bridging skills" that will facilitate communication across cultures. I believe these changes will permit Puerto Ricans to attain genuine multiliteracy and allow them to move successfully in a multitude of cultures.

REFERENCES

Anderson, A. B., Teale, W. B., & Estrada, E. (1980). Low-income children's preschool literacy experience: Some naturalistic observations. *The Quarterly Newsletter of the Laboratory of Comparative Human Cognition 2*(3), 59–65.

Arnove, R. F., & Graff, H. J. (Eds.). (1987). *National literacy campaigns: historical and comparative perspectives*. New York: Plenum Press.

Centro Journal. (2001). *The Puerto Rican community in Chicago*. *Centro Journal, 13*(2).

Chiseri-Strater, E. (1991). *Academic literacies: The public and private discourse of university students*. Portsmouth, NH: Boynton/Cook Publishers.

Cummins, J. (1986). Empowering minority students: A framework for intervention. *Harvard Educational Review, 56*(1): 18–36.

Del Valle, T. (2002). *Written literacy features of three Puerto Rican family networks in Chicago*. New York: Edwin Mellen.

Farr, M. (1994). *En los dos idiomas*: Literacy practices among Chicago *mexicanos*. In B. J. Moss (Ed.), *Literacy across communities* (pp. 9–47). Cresskill, NJ: Hampton Press.

Fernandez, R. R., & Velez, W. (1989). *Who stays? Who leaves?* Findings from the ASPIRA five cities high school dropout study (pp. 7–17). Washington, DC: ASPIRA Association.

Geertz, C. (1988). *Works and lives: The anthropologist as author*. Stanford, CA: Stanford University Press.

Goody, J. (1986). *The logic of writing and the organization of society*. New York: Cambridge University Press.

Goody, J. (1987). *The interface between the written and the oral*. New York: Cambridge University Press.

Greene, S. (1990). Toward a dialectical theory of composing. *Rhetoric Review, 9*, 149–172.

Heath, S. B. (1982a). Protean shapes and literacy events: Ever-shifting oral and literate traditions. In D. Tannen (Ed.), *Spoken and written language* (pp. 91–117). Norwood, NJ: Ablex.

Heath, S. B. (1982b). What no bedtime story means: Narrative skills at home and in school. *Language in Society, 11*, 49–76.

Heath, S. B. (1983). *Ways with words: Language, life, and work in communities and classrooms*. New York: Cambridge University Press.

Hymes, D. (1974). *Foundations in sociolinguistics: An ethnographic approach*. Philadelphia: University of Pennsylvania Press.

Kyle, C. L., & Sufritz, E. (1989). *Indivisible good schools = healthy economy; Poor academic achievement = increased unemployment: A longitudinal study on the relationship between job growth and school performance in 15 of Illinois' largest counties*. Chicago: Loyola University School of Education.

Padilla, F. M. (1987). *Puerto Rican Chicago*. Notre Dame, IN: University of Notre Dame Press.

Perez, G. (2000). *Near northwest side story: Gender, migration, and everyday life in Chicago and San Sebastian, Puerto Rico*. Unpublished doctoral dissertation, Northwestern University, Evanston, IL.

Ramos-Zayas, A. Y. (2003). *Performing the nation: The politics of race, class and place in Puerto Rican Chicago*. Chicago: University of Chicago Press.

Rodriguez, C. E. (1991). *Puerto Ricans born in the USA*. Boulder, CO: West View Press.

Rua, M. (2001). Colao Subjectivities: PortoMex, and MexiRican perspectives on language and identity. *Centro Journal, 13*(2), 117–129.

Rua, M., & Garcia, L. (2001, September). *Latinidad in motion: Mapping Latino urban landscapes through Chicago ethnic festivals*. Paper presented at the meeting of the XXIII International Congress of the Latin American Studies Association, Washington, DC.

Shuman, A. (1986). *Storytelling rights: The uses of oral and written texts by urban adolescents*. New York: Cambridge University Press.

Taylor, D., & Dorsey-Gaines, C. (1988). *Growing up literate: Learning from inner-city families*. Portsmouth, NH: Heinemann.

Walsh, C. E. (1991). *Pedagogy and the struggle for voice: Issues of language, power, and schooling for Puerto Ricans*. New York: Bergin and Garvey.

Zentella, A. C. (1997). *Growing up bilingual*. Malden, MA: Blackwell Publishers.

PART

III

At School

Photograph by Irma Olmedo.

5

The Bilingual Echo: Children as Language Mediators in a Dual-Language School

Irma M. Olmedo
University of Illinois at Chicago

Research into young children's linguistic abilities shows that they are sensitive to the language skills of their peers and can adjust their language to facilitate comprehension and communication. This article discusses findings of a research project on young children's bilingual development in the context of a dual-language school in Chicago.[1] The study explores how children use their two languages in that setting, how they develop their bilingualism, and in what ways they manifest their metalinguistic and metacommunicative skills in the classroom. One aspect of their developing bilingualism is demonstrated in the ways that they collaborate with each other and serve as mediators for the language and concept learning of their peers. This article demonstrates aspects of the interactive work of negotiating shared meaning in the classroom by children of varying degrees of bilingualism and those just starting to develop their bilingual skills. Findings of this research show that even children as young as kindergarteners recognize their peers' level of bilingual skills, monitor each other's comprehension and production skills, and provide scaffolds for maximizing the comprehension and communication of their peers.

In elementary classrooms, it often is the case that children learn more from each other than they learn from the teacher. This learning from peers is especially critical in classrooms wherein children have opportunities to interact with native speakers of a second language as they themselves are learning that language. The teacher in the classroom researched in this study recognized that peer interaction is a critical component of second language development. Therefore, this classroom was rich with children's talk, a wonderful setting for a researcher. The children's talk analyzed for this article demonstrates how the children are developing their bilingual skills and how their use of their two languages exemplifies their developing metalinguistic and metacommunicative awareness.

THEORETICAL FRAMEWORK FOR UNDERSTANDING CHILDREN'S BILINGUALISM

The theoretical background for this research on children's bilingual development comes from three different sources. These sources include psycholinguistic research on child language, sociolinguistic research on bilingualism, and research on second language development in the context of schooling. One important source for psycholinguistic research is case studies of bilingual children. Many of these case studies have been conducted by parents, linguists, and language researchers (Fantini, 1985; Hakuta, 1986; Hoffman, 1991; Homel, Palij, & Aaronson, 1987; Leopold, 1949). The case studies point to the ability of even very young children to learn the languages to which they are exposed in their environment. Although children progress through a stage in which their different languages may be mixed, this stage often is very short. Children at an early age can differentiate their two languages, make judgments about which language to use with which speakers, and even when it is acceptable to use both languages.

These case studies are a very rich literature for understanding childhood bilingualism. One characteristic of these case studies, however, is that they are predominantly of middle-class children from highly literate families who have had opportunities to live and travel in countries where the two languages are spoken. Often, the parents are well educated and themselves fluent in several languages. There are few such case studies of Spanish–English bilingual children from working-class or inner-city backgrounds, or descriptions of European American and African American children learning through the medium of a second language in American classrooms. This was the population in the classroom investigated in this research.

A second source for this research consisted of studies on the relation of bilingualism to cognitive and metalinguistic development. Recent studies of child bilingualism have tried to document a variety of areas in children's language development, including the possible effect of their bilingualism on their cognitive development, and their metalinguistic awareness. Metalinguistic awareness refers to speakers' knowledge of "certain properties of language and their ability to analyze linguistic input, i.e., to make the language forms the objects of focal attention and to look at language rather than through it to the intended meaning" (Cummins, 1987, p. 57). According to Chaney (1994), "Metalinguistic awareness [is] a highly decontextualized linguistic skill that requires not only an ability to comprehend and produce language in a communicative way, but also an ability to separate language structure from communicative intent, ... the ability to think explicitly about structural features of language (e.g., phonemes, words, and sentences) and to focus on the forms of language separately from the meanings" (p. 372). Such knowledge can include the ability to make judgments about one's language usage and the linguistic fluency of other speakers.

Many linguists and some psychologists have studied the relation between metalinguistic awareness and cognition. Vygotsky (1962), for example, claimed that there was a connection between metalinguistic awareness and children's ability to control their cognitive processes. He proposed that access to two linguistic systems would hasten the development of metalinguistic skills in young children. According to Vygotsky (1962), in learning to use a foreign language "the child learns to see his language as one particular system among many, to view its phenomena under more general categories, and this leads to awareness of his linguistic operations" (p. 110). This seeing of one's language as a system different from others and this awareness of language operations are both components of metalinguistic awareness, the understanding of what it means for a language to be a system. A child's ability to reflect on his or her language usage and to articulate reasons for using some language forms rather than others would be indicative of a high level of metalinguistic awareness.

Bilingual children, as a result of their early exposure to two language systems, should have more highly developed metalinguistic awareness at an earlier age than monolingual children. This also should be the case for young monolingual children exposed to a second language early in their linguistic development, especially in a setting wherein they can interact with native language–speaking peers who are using the other language for communication. In these situations, children's metacommunicative skills also are developed as the children become aware that the second code is used to carry out functions similar to those they themselves engage in when they use their own language. Therefore, the second language can serve a variety of functions for them, as a code for making their wishes known and engaging others in work and play, in short, an aspect of their linguistic capital.

Research on children's bilingual development in a range of languages points to positive effects on metalinguistic awareness resulting from the early introduction and use of two languages (Ben-Zeev, 1977; Grosjean, 1982; Leopold, 1949; Tunmer & Myhill, 1984; Vygotsky, 1962) Some findings from this line of research attribute the following advantages to bilingualism in children: greater cognitive flexibility, more complex analytical strategies in dealing with their languages, greater awareness of linguistic operations, and positive effects on divergent and creative thinking (Ben-Zeev, 1977; Bialystok, 1988, 1991, 2001; Diaz, 1983). Qualifications on these findings are made with reference to considerations related to sociocultural factors in the language learning context, including issues such as the status of the languages.

A third source of research for this project was that of second language learning theorists. These theorists argue that opportunities for peer interaction with speakers of the second language are critical for optimal learning of that second language (Fillmore & Valadez, 1986; Krashen & Terrell, 1983; McLaughlin, 1984, 1985). They recognize that effective participation in classrooms requires another level of understanding communication. This understanding can be referred to as metacommunicative awareness. Whereas metalinguistic awareness relates to the speaker's understanding of language as a system, metacommunicative awareness is broader. Bateson (1972) argued that in metalinguistic messages, "the subject of discourse is the language," whereas in metacommunicative messages, "the subject of discourse is the relationship between the speakers" (p. 178). Thus, metacommunicative awareness would include judgments about the interlocutors, knowledge and understanding of the stated and unstated rules for interaction, and appreciation for how contextual and paralinguistic cues can help to facilitate communication. In the classroom, this might entail monitoring the physical environment and assessing the linguistic fluency and language proficiency of classmates to resolve instances of miscommunication. This awareness can be developed by young children through the ways that classroom instruction is structured and as they become active participants in that environment.

Sociocultural theories of child development inform the perspective of many second language acquisition (SLA) researchers (Toohey, 1998; Tse,

1996; Vine, 2003; Willett, 1995). Toohey (1992), for example, showed how learners of English as a second language (ESL) adopted community practices from interaction patterns in the classroom to develop their skills. Even the classroom seating arrangements curtailed opportunities for children to learn from peers. Willett (1995) focused on the communicative event known as phonics seatwork to demonstrate how ESL learners not only developed their linguistic competence but also constructed social relations and identities as able learners. Vine (2003) examined the role of partner practice as a significant opportunity for joint activity facilitating second language acquisition.

As bilingual education researchers examine the optimum educational settings for children to develop their bilingualism, dual-language programs offer certain attractions. In this program model, sometimes also known as dual-language immersion, native speakers of both languages are integrated into the same classrooms for instruction (Christian, 1994; Christian & Whitcher, 1995; Christian, Montone, Lindholm, & Carranza, 1997; Genesee, 1987; Lindholm, 1992; Lindholm-Leary, 2001; Smith, 2001). This means that students have opportunities to interact with native speakers of each of the languages. The expectation is that in these situations children will learn the second language not only from the teacher nor predominantly through formal lessons, but also in the natural course of interaction with their peers. This is the theoretical assumption of this educational model, although as Potowski demonstrates in chapter 6 of this volume, the hegemony of English is so strong that students' use of Spanish in the dual-language school she researched often was restricted to conversations with the teacher on academic content.

DESCRIPTION OF A DUAL-LANGUAGE SCHOOL

The school in which this research was carried out is a dual-language magnet public elementary school in Chicago. Because this school offers a magnet program, enrollment is voluntary, and parents who elect to send their children there do so because of the dual-language curriculum. The school curriculum calls for approximately 80% of the instructional time in the kindergarten to be in Spanish, with increasing percentages of English in the higher grades until the percentages of both languages reach 50/50 by fifth grade. To ensure that English-speaking students have an opportunity to develop bilingual skills and that native Spanish speakers do not develop a form of subtractive bilingualism, more intensive exposure to Spanish needs to be provided in the lower grades. The rationale for this type of language distribution is the need to counter the hegemony of English in society, which militates against children's bilingual development.

The dual-language model is considered to be an enrichment model of bilingual education because its proponents believe that bilingualism is a good thing for all children. Although many advocates of bilingualism support bilingual education programs, the reality is that most of these programs are not maintenance programs, but transitional ones, in which the development of the home language is secondary to the goal of English language proficiency. The main objective of these programs is to move students as rapidly as possible into the English-only curriculum of the school, using the home language only where absolutely necessary to ensure that students do not fall behind in their academic learning while they are developing their English skills. For this reason, most children in bilingual programs have access to instruction in the home language at the most for only 3 years. In contrast to most transitional bilingual programs, in the dual-language model, children continue to receive instruction in both languages even after becoming proficient in English.

Another feature of dual-language programs is the principle that the most effective way to learn a second language is to integrate it into the teaching and learning of other academic content. In these programs, the second language is not an "add on," a kind of frill unconnected to the real business of learning the curriculum. It is part and parcel of such curriculum learning. As such, the second language serves multiple functions in the classroom, and potentially all the same functions that the first language can serve.

The kindergarten class for this research, with its 21 children, was ethnically, racially, and linguistically diverse. Eight of the children were English monolinguals, including three African Americans. The bilingual speakers included seven English-dominant and two Spanish-dominant Spanish speakers, three speakers considered to be more 'balanced' bilinguals because they could interact almost equally well in English and Spanish, and one Portuguese–English speaker. The classifications of language dominance were based on judgments made by the teacher, who took into account information provided by the parents on the home language usage of the children as well as classroom observations of the children's language usage.

The data reported for this article focused on 12 of the children, all between the ages of 5 and 6 years. The Latino children who were native Spanish speakers (Margie, Samuel, Carlos, Flor, Nancy, and Norberto) were of varying ethnic groups and included a Cuban, a Puerto Rican, a Mexican and a Colombian child (all names are pseudonyms). The English monolinguals included two African American children (Brad and Eddie) and three European American whites (Millie, Abe, and Kathy). Abe, one of the more precocious, came from a home in which the mother spoke several languages and traveled extensively abroad. Clara, the Portuguese- speaking child from Brazil, was becoming trilingual. She spoke Portuguese at home and was being instructed in Spanish and English in school. Some of the children had attended bilingual preschool in the same school, and therefore had been exposed to instruction in both languages before kindergarten.

The teacher was a very fluent, although nonnative, Spanish speaker. She had taught kindergarten for a number of years at the school, and subsequent to this research was recognized in a regional outstanding teaching competition. She organized what would be considered a very open, interactive classroom in which children had a range of activities going on simultaneously in various areas of the room. Typical of many kindergarten classrooms, the room had a play corner in the form of a house, a reading corner with books in English and Spanish, an art corner with supplies, and a variety of other learning centers that changed according to the curricular themes being covered. Because there was so much talk in this classroom, it often was difficult to make good classroom videotapes of children when they were interacting in small groups in these various centers. Therefore, many of the examples used for this research were taken from whole-class episodes in which the teacher had greater control of the interaction. It is possible, therefore, that the linguistic data analyzed for this article may underestimate the language mediation skills of the children.

ANALYZING DATA ON CHILDREN'S LANGUAGE USAGE

The data collected for this research comprised analyses of audio- and video-taped samples of kindergarten children's speech and classroom episodes in which the children worked with others of varied language backgrounds in whole-class or small groups. The data collection focused on situations in which Spanish was the primary language of instruction. There was only one Spanish monolingual student in the class, but she remained for less than a month, and we were unable to videotape interactions with her.

Efforts were made to record episodes as they were occurring naturally in the classroom to document the usual and normal interaction among classroom participants. Although the children initially were very conscious of the videotape camera and the audiotape recorder, after several taping sessions, they appeared to proceed with their classroom activities without focusing on the taping. Videotaping and audiotaping took place between October and May of one academic year, generally in the mornings once a week or every other week. The video- and audiotaped data were supported with field notes of classroom events and background information about the children provided by the teacher.

In addition to videotapes of classroom interaction, data also were collected from structured interviews with the children conducted in English, Spanish, or both and communication tasks involving both languages. These tasks included storytelling, picture identification, sentence repetition, and sentence completion tasks. The interviews and tasks were carried out with the 12 focus children. The interview questions were intended to elicit the knowledge that these children had about the languages in their environment and their attitudes toward them. The children were asked about the linguistic fluency and comprehension skills of their classmates as well as their consciousness of the strategies they used to learn their languages, to understand, and to make themselves understood. One question elicited the strategies the child would use when someone in the class did not understand what someone else was saying. These interview questions were a way to examine the children's metalinguistic and metacommunicative awareness and their consciousness of their language mediation skills.

Analysis of the tapes included identification of episodes in which a child appeared to misunderstand and another child intervened to facilitate comprehension. This included situations in which a child failed to answer or respond to the teacher's question or a peer's comment and another child spontaneously entered the interaction. Focusing on these episodes was a way of exploring the children's metacommunicative skills to identify how they interpreted instances of miscommunication and how they behaved in such cases. This analysis was aimed at identifying the ways that the children became language mediators for peers in the classroom.

CHILDREN AS LANGUAGE MEDIATORS

Important aspects of data analysis involved exploring how these children developed their two languages and how they interacted in the classroom when instruction was unclear for any member of the class. Given that during most of the active teaching time, instruction was carried out in Spanish and that about one third of the children were just beginning to learn it, there were many instances of a child not understanding the teacher's talk. How children handle instances of miscommunication can be considered part of their metacommunicative skills because their responses require that they consider not only language structures, but also various meta-level aspects of the communicative act.

Because the class was heterogeneous in terms of language fluency, this classroom provided many opportunities for children to serve as language mediators or brokers for the learning of their peers. This occurred not only with the bilinguals, who are able to interact in both languages, but also with the native speakers of each language, who could model native language usage in their first language for their peers. Both native Spanish speakers and native English speakers occasionally code-switched or alternated between the two languages. The children were aware of the varying proficiency levels in each of the languages of their peers. When asked to identify the most fluent Spanish speakers (i.e., "who speaks Spanish the best?"), the most fluent English speakers, and the most fluent bilinguals, the children generally named the same speakers identified by the teacher.

Transcripts of the classroom conversations showed the frequency with which the children spontaneously took on the role of translators or language mediators to ensure that their peers understood what was occurring. This was the case even for children who may not have developed much fluency in the second language, but nevertheless were conscious of instances in which their classmates were not comprehending the communication.

USE OF THE BILINGUAL ECHO FOR LANGUAGE MEDIATION

An example of the aforementioned language-mediation process is what I reference as "the bilingual echo," a phenomenon that demonstrated these children's growing bilingualism, as well as their metalinguistic and metacommunicative awareness. The bilingual echo is a process in which a child spontaneously assists in the language and concept learning of a peer through a variety of linguistic and paralinguistic strategies. Whereas an echo generally is an exact replication of an original statement, the "bilingual echo" is not such a repetition of the original communication. I use the term "echo" as a metaphor because the child's message follows that of another speaker who has already communicated a request or intent.

The bilingual echo is characterized by the following steps:

Step 1. The child (language mediator) must understand another speaker's communicative intent in whatever language it is expressed.

Step 2. The child must monitor the behavior of a peer or peers to ascertain that they have not understood the speaker's message.

Step 3. The child must decide on a strategy to ensure that the message is comprehensible for the peer.

Step 4. The child must address the peer or peers using that strategy.

These children used several strategies in the language-mediation role or several versions of the "bilingual echo." These strategies included the following:

- Translating or paraphrasing the message, sometimes using code-switching.
- Scaffolding the message in one or both languages by giving both linguistic and paralinguistic cues.
- Modeling the appropriate behavior or providing a response to the request.

PREFABRICATED LANGUAGE AND LINGUISTIC ROUTINES

One aspect of instruction in this classroom that facilitated this language-mediation role was the use of prefabricated language as an important feature of classroom routines. Some language researchers have pointed to the use of linguistic routines and formulaic speech as an important strategy for facilitating the development of second language skills (Cazden, 1992; Perera, 2001; Wong-Fillmore, 1991). This formulaic language is powerful because it is associated with recurring classroom tasks or routines and is used to get things done. It facilitates children's comprehension and interaction in the classroom. Examples of such routines include attendance checking, distribution of classroom materials, assignment of tasks, use of common procedures for classroom control, snack time, and cleanup activities. The vocabulary and linguistic structures of these classroom routines include areas such as common requests and directives, use of politeness terms, numbers, days of the week, months, weather terms, colors, food, toys, and common games.

This formulaic language can be used to make one's needs and preferences known to others, and to facilitate participation in the ongoing activities of the group. This "prefabricated language" also is easy to acquire if it is presented in a context in which the extralinguistic cues are clear. It provides a readily available way for monolinguals to use the second language, to enhance their comprehension skills, and to participate actively in classroom activities. In the classroom used for this study, the teacher used linguistic routines regularly to attract the children's attention, to maintain classroom control, to make transitions between activities, and to carry out a range of other functions.

CHILDREN'S STRATEGIES FOR LANGUAGE MEDIATION

The most common way that children perform as language mediators involves translation of a message. Many of these translations are evident during classroom routines. In addition to content teaching, the kindergarten teacher stresses appropriate behavior in the classroom, especially in terms of listening to others and raising hands for permission to speak.

For example, one morning when the children in the classroom were especially noisy, the teacher stopped to stress the classroom rules: *"¿Quién va a respetar las reglas hoy? Levanta la mano si vas a respetar las reglas hoy"* ("Who is going to respect the rules today? Raise your hand if you are going to respect the rules today.") Norberto noticed that the teacher was waiting for responses, and that not all the children had raised their hands. He appeared to have concluded that they did not understand her request. He echoed the teacher's request and translated her message by saying to the class, "Raise your hand if you want to respect the rules."

These translated interventions were the most common examples of the "bilingual echo." Frequently, the children either repeated what the teacher had said or translated it for the class or for specific others who may not have understood or responded.

Sometimes the children scaffolded a message for a peer through a variety of strategies. One strategy is the use of paralinguistic cues to accompany speech, using gestures to facilitate comprehension. Children learned this common strategy from their teacher, who often used gestures as contextual cues to support comprehension.

In the classroom used for this study, mediation through paralinguistic cues was evident in examples such as the following. The class was seated in a circle and the teacher told the children: *"Levanten la mano."* This was a classroom routine used to indicate that the children were ready for the transition to the next activity. Flor noticed that Carl had not raised his hand, so she said to him, "Do like this" as she raised her hand.

When the children completed an activity, it was necessary for them to pick up their materials and clean up. Eddie, an English monolingual speaker, went over to the light switch, turned it off, and shouted *"A recoger"* (Let's pick up) to ensure that the children knew what to do next. Samuel finished cleaning up, sat down in the circle, and said loudly, *"Es hora de limpiar"* (It's time to clean up). The children observed him, listened, and hurried to clean up and sit in the circle.

When Eddie spoke out of turn, the teacher scolded him by saying, *"Eddie, cuando yo estoy hablando, ustedes escuchan"* (Eddie, when I'm speaking, you listen). Carlos, who was sitting next to Eddie, repeated *"escucha"* (listen) after the teacher, and cuffed his hand behind his ear in a gesture to reinforce the verbal message.

Classroom chores are another venue for using prefabricated language at the same time that curricular concepts are being taught. Snack time is one of these occasions. Children count napkins, cups, and cookies when they get ready for snack, often in Spanish, and solve math problems in the process. In the classroom used for this research, they learned to subtract from 21 when some of the children were absent, and learned to divide the snacks when there were not enough for all the children.

For example, when Janice was responsible for counting the cups, three children were absent, so the teacher said to her, *"Tienes que quitar tres."* Janice looked around to one of the Latino children, who said to her "take away three," thus translating the teacher's message.

When the teacher asked Grace in Spanish to feed the fish and pointed to the sign on the wall for each person's chores, Grace appeared not to understand. She turned to Miriam, who said to her, "She wants you to feed the fish." The teacher added, *"Pero un poco,"* making a gesture with her hand by bringing together two of her fingers to indicate a little bit, and Miriam translated for Grace, "just a little." The children had learned that certain gestures and paralinguistic cues accompany certain vocabulary and language functions. Learning to interpret and use the appropriate gestures was becoming part of their communicative skill repertoire.

The children's language mediation role was not limited merely to clarifying messages. As language mediators the children also were able to support the concept learning of their peers. A good example of scaffolding a message came from another snack time episode. The teacher often took advantage of common classroom activities to teach content area concepts such as those in math and science. During one snack time, she discovered that the cookies a mother had sent for snack were very large. She decided to divide them in half and give one half to each child. At the same time, she decided to use this activity to teach the children the concept of one half.

The teacher, drawing a circle on the board to represent a cookie, asked the class in Spanish, *"Si te quiero dar la mitad de la galleta, la mitad de la galleta porque no puedes comer todo, ¿cómo lo voy a hacer?"* (If I want to give you half of the cookie, half of the cookie, because you can't eat the whole thing, how do I do it?)

Samuel replied, *"Tienes que poner una raya"* (You have to put a line).

The teacher ignored Samuel's response and called on Norberto, one of the more balanced bilinguals, to the board, gave him a marker, and asked him to show her and the class. Although Norberto understood Spanish, he seemed perplexed by the task and looked around at his classmates. Several children shouted out "a half" or *"la mitad."* When Norberto still appeared not to know what to do, Flor said, *"Pon una rayita* and color it on the other side" (Put a line). She made an imaginary line across the circle. Chris also went up to board and gestured to show Norberto how to draw the line.

If we analyze what skills were involved in this language mediation role, we see that the children had to understand the teacher's linguistic message given in Spanish, the teacher's communicative intent, the cognitive demands of the task, and how to depict half of the circle. They had to understand that the circle drawn on the board represented a cookie the teacher was trying to divide in half. They also had to monitor the behavior of Norberto to know that he either did not understand the question because of the language or did not know how to answer it. In this case, some children shouted out "a half," thus translating the teacher's Spanish *"la mitad."* One student, Samuel, told him what to do in Spanish—that he should draw a line. Flor proceeded to alternate between both Spanish and English, or code-switch, telling him to draw a line and shade in one side to indicate a half. Chris went to the board and drew an imaginary line across the circle, thus modeling the answer to scaffold the cognitive demand. The children were actively reading the environment, assessing when a communication breakdown had occurred, and intervening to ensure that their peers could understand and respond.

The children used contextual and situational cues to play the language mediation role and interpret the teacher's message. Another example involved an activity that found the children preparing to make fossils by first mixing their own play dough. The teacher planned to use this play dough cooking activity as a way to teach vocabulary and mathematics concepts.

She had a copy of the recipe and instructions on a large sheet of poster paper. She read these instructions aloud in Spanish to the children and had them follow the steps for mixing the ingredients and kneading the dough. The teacher planned to take the liquid mixture into the cafeteria kitchen for cooking after the children had mixed the ingredients. When they reached the last step, she read, *"Poner al fuego"* (Put on the fire or stove).

Brad:	*"¿Qué es fuego?"*
Carlos responded:	"Fire."
Brad:	"How we gonna get fire?"
Teacher:	*"En la cocina"* (in the kitchen).

Brad looked confused and mumbled something as he looked toward the play kitchen area in the kindergarten room.

Teacher:	*"No, en la de verdad"* (no, in the real one).
Brad:	"Oh, you mean [pause].... Everybody get your shoes on, we gonna get fire."

Brad may not have understood the teacher's expression *la de verdad* in reference to the real kitchen down the hall where the cooking would take place versus the play kitchen in the classroom. But he made judgments from the contextual and situational cues to interpret the teacher's message that they would have to go somewhere else to cook the dough. And he promptly communicated this knowledge to his peers. If they were to leave the room and go to where the real stove was to cook the mixture, they would have to put on their shoes.

Because two languages were used in the classroom some children appeared to have internalized the idea that it is important to learn what things mean. Therefore, even in situations wherein they were not addressed directly or expected to respond, the children actively sought meaning. Abe demonstrated this search for meaning when the teacher said, *"Janice está pasando papel."* Although the teacher was merely making the statement, "Janice is passing out paper," and not expecting any particular response from any student, Abe asked, "What does that mean?" The teacher repeated, *"Janice está pasando papel."* She frequently repeated her message in the same language instead of translating immediately for the children. Carlos proceeded to translate, "Janice is passing out the paper."

Although translation is one principal strategy for language mediation, another strategy involves paraphrasing a message to enhance comprehension. The children had learned that there are alternative ways of delivering the same message. One of these alternatives is to translate but also to paraphrase, thus perhaps simplifying, or scaffolding, by providing support for understanding a message. An example of this strategy comes from a conversation between several children during a calculator activity.

The teacher wanted to know what had happened to one of the calculators that was not working. She addressed Eddie, an English monolingual child, who was holding the calculator:

Teacher: *"Y¿cómo pasó que se rompió.¿Qué le hiciste que se rompió?"* (And how did it happen that it broke? What did you do to it that it broke?).

Norberto observed the interaction and noticed that his classmate Eddie was not responding. He understood the teacher's questions given in Spanish and translated them, communicating the intent in a much more direct way:

Norberto: "How did you break it?"

In this example, it is clear that Norberto was not giving a literal translation of the teacher's communication, but rather interpreting the intent in the message and using the resources of the other language to do so. Norberto's directness was typical of the way many of the children interacted among themselves. The indirectness that characterized some of the teacher's talk may have been developmentally more challenging to these 5- and 6-year-olds.

An interesting aspect of the children's interactional cooperation and mediation in this classroom was that the strategic use of the language-mediation role was not confined to bilingual children. Even English monolinguals were able to participate when they understood some portion of what the teacher had said and relied on contextual cues to interpret the remainder of the message. For example, the teacher frequently asked questions at the beginning of a class session. Some of the questions become rather routinized, a teaching strategy intended to maximize the participation of all the children in whole-class sessions. Such routines also can be a way of maximizing "context-embedded" communication and thus enhancing comprehensible input (Cummins, 1991; Krashen, 1982). Hakuta (1976) explained that "the learner will employ a strategy which 'tunes in' on regular patterned segments of speech, and employs them without knowledge of their underlying structure, but with the knowledge as to which particular situations call for what patterns" (p. 331). Many situations involving classroom routines elicit that type of response from the children.

Common classroom routines with attending formulaic speech include discourse on dates, weather, counting, class attendance, illness and health, clothing children are wearing, colors, and the like. Discussions of birthdays combine a variety of routines that include counting and giving dates.

In one whole-class session, the teacher of the classroom in this study asked, *"¿Quién celebró un cumpleaños hace poquito?"* (Who celebrated a birthday very recently?)

Many of the children raised their hands. Eddie pointed to Miguel, who had not raised his hand to volunteer that "he had a birthday." Eddie understood not only that the conversation had to do with birthdays, but also that the teacher was not asking whose birthday it was that day, but who had already had a birthday. These kindergarteners had not studied verb tense in any formal way. Part of Eddie's comprehension may have come from the fact that series of questions about birthdays was a regular classroom routine. Therefore, even the English monolingual children were able to internalize the meaning of the message from the sequence in these routines, and thereby participate in the interaction.

The preceding examples illustrate the value of classroom routines, prefabricated language, or formulaic language in the development of the children's bilingualism and metacommunicative awareness. Not only is there considerable vocabulary associated with the language of the classroom, but these routines also include the use of many language functions important for developing higher levels of linguistic fluency. The children were able to develop their receptive and productive language in a variety of language functions, such as giving directives and requests, expressing preferences, agreeing and disagreeing, giving directions, and asking for clarification. In this kindergarten study, as early as November, I heard even English monolinguals using the language of classroom routines in Spanish on a regular basis and with a native-like accent.

SUMMARY AND CONCLUSIONS

The examples described in this chapter demonstrate that participation in this dual-language program, with its focus on exposing children to content in both languages, not only taught children that content, but heightened their metalinguistic and metacommunicative awareness. The children in the reported study were able to assess the linguistic proficiency of their peers, and often responded appropriately to serve as language mediators for them and thus resolve instances of miscommunication. The English monolinguals, although rather limited in their ability to carry out conversations in Spanish, were developing their receptive language skills in Spanish. They were therefore able to comprehend much of what was occurring in class, as evidenced by their ability to respond appropriately to directives and instructions. The Spanish speakers were improving on their proficiency in English and also using their Spanish fluency to serve as language mediators for their peers.

Various researchers have argued that there is a relationship between exposure to two languages in childhood, the early development of meta-linguistic awareness, and more general cognitive abilities. Researchers should turn to this area to find support for the benefits of this early exposure to dual-language instruction. Both groups of children involved in such a program develop knowledge of language as a system that goes beyond the specific knowledge of each one. They are sensitive to the presence of different languages in their environment and make judgments about the linguistic proficiency of their peers. They become language mediators for their peers by monitoring their peers' comprehension, observing contextual and situational cues, and using a variety of strategies in both of their languages as well as paralinguistic cues to facilitate comprehension. Young children can absorb and manipulate a great deal of the linguistic input to which they have access. Placing them in situations with a diversity of language backgrounds and opportunities for peer interaction facilitates the growth of their proficiency and comprehension.

The research raises some questions worthy of further study. How would the language mediation strategies change if several of the children were monolinguals in each language? Because all the children in the class could speak some English, they all shared this language. The need for language mediation would be greater if there were a group of monolinguals in each language trying to interact with those in the other language group. Such a situation would create greater challenges for both groups to participate in the language mediation role.

Another question concerns the range in individual differences among the children in their metacommunicative awareness. Some of the children in the reported study appeared to have a more sophisticated understanding than others about how to use the resources of both languages to serve as mediators. In addition, during the interviews, some were better able to articulate what strategies they used when someone did not understand.

A further question asks how these children's metacommunicative skills compare with those of monolingual kindergarteners whose schooling is conducted through only one language. How much of these children's skills can be attributed to participation in dual-language instruction? It may be the case that these skills develop as they are put to use in situations that call for them.

A final question asks what effect these skills might have on the literacy development of these children. Because so much of the academic content of schooling is based on literacy, it would be important to explore what impact these skills might have on reading and writing processes. Would the sensitivity that these children are developing to contextual cues in the environment transfer to the reading process such that they become more conscious of context cues in written texts enabling them to decode what they are reading and interpret those texts?

One concern about the bilingual development of these children is that it appears, at least from audio- and videotapes of children in the classroom, that the English monolinguals are not able to carry out conversations in Spanish. To a certain extent, it can also be observed that Spanish-dominant children exhibit symptoms of native language loss. During the interview portions of the data gathering in the reported study, the English monolinguals were rarely able to say more than isolated words in Spanish, although they were able to comprehend quite a bit. By April and May, when the interviews were carried out, the Spanish-dominant children, in responding to the interview questions in Spanish, manifested many hesitations in speech, occasional use of code-switching into English for vocabulary, and in general, a lower level of fluency in Spanish than in their English conversations. Such hesitations in speech and one-way code-switching or alternating from Spanish to English could be signs that their English fluency was developing and their Spanish fluency was not keeping pace.

For supporters of dual-language programs as a model for the bilingual development of children, these results are sobering, especially given the fact that in the school and the kindergarten classroom, approximately 80% of the curriculum was to be carried out in Spanish. Moreover, the school was consciously oriented to providing curriculum and activities that affirmed Spanish as an important language for all children. Longitudinal studies of bilingual development in these types of programs would be needed to examine how far English monolinguals are able to progress with the development of their second language and how far Spanish native speakers progress in maintaining their bilingualism.

Nevertheless, the dual-language school or two-way immersion programs may be a sound educational model for enhancing children's bilingual development. This model can have benefits not only for language-minority children, but also for native English speakers, who can develop fluency in the second language as they learn content through the medium of the second language. Nevertheless, the hegemony of English manifested itself in a variety of ways in this classroom even in a program actively geared toward developing bilingualism. Although this should provide reassurance to those concerned about the development of English skills in bilingual programs, it should be sobering to advocates of bilingualism who believe that it can be promoted by educational programs. The development of bilingual skills cannot be left to the school alone. Schools that attempt to promote bilingualism will need to seek allies in the broader community if they are to be successful in this endeavor.

REFERENCES

Bateson, G. (1972). *Steps to an ecology of mind.* New York: Ballantine Books.

Ben-Zeev, S. (1977). The influence of bilingualism on cognitive development and cognitive strategy. *Child Development, 48,* 1009–1018.

Bialystok, E. (1988). Levels of bilingualism and levels of linguistic awareness *Developmental Psychology, 24*(4), 560–567.

Bialystok, E. (1991). Metalinguistic dimensions of bilingual language proficiency. In E. Bialystok (Ed.), *Language processing in bilingual children* (pp. 113–140). Cambridge, England: Cambridge University Press.

Bialystok, E. (2001). *Bilingualism in development: Language, literacy and cognition.* Cambridge, England: Cambridge University Press.

Cazden, C. (1992). Adult assistance to language development: Scaffolds, models, and direct instruction. In C. Cazden (Ed.), *Whole language plus* (pp. 99–113). New York: Teacher College Press.

Chaney, C. (1994). Language development, metalinguistic awareness, and emergent literacy skills of 3-year-old children in relation to social class. *Applied Psycholinguistics, 15,* 371–394.

Christian, D. (1994). *Two-way bilingual education: Students learning through two languages.* Washington, DC: Center for Applied Linguistics.

Christian, D., Montone, C. L., Lindholm, K. J., & Carranza, I. (1997). *Profiles in two-way immersion education.* Washington, DC: ERIC/Center for Applied Linguistics.

Christian, D., & Whitcher, A. (1995). *Directory of two-way bilingual programs in the United States.* Washington, DC: Center for Applied Linguistics.

Cummins, J. (1987). Bilingualism, language proficiency, and metalinguistic development. In P. Homel, M. Palij, & D. Aaronson (Eds.), *Childhood bilingualism: Aspects of linguistic, cognitive, and social development* (pp. 57–73). Hillsdale, NJ: Lawrence Erlbaum Associates.

Cummins, J. (1991). Interdependence of first and second-language proficiency in bilingual children. In E. Bialystok (Ed.), *Language processing in bilingual children* (pp. 70–89). Cambridge, England: Cambridge University Press.

Diaz, R. (1983). Thought and two languages: The impact of bilingualism on cognitive development. *Review of Research in Education, 10,* 23–54.

Fantini, A. E. (1985). *Language acquisition of a bilingual child: A sociolinguistic perspective*. Clevedon: Multilingual Matters.

Fillmore, L. W., & Valadez, C. (1986). Teaching bilingual learners. In M. C. Wittrock (Ed.), *Handbook of research on teaching* (3rd.ed., pp. 648–685). New York: Macmillan.

Genesee, F. (1987). *Learning through two languages: Studies of immersion and bilingual education*. Cambridge, MA: Newbury House.

Grosjean, F. (1982). *Life with two languages*. Cambridge, MA: Harvard University Press.

Hakuta, K. (1976). A case study of a Japanese child learning English. *Language Learning, 26,* 321–351.

Hakuta, K. (1986). *Mirror of language: The debate on bilingualism*. New York: Basic Books

Hoffman, C. (1991). *An introduction to bilingualism*. New York: Longman.

Homel, P., Palij, M., & Aaronson, D. (1987). *Childhood bilingualism: Aspects of linguistic, cognitive, and social development*. Hillsdale, NJ: Lawrence Erlbaum Associates.

Krashen, S. (1982). *Principles and practices of second language acquisition*. Oxford: Pergamon Press.

Krashen, S., & Terrell, T. D. (1983). *The natural approach: Language acquisition in the classroom*. San Francisco: The Alemany Press.

Leopold, W. F. (1949). *Speech development of a bilingual child* (vol. 3). Evanston, IL: Northwestern University Press.

Lindholm, K. (1992). Two-way bilingual/immersion education: Theory, conceptual issues, and pedagogical implications. In R. V. Padilla & A. H. Benavides (Eds.), *Critical perspectives on bilingual education research* (pp. 195–220). Tempe, AZ: Bilingual Press.

Lindholm-Leary, K. J. (2001). *Dual language education*. Clevedon: Multilingual matters.

McLaughlin, B. (1984). *Second-language acquisition in childhood: Vol. 1. Preschool children* (2nd ed.). Hillside, NJ: Lawrence Erlbaum Associates.

McLaughlin, B. (1985). *Second language acquisition in childhood: Vol. 2, School-age children* (2nd ed.). Hillside, NJ: Lawrence Erlbaum Associates.

Olmeda, I. (2003). Language mediation among emergent bilingual children. *Linguistics and Education, 14*(2), 143–162.

Perera, N. S. (2001). The role of prefabricated language in young children's second language acquisition. *Bilingual Research Journal, 25*(3), 327–356.

Smith, P. (2001). Community language resources in dual language schooling. *Bilingual Research Journal, 25*(3), 375–404.

Toohey, K. (1998). Breaking them up, taking them away: ESL students in grade I. *TESOL Quarterly, 32*(1), 61–84.

Tse, L. (1996). Language brokering in linguistic minority communities: The case of Chinese and Vietnamese-American students. *Bilingual Research Journal, 20,* 485–498.

Tunmer, W. E., & Myhill, M. E. (1984). Metalinguistic awareness and bilingualism. In W. E. Tunmer, C. Pratt, & M. L. Merriman (Eds.), *Metalinguistic awareness in children: Theory, research, and implications* (pp. 169–187). Berlin: Springer-Verlag.

Vine, E. W. (2003). My partner: A five-year-old Samoan boy learns how to participate in class through interactions with his English-speaking peers. *Linguistics and Education, 14*(1), 99–121.

Vygotsky, L. S. (1962). *Thought and language*. Cambridge, MA: MIT Press.

Willett, J. (1995). Becoming first graders in an L2: An ethnographic study of L2 socialization. *TESOL Quarterly, 29*(3), 473–503.

Wong-Fillmore, L. (1991). Second language learning in children: A model of language learning in social context. In E. Bialystok (Ed.), *Language processing in bilingual children* (pp. 49–69). Cambridge, England: Cambridge University Press.

ENDNOTE

1. This chapter is a slightly different version of Olmeda (2003).

Photograph by Joanne Spyridakos.

6

Latino Children's Spanish Use in a Chicago Dual-Immersion Classroom

Kim Potowski
University of Illinois at Chicago

United States public schools offer several programs for language-minority students learning English at school. Most of these programs seek to transition students to all-English classrooms as soon as they have reached a certain level of English proficiency (for a description of bilingual education programs, see Crawford, 1995). But some programs, including dual-immersion or two-way bilingual immersion programs, encourage the development of students' first language (L1) as well as their English by imparting the curriculum in both languages.[1] These schools also target language *majority* students. Ideally, half of the students in the classroom are native English speakers learning the minority language, in this case Spanish, as a second language (L2). Theoretically, when approximately equal numbers of native speakers of both languages are present, opportunities are provided for English and Spanish learners to communicate with each other instead of with the teacher alone (Christian, 1996).

As of September 2001, there were at least 260 dual-immersion programs operating in U.S. elementary schools in 10 different languages, with 244 operating in Spanish (Center for Applied Linguistics, 2001). Several studies indicate that dual-immersion the academic achievement of students reaches levels higher than local norms (Christian, Montone, Lindholm, & Carranza,

1997; Lindholm & Aclan, 1991; Thomas & Collier, 1997), and that their Spanish and English proficiency also are high (Christian et al., 1997).[2]

Despite these encouraging findings, we know very little about students' language use in dual-immersion classrooms. Tarone and Swain (1995) found the lack of in-depth observation of language use and interaction in immersion classrooms striking, given the "ample evidence that social context can cause the speech of second-language learners to vary substantially in its grammatical and phonological structure" (p. 176). The research that has been done in "regular" immersion classrooms (in which all students have the same L1 and are learning the L2 for the first time) indicates that students increasingly avoid using their L2 in peer interactions as they move to higher grade levels (Broner, 2000; Tarone & Swain, 1995). More specifically, French immersion students were found to use French only for academic purposes and English for almost all social purposes. Tarone and Swain (1995) called this a type of *diglossia*, reconceptualized by Fishman (1967) as a separation of two languages in a society in which one language, learned formally in schools, serves literary and official functions while another language, learned at home, serves daily vernacular functions. Tarone and Swain proposed that in immersion classrooms, English becomes the vernacular and the L2 is the "superordinate" language for official business.

In attempting to explain these findings, Tarone and Swain (1995) suggested that immersion students carry out the social functions of play, competition, and arguing in the L1 for two reasons: (a) They do not know how to do so in the L2, given that they do not receive such input from their teachers, and (b) their need to perform these functions is more important to their social identity than whatever need they feel to stay in the L2. Expanding further on this sociolinguistic explanation of immersion students' classroom language use, Tarone and Swain drew on the work of Labov (1972), who proposed that members of an adolescent African American speech community risked being marked nonmembers, or "lame," if they used the superordinate speech style of standard English. Applying this to the immersion classroom, Tarone and Swain proposed that students who used French with their peers for nonacademic purposes risk social exclusion. They further suggested that dual-immersion classrooms may exhibit a similar phenomenon, although no one had yet examined dual immersion in this way. What makes the study of language in dual-immersion classrooms particularly interesting is that, by design, a large number of students actually are monolingual or bilingual Spanish speakers. One might therefore predict higher levels of Spanish use than in regular immersion, wherein all students are learning Spanish as an L2.

Some of what we do know about language use in dual-immersion settings rests on unquantified observations. Christian et al. (1997) indicated that "in general," the dual-immersion students they observed used Spanish with the teacher and while engaged in academic activities. In the lower grades, students were "sometimes" observed addressing the teacher in English during Spanish time, but this was less common in the upper grades. The use of Spanish during English time was very rare, occurring most frequently among Spanish-dominant children. In contrast, English often was used during Spanish time for social interactions among peers of both language backgrounds, even among Spanish L1 students, especially when the teacher was not within earshot. The authors contended that the use of English during Spanish time did not reflect students' inability to express themselves fully in Spanish, but rather was "clearly a deliberate choice" (Christian et al.,1997, p. 58). Other studies have found similar avoidance of Spanish by Latino students in dual-immersion classrooms (Delgado-Larocco, 1998; Freeman, 1998; McCollum, 1995). Several recent studies quantified Spanish use in dual-immersion classrooms and found that students are using less Spanish than educators might have thought. Fortune (2001) found that students used Spanish 33% of the time during Spanish lessons, and Carrigo (2000) found that students initiated comments to the teacher in Spanish only 26% of the time and responded to teachers' Spanish comments in Spanish 72% of the time.

These findings suggest that although dual-immersion classrooms provide students with plenty of opportunities to speak Spanish, there is no guarantee they will do so. Yet, to understand the potential of a dual-immersion classroom, we need to examine how much Spanish actually is being used, with whom, and for what purposes. Second language acquisition (SLA) research has acknowledged the need for input (Krashen, 1981), interaction (Long, 1981), and output (Swain, 1985) for SLA to take place. Similarly, although we still lack formal theories of heritage language development, it is reasonable to assume that for bilingual Latinos raised in the United States to maintain Spanish proficiency, they must engage in listening to Spanish and speaking it. Furthermore, Delgado-Larocco (1995) noted that it is essential to be aware of the real extent to which English dominates daily classroom exchanges, or English hegemony can become part of the school's hidden curriculum. The current study sought to quantify how much Spanish is spoken, with whom, and for what purposes in a dual-immersion classroom, and to explain the reasons behind the language use of two Latino students through ethnographic inquiry.

SETTING

According to the 2000 Census, Chicago's Latino population of 26% makes it the city with the third largest Latino population in the United States, and the composition of this population is 69% Mexican, 17% Puerto Rican, 2.5% Guatemalan, 2% Cuban, and 12% other groups (Census, 2000). As of late 1998, Chicago's public schools offered 10 dual-immersion programs.[3] This study took place at the Inter-American Magnet School (IAMS), which, founded by parents in 1975, is one of the oldest dual-immersion programs in the United States. The school is located in an affluent neighborhood on the north side, but because of its magnet charter, it serves children from all corners of the city and reflects its diversity: 65% of the children are His-panic; 19% are European American; 14% are African American; and 60% receive free or reduced lunch. Student achievement on standardized tests regularly exceeds state, city, and district norms, and the school has seen five Golden Apple teaching award winners, one Illinois Teacher of the Year, and more than two dozen newspaper and magazine articles.

In preschool through third grade, 80% of the curriculum is taught in Spanish and 20% in English. In grades 4 through 6, Spanish is used for 60% of the curriculum, and grades 7 and 8 are split fifty-fifty. The two languages are divided by subject. For example, in fifth grade, Spanish language arts, math, and half of the social studies curriculum are taught in Spanish, whereas English language arts, science, and the other half of the social studies curriculum are taught in English.

One of the three dual-immersion schools profiled in a study by Christian et al. (1997) IAMS. The researchers noted:

> As at the other two sites, English was clearly the preferred language for social purposes for those students who had achieved a certain level of fluency in it. At IAMS there appeared to be an even greater use of English by students when speaking among themselves. (pp. 85–86)

Christian et al. (1997) also noted that the level of English proficiency ex-hibited by the native Spanish speakers at IAMS was higher than at the other two schools. Only 35% of the students at IAMS' were determined to be lim-ited English proficient, as compared with 40% and 54%, respectively, at the other two sites, and roughly 45% of the Hispanic students entered IAMS already bilingual (although no definition of the term bilingual was provided). In their conclusions, Christian et al. (1997) wrote that at the IAMS,

> getting the Spanish proficiency of both language groups to meet [their] English proficiency levels has been a challenge. While some English-dominant students excelled in Spanish, many did not see the need to learn Spanish (at least in the earlier grades) and were *not motivated to learn it*. The Spanish-dominant students, too, were so drawn by the dominance of English in society that they were *not motivated* to improve their Spanish language skills beyond oral proficiency. (p. 86, emphasis added).

Motivation has been formalized as a construct to help explain SLA (Gardner, 1985; Gardner & Lambert, 1972). Recent work in the field of English as a second language (ESL) has expanded on motivation with the concept of *investment* (McKay & Wong, 1996; Norton, 2000), which recognizes that peoples' reasons for speaking a given language are inextricably linked to their immediate social surroundings and the facets of their identity they wish to present. After describing the Spanish expectations in the school and the classroom and presenting the language use findings, I offer interpretations of the students' language use based on their various and sometimes competing identity investments.

SPANISH USE IN THE SCHOOL

Knowledge of written and oral Spanish was not only advantageous, but at times also crucial within the school building. The hallways on all three floors exhibited students' work on current topics of study almost entirely in Spanish. I routinely observed school staff directing or disciplining children in the hallways in Spanish. Even more notably, public announcements during the school day often were given in Spanish without an English repetition, including summons for students to report to the main office or requests that visitors move their vehicles. The lack of repetition in English indicated that the building was a Spanish-speaking space. During open house nights, I saw several teachers display a tenacious dedication to Spanish. When one third-grade parent requested that homework be sent home with an English translation so she could help her child, the teachers replied that such a practice would undermine the need for the child to force himself to comprehend the Spanish instructions. Teachers also described ways in which parents could foster their children's Spanish development.

However, it was apparent that English was the dominant and more highly valued language in the school. For example, I routinely observed teachers using English during lessons that, according to the official classroom schedule, were supposed to be in Spanish. Some teachers explained that the books were in English, or that it was more important for students to know the material in English for upcoming standardized tests. Additionally, the "resource" classes of music, gym, and computers were taught in English, and several teachers complained that this eroded the percentage of Spanish instruction that students were supposed to receive each day. Only school-wide competitions such as the science fair, history fair, and storywriting competition, whose winners would proceed to a city-wide competition, were completed in English only. Whereas ESL classes were taught by a language acquisition professional who regularly presented at national conferences, the teacher of Spanish as a second language (for students struggling with Spanish) had no SLA training, claiming that she needed none. On the days I observed her class, the students colored items on vocabulary sheets and produced very little Spanish. There were Spanish L2 students in their eighth year of the program whose oral Spanish production was extremely halted, at levels far below the English of their Spanish L1 classmates. Despite the school's goals espousing equality of Spanish and English, there was clearly "leakage" (Freeman 1998) from the outside English-dominant world.

SPANISH IN MS. TORRES' CLASSROOM

I focused on Ms. Torres'[4] fifth-grade classroom because findings show that language use in "regular" immersion classrooms begins to shift to English at about the fourth- or fifth-grade level (Blanco-Iglesias, Broner, & Tarone, 1995; Met & Lorenz, 1997, p. 258; Tarone & Swain, 1995) and that by fifth grade, Spanish language learners in dual-immersion programs scored as "fully proficient" in Spanish (Christian, 1996). Ms. Torres' family had immigrated to Chicago from Mexico when she was 14 years old, and she currently is a very fluent Spanish-English bilingual.

Students needed a high level of Spanish comprehension to be successful in Ms. Torres' classroom. She spoke at a native pace similar to what I have observed in Mexican elementary schools, and did not appear to "water down" her vocabulary (Valdés, 1997). In fact, she commented that at the beginning of the school year, even L1 Spanish students complained that she spoke Spanish very fast. The students' social studies textbook and almost all of their math materials were in Spanish, and the students read three novels in Spanish during the year, had animated discussions about them, and wrote written responses that included new vocabulary items. Even students who could not produce much accurate oral Spanish seemed to understand most of what they heard and read in their language arts, math, and social studies classes taught in Spanish.

However, as in the school generally, Spanish lost out to English. Fifth-grade classrooms were supposed to be 60% Spanish and 40% English, but according to my observations, Spanish was the official class language during only 40% to 50% of the week. The importance of standardized tests was evident as well. Near the time of the Iowa Test of Basic Skills and the Illinois State Achievement Test examinations, Ms. Torres had students complete reading and math journals in English, although math was supposed to be taught in Spanish. When students spoke to her in English during Spanish lessons, she sometimes required them to repeat themselves in Spanish, but she often allowed English use to go without comment. Anyone who has observed an immersion classroom knows how challenging it can be to juggle the tasks of maintaining order, keeping students on task, and using the target language for several hours, including the constant deliberation and decision whether to focus on what the student said to advance the lesson or to focus on the way it was said. Many teachers I interviewed struggled with this issue.

Following Willett (1995) and Norton (2000), who examined how individual ESL learners valued English, I sought to understand whether students felt a need to acquire high levels of Spanish proficiency. Ms. Torres clearly stated her belief that the students did not value Spanish enough for high or low proficiency levels to influence their status in the classroom. Students' comments about each other's Spanish seemed to corroborate that it was not a large factor in their popularity. However, Spanish did bestow two specific classroom benefits during teacher-fronted lessons: Using Spanish seemed linked to a student's identity as academically successful, and proficiency in spoken Spanish seemed to enable students to be more successful at getting and keeping the floor during teacher-fronted lessons, a point examined later.

METHODS AND FINDINGS

I audio- and videorecorded 12½ hours of classroom data from four students during Spanish language arts and Spanish social studies lessons over a period of 5 months. On the recordings, students routinely went off task, spoke English during Spanish time, and sometimes used swear words, lending confidence to my belief that they did not see me as an authority figure or someone for whom they had to perform in a certain way. A total of 2,203 turns were coded according to nine sociolinguistic variables, which are described in Appendix A. The code-switched turns (turns that mixed Spanish and English in chunks larger than one word) formed 5% of the corpus and were removed for separate analysis. I focus on the language use of two Latino students, Carolina and Matt, although some data from Melissa and Otto, two second-language learners, are presented for comparison. Both Carolina and Matt learned Spanish as their L1 and entered school Spanish-dominant, but by the time of this study, they were English dominant.

Carolina, one of the most fluent Spanish speakers in Ms. Torres' class, had no trouble expressing herself orally in either language, although she occasionally used English lexical items in her Spanish (e.g., *"Está wrestling con un cocodrilo"*). She was one of the most active participants in the classroom in all subject areas, volunteering answers to the teacher's questions and helping other students with vocabulary. Her mother was from Ecuador and her father from Honduras, and she spoke Spanish daily at home with her parents, her grandparents, and her younger sister.

Matt's oral Spanish was very native-like, although he often borrowed English words, code-switched to English for larger parts of sentences, or shifted into English entirely. He was beyond his peers in both analytical skills and knowledge of school-related subjects, and he participated frequently in class, but toward the end of the school year he was beginning to exhibit resistance to homework and to school in general. His mother had immigrated from El Salvador when she was 18 years old, and his Euro-American stepfather did not know Spanish. Matt spoke Spanish at home each day for a short time before and after school with his maternal grandparents and with his maternal great-grandmother, but his mother said that he regularly responded in English when she spoke to him in Spanish. He used English with his younger sister.

Table 6.1 presents Carolina's and Matt's percentages of Spanish and English use, and also that of the Spanish L2 students, Melissa and Otto, during the 12.5 hours of data.

The students averaged 56% Spanish use overall, which was 12% more often than they used English, but much less than the 100% expected during these Spanish lessons. I had predicted that the presence of Latino-heritage

TABLE 6.1

Overall Language Use

Spanish	English	Total
56% (1,141 turns)	44% (909 turns)	100% (2,050 turns)

Spanish speakers would result in greater Spanish use than has been found in "regular" Spanish immersion programs. It was surprising to find that Spanish was used slightly less often in this dual-immersion classroom than the 63% found by Broner (2000) in a regular-immersion classroom. This may be attributable to differences in language rule enforcement by the teachers in the two classrooms, but this has not been formally examined. It also may be that bilingual Latino students perceive and attempt to conform to the language expectations of mainstream society by asserting their English competence as often as possible. Teachers at IAMS commented that even students recently arrived from Latin America with low English proficiency preferred to speak English, and often were the most difficult students to get to use Spanish in class. However, there is no empiric support for these explanations.

Table 6.2 presents findings concerning the language use of the four students according to their L1:

Table 6.2 shows that the students' L1 did not influence their classroom language use. That is, the students who had Spanish as their L1 did not use more Spanish than Spanish L2 students. More relevant to Spanish use was the students' gender, as shown in Table 6.3:

TABLE 6.2

Language by Student

	Spanish L1		Spanish L2		
(N = 2,050)	Carolina (N = 590) n (%)	Matt (N = 527) n (%)	Melissa (N = 340) n (%)	Otto (N = 593) n (%)	Total
Spanish	393 (67)	248 (47)	219 (64)	281 (47)	1,141 (100)
English	197 (33)	279 (53)	121 (36)	312 (53)	909 (100)
Total	590 (100)	527 (100)	340 (100)	593 (100)	2,050 (100)

TABLE 6.3

Language Use by Gender

	Girls (N = 930) n (%)	Boys (N = 1,120) n (%)
Spanish	612 (66)	529 (47)
English	318 (34)	591 (53)
Total	930 (100%)	1,120 (100%)

The girls averaged 66% Spanish use and the boys averaged 47% Spanish use. The girls, therefore, conformed to the language rules more than the boys, echoing other classroom research showing that girls in elementary schools tend to exhibit behaviors that are more acceptable to the teacher (Toohey, 2000; Willett, 1995). Ms. Torres did not consider either Otto or Matt to have serious behavioral problems, but they routinely teased and tried to subordinate their peers. If boys generally tend to be more rambunctious in class, it may follow that in a dual-immersion context they choose to flout the language rules more often than girls. However, there were six girls in the classroom (two L1 and four L2) who resisted using Spanish, and there were three boys (two L1 and one L2) who seemed to enjoy using Spanish and rarely used English publicly during Spanish time. Therefore, gender explanations of language choice must be tempered by an examination of individual students' language choices.

Whether the students' interlocutor was the teacher or another student also was related to their language choices, as seen in Table 6.4:

When talking to the teacher, the students used Spanish 82% of the time, indicating a general willingness to follow the language rules with the teacher. But during group work, when their language use was usually unmonitored, students tended to use English whenever possible. Of the 1,085 turns directed to peers, 68% were in English and only 32% were in Spanish, a considerable drop from the 82% Spanish use with the teacher, suggesting a diglossic situation such as that described by Tarone and Swain (1995) in regular-immersion classrooms. To explain the high levels of English use found in a dual-immersion classroom she studied, Carranza (1995) suggested that students experienced a "feeling of 'pretense' when two people communicate in one language knowing that both can be more

TABLE 6.4

Interlocutor

	Spanish n (%)	English n (%)	Total n(%)
To teacher (47% of corpus)	794 (82)	171 (18)	965 (100)
To peers (53% of corpus)	347 (32)	738 (68)	1,085 (100)
Total (100% of corpus)	1,141	909	2,050

effective in another" (p. 174). Given Carolina and Matt's high levels of English proficiency, speaking in Spanish with their peers may have felt just as "pretentious" as it would have to Melissa or Otto. An interesting area for future study is whether the Spanish proficiency of peer interlocutors affects language use. For example, on several occasions, I noticed Carolina using more Spanish than usual when seated with highly Spanish-proficient Latino classmates. However, the students changed tablemates so often that quantification of this variable was impractical for this study.

Table 6.5 breaks down individual students' language use with the teacher and with peers:

TABLE 6.5

Individual Students' Language Use by Interlocutor

	To Teacher			To Peers		
	Spanish (N = 794) n (%)	English (N = 171) n (%)	Total (N = 965) n (%)	Spanish (N = 347) n (%)	English (N = 738) n (%)	Total (N = 1,085) n (%)
Carolina	270 (91)	26 (9)	296 (100)	123 (42)	171 (58)	294 (100)
Matt	195 (83)	41 (17)	236 (100)	53 (18)	238 (82)	291 (100)
Melissa	112 (88)	15 (9)	127 (100)	107 (50)	106 (50)	213 (100)
Otto	216 (71)	89 (29)	305 (100)	65 (23)	223 (77)	288 (100)

Students' language use with the teacher was fairly homogeneous. All the students except Otto used Spanish 83% to 91% of the time when speaking with the teacher, and even Otto's language use with the teacher was almost three fourths in Spanish. Students' language use with peers showed more variation, particularly in relation to gender. Again, the girls used more Spanish than the boys, but some differences merit description.

Compared with Melissa, Carolina used slightly more Spanish with the teacher, but slightly less with her peers. Carolina's high oral Spanish proficiency would have allowed her to use Spanish with her peers more often than she did, but her interview and journal comments indicated that she was unwilling to risk social exclusion. Her classmates requested her as a tablemate more often than all the other girls in the classroom except one, indicating that she was quite popular. Melissa, on the other hand, experienced a degree of social exclusion and mild teasing because of her intense academic focus and her insistence on using Spanish. She often answered her peers' English in Spanish, which no other students in the corpus did, and even occasionally admonished them to use Spanish.

Matt's level of Spanish use with the teacher was close to that of the girls. Additionally, during teacher-fronted lessons, his frequent volunteered answers and offers to help the teacher reflected his investment in a public identity as a conscientious student. However, when talking with his peers out of the teacher's earshot, he used the least Spanish of all four students, and his comments very clearly sought to identify him as resistant to the academic demands placed on him. Such comments would logically take place not in Spanish, which was the schoolwork language, but in English, the adolescent vernacular of the classroom.

The final variable linked with Spanish use was the topic of the turn. Students' turns were coded as "on-task" when they were about academic content, "management" when they regulated the completion of an academic task, and "off-task" when they were unrelated to academic content or tasks. Table 6.6 shows the amount of Spanish and English used for each type of topic:

Most of the children's on-task turns (68%) were made in Spanish. These 935 on-task Spanish turns accounted for fully 88% of the entire Spanish corpus. This is not surprising, because on-task turns were related directly to academic work based on texts written in Spanish. However, students greatly preferred English for off-task topics. Only 15% of the total turns in the corpus were off-task, but 83% of them were in English. Noting this

TABLE 6.6

Topic

(N = 2,050)	Spanish n (%)	English n (%)	Total n (%)
On-task (67% of corpus)	935 (68)	436 (32)	1,371 (100)
Management (16% of corpus)	144 (43)	193 (57)	337 (100)
Off-task (15% of corpus)	54 (17)	258 (83)	312 (100)
Unknown[5] (1% of corpus)	9 (30)	21 (70)	30 (100)

trend, I examined the specific topics and functions of students' off-task English turns and compared them with their off-task Spanish turns. Although this lacked the rigor of a thorough discourse analysis, it was apparent that students used English to talk about movies, TV shows, and popular culture, and to carry out functions such as fighting, teasing, and complaining about school. Students' off-task peer Spanish, however, carried out a much more limited range of functions. For example, one student was recorded singing absentmindedly to himself the Spanish song the students had learned in chorus. Another student once referred to the Power Rangers in Spanish and to the *día del niño*. These turns differed from the off-task turns in English because they lacked an obvious interlocutor and communicative intent. Significantly, there were no references to TV, music, or movies, nor any fighting, teasing, or slang in Spanish.

The finding that most social talk was conducted in English and most Spanish was used with the teacher for academic topics supports Tarone and Swain's (1995) proposal that a type of diglossia can exist in immersion classrooms, but in this case, it existed even in a dual-immersion classroom.[6] Interestingly, this language use pattern represents an inversion of the larger diglossic situation of Spanish in the United States, in which English is the language for official and academic work and Spanish is reserved for social and informal situations. The fact that these students carried out challenging academic curriculum in Spanish is important because it opposes the messages of larger society about the inferiority of Spanish. In

Cummins' (1984) terms, these students were developing cognitive academic language proficiency in Spanish, if not many basic interpersonal communicative skills. As Tarone and Swain (1995) have noted, it may not be crucial that dual-immersion students use Spanish for social interactions to develop respectable levels of proficiency. Dual immersion provides opportunities for literacy development in Spanish that many children in the United States, both Spanish- and English-speaking children, do not receive in the home.

However, Tarone and Swain (1995) also claimed that immersion students use their L1 for social functions because they do not know how to carry them out in their L2. They argued that if students were able to use their L2 for these social functions, they would. I did not verify whether Carolina and Matt knew how to say in Spanish the exact things they had produced in the English corpus, but my speech samples suggest that they did, although they probably would not have known much Spanish slang because they were English-dominant heritage Spanish-speakers who grew up entirely in the United States. I offer an alternative interpretation, proposing that even if these two Latino students had been able to carry out these social functions in Spanish, doing so would have made them stand out from their peers, compromising their identity investments in peer group status. Melissa is a counterexample because it seemed that the identity she sought to promote was precisely that of a Spanish speaker, which, combined with her intense academic focus, seemed to outweigh any need to perform social functions such as playing or talking about adolescent themes, and she suffered a degree of social exclusion as a result.

The only language use that appeared to be connected to students' L1 was their bidding strategies. "Bidding" refers to the ways that students gained permission to speak during a teacher-fronted lesson. When the teacher was leading a lesson, students could speak publicly either by shouting out their comments or by bidding for and being granted the floor. Students could bid for the floor by raising their hands, by saying something like "Ooh!" or "I know!," or by doing both at the same time. When shouting out, students used Spanish 81% of the time, but when they had been selected, their Spanish use rose to 96%. This is likely because after taking the trouble to bid for the floor, and winning it over competing students' bids, students may have felt more pressure to use Spanish than if they had just shouted out. As indicated in Table 6.4, students who spoke more during teacher-fronted lessons were more likely to produce Spanish, which prompted me to examine students' bidding strategies and how often they were successful.

The Spanish L1 students had a higher percentage of their verbal bids selected by the teacher (52%) than did the Spanish L2 students (14%). Carolina and Matt used a strategy that Melissa and Otto did not use. When the teacher posed a question, Carolina and Matt began saying their answer in Spanish (e.g., *"Oh, es como ... "* or *"Los que, los que ... "*), which seemed to attract the teacher's attention over competing bids such as "Ooh!" or *"¡Yo sé!"* Melissa and Otto did not use this strategy.

If language production is a component central to language development (Swain, 1985), these Spanish L1 students possibly were reaping more linguistic benefits than their Spanish L2 counterparts. That Spanish L2 students were less successful at verbally gaining the floor also suggests that their teacher expected and rewarded native-like participation during teacher-fronted lessons, a finding that runs counter to the Valdés' suggestion(1997) that dual immersion serves the needs of Spanish L2 students more than the needs of Latinos. Further systematic study of teachers' selection of students' bids in dual-immersion classrooms is necessary because, as suggested by Carranza (1995), access to the floor is an important resource that not only affects the learning of content, but also constitutes opportunities to use, practice, and learn Spanish.

QUALITATIVE FINDINGS

Each of these students brought to the classroom different personal and linguistic relationships to Spanish, and each was likely to be treated by and react differently to the environment created by Ms. Torres and by the other class members. It is reasonable to posit that students' classroom language choices reflected these differences. A growing body of research in ESL (McKay & Wong, 1996; Norton, 2000; Norton Peirce, 1995; Willet, 1995) has used case studies to analyze how students' identity investments, power relations vis-à-vis other people, and social interactions affect their language learning experiences both inside and outside the classroom. Norton (2000) used the term "identity" to reference the way individuals understand their relations to the world, how those relations are constructed over time and space, and how they understand possibilities for the future. McKay and Wong (1996) argued that learners' negotiations of identity are "not simply distractions from the proper task of language learning.... Rather, they must be regarded as constituting the very fabric of students' lives and as determining their investment in learning the target language" (p. 603).

Although the field has not yet tested theories of heritage-Spanish development, it is logical to assume that heritage speakers need actually to produce Spanish for their Spanish linguistic systems to develop (Swain, 1985). It is therefore crucial to understand that "a learner's motivation to speak is mediated by other investments that may conflict with the desire to speak—investments that are intimately connected to the ongoing production of the learners' identities and their desires for the future" (Norton, 2000, p. 120). Norton proposed that learners "invest" in a language when they feel they will acquire a wider range of symbolic and material resources (e.g., friendship, education, and money) as well as access to things previously unavailable to them. Additionally, they must see the return on their investment as worth the effort expended. Norton's collective case study provides evidence that a person's investment in using a language can appear contradictory, depending on the momentary conditions in which speaker–learners find themselves.

To develop an accurate interpretation of the reasons behind these students' language use, I observed them over 100 hours in the classroom, gym, lunch, recess, computer use, music, and academic classes taught in English over a period of 9 months. In addition to participant observation and notetaking, I used a written questionnaire to explore students' attitudes toward Spanish, and I interviewed students, parents, and the teacher. The descriptions that follow seek to produce a balanced portrait of students' home and classroom language use to foster an understanding of the reasons behind their language choices.

CAROLINA

The Padilla family's home was located in a northwestern neighborhood of the city that held spacious houses and yards reminiscent of the suburbs. Carolina's mother, a human resources professional, came to the United States from Ecuador when she was 5 years old, and her father came from Honduras after completing high school there. Carolina lived with her parents, her two sisters, and her two maternal grandparents. Mrs. Padilla had chosen the Inter-American for Carolina's older sister Natalie. Mrs. Padilla wanted her children to be "really bilingual," citing her own success upon entering the job market as proof of the importance of knowing Spanish.

Despite a recognition of her own tendency to use English, Mrs. Padilla said she found it surprising "that all these kids, despite the fact that they speak Spanish, when they speak to one another they only speak English," which she routinely observed between Carolina and her friends when they came to the house. She posited that "it's a comfort level; maybe, it's what they see out there; it's on TV; it's the culture that they live in. And I think they won't appreciate it until they get older. I know I didn't." She asked me how parents can reinforce Spanish both inside and outside the home, which I found somewhat in contradiction to her preference that her daughters discontinue their formal study of Spanish in high school and "pick up a third language." She commented that Natalie planned to study French in high school, "which is fine, because we use Spanish at home, and she's very comfortable and articulate. I think sometimes more than I am. So she wants to learn a third language." She also commented that she will let Carolina decide what language to study in high school, although she admitted: "I don't know if I would even encourage her to continue in Spanish, because I think that she has a solid foundation, going to Inter-American all these years." However, when asked, she commented that she had seen clear improvements in Carolina's English vocabulary, but had not noticed the same phenomenon in her Spanish.

In tune with the educational priorities and demands in the United States, Mrs. Padilla showed considerably more concern about her daughters' English development. She once took Natalie to be tested:

> and they found that her English grammar was not good. The person that tested her was bilingual and it seemed that they confuse the grammar, so I had to sign her up for tutoring in English so she wouldn't fall behind, especially because I was having her tested to go to high school. And with Carolina, I had her tested and it was the same thing, so I put her in the tutoring program. So that's one thing I'm concerned about, that they may not be learning English well enough to compete outside of Inter-American.

For Mrs. Padilla, Spanish development was important as long as her children's English did not suffer, a very reasonable response to the English-dominant environment in which she and her family live. Carolina's classroom language choices may have reflected these competing demands. In an interview, Carolina stated that she would not be happy at a school that taught only English because she "might forget Spanish," but her language use, as presented in the previous section, shows that she did not take full advantage of classroom opportunities to speak Spanish. Carolina admitted that she and her classmates used English during Spanish lessons, indicating that it was because they "forgot" or "they're sometimes more comfortable, and they use it a lot. Because, I mean, when we're in recess, we all wanna just speak English." In class, she used English when displaying her knowledge of popular music, radio stations, and television shows, and occasionally to complain about school. She said her own use of English during Spanish lessons was because outside of class, "I talk English most of the time. I don't really, like, use the Spanish that much."

During the year of this study, Carolina's report card grades were high and her standardized test scores were above national norms. She was one of the most participatory students in Ms. Torres' class, and also one of the most fluent Spanish speakers, receiving the highest ratings on an oral Spanish assessment performed by the Center for Applied Linguistics. However, Carolina claimed, "I'm not good like people think in Spanish because people keep on like judging me that I should really know a lot of Spanish since I come from a Spanish family. But sometimes it's not true, because you keep talking all this English and you start forgetting your Spanish." This reluctance to accept a position as a superior Spanish speaker by virtue of coming from a Spanish-speaking family is noteworthy. Melissa did just the opposite. She enjoyed receiving praise for her Spanish precisely because it was not expected of her as a nonnative speaker. Melissa had to work harder for her Spanish, and both she and her mother enjoyed the praise it brought. As mentioned earlier, Melissa insisted on using Spanish with her peers as much as she did to fortify her investment in an identity as a Spanish-speaker (for more details on Melissa and Otto, see Potowski 2002), whereas Carolina did so through using Spanish with her family and with Ms. Torres.

In summary, Carolina used Spanish with the teacher very consistently (91% of the time). Her daily use of Spanish with her family, particularly with her monolingual grandparents, and the family's trips to Spanish-speaking countries contributed to her Spanish language proficiency and positive identity as bilingual. This, combined with her high level of classroom participation, positioned her as a successful Spanish speaker. She was willing and able to conform publicly to Ms. Torres' language expectations. In return, Ms. Torres frequently gave Carolina the floor. With her peers, Carolina did use Spanish 42% of the time, but because the students generally preferred English, she used it with them 58% of the time to remain in good social standing. Her investment in an identity as a good student promoted her Spanish use, whereas her investment in her status among her friends (who used slang and talked about preadolescent topics in English) motivated her English use.

Matt

Matt's mother, Mrs. Castillo, came to the United States from El Salvador when she was 18 years old. Her husband, Matt's stepfather, was Euro-American and did not speak Spanish. Mrs. Castillo chose the Inter-American because some friends highly recommended it. She commented that the bilingual programs in other schools did not teach Spanish well, whereas at the Inter-American, *"el primero es español"* ("Spanish is first"). She said this was important in her decision because

> *A veces es muy difícil para uno que trabaja estarles enseñando.... Se lo puede enseñar uno a hablar, pero ya para escribirlo bien y leerlo bien es bastante difícil. Ellos no lo aprenden eso estas escuelas de acá.... El inglés, siempre lo van a aprender. Pero el segundo idioma, que es el de la familia y de donde uno viene, es bastante difícil porque uno esta en un ambiente donde más inglés se habla que el idioma de uno.*

> (Sometimes it's very difficult for someone who works to teach them.... One can teach them to speak, but to write it well and read it well, it's quite difficult. They don't learn that in these schools around here.... English, they're always going to learn. But the second language, which is the one of the family and where one comes from, it's very difficult because one is in an environment where more English is spoken than one's own language.)

It is interesting that she referred to Spanish as the children's "second" language, although they chronologically learned it first. Spanish was indeed second in both proficiency and importance in their lives. Mrs. Castillo said that her son and his friends identified more with English than with Spanish: *"Ellos dicen, 'De aquí somos, aquí nacimos y éste es el idioma de nosotros, el que necesitamos más'"* (They say, "We're from here; we were born here and this is our language, the one we need more"). However, Mrs. Castillo wanted Matt to know Spanish because *"Es de donde él viene. El background de él, ¿no? De donde él desciende, aunque aquí nazca. Quiero que conozca la cultura y el idioma y todo"* (It's where he comes from. His background, no? Where he descends from, although he was born here. I want him to know the culture and the language and everything).

Mrs. Castillo told me that when she spoke to Matt in Spanish, he almost always answered her in English or indicated that he did not understand what she said. "And I have to tell him in English," she said. She noticed that his Spanish vocabulary and syntax had declined over the past year. Both Matt and his mother said that the television programs he watched and the music he listened to were all in English, and that Matt left the room whenever she put on Spanish television programs, although he did watch an occasional soccer news show in Spanish. Half of the library books that Mrs. Castillo regularly brought home for Matt were in Spanish, but she said that he read more in English. She also indicated that he might not want to continue studying Spanish in high school. Despite her positive feelings about the Inter-American, Mrs. Castillo shared some of the same fears Carolina's mother expressed about her son's English development, which may have been what caused her not to insist that her son use Spanish with her. Despite this preference for English, when Matt's parents mentioned moving to the suburbs and told him that he would find only English-speaking children there, *"Me dice, '¿No voy a hablar español o qué?' Se quedó pensativo, como que no le gusta mucho la idea"* (He says to me, "I'm not going to speak Spanish or what?" He was pensive, like he doesn't like the idea very much). His mother also said that Matt pays attention to entertainment figures such as Jennifer Lopez, Ricky Martin, and Christina Aguilera, and can identify their Latin origins.

Matt was successful and well adjusted at school. According to his mother, *"se siente como en familia, se siente muy identificado con todos"* (He feels like he's in a family, he identifies with everyone). He received high grades, particularly in math and science, although, like Carolina, he disliked writing in English or Spanish. When I asked Ms. Torres to name students with high Spanish proficiency, the first student she mentioned was Matt, saying that he was "fabulous." However, in the second interview a few months later, she rated his listening and reading comprehension highly but lamented what she considered his underutilized Spanish skills: *"Y sí lo sabe hablar bien, pero ya mete mucho inglés. También la mamá, si no se esfuerza le habla más en inglés"* (He does know how to speak it well, but he puts a lot of English in there now. Also his mom, if she doesn't work at it, he speaks to her more in English).

Matt exhibited ambivalence toward Spanish. In his journal he wrote that it was important to know Spanish *"porque es el idioma de tu cultura y hay cosas en español que tenemos que leer"* (because it's the language of your culture, and there are things in Spanish that we have to read). On the questionnaire, he indicated that Spanish was important on various levels (for a good job, for his future spouse and children, and in Chicago), but that he liked speaking Spanish slightly less than speaking English. When asked in an interview what was important to succeed at the Inter-American, Matt was the only student who mentioned "knowing Spanish and English." Despite these pro-Spanish responses, he also said that there was "too much Spanish" at the school, particularly because the standardized Iowa math tests were in English: "Sometimes [having math class in Spanish] is bad, because in the Iowa tests, there's these words in English that they never told us, and like at the last minute they give us these sheets that say some words in English." He also said he would prefer that science be taught in English because it would be easier. "There are some words I don't know in Spanish, in science. "Moreover, in his interview, he commented that learning Spanish was important at school only for Spanish class, nothing more, and that Spanish class was so boring that he "almost fell asleep once."

Matt made an interesting observation when I asked him to rate Melissa's Spanish as low, medium, or high: "She's high, because she talks very little in English during Spanish class. I think she's better than me in Spanish. Not like in the words because she doesn't know a lot of words, but she's better in controlling her language." Matt knew he had higher Spanish proficiency than Melissa, but also was aware that she used Spanish more than he did. When asked why he used English during Spanish lessons, Matt replied, much like Carolina, that he was "used to talking in English."

Although Matt was the first student Ms. Torres mentioned for high Spanish proficiency, she did not consider his attitudes toward Spanish as very positive. It was while discussing Carolina's attitudes that Ms. Torres first revealed her opinions about Matt's attitudes:

> Yo pienso que [a Carolina] le gusta. Y que se siente orgullosa de poder hablarlo, y poder comunicarse en el español, sí. Pero Matt es diferente. [risa] Él niega más. Pero es por la edad ahorita, yo creo que él está más rebelde.

> (I think that [Carolina] likes Spanish. And she feels proud to be able to speak it, to be able to communicate in Spanish, yes. But Matt is different. [laughter] He refuses more. But it's because of their age right now, I think he's more rebellious.)

Matt was one of the five students Ms. Torres mentioned whom she most frequently sanctioned for speaking English.[7] When asked how students felt when this happened, she replied:

> No les gusta. "Oh, pero yo no estaba hablando." "No, pero es que él me preguntó en inglés." Lo niegan. Ay, sobre todo Matt. Siempre está batallando. Se les ve la cara, el enojo. Y muy claro lo veo yo, sobre todo en Otto. Y claro, Matt, no tengo que verlo. Él me lo dice. Es muy defensivo. Él siempre está defendiéndose.

(They don't like it. "Oh, but I wasn't talking." "No, but he asked me in English." They deny it. Aye, especially Matt. He's always fighting. You can see the anger on their faces. I see it very clearly, especially in Otto. And of course Matt, I don't have to see it. He tells me. He's very defensive. He's always defending himself.)

Although Matt disliked being publicly reprimanded for speaking English, Ms. Torres noted that when he was caught, he did not make an effort to change his linguistic behavior and speak Spanish, which my observations and recordings corroborated. However, Ms. Torres was generally satisfied with Matt's level of participation in both languages.

In public, Matt wanted to be perceived as a conscientious and helpful student, which was evident when he volunteered to lower the overhead screen, and fought to hold a classroom job. It was also evident in the following two responses. When Ms. Torres asked the class why they thought she was making them read a lot of Spanish, Matt answered, *"Para mejorar"* (To improve), and when she reminded them that she was going to take away *canicas*[7] if they kept using English, he suggested that she take away a dollar instead. These comments, even if insincere, seemed to indicate a desire to be perceived publicly as a good student. Both Ms. Torres and Mrs. Castillo indicated that there were serious consequences at home if Matt got into trouble at school, which prompted Matt to use just enough Spanish to avoid getting in trouble. However, Matt in his comments with his peers clearly sought to identify himself as resistant to the academic demands placed on students. He said he did "busywork," not homework, and sometimes bragged about how little interest he had in academic pursuits. He also occasionally subordinated his peers by saying that he was more intelligent or that they did not know how to do things correctly (all of which was done in English).

In summary, Matt used Spanish with the teacher 83% of the time, but with his peers only 18% of the time. Despite his familial identification with Spanish, he used only English with his stepfather, and preferred to use English with his mother, sister, and friends. He also spent less time with his Spanish-speaking grandparents than did Carolina. His peer English use reflected his desire to fit in with his peer group.

CONCLUSIONS

Although to date there are no empirically based theories of heritage language development, heritage speakers need interaction with fluent speakers to maintain their Spanish. In this classroom described, heritage speakers had regular contact with other heritage speakers and with native-speaking teachers and texts, and they were expected to use Spanish during a large portion of the school day. Although Carolina and Matt used Spanish an average of 87% of the time with the teacher, together they averaged just 30% Spanish use with peers. Half of their peers were Spanish L2, and, like Carolina and Matt themselves, all of the Spanish L1 students who entered school Spanish-dominant were now English-dominant. Research in dual-immersion classrooms with more Spanish-dominant students likely would produce different results.

This preference for English suggests that there was "leakage" (Freeman, 1998) into the classroom of the dominant language patterns in the wider community. That is, despite the school's goals of using and valuing Spanish and English equally within the building, practices of English dominance outside the building found their way into the school. Freeman (1998) noted that

> English is naturally the language of choice for ... students because languages ... other than standard English tend to be stigmatized in mainstream U.S. society and because English is what the students hear on television and in the popular music that they listen to. Although the school goes to great lengths to create an environment in which English and Spanish are valued equally, the same conditions simply do not exist outside the school's discourse. (p. 578).

Although English L1 students in this study did understand grade-level academic texts and conversations in Spanish, and although most could use Spanish to express their basic ideas orally and in writing, their fluency and accuracy was overall lower than the English of their Spanish L1 counterparts. Leakage was also apparent in their teachers' use of English during Spanish lessons, the importance given to English-language standardized tests, the parent meetings conduced in English despite the presence of Spanish-dominant parents, and the higher quality of ESL instruction compared with that for Spanish as a second language. However, the finding that heritage speakers' bidding strategies were more successful at gaining the floor suggests that opportunities to produce Spanish output may be slanted in favor of these students, and that their linguistic knowledge does have value in these classrooms (Valdés, 1997).

Freeman (1998) argued that dual immersion is an attempt at language planning, and according to Fasold (1984), a successful language planning policy includes measures to influence people's self-identification so that the identity of the target language population becomes desirable. In this study, students' investments in identities as Spanish-speakers appeared to be more relevant to their language choices than their backgrounds as Latino or having had Spanish as a first language. The wide variation in language use displayed by individual students highlights the usefulness of ethnographic case studies in illuminating data often overlooked in the compilation of group data, particularly in environments as complicated as classrooms. If bilingual youth are to maintain their Spanish language skills to a degree sufficient for them to transmit the language to their own future children, not only must dual-immersion educators pay close attention to the amount of Spanish being used in class and for what purposes; they also must find ways to encourage students to invest in identities as Spanish speakers.

APPENDIX A

Procedures for Coding Students' Turns

Turn.   A turn was defined as the time when an interlocutor stopped talking or was interrupted by another interlocutor's turn (Ellis, 1994; Levinson, 1983). In example 1, each numbered line represents a separate turn. Matt was assigned a total of four turns in this exchange: lines 2, 4, 6, 8, and 9 (which formed one turn that extended to two written lines).

(1)

1	Ms. Torres:	¿De qué otros lados vienen las historias y los cuentos? [From where else do stories and tales come from?]
2	Matt:	Oooh!
3	Ms. Torres:	Matt.
4	Matt:	*De ... cosas que existen y/* [From ... things that exist and/]
5	Ms. Torres:	*De cosas que existen pero ¿dónde?* [From things that exist, but where?]
6	Matt:	*... y que no existen. Como/* [... and that don't exist. Like/]
7	Ms. Torres:	*De cosas que existen/* [From things that exist/]
8	Matt:	*Uh ... como.... um ... como ... son como ... como una*
9		*leyenda, dice de, del sol, and how it was made and, y cosas así.* [Uh, like ... um ... like ... they're like ... like a legend, it says, about the sun, and how it was made, and things like that.]

Gender and LI. There were two girls (one Spanish L1 and one Spanish L2) and two boys (one Spanish L1 and one Spanish L2). However, as mentioned previously, the Spanish L1 students were English dominant, which was likely very a significant factor in their language use.

Language. Turns were coded by language as either Spanish or English. A turn with a single lexeme mixed in from the other language, what Myers-Scotton (1993) calls an ML + EL lexeme, was coded according to the matrix language. Therefore, the turn *"No tenían muchos weapons" was coded as* "Spanish" and the turn "I don't get the *mensaje"* was coded as "English." Turns with larger mixed constituents, called ML + EL islands (Myers-Scotton 1993) such as *"Como una leyenda, dice de, del sol,* and *how it was made and, y cosas así,"* and turns with intersentential codeswitches (both of which formed only 5% of the corpus) were eliminated for this analysis. A small number of turns were coded *"null,"* including bids to get the floor such as "Oh!" (but *"¡Oh, yo sé!"* was coded as "Spanish") as well as turns that consisted of only a name such as "José" or "Ellen."

Broner (2000) and Fortune (2001) coded for language using different criteria, making our findings not entirely comparable.

Interlocutor. Turns were coded *"to teacher"* when students answered questions aloud during teacher-fronted lessons or directed turns to her during groupwork, and *"to peer"* when students directed turns to their classmates but not to the teacher. It usually was obvious who the intended interlocutor was, but sometimes it was not entirely clear whether a turn was intended for the teacher to hear. I used the turn's volume as a criterion: If the speech was picked up by the videocamera in the corner of the room, it was labeled *"to teacher"* because it was loud enough for me to assume that she was an intended interlocutor (although the turn obviously was intended for classmates to hear as well). If a turn was picked up only by the tape-recorder on the desk, it was not loud enough for the teacher to be a likely intended interlocutor, so the turn was labeled *"to peers."* If the student actually was talking to the teacher while she was near his group, close enough to be picked up by the tape-recorder, the turn was coded *"to teacher."* This criterion relied on some degree of subjective interpretation.

Topic. I used the term "on-task" when the content of turn was related directly to the official activity assigned by the teacher and "off-task" when students were talking about something completely unrelated to the official lesson. I used a third term, "management," for turns that regulated academically oriented activity. While carrying out on-task activities, students said things like "You go first," "Let me see that," and "Give me the red marker," which are not comments related to the academic content itself but did serve to manage the completion of the task. Tarone & Swain (1995) and Blanco-Iglesias et al. (1995) used the dichotomy "academic topics" versus "socializing." It may seem appropriate to equate on-task with academic talk and off-task with social talk, but in fact much of the language students use to regulate academically oriented activity (which I have termed "management") appears more similar to social talk than to academic talk. Broner (2000) and others have recognized how difficult it is to decide whether a student is on-task or off-task. The main criteria I used was whether the teacher would likely have approved of the utterance in the context in which it occurred.

However, Fortune (2001) noted that describing tasks over many hours of observation in an elementary school, judging whether students' utterances are on or off task, and comparing tasks in one classroom with those in another is impossible to do in an entirely reliable manner.

Selectedness.   I began to notice patterns in how students gained the floor during teacher-fronted lessons. Because no immersion studies to date have examined this phenomenon, I created the term "selectedness." "Selected" meant that the student had bid to speak and was selected by the teacher to take the floor. Bidding refers to the ways in which students gain permission to speak during a teacher-fronted lesson. Students usually bid for the floor by raising their hands, by shouting something like "Ooh!" or "I know!," or by doing both at the same time. "Unselected" meant that the student shouted out without bidding or being selected by the teacher. I excluded entirely choral answers (shouted out by more than one student) because they usually were only one word long, such as *"sí"* or "no," and represented one of very few possible responses, so I did not feel they said much about students' language use.

REFERENCES

Blanco-Iglesias, S., Broner, J., & Tarone, E. (1995). Observations of language use in Spanish immersion classroom interactions. In L. Eubank, L. Selinker, & M. Sharwood Smith (Eds.), *The current state of interlanguage* (pp. 241–254). Philadelphia: Johns Benjamin.

Broner, M. (2000). *Impact of interlocutor and task on first and second language use in a Spanish immersion program*. Unpublished doctoral dissertation, University of Minnesota.

Carranza, I. (1995). Multilevel analysis of two-way immersion discourse. In J. Alatis, C. Straehle, B. Gallenberger, & M. Ronkin (Eds.), *Georgetown University round table on languages and linguistics* (pp. 169–187). Washington, DC: Georgetown University Press.

Carrigo, D. (2000). *Just how much English are they using? Teacher and student language distribution patterns, between Spanish and English, in upper-grade, two-way immersion Spanish classes*. Unpublished doctoral dissertation, Harvard University, Cambridge, MA.

Census 2000. www.census.gov.

Center for Applied Linguistics. (2001). *Directory of two-way immersion programs in the U.S.* Retrieved March 19, 2002, from http://www.cal.org/twi/directory.

Christian, D. (1996). Two-way immersion education: Students learning through two languages. *Modern Language Journal, 80*, 66–76.

Christian, D., Montone, C., Lindholm, L., & Carranza, I. (1997). *Profiles in two-way immersion education*. McHenry, IL: Delta Systems.

Crawford, J. (1995). *Bilingual Education: History, Politics, Theory and Practice* (3rd ed.). Los Angeles: Bilingual Educational Services.

Cummins, J. (1984). Wanted: A theoretical framework for relating language proficiency to academic achievement among bilingual students. In C. Rivera (Ed.), *Language Proficiency and Academic Achievement* (pp. 2–19). Clevedon, England: Multilingual Matters.

Delgado-Larocco, E. (1998). *Classroom processes in a two-way immersion kindergarten classroom*. Unpublished doctoral dissertation, Davis: University of California.

Ellis, R. (1994). *The study of second language acquisition*. Oxford: Oxford University Press.

Fasold, R. (1984). *The sociolinguistics of society*. New York: Blackwell.

Fishman, J. (1967). Bilingualism with and without diglossia; diglossia with and without bilingualism. *Journal of Social Issues, 23*, 29–38.

Fortune, T. (2001). *Understanding immersion students' oral language use as a mediator of social interaction in the classroom*. Unpublished doctoral dissertation, University of Minnesota, Minneapolis.

Freeman, D. (1998). Bilingual education and social change. Clevedon, England: Multilingual Matters.

Gardner, R. (1985). *Social psychology and second language learning: The role of attitudes and motivation*. London: Edward Arnold.

Gardner, R., & Lambert, W. (1972). *Attitudes and motivation in second-language learning*. Rowley, MA: Newbury House.

Krashen, S. (1981). *Second language acquisition and second language learning*. Oxford: Pergamon.

Labov, W. (1972). *Language in the inner city* (pp. 255–292). Philadelphia: University of Pennsylvania Press.

Levinson, S. (1983). *Pragmatics*. Cambridge: Cambridge University Press.

Lindholm, K., & Aclan, Z. (1991). Bilingual proficiency as a bridge to academic achievement: Results from bilingual/immersion programs. *Journal of Education, 173*(2), 99–113.

Long, M. (1981). Input, interaction, and second language acquisition. In H. Winitz (Ed.), *Native language and foreign language acquisition* (pp. 259–278). *Annals of the New York Academy of Sciences, 379.*

McCollum, P. (1994). Language use in two-way bilingual programs. *IDRA Newsletter, XXI*(2), 1, 9–11.

McKay, S. L., & Wong, S. C. (1996). Multiple discourses, multiple identities: Investment and agency in second-language learning among Chinese adolescent immigrant students. *Harvard Educational Review, 66*(3), 577–608.

Met, M., & Lorenz, E. (1997). Lessons from U.S. immersion programs: Two decades of experience. In R. K. Johnson & M. Swain (Eds.), *Immersion education: International perspectives* (pp. 243–264). Cambridge, England: Cambridge University Press.

Myers-Scotton, S. (1983). *Dueling languages: Grammatical structure in Codeswitching.* Oxford: Clarendon.

Norton, B. (2000). *Identity and language learning: Gender, ethnicity, and educational change.* Essex: Pearson Education Limited.

Norton Peirce, B. (1995). Social identity, investment, and language learning. *TESOL Quarterly, 29*(1), 9–31.

Potowski, K. (2002). *Language use in a Spanish–English dual immersion classroom.* Unpublished doctoral dissertation, University of Illinois, Urbana-Champaign.

Schumann, J. (1978). The acculturation model for second-language acquisition. In R. C. Gringas (Ed.), *Second language acquisition and foreign language teaching* (pp. 00–00). Washington, DC: Center for Applied Linguistics.

Swain, M. (1985). Communicative competence: Some roles for comprehensible input and comprehensible output in its development. In S. Goss & C. Madden (Eds.), *Input in second language acquisition* (pp. 235–256). Rowley, MA: Newbury House.

Tarone, E., & Swain, M. (1995). A sociolinguistic perspective on second language use in immersion classrooms. *The Modern Language Journal, 79*(ii), 166–178.

Thomas, W., & Collier, V. (1997). *School effectiveness for language minority students.* Washington, DC: National Clearinghouse for Bilingual Education.

Toohey, K. (2000). *Learning English at school: Identity, social relations, and classroom practice.* Clevedon, England: Multilingual Matters.

Valdés, G. (1997). Dual-language immersion programs: A cautionary note concerning the education of language-minority students. *Harvard Educational Review, 67*(3), 391–429

Willett, J. (1995). Becoming first graders in an L2: An ethnographic study of L2 socialization. *TESOL Quarterly, 29*(3), 473–503.

ENDNOTES

1. Dual immersion is an offshoot of the Canadian immersion programs developed in the 1960s in response to parental pressure for better French instruction for their children. In such "regular" immersion programs, all children are English speakers learning the second language for the first time, and the teacher is the sole native speaker model.

2. On a more critical note, Valdés (1997) reminded us that introducing native-language programs will not automatically solve Latino students' educational problems.

3. Not all schools using the label "dual immersion" fulfill the descriptions provided in the introduction. For example, one school had a 98% Latino population, which very likely does not represent an equal balance between native speakers of Spanish and English unless half the students were in fact English dominant.

4. All names are pseudonyms, except for the name of the school, which is used with permission.

5. In the 34 turns coded "uinknown," the preceding turn was not entirely audible, making the topic impossible to determine.

6. However, this classroom did not appear to be entirely diglossic, because academic topics were carried out in English 32% of the time (even during these Spanish lessons) and 17% of off-task turns were in Spanish. Because Ms. Torres also taught English lessons, students were accustomed to speaking English with her for academic lessons. Spanish, therefore, was not the only "on task" language in this classroom.

7. Students could earn *canicas* (marbles) for finishing their work on time, for using Spanish during group work, and for other behaviors the teacher sought to reinforce. Students lost *canicas* primarily for using English during Spanish time.

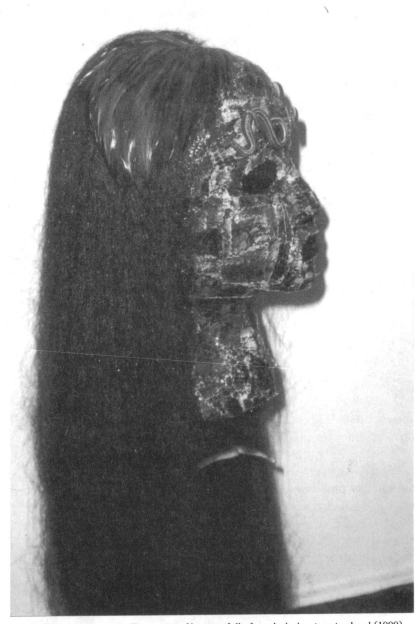

Asymmetry: Artword by Flora, part of her portfolio for admission to art school (1999).
Photograph by Elaine Foin.

7

Global Links From the Postindustrial Heartland: Language, Internet Use, and Identity Development Among U.S.-Born Mexican High School Girls

Jennifer L. Cohen
DePaul University

Research on Internet chat room use, especially regarding role play with online identities, tends to focus on the implications of users' online fantasies for their present-day lives (Turkle, 1995; Wallace, 1999). Because access to Internet chat rooms can give participants opportunities to experiment with new identities or simply interact with people they might not otherwise meet, research on chat room use is relevant to understanding identity processes. This is particularly important to educational research on the importance of identity work to student achievement (Hemmings, 2000). However, the existing emphasis on the role of Internet chat rooms in users' current lives overlooks the vital connection between Internet chat room use and future identity roles. This is an important extension of existing research on the role of the future in students' current educational decisions (Yowell, 1999).

I spent two and a half years, from 1998 to 2001, researching identity processes and school achievement in a group of seven U.S.-born Mexican students attending an underresourced urban high school. This article is based on one student, Flora, and her talk about her experiences participating in online chat rooms. Most often, she described her experiences to me in conversation with her friend, Lidia, who also often participated in chat rooms.[1] I analyze how Flora's participation in this linguistically based environment shaped her identity in high school and influenced her educational ambitions. Most significantly, this chapter examines how Flora used Internet chat rooms to engage in anticipatory socialization (Fuchs Ebaugh, 1988) regarding her desired future role identity as a college student in Los Angeles. Online, Flora learned about the norms and expectations associated with the role identity of college a student in Los Angeles and brought that information to bear on her current educational and personal decisions. She also used the Internet to develop a relationship with a boyfriend in Los Angeles, who was an initial point of contact for her anticipatory socialization. Through him, she began to assemble a social network in Los Angeles, which was an additional important step in her plans to move to there. Finally, the Internet offered Flora access to cosmopolitan experiences that she used to cultivate a new role identity, the "black sheep." Asserting herself as a black sheep helped her as she attempted resolve deep conflicts between two current role identities: as a working-class Mexican daughter whose family wanted her to stay close to home and an ambitious student who wanted to travel across the country for art college.

Research on Internet use tends to focus on how people in more affluent families and schools use the Internet for education and socializing (Garner & Gillingham, 1996; Turkle, 1995). Less is known, however, about the independent computer habits of working-class and lower working-class students of color living in urban neighborhoods. Yet, my research suggests that computers and Internet connections are becoming more financially accessible, even in underresourced urban neighborhoods. This was especially true for students in the honors program at Yates High School (a pseudonym), who were likely to pursue getting a computer on their own, or have access to a computer account because they had a sibling in college. Therefore, it is important to learn about the personal and cultural implications of increasing online experiences for working-class and lower working-class students who use the Internet to understand better the relation between their identity development and educational achievement. In Flora's case, she used the Internet to develop a significant educational opportunity for herself. Pursuing this opportunity created role identity conflicts for her, which she also tried to reconcile using the Internet.

THE SITE

Flora attended Yates high school, a public school on the southeast side of Chicago. The area is known for and shaped by the steel mills that dominated the economy for a century. Flora lives in one of a cluster of neighborhoods around these old steel mills. The neighborhoods served as housing for the main steel mills and other industry in the area, including the salvage plants and the docks in the international harbor for the ships that bring in the raw supplies for the industries. The steel industry shaped the area, from the landscape to the economy to the boundaries of the neighborhoods themselves: rivers used for shipping, steel plants, ports, railroads, and highways.

But when the U.S. steel industry declined in the 1980s, most of these mills closed, ending a century of relative prosperity and stability. The neighborhoods are left with large tracts of abandoned land, some of the mills torn down and others standing empty, proliferating landfills, and a stagnant economy.[2] I had grown up not more than 30 minutes away by car, but had never traveled to the area, never considered it a place I might go, and never considered in any depth who, if anyone, might live there. It was not only I who was isolated from the neighborhood. Historically, the entire area has been isolated from the city itself, cut off by the city's disdain for the inevitable stink and dirt of the pollution from the steel mills (Bensman & Lynch, 1987; Geoghegan, 1992). Outsiders sometimes lump the neighborhoods together under the name "Southeast Chicago." The students and teachers never used this term, however, referring instead to specific neighborhoods and their specific characters, especially in terms of their desirability and racial demographics.

Southeastern Chicago was dominated originally by immigrant workers from Eastern Europe, Ireland, and Sweden. The area became integrated in the early 1900s with African Americans and Mexicans as jobs in the mills increased, and consequently the need for workers to provide unskilled labor (Chicago Fact Book Consortium, 1995; Año Nuevo Kerr, 1976). Mexicans originally came to the area to work on the railroads, but stayed to work in the mills. The area, home to the first Mexican church in Chicago, remains the oldest, if not the best-known, Mexican neighborhood in the city (Año Nuevo Kerr, 1976). In 1990, Hispanics made up one third of the neighborhood's population, but the demographics are shifting, with a dramatic increase in the number of Black people moving to the area.[3] Flora and Lidia described this change as being of concern to their parents, who discussed moving out of the neighborhood.[4]

Yates high school is a midsized public school in distress. The school has been targeted for the district's severest remediation because of its persistently low test scores. The student population is approximately half Mexican and half African American, with smaller populations of Haitian immigrants, Central Americans, and Puerto Ricans. The school roster indicated that there were four White students attending at the time I did my research, but a school administrator reacted with surprise that there would be that many listed. She explained to me that many students are assigned an ethnicity on their school forms by counselors who "just take a look and write something down"—in other words, on the basis of phenotype. Although there were a number of mixed-ethnicity students in the classrooms I observed, there was no visible group of students who could be identified as White.

BACKGROUND

I conducted my research at Yates from the time I met Flora, when she was a sophomore, to her graduation. I met Flora when I asked a teacher whether there was anything I could help him do while I was observing his class. He asked that I sit with a "group of gigglers" at the back of the classroom and help to keep them on task. Those gigglers turned out to be an unusually integrated peer group at Yates High School. It included African American and U.S.-born Mexican girls, relatively high and relatively low achievers, and Spanish speakers and non-Spanish speakers. They all were in an honors track at the school. Whereas some of the students' grades put them in the top 20 graduating seniors and about half graduated with honors, others ultimately dropped out of honors or were dropped from the program because of their low grades, and two did not graduate at the end of their senior year.

Flora viewed herself as an outsider among her peers, in her school and in her neighborhood, and for that reason her identity work was particularly important to her. She discussed her identity often. Flora saw herself as going beyond the usual expectations for her peers, doing what she could to cultivate links with people outside her neighborhood (e.g., chatting online, taking art classes downtown, attending summer school in Los Angeles). Flora's sophisticated computer use, interest in Spanish-language subculture in Mexico and the United States, and efforts to expand her experiences beyond the immediate neighborhood made her stand out among the students I met at Yates High School. She stood out physically, too, because she was taller than all her friends. Even more, Flora dressed and presented herself in a way that incorporated her interest in crossing social, cultural, and racial lines. She dyed her long hair with brighter, lighter orange highlights than the others and wore green contact lenses, which were duly noted by her mother.[5] "Ever since I wore these," she told me, "my mother calls me 'the girl with the green eyes' all the time. Just that. When I eat my breakfast she says 'Oh, look at the girl with the green eyes at my table.'" Among peers who regularly wore the school uniform and sneakers, Flora added to her uniform a leather bracelet with the name of her favorite *rock en español* band, *Los Jaguares;* a necklace with the Mayan calendar on it; and black leather shoes with shiny silver zippers across the toe. I watched those shoes on the stairs ahead of me when Flora first took me up the four flights of stairs to the art studio space where she was working on a piece to add to the portfolio she was preparing for her application to art schools.

Academically, many of the teachers with whom I spoke singled out Flora for her sensitive, analytical mind, artistic talent, and educational ambitions. These assessments fit with my own experience of Flora. From the time I met her, Flora described herself to me and to her friends as a "black sheep," one destined to leave home and go a different way. Her vision of herself as a black sheep supported her primary educational and social ambition, which was to attend college at an art school in Los Angeles. It is not unusual—although it's no guarantee—for students who graduate in one of the school's two honors tracks to attend college. Most enroll in nearby colleges, and some go as far as the large state school in the southern part of Illinois, where their older siblings often are already enrolled. It is very unusual, however, for a student independently to make the connections necessary to enroll in an out-of-state school. More unusual still, Flora applied to an art school in Los Angeles, California, and was admitted with a four-year scholarship. This article analyzes Flora's talk about her experiences to better understand how she achieved this ambitious success— and why she chose not to go.

ROLE IDENTITY THEORY

The findings here are relevant to researchers and educators who want a better understanding of students who stay in school despite factors that put them at risk, to learn how students who statistically might have dropped out of high school instead remain as successful students (Darder,

Torres, & Gutíerrez, 1997). Much of the literature on successful, at-risk students describes and analyzes students' varying strategies for staying in school, with an emphasis on the role of identity formation in students' developing strategies (Cordeiro, 1990; Flores-Gonzalez, 2002; Hemmings, 2000; McGinty, 1999). This article brings to this body of research a detailed discussion on the role of Internet use, specifically participation in online chat rooms, in one successful student's developing identity and educational strategies.

I concur with researchers who argue that an understanding of identity is essential to understanding educational success and failure (Flores-Gonzalez, 2002; Hemmings, 2000; Saravia-Shore & Martínez, 1992; Yowell, 1999). I use the ethnography of communication as an interpretive framework that gives priority to language use. This approach facilitates a focus on the interpersonal experiences that make up the larger cultural processes associated with identity development and educational achievement. Indeed, as ethnographers Richard Bauman and Joel Sherzer (1989) assert, "the unifying principle [of the ethnography of communication] is that society and culture are communicatively constituted, and that *no* sphere of social or cultural life is fully comprehensible apart from speaking as an instrument of its constitution" (p. xi).

My understanding of the personal conflict Flora faced as a result of her educational ambitions is based on role identity theory. Role identity theory draws on a wide range of sociological theories that explore the relationship between the individual and society. These theories differ in the degree of control over interpersonal relations that they attribute to human beings. That is, within sociological theory there is a struggle over the degree to which social identity roles are fixed in society, with individuals filling roles constrained by preexisting material conditions, and the degree to which we make our roles through constant evaluation, negotiation, and discovery of new roles (Stryker, 1980; Waters, 1994; Zurcher, 1983). Although these may seem to be contradictory positions, for the most part, as Louis A. Zurcher (1983) points out, "The structuralist position emphasizes the effect of historical factors, power distributions, and cultural values on role enactment. The symbolic interactionist view assumes that roles emerge from or are significantly shaped by interactions in specific social settings" (p. 14). These schools represent differing analytical foci, however, rather than mutually exclusive arguments (Fuchs Ebaugh, 1988; Zurcher, 1983). The tension Zurcher describes between the structuralist and the symbolic interactionist views in role identity theory echoes what

Bauman and Sherzer (1989) characterize as "the heart of the deepest problem in the social disciplines: the dynamic interplay between the social, conventional, ready-made in social life and the individual, creative, and emergent qualities of human existence" (p. xix). Each description suggests that we do not experience life in terms of one or the other extreme, but as a dynamic interplay between them. My research confirms this interplay, which Flora chose to negotiate by working within the tensions to develop a role identity that might enable her own ambitions.

Whether an individual is filling a role or making one, she will experience role conflict (Flores-Gonzalez, 2002; Fuchs Ebaugh, 1988), or what William S. Goode (1960) calls "role strain." In Flora's case, she often referred to her roles as daughter in a Mexican family and as ambitious student in a bad high school because she felt conflict between the expectations for these roles. She dreamed of going to college in Los Angeles, but attended a high school that "makes me stupider the longer I'm here." She longed to leave Chicago, asserting again and again that "It's just not home here. It doesn't feel home to me," "I'm a lost soul without a home," and "my heart is set out West; I have come to my term and I really hate it here." Yet, when I asked her why she might not go, given that she had such a generous scholarship, she asserted, "Because I'm a good Mexican daughter!" Flora knew that when she said, "I'm a good Mexican daughter!" it meant her family expected her to attend school close by and live at home. As Flora also said, "Family first and then career; that's what you're brought up to."

As I show, in statements such as "I'm a good Mexican daughter," Flora acknowledged that she had a role to fill and a desire to fill it well. In the end, the traditional expectations for a good Mexican daughter conflicted with her own educational ambitions and desires. Because she did not want to exit either role, she had to try to find a way to reconcile this conflict.

EXITING A ROLE

Many of Flora's behaviors confirmed Helen Rose Fuchs Ebaugh's (1988) description of the process individuals go through as they try to exit one role and enter another. Fuchs Ebaugh defines role exit as "[t]he process of disengagement from a role that is central to one's self-identity and the reestablishment of an identity in a new role that takes into account one's ex-role" (p. 1). Understanding this theory of role exit helps to illuminate the larger significance of some of Flora's pursuits, such as joining California college chat rooms online. Flora's participation in these chat rooms constituted more than curiosity in an outgoing young woman. Chatting with college students was a way for Flora to engage the new role she desired. This "anticipatory socialization" (Fuchs Ebaugh,1988, p. 7) through her on-going access to the chat rooms, and later by attending summer school in Los Angeles, allowed Flora to learn about the values and orientations of the group she wanted to join. Fuchs Ebaugh (1988) explains, "By identify-ing with a group that one hopes to join, the person begins to be like mem-bers of the group in value orientation and normative expectations before actually entering the new role" (p. 7).[6]

ASSESSING FUTURE ROLE IDENTITIES

Possible selves theory (Markus & Nurius, 1986) is an important comple-ment to role identity theory because it emphasizes that we develop a sense of identity diachronically as we grow over the years and synchron-ically as past, present, and future come together to influence our current decisions. Furthermore, possible selves theory highlights the affective ele-ment of identity development: the centrality of our hopes and fears as we imagine ourselves in the future. The possible future selves we imagine can be positive or negative. Our feelings and beliefs about these possible selves are central to the decisions we make. Possible selves "represent specific, individually significant hopes, fears, and fantasies" (Markus & Nurius, 1986, p. 954). They encompass the many ways we can imagine growing in the future: our "hoped-for" selves, which we imagine in our dreams and fantasies; our "expected selves," which we can enact through specific scripts and strategies, and our "feared selves," which we seek to avoid. These various possible selves influence and regulate our behavior, particularly regarding our ability to achieve our goals.

Flora articulated her possible selves quite clearly. She feared staying in the neighborhood, dependent on her parents. She dreamed of traveling and moving to Los Angeles to become an artist. Although all possible selves are imagined future selves, they have a direct relation to an individual's current actions and motivations when that person develops "specific scripts, plans, and affect for goal actualization." This is how hoped-for selves can develop into expected selves (Yowell, 1999, p. 4). Other girls in Flora's peer group may have dreamed of going to college or graduating from high school, but did not take specific steps to realize these dreams (such as taking the neces-sary standardized tests, turning in work to pass classes, or finding out about college life). Flora, however, did develop the specific scripts and strategies.

The opportunity to experiment with the role of a California college student was part of a process that gave Flora tools she needed to develop this role from a hoped-for self to an expected self and the procedural knowledge important to taking real steps to secure her goal.

THE BLACK SHEEP:
"I HAVE MY LUGGAGE PACKED IN MY HEAD"

Participating in college chat rooms, along with other steps Flora took, allowed her to develop a hoped-for self into an expected self, and to engage in anticipatory socialization by building a new reference group (Fuchs Ebaugh, 1988, pp. 107–108). This is a necessary part of building a new role identity. At the same time, however, Flora remained committed to her current role identity as a good Mexican daughter, although her mother adamantly opposed her plans to move to California and to study art. Fuchs Ebaugh (1988) reports that people who encounter strong negative reactions to their planned role exit from significant people in their lives usually stop the process and reevaluate their role situation (p. 98). Citing additional research, she suggests that, "role entrapment is a common occurrence" (p. 100).

During her time in high school, and through the summer after her graduation, however, Flora responded to this pressure by cultivating an alternative role, which she called being "the black sheep." Being the black sheep was an attempt to reconcile the role conflict she encountered. As a black sheep, Flora was still in the fold, so to speak, but clearly different. As she said, "I am a dreamer. Dreamers like me are black sheep because we don't have our feet firmly on the ground." As the black sheep, she could remain a recognized daughter, but one with a different script. Thus, during high school she neither interrupted the exiting process nor became entrapped, but continued trying to balance her many conflicting desires and the expectations of the significant people in her life.

IDENTITY PLAY ONLINE

Chat rooms are important environments to understand, because in chat rooms written language provides the only clues to identity, rendering the physical body invisible (although this will change as digital camera and other technologies become widely accessible). For many Internet users, both educators and game players, the invisibility of the physical body has been taken as a liberating step that allows participants to experiment with new and different identities. The notions underlying this expectation of freedom are that the visible, physical body fixes our identities and that language is neutral. Chat rooms invite identity play because participants know each other only through verbal self-descriptions. For many Internet users, this opportunity for pure linguistic self-representation seems utterly freeing. As Sherry Turkle (1995) says of online interactions, "When we step through the screen into virtual communities, we reconstruct our identities on the other side of the looking glass. The reconstruction is our cultural work in progress" (p. 177). As Turkle describes it, participants in chat rooms and online fantasy games experiment with different identities in a prototypical postmodern state.

Although I agree that participation in chat rooms constitutes both cultural and personal identity work, Flora's narratives of her own online experiences contradict the expectation that the Internet opens onto a looking-glass world governed by different social and physical rules. Her encounters challenge many assumptions that one can necessarily self-represent more freely online in a written, verbal rather than a visual, physical medium (Turkle, 1995, p. 184). As Flora's experience shows, even in Spanish language chat rooms, readers adeptly identify others' lexical and morphologic variations without visible, embodied clues. As Flora described it, people remained obsessed with stabilizing identity and used the linguistic variation present in chat room writing to recreate national, cultural, gendered, and linguistic hierarchies in force in the nonvirtual world. In many conversations about their Internet experiences, Flora and Lidia related that other participants readily discerned their linguistic regionalisms, cultural knowledge, and specific uses of grammar and vocabulary.[7] All these shaped Flora's online experiences and, consequently, her identity work.

Flora told me that she went online to participate in chat rooms, and that because she was most confident in her Spanish writing ability, she was most comfortable in the Spanish-language chats. She participated in international Spanish-language chat rooms, sometimes general in focus, sometimes specific, such as *rockero* chat rooms dedicated to underground Mexican rock music. Flora's facility in written Spanish and her choice of Spanish-language chat rooms reflected how deeply she valued her Mexican identity and her strong connection to her family. Flora indicated this as she and I discussed her impressions of the neighborhood one day in the school library. Flora's talk about her fluency in Spanish confirmed "how central language is to the identification of self and group"

(Wolfram, 1991, p. 14). Knowing Spanish indexed Flora's pride in her up-bringing and connection to her culture. In turn, Flora indicated, culture and family insulated her from the undesirable people in the neighborhood she and her peers called "ghetto." From my own observations, they used the term "ghetto" as a signifier whose meaning shifted in different con-texts. (A fuller discussion of this term and their usage of it follows later in this chapter.) Generally, it is important to note that as Flora, Lidia, and I spoke in the library that day, Flora's Spanish fluency indexed her identifi-cation with her culture, and that her cultural identity insulated her against the threat of being like the "ghetto" people around her, both in the school and in the neighborhood.

F: And it's like different because me, how [?] was brought up I was never . around .
        people .. like ghetto people. Like I was never

J: You didn't go to school with them?

F: I did but

J: Well, you do now.

F: No, I went to bilingual. I was more associated with *my culture.*[8]

Flora and her parents had to make an effort to ensure that she, as a U.S.-born transnational, would be fluent in spoken and written Spanish, and they used a bilingual program in the public schools to accomplish that. Flora's formal education in the Spanish language helped her be more con-fident writing in Spanish than in English. Beyond that, she confirmed that her fluency in written and spoken Spanish was an expression of a cultural identity closely affiliated with Mexico, underscoring the close relation between language and culture.

Flora's fluency in spoken and written Spanish served her in two ways. At the same time that fluency in Spanish reflected and strengthened her com-mitment to her culture and family, it also allowed her to cultivate an inde-pendent and alternative cultural identity online. In Spanish-language chat rooms, Flora could engage in anticipatory socialization with outside groups, which helped her work to avoid negative possible selves in the neighborhood. Spanish-language chat rooms on the Internet gave Flora a place to roam away from her neighborhood and her family as the "black sheep," while staying close to her Mexican identity, language, and culture.

Students at Yates increasingly use e-mail, but fewer than half of the stu-dents in Flora's class had access to computers at home in their senior year of high school. The students I spoke with who used e-mail described their primary interest as writing to friends and family they already knew. Some limited themselves to these correspondences, while others described themselves and their older siblings as using the Internet to meet new people and sometimes to look for dates. Like them, Flora used the Internet to meet new people. The Internet served to connect Flora to chat room participants in Latin American countries, including Colombia, Ecuador, Argentina, and Mexico, and with Chicanos in Los Angeles. Flora's stories of her experiences on the Internet highlight the interactive, socially defined, and contingent processes of making and remaking borders within an individual. Especially online, Flora encountered a more global perspective on Mexican identity than the one she described learning at home. Communication with such a range of Spanish speakers at times challenged Flora's experience of her own Mexican identity as she encountered hierarchical attitudes among other Latinos who denigrated Mexicans. But it also allowed her to enter into these exchanges as an active participant who shared her own views and simultaneously was able to develop them in response to those she encountered online.

Flora took this experimentation further, however, by tapping into the possibility for identity play online: inventing new personae and representing herself online as someone other than who she was in her daily life. In the school library, for example, I observed Flora going into a chat room for students at a California college and posing as a college student who also was a member of a rock band. She told me stories of other experiences posing as a resident of Los Angeles and a suburb of Mexico City, as a college student, as a member of a rock band, and as a woman older than she really was. For Flora, the Internet brought out the potential to explore the malleability of identity, and to encounter its resistances.

During one of our whispered conversations in the library, Flora told me she used the Internet to research and create an identity as a resident of a Mexico City suburb. She wanted to represent herself as Mexican and "pass" in a chat room restricted to Mexico City residents. Although Flora used information she got online to establish an address and a phone number, and even to determine landmarks and major businesses in her chosen neighborhood, she was unable to convince the other participants of her chosen identity. In this chat room, unlike others she and Lidia described in which participants were thrown out in a barrage of insults, Flora knew she had been unsuccessful when she was excluded by being formally ignored. Participants were able to register with the moderator that they were ignoring her posts intentionally. Because more than half of the participants had registered this verbal exclusion, the moderator rejected her from the chat. Flora told me that she never found out specifically why she was excluded in this way, and she did not mention trying this type of exclusive chat room again. In fact, she was generally reluctant to speak in any detail about this experience, especially in comparison with her eagerness to tell me about other online exploits in which she was more successful.[9] As I discuss in greater detail later, Flora's reticence regarding her exclusion points to the importance of these chat room experiences in Flora's fears and ambitions regarding her possible future identities.

Although Flora's efforts to participate in that exclusive chat room were stymied, her description of the experience highlighted the way in which, without leaving her neighborhood, she was able to use identity play to experiment with her national and class identities as a Mexican and as a resident of a neighborhood different from her own in Chicago. Her interest in the chat room reflected her desire to be able to cross borders in her own identity work. Her failure suggests that the national border between Mexico and the United States is indeed contingent, not in this case on being able to fool a border guard, as many Mexicans must do to enter the United States, but on differing expectations for cultural and linguistic knowledge related to a Mexican identity on either side of the border. Even on the other side of the looking glass, as Flora's experience in the Mexico City chat room illustrates, people remain obsessed with stabilizing identity in order to place individuals within power relationships, including an ironic inversion of power between the United States and Mexico in the control of people's movement across the border.[10]

LINGUISTIC CUES ONLINE

Written language online is conversational and thus more open to lexical variation than standardized written language (de Beaugrande, 1984). For Flora and Lidia, writing in the chat rooms seemed to highlight the use of language as a marker of social status and national and ethnic identity, which they and others interpreted through instances of lexical variation (e.g., *vos*), morphologic variation (e.g., "finnin' to go") and uses of slang terms (e.g., *chale*), each of which I discuss as they appear in the transcripts later. As Walt Wolfram (1991) points out, "[s]lang is one of those labels that gives dialectologists fits" because it is an imprecise term used loosely in everyday speech (p. 46). Although the exact nature of slang cannot be characterized precisely, Wolfram (1991) advocates the usefulness of the concept in general for characterizing certain social behaviors. The term is useful, he continues, because "[w]hat distinguishes items classified as slang is their sociopsychological role rather than their linguistic composition" (p. 47).

In this context, the sociopsychological function of slang puts a linguistic spin on the processes role identity theorists have described in other contexts by highlighting the role of language in our experiences of and responses to social roles. In other words, just as there is a direct relation between the way a dialect is judged by others and the social position of its speakers (Wolfram, 1991, p. 5), there is a direct connection between the uses of slang and the social roles of its speakers. This means, on the one hand, that what is "one person's slang may be another person's conventional lexicon" (Wolfram, 1991, p. 49). That is, a dominant group may judge speech as slang (e.g., nonstandard, incorrect) that a nondominant group considers conventional. By the same token, however, speakers can use slang terms to create or indicate in-group belonging and to differentiate themselves from a dominant group (Wolfram, 1991, p. 46).

In Flora's and Lidia's descriptions of their online experiences, both lexical variation and what I call slang terms were important either as part of efforts to establish hierarchy or as in-group markers. Flora and Lidia sometimes displayed their knowledge of a slang term. But Flora, in particular, sometimes denied it, as a way to assert that she was not part of a group. In the example later, they refer to Argentineans who use *vos* for the second person plural pronoun in Spanish, which is a regionally specific lexical variation[11] (Castillo & Bond, 1987, pp. 29–30). They then discuss the meaning of *chale,* a slang term, and highlight its variable and context-specific meanings. In both instances, the ability to read linguistic variation establishes insider and outsider status. The use of *chale,* for example, is very popular among working- and lower working-class residents of Mexico City. Thus it indexes regional, class, and national differences.[12]

For Flora, the tendency of participants to scrutinize her vocabulary sometimes indexed a broader dynamic of hierarchical judgments among Latin American Spanish speakers in which Mexicans and Mexican Spanish were denigrated by South Americans. In the following transcript, Flora and Lidia described encountering such judgment from Argentineans, whom they felt sneered at them for being Mexican. At the same time that they described being judged by the Argentineans, they also showed that they are aware of how others are identified by their language use, and in later transcripts actually engaged in identifying and judging others. At different times, they were able to participate as both subjects and objects of this verbal scrutiny. In this conversation, we were talking during their lunch period at Yates. They had already told me that chat room participants could identify each other by the language they used, and I asked them directly for some examples.

F: They talk /?/ . They go *"vos?"* you know?

L: Oh yeah.

F: And they'll go like right away, "You're Mexican" [sneering intonation]. Umhm. Yeah.

J: 'Cause you don't use *vos?*

L: Yeah.

J: They can notice that right away?

L: They can notice by .. what you write. Like, um, for instance, they could they know you're like … from Mexico City you go if you put like *chales* or something.

J: Uhmm.

L: *Chale* like "damn" or

F: How?

L: *Chale* is like damit or something, right?

F: I think it would be, it depends how you use it. *Chale* could be "OK."

J: It could mean OK or it could mean dammit?

F: Not dammit.

L: Like "darn" or something.

The girls' narrative shows that they, like other readers in the chat rooms, situate participants on the basis of their particular uses of Spanish. Here they do not attach any valence to the use of the term *chale,* but in other conversations they do make direct or implicit judgments, as we will see in later transcripts. Flora and Lidia know that the term *chale* is associated with Mexico City, but they struggle over its exact meaning. They cannot say precisely what *chale* means because, as Flora pointed out, "It depends how you use it." In other words, the use of *chale* can be considered flexible and multifunctional. It is an expression that usually communicates disappointment, like the English "Aww, come on," but also can communicate other feelings, such as disbelief, sometimes with a sense of affront, as the English "You're putting me on, right?"[13] Elias Dominguez Barajas explains,

> [*Chale*] can also be used to communicate urgency as if something unexpected happens and there is no other immediate word to call attention to it;

for example a fight or scuffle suddenly breaks out, and in an effort to mobilize and direct the attention of his companions, one of those involved quickly utters the string, *"Chale, chale, chale"* while pointing and pushing in the direction of escape or of the confrontation. It can [also] communicate slight annoyance, as in *"Chale, cabrón, ya pírale"* [Shit man, quit it].[14]

Their struggle also indicates that they are not members of the in-group most likely to use this word. Both girls identify strongly as Mexicans, knowledgeable about Mexican culture and the Spanish language. Exchanges such as the preceding one, however, underscore that the Internet brought them into contact with different aspects of Mexican culture than they encountered through their family connections alone, which tended to limit them to the *ranchos* (small rural communities) and some tourist travel with family in Mexico. As Flora's conversation shows, knowing—and not knowing—the right slang is integral to her understanding of social and economic identity.

FLORA'S BOYFRIEND

The conflicts in Flora's Mexican identity, which affiliated her with a people and a culture she esteemed but also quite pointedly differentiated her from a large group of undesirable peers in her neighborhood, deepened as her Internet use brought her into contact with Chicanos in Los Angeles. Throughout high school Flora was very careful about whom she counted as a peer, and attributed to peers central importance in her identity work. So it is not surprising that Flora used the Internet to develop social relationships. Many were temporary, but her relationship with Diego, a self-described Chicano living in Los Angeles, was lasting and formative.

Flora met Diego online in a *rockero* chat room visited by fans of underground Mexican rock music. Flora initially described herself as older and as a college student (Diego is about 6 years older than she). She and Diego corresponded regularly in the chat room and privately for a year, eventually shifting over to regular phone conversations and then face-to-face visits. Their relationship lasted 3 years, through Flora's high school graduation.

Flora's descriptions of Diego suggested that their relationship involved conflicting desires for her and functioned as a contested site for her identity work. Flora and Diego shared a deep identification with Mexican culture, which Flora made clear was important to her. And Diego's location in and knowledge of Los Angeles was important to Flora's ambition to attend art school there. Flora knew Diego would be there the year she was accepted into the summer program at her chosen school in Los Angeles. She chose to go even though she had very little family support. In the face of her mother's very gendered protestations that "You'll come back pregnant!" Flora traveled to Los Angeles and met up with Diego.

Flora described to me that Diego was an intimate contact that summer who helped orient her to the city, came to get her when she got lost, and ultimately pushed her to learn her own way around and budget her money carefully (she proudly told me that she budgeted so well that she came home with $200 unspent). He was both a familiar point of contact in an unfamiliar and intimidating city and an influence pushing her toward the independence she would need to consider attending college so far from home without family support.

When Flora came back to school the next year, her self-pride in her new independence was evident in her eagerness to tell her stories of her experiences in Los Angeles. Additionally, she took on the role of a more knowledgeable peer, admonishing the others to take more responsibility for their actions and decisions, and not to depend on their parents to make things easy for them.

BUILDING A SOCIAL NETWORK: THE DILEMMA OF PROXIMITY AND BEING "GHETTO"

Flora's relationship with Diego seemed to present a dilemma for her because while he offered her so much interest and independence, he also brought her in proximity with the Chicano culture of Los Angeles. Flora indicated in her narratives how this was a dilemma by linking Diego and Chicanos with being "ghetto." Even far from home, she risked being taken as "ghetto" if she allowed herself to be associated with the wrong peers. Being close to Diego supported her ambitions, but also threatened them.

The emic meaning of the term "ghetto" for the students in Flora's peer group, like the term *chale* for young people in Mexico City, depends for its significance on the context in which it is used. When I asked Flora and Lidia directly what being ghetto meant, they asserted that it was not, as I had imagined, tied to racial or even to class identity. Being ghetto, they explained, had to do with one's attitudes and behavior. "Ghetto," similar in the meaning to "low life" among Puerto Rican youth (Flores-Gonzales, 2002), suggests someone who does not take care of her or his physical appearance, does not plan for the future, is loud or rowdy in public, spends time in the street, is perhaps involved with gangs, and frequently gets into trouble with authorities. Someone who is "ghetto" clearly is "going nowhere." Although, among themselves, Flora and most of her peer group adamantly defined themselves against a ghetto identity, they also were very aware of their proximity to those whom they consider ghetto. This group, which is large, includes a few members of their school-based peer group and many of the other young people in their school and neighborhood. They know that, especially to outsiders, they, as Mexicans from South Chicago, are likely to be classified along with the others as ghetto.

When I went with them on a class trip to a university in a rural and predominantly White part of the state, this anxiety was evident. Flora and others laughed nervously as they sat in the crowded cafeteria. As they looked around at the mostly White students eating there, they talked among themselves about how the other students were sure to think they were ghetto by judging their appearance. It mattered to them that they had driven up in a new tour bus. They laughed that they had not shown up "looking ghetto" as had students from other schools who had come in simple school buses. Although being "ghetto" was not strictly tied to class (one can be poor, but not "ghetto"), class figured as one way that a person or group could appear "ghetto." But that point of distinction meant someone had to have seen them get off the bus. Looking around the cafeteria later, Lidia said in so many words, "They think we're ghetto, right?" and then laughed. Their self-consciousness suggested that they perceived their nonghetto identities to be fragile, because they were susceptible to being defined by outsiders, whether college students, teachers, administrators, or friends' parents. It was important to many of the girls to differentiate themselves from their "ghetto" peers, but Flora placed a particularly high premium on countering this threat.

Flora's conversations about Chicanos in Los Angeles, both in person and online, showed that she felt a greater proximity and a more invested sense of identity with them than with the South Americans with whom she chatted. This proximity brought on identity-based anxieties about the social significance of being "Chicano" versus being "Mexican." Flora responded by using linguistic cues to distance herself from what she called the "ghetto" aspects of being Chicano. In Flora's discussions of Diego she distinguished differing points of identification within a sense of shared cultural identity. Her reports of conversations with and about him, therefore, may have served the simultaneous purposes of proving her proximity to him as part of her independence from her neighborhood and the people there; proving her difference from him, a Chicano close to "ghetto" culture; and demonstrating her own interest in and knowledge of a range of cultures. That is, knowing about Chicano culture *as an outsider* made it clear she was not one of them while it enhanced her cosmopolitan image.

As Flora described Diego to me, he was a Chicano who played in a rock band. He also worked and attended classes at a local community college, but was not able to graduate. He failed some of his classes each term he was enrolled. His proximity to being "ghetto" came up in a conversation about their computer experiences, in which I followed up on Flora and Lidia's comments that other chat room participants could tell they were Mexican by the way they used words. Flora told me that "well, only the Hispanic ones [could tell]." Then she added that participants also could tell who was from California, and she and Lidia mentioned some of the particular words that marked a Spanish speaker from California.[15]

F:	Also you can tell which one is from California.
L:	Oh yeah! 'Cause of how they talk out there.
J:	Like what?
L:	They say like, *sabanas,* that's like, bye? Um ...[16]
J:	*Sabanas?*
F:	*Chale* they say.
L:	Yeah.
F:	*Transa, ¿qué transa?* [?] like she was saying.[17]
L:	Um .... they say *orale*.
J:	What's that mean?
F:	*Chale.*
L:	Like, um ...... Like ...
F:	OK.
L:	Like heeeey! Or something like that.

As they continued to think of words that marked a participant in some way, they came to what Lidia called "*cholo* types," who they agreed were "really ghetto," "very ghetto."[18]

F:	I know this from Diego.
L:	Hee hee.
J:	Diego is ghetto?
F:	Yeah, he's from Echo Park and [?].
J:	Say no more, right?

F: Say no more.

L: And some people in the chats are, like, some from California even write, like, the
          ... Black people like, "Ya, I'm finnin' to go" like.

In this conversation, when Lidia introduced the topic of being ghetto, Flora immediately referred to Diego who, living in Echo Park, a neighborhood in Los Angeles known in part for its poverty and Mexican gangs, was in a position to teach her about it. It also meant Diego was in close enough proximity to risk being in some way ghetto himself. Flora and Lidia told me that the Spanish speakers in California whom they met in chat rooms were mostly "Chicanos, like in the *barrio* [neighborhood]." As Lidia pointed out, "[They] even write like the Black people."[19] Lidia's comment complexly linked Chicanos and Blacks, race and culture in an assessment of "ghetto" identity (and echoes Flora's mother's criticism that Diego was" "too dark"[20]). Lidia's ready semantic link pointed to a slippage among these categories of identity, which the students either had not fully articulated to themselves or were unwilling to articulate to me. Although they did not explicitly state their relation to Blacks in the neighborhood, their identification as not Black and their parents' desire to move to avoid living with Blacks pointed to a tendency for Mexicans in the area to associate with Whites, rather than to identify with Blacks, despite a shared history of housing and employment restrictions (Año Nuevo Kerr, 1976).[21]

Online, semantic cues are paramount as social markers that allow Flora and Lidia to mark Chicanos who reveal their social proximity to Blacks by adopting their speech patterns as ghetto. This linkage of ghetto and Black slang also reflects Flora's and Lidia's persistent social anxiety about Blackness and the resulting distance they try to keep from most Black people in their neighborhood and school. In both instances, whether they were worried about Blackness or ghettoness, establishing what they were *not* was essential to their identity work.

The sum of my observations and the students' comments does not bring a clear definition of ghettoness into relief. "Ghetto" is a term that serves many social purposes and can shift its meaning depending on the context and audience. It can be a class marker, a race marker, and a culture marker, yet marks none of these groups definitively. For Flora, however, the term "ghetto" additionally seemed to suggest a static mentality, without the expectation of social mobility and cultural sophistication. It is possible that Diego's social situation was similar to the one Flora described for herself: not ghetto but living in a ghetto neighborhood. Still,

Flora's concern that at 26 years of age, he had not graduated from community college and the teasing she described suggested that she identified closely with him, and also felt the need to clarify how she was different through points of differing identification. Once again, she used slang as a marker of identity.

F: And Diego told me "[?]" and I'm like, "What?" "[?]!"[22] [Her tone shows that he is admonishing her for not knowing what that word means.] He goes, "It's a really common word." And I'm like "excuse me, I don't know your slang. I'm not from the gheettooo." Diego thinks I'm conceited but ..

J: I was going to say, what did he say when you said that?

F: And I make fun of him. I go, like, .. I call him Little Killer or El D.

L: Oh yeah, 'cause you know they use them
                                        [
F: Little Teardrop.

L: Names like, um. Little *Payaso* [clown] and all that stuff.

F: *Payaso,* Little Teardrop
                    [
L: They put names like that over there.

F: I go I go sometimes I go like "Well are you going to go chill in your lowrider?"

Flora and Diego came together through their shared identifications with aspects of Mexican identity, notably music, language, and cultural knowledge of Mexico. In this description of their conversations, however, Flora was careful to clarify an important difference between them, both to Diego and to her audience in Chicago, Lidia and me. Whereas Flora took pride in knowing Mexico City slang such as *chale,* she pointedly asserted her ignorance of Diego's slang and drew out her pronunciation of the word "ghetto," to draw attention to it further. She used language to associate Diego further with what she considered to be the ghetto aspects of Chicano culture by giving him the kind of nicknames used by gang members "over there," as Lidia pointed out. Flora's reference to Diego's lowrider, which he may or may not actually own, further indexed both class and cultural aspects of Chicano identity. All of this teasing served to distance her own identifications within U.S.–Mexican culture from his. He was intimate to her life, but lived in the Los Angeles of Chicano barrio culture. By asserting her ignorance of that culture she affirmed her ambition to attend art school there and thus to inhabit the Los Angeles of both higher education and formally educated art culture.

Flora's dilemma seemed to be how to maintain proximity to Diego without becoming associated with his culture.

CONCLUSION

Flora's ambition to attend art school in Los Angeles indicated her desire to shift her social class as well as her geographic locale. The school she chose was private, mostly White, and in a wealthy part of town. Flora's mother, on the other hand, was concerned that her children graduate from college, but stay close to home. Her concerns reflected the dangers of their neighborhood, in which competing gangs were active and it was a real risk to be on the street. Her mother's desire to keep her children home also reflected a cultural expectation that good children, especially good girls, stay close within the family sphere (Guerra, 1996). As the only daughter, Flora's desire for travel and art education challenged this cultural expectation. The deep conflicts her desires created remind us that expectations for higher education are culturally situated. For most poor or working-class students, students of color, and women, pursuing postsecondary education entails a cultural shift that can require or result in a break with their home culture (Belenky, 1986; Garcia, 2004; Rose, 1989; Willis, 1977).[23] Flora experienced significant role strain as a result of this conflict. By exploring her perceptions of the causes of that strain, we can better understand the creative agency she also employed as she tried to resolve the strain.

Possible selves theory reminds us that at any given moment, an individual takes into account many different aspects of her identity work in making her decisions. Each of these selves is complex, but they are subject to differing constraints. The "now self" must account for the very real social constraints, both limiting and enabling, that an individual experiences. In Flora's case, such constraints included cultural and class-based family pressure to stay close to home, her parents' commitment to their children's well-being and expectations for educational achievement, her own desire to be accepted by her family, the cost of moving away from home and her fear that she would not make it, and the limited financial and educational resources for her as an urban, working-class youth of color.

Flora's relationship with Diego—and the distinctions she made within that identification—helped her to bridge her now self with her possible future selves, both desired and feared. Although she set her sights on a predominantly White school, she preferred Diego's company, and returned critical of the White students there. In every way, she sought to minimize the cultural break that attending this school might entail. Flora's narratives did not assert her proximity to White culture, but rather differentiated her from Chicano and ghetto culture. For example, Flora described her interactions with White students as troubling, both in Chicago art workshops outside of her neighborhood and at the summer program in Los Angeles. As she said, "Being with those kids, I learned my education was deprived. On the first day I learned that. My education was deprived. But I'm cool with them, they like me." During the summer program, she had to work very hard on her writing, revising many times and staying up late to complete papers. "But we had a good connection, the professor and I," she asserted. "I worked really hard and she helped me, and she gave me a book on writing good papers." Yet, back in her neighborhood for her final year of high school, she also was critical of those students, saying that they thought they knew everything. Yates students knew more than she had given them credit for, she said, and she was surprised to come back with a new respect for them.

It clearly was important to Flora to be successful in Los Angeles, with the teachers and the other students, but she did not celebrate their culture over her own. Flora's comments were consistent with the interests she pursued over time: her desire to be a cosmopolitan person, but to reinforce and develop her connections with her Mexican identity. Flora's use of the Internet was essential to this process, but it also brought her into closer proximity to Chicano culture. Because this provoked additional feared possible selves, she scrupulously differentiated herself from Chicanos in Los Angeles, whom outsiders would stereotype as gang members and low riders—in other words, as ghetto. Although she had to negotiate this increased proximity to "ghetto" culture as a result, Flora embraced a more detailed and expansive knowledge of Mexican culture as a means of renegotiating some of the traditions in her family and neighborhood and trying to create a new role for herself that could accommodate both her ambitions and her devotion to home. Flora's experiences bring to light the personal struggles young people face that often lie unseen beneath the surface. In Flora's case, many of her most significant experiences took place away from school and family, in the privacy of online communication. More research on such young people's use of the Internet, focusing on the ways the Internet is important to them, are necessary to understand the powerful changes in national and ethnic identity for U.S.-born Mexicans, and the role the Internet can play in these complex social processes.

ACKNOWLEDGMENT

I would like to acknowledge the support I received for the research and writing of this project from the Spencer Foundation's Dissertation Fellowship for Research Related to Education, the University of Illinois at Chicago Department of Sociology's Rue Bucher Memorial Award for Qualitative Research in Social Processes, and the University of Illinois at Chicago Department of English's Dissertation Fellowship.

REFERENCES

Año Nuevo Kerr, L. (1976). *The Chicano experience in Chicago, 1920–1970.* Unpublished doctoral dissertation, University of Illinois at Chicago, Chicago, IL.

Bauman, R., & Sherzer, J. (1989). Introduction. In R. Bauman & J. Sherzer (Eds.), *Explorations in the ethnography of speaking* (pp. ix–xxvii). New York: Cambridge University Press.

Belenky, M. F. (1986). *Women's ways of knowing: The development of self, voice, and mind.* New York: Basic Books.

Bensman, D., & Lynch, R. (1987). *Rusted dreams: Hard times in a steel community.* New York: McGraw-Hill.

Castillo, C., & Bond, O. F. (1987). *The University of Chicago Spanish dictionary.* Chicago: University of Chicago Press.

Chicago Fact Book Consortium (Eds). (1995). *Local community fact book: Chicago metropolitan area 1990.* Chicago: Academy Chicago Publishers.

Cordeiro, P. A. (1990). *Growing away from the barrio: An ethnography of high achieving at-risk Hispanic youths at two urban high schools.* Unpublished doctoral dissertation, University of Houston, Houston, TX.

Darder, A., Torres, R. D., & Gutíerrez, H. (1997). *Latinos and education: A critical reader.* New York: Routledge.

de Beaugrande, R. (1984). *Text production: Toward a science of composition.* Norwood, N.J.: Ablex.

Farr, M. (in press). *Playing with race in transnational space: Rethinking* Mestizaje. In C. Evans Davies, J. Brutt-Griffler, & L. Pickering (Eds.), *English and ethnicity.* New York: Palgrave Macmillan.

Flores-Gonzalez, N. (2002). *School kids, street kids: Identity development in Latino students.* New York: Teachers College Press.

Fuchs Ebaugh, H. R. (1988). *Becoming an ex: The process of role exit.* Chicago: University of Chicago Press.

Garcia, A. M. (2004). *Narratives of Mexican American women: Emergent identities of the second generation.* Walnut Creek, CA: Alta Mira.

Garner, R., & Gillingham, M. G. (1996). *Internet communication in six classrooms: Conversations across time, space, and culture.* Mahwah, NJ: Lawrence Erlbaum Associates.

Geoghegan, T. (1992). *Which side are you on? Trying to be for labor when it's flat on it's back.* New York: Plume.

Goode, W. S. (1960). A theory of role strain. *American Sociological Review, 25,* 483–496.

Guerra, J. (1996). "It is as if my story repeats itself": Life, language, and literacy in a Chicago comunidad. *Education and Urban Society, 29,* 35–53.

Hemmings, A. (2000). Lola's links: Postoppositional identity work of urban youths. *Anthropology and Education Quarterly, 31,* 152–172.

Ignatiev, N. (1995). *How the Irish became White.* New York: Routledge.

Jones-Reid, M. F., Lopez, C., & Robinson, L. H. (2000). *Mexican slang plus graffiti.* Round Rock, TX: Bueno Books.

Lea, C., Caravajal, C. S., Britton, M., & Horwood, J. (2001). *The Oxford Spanish dictionary and grammar.* New York: Oxford University Press.

Markus, H., & Nurius, P. (1986). Possible selves. *American Psychologist, 41,* 954–969.

McGinty, S. (1999). *Resilience, gender, and success at school.* New York: Peter Lang.

Paredes, A. (1977). On ethnographic work among minority groups: A folklorist's perspective. *New Scholar, 6,* 1–33.

Rose, M. (1989). *Lives on the boundary: A moving account of the struggles and achievements of America's educationally underprepared.* New York: Penguin Books.

Saravia-Shore, M., & Martínez, H. (1992). An ethnographic study of home/school role conflicts of second-generation Puerto Rican adolescents. In M. Saravia-Shore & S. F. Arvizu (Eds.), *Cross-cultural literacy: Ethnographies of communication in multiethnic classrooms* (pp. 227–251). New York: Garland Publishing.

Stryker, S. (1980). *Symbolic interactionism: A social structural version.* Menlo Park: CA: Benjamin/Cummings.

Tannen, D. (1989). *Talking voices: Repetition, dialogue, and imagery in conversational discourse.* New York: Cambridge University Press.

Turkle, S. (1995). *Life on the screen: Identity in the age of the Internet.* New York: Simon & Schuster.

Valenzuela, A. (1999). *Subtractive schooling: U.S.–Mexican youth and the politics of caring.* Albany, NY: SUNY Press.

Wallace, P. (1999). *The psychology of the Internet.* New York: Cambridge University Press.

Waters, M. C. (1990). *Ethnic options: Choosing identities in America.* Berkeley, CA: University of California Press.

Waters, M. (1994). *Modern sociological theory.* London: Sage Publications.

Willis, P. (1977). *Learning to labor: How working class kids get working class jobs.* New York: Colombia University Press.

Wolfram, W. (1991). *Dialects and American English.* Englewood Cliffs, NJ: Prentice-Hall.

Yowell, C. (1999, Fall). The role of the future in meeting the challenge of Latino school dropouts. *Educational Foundations,* 1–24.

Zurcher, L. A. (1983). *Social roles: Conformity, conflict, and creativity.* Beverly Hills, CA: Sage.

ENDNOTES

1. To ensure their anonymity, I have changed the names of all the people who were part of my research and the name of the school.

This article is drawn from a larger ethnographic study. My analysis is in keeping with ethnographic methodology including participant observation and triangulation of my observations with other community members. Nonetheless, ethnographic work among U.S.–Mexicans presents certain challenges, especially to the Anglo researcher. This is especially true in terms of limits on the ethnographer's ability to recognize the cultural context for a given statement and therefore misinterpret it, or to recognize certain acts of verbal performance intended to influence the researcher's conclusions or appeal to her pre-existing biases. I address this issue more fully in the larger study and acknowledge it here as an essential consideration in my analysis. For a careful discussion of these research risks to the Anglo ethnographer, see Paredes (1977).

2. The last mill, the USX South Works steel mill, closed in 1992, but by then it employed only 600 workers, compared with the more than 20,000 it had employed 50 years before (Chicago Fact Book Consortium, 1995, p. 146).

3. Between 1970 and 1990, the Black population (including African Americans and Haitian immigrants) increased to 62% of the total residents. Hispanics made up one third of the population in 1990, although the majority of these were not immigrants. The area around Yates has the highest concentration of Hispanics (75%), but only 25% of that population was foreign born (Chicago Fact Book Consortium, 1995, pp. 146–147).

4. This seems to be representative of many non-Black people in South Chicago. From 1980 to 1990 the population of Blacks increased by 2,830 people, whereas the population of non-Blacks decreased by 8,607 (Chicago Fact Book Consortium, 1995, p. 355).

5. As I discuss later in the chapter, although Flora lightened her hair and eyes, she did not talk about integrating into White culture. Her decisions about how to present herself index her awareness that she desired to move up in a class hierarchy in which Whites dominate the upper classes. In the United States and Mexico, therefore, identifying with a higher social class means identifying with, or in some way addressing, White culture and the racial notion of whiteness.

6. Fuchs Ebaugh continues, "The person, in a sense, psychologically becomes part of the group before he or she actually becomes a member" (p. 109), which describes the shift Flora was trying to accomplish quite accurately.

7. Like many women who have reported their online experiences, Flora and Lidia also described being sexually harassed (e.g., being asked what they were wearing and other more explicit questions) on the basis of their gender (Turkle, 1995; Wallace, 1999). They also reported frequent instances of participants using

anti-gay comments to harass other participants or try to intimidate them out of a chat room.

8. I follow Tannen's (1989) transcription conventions, which I describe in the Appendix.

9. I asked her about this experience repeatedly over the course of a year and never got her to offer any more detail than what I have shared here.

10. Flora and Lidia described examples of other girls in their peer group being rejected by Mexican men, such as the friend who had been asked to dance by a recent Mexican immigrant at a concert. After a few moments of conversation, however, he turned away from her, calling her *"muy Americanizada"* ("too Americanized"; see also Valenzuela, 1999, p. 182 for perspectives from immigrant students in the United States).

11. *Vos* is the second person singular familiar personal pronoun in Spanish. The alternate form of this personal pronoun is *tú*. *Vos* is not universally used among Spanish-speaking countries and not at all in Mexico, where *tú* is used exclusively, or in the Caribbean. In most of Central America and Argentina, *vos* is considered correct among all social groups. According to the *Oxford Spanish Dictionary and Grammar*, it is considered "'unrefined'" elsewhere in Latin America (Lea, Caravajal, Britton, & Horwood, 2001, p. 109). The *University of Chicago Spanish Dictionary* is more specific. It states that the use of *vos* has class connotations only in Chile, where it is associated with lower economic classes (Castillo & Bond, 1987, p. 30). It locates the use of *vos* in Central America and parts of Venezuela, Colombia, Ecuador, Peru, Bolivia, and Uruguay, and all of Paraguay, Argentina, and Chile.

12. Elias Domínguez Barajas, personal communication, June 5, 2002.

13. I heartily and sincerely thank my colleague Elias Dominguez Barajas, who deepened my understanding of the term *chale* considerably. In addition to his own knowledge of the term as a Mexican Spanish speaker, he gathered information from an older brother in Mexico. Elias brought more to my understanding of the word's many uses than any dictionary could. Indeed, a dictionary of Mexican slang reports only that *chale* "indicates disbelief as in 'Oh sure,' 'No way,' 'Nice try' or 'Tell me another one'" (Jones-Reid, Lopez, & Robinson, 2000, p. 39).

14. Domínguez Barajas adds that his older brother has a sense that the term derives from a slang term for Asians, particularly the Chinese immigrants, *chales*. They were considered gullible (because they were unfamiliar with the language and culture of Mexico). The term *chale,* then, could be a truncation of the phrase, "Do I look like a *chale* to you?" meaning, "Do I look gullible to you?" There is an ironic link among the idea that the term Flora and Lidia are discussing has its

roots in immigration and ethnic discrimination in Mexico, their experience of insider–outsider status, and Flora's later description of her unsuccessful effort to enter an exclusive Mexican chat room by passing as a Mexican.

15. They did not specify, in their own words, who made up this particular group of Californian Spanish speakers, although, of course, Spanish speakers in California come from many countries, and include nonimmigrants like themselves.

16. Jones-Reid, Lopez, and Robinson (2000) include *sabanas* among slang words for *"sí"* (yes) (*Mexican Slang,* p. 102).

17. Jones-Reid, Lopez, and Robinson (2000) include *¿qué transas?,* with an *s,* among slang words for greetings (*Mexican Slang,* p. 101).

18. Jones-Reid, Lopez, and Robinson include *cholo* in their discussion of border slang. They acknowledge that the word is "ill-defined" but offer that "[c]*holos* are variously Los Angeles street punks, Mexican American gangsters, or (according to Mexicans) any sort of low rider low-life that come south of the border" (*Mexican Slang,* p. 95).

19. Lidia and Flora also referred to the Mexicans who lived in their neighborhood and who used African American Vernacular English (AAVE) inflections when they spoke English as "ghetto."

20. Flora told me she argued with her mother on this point, accusing her of seeing only the surface whereas Flora appreciated the beauty within. Nonetheless, Flora's mother's comment indexes complex valuations of social status based on skin color. In Mexico, darkness is associated with Indianness in a social structure that marks Indians as the "other." In the United States, darkness is associated with blackness in a hierarchical social structure that differentiates White and other, with the Black as the salient other (Farr, in press).

21. Historically, Mexicans' association with Whites shifted from excluded other to insider status when Blacks began moving into the neighborhood. Housing restrictions against Mexicans relaxed as Mexican residents were increasingly welcomed by Whites in a context of even greater social discrimination against Blacks (Año Nuevo Kerr, 1976). This phenomenon repeats a history of immigrant groups identifying against Blacks as a way of shifting ethnic/racial identity toward Whiteness and thus gaining social privileges restricted to Whites (Ignatiev, 1995; Waters, 1990).

22. I cannot discern what this word might be from the tape.

23. Flora also had wanted to attend a particular, and better, magnet high school outside her neighborhood. Then, too, she told me, her parents expressed concern that leaving the neighborhood would be difficult and dangerous, and did not give her the necessary permission to go.

APPENDIX

To transcribe my tapes, I followed Deborah Tannen's (1989) transcription conventions as she outlines them in *Talking Voices* (pp. 202–203). This means that punctuation represents intonation rather than grammatical conventions. I have not transcribed certain expressions, such as "gonna" but rather "going to." Tannen (1989) argues that "reduced phonological realizations are standard in casual speech," but that research has shown that readers consistently rank the social class of the speakers lower when they see these reduced phonologic realizations in writing (p. 202). Thus, she argues that "representing them by a nonstandard spelling misrepresents them," and, further that it usually is applied inconsistently (p. 202). In this chapter, the following transcription conventions are used:

.	One dot indicates sentence final falling intonation.
,	A comma indicates clause-final intonation.
...	Three dots indicate a pause of a half second or more.
..	Two dots indicate a pause of less than a half second.
[	Brackets show overlap.
""	quotation marks highlight dialogue.
/words/	Text in slashes shows uncertain transcription.
/?/	A question mark in slashes indicates inaudible utterance or an utterance I could not discern from the tape.
!	An exclamation mark indicates exclamatory intonation.
italics	Italics indicate added intonational stress.

Photograph by John Paul Spicer-Escalante.

8

Writing in Two Languages/Living in Two Worlds: A Rhetorical Analysis of Mexican-American Written Discourse

María Spicer-Escalante
Utah State University

It is 9:40 in the morning and the warm late August wind blows in Luis's face as he crosses the campus at the University of Illinois at Urbana-Champaign. Luis is a freshman. This morning, he is tense because in less than 20 minutes he will be—for the first time in his life—in a Spanish language class. This seems odd to him because he has spoken Spanish all his life, at home, with all his friends in Chicago, and around *Pilsen* and *La Villita*. Moreover, he listens to music and sings in Spanish, has traveled to Mexico to visit his relatives, and sometimes flips through Latino television channels, *Univisión* and *Telemundo*. So far, he has had no problems speaking, understanding, and even reading Spanish-language magazines and newspapers. However, he has never attended a Spanish class in his life and that makes him feel uncomfortable and insecure about his language abilities.

Luis's nervousness increases when he arrives in the classroom and the teacher asks the students to write a short autobiography of themselves. Luis is confused and speechless. At this moment, he realizes that he has never written *en español,* not even a postcard or an e-mail to his friends or relatives in Mexico. At school, he learned how to read and write only in English.

Luis is astonished and starts to sweat. He is afraid because he does not know how to write certain words in Spanish. He knows that some have an accent mark in Spanish, but he does not know what words need an accent and which ones do not. Even worse, he recognizes that he does not know how to spell some words or to distinguish the boundaries between them. As Luis writes down his autobiography, feelings of fear and shame consume his mind.

Luis's experience is a very common situation among Spanish heritage speakers (SHS)[1] in the United States in general, and among students of Mexican origin in particular. Students such as Luis grow up speaking Spanish at home and in their community, but most of them do not receive formal instruction in writing in Spanish because academic contact with written Spanish is rare and underemphasized in their home and community contexts. Consequently, in such an environment, they have the opportunity to improve their oral, but not their written, Spanish skills. Thus, their writing has been commonly identified as the weakest area of their Spanish language abilities (Hidalgo, 1993; Merino & Samaniego, 1993; Teschner, 1981). The difficulties of SHS students are compounded by the fact that when they later arrive at a University and take Spanish language classes, they frequently are required to write in Spanish. However, for many of them, as for Luis, this is the first time they face such a task in their lives. Thus, Luis's Spanish texts point not only to the gap between oral and written abilities for SHS students, but they also show highly unique rhetorical characteristics that need to be explored further.[2]

With this idea in mind, I started to look more closely at Luis's Spanish and English written texts, realizing that they somehow were different from those written by both Anglo students and by Spanish native speakers from Mexico. However, although I perceived the differences, I could not specifically identify or classify them, locate them in the text, or characterize them. To examine the rhetorical features that the Spanish and English writings of SHS display further, it seemed necessary to compare them with the Spanish and English texts produced by other, non-SHS students.

To carry out this project, I designed a study that would reveal some particular characteristics of the rhetorical features used by SHS when composing a text in both Spanish and English. I collected writing samples from 41 students, ranging in age from 19 to 23 years. My informants originated from both the United States and Mexico, and belonged to three diverse linguistic groups: Spanish heritage speakers in the United States (SHS), Spanish second language learners who also are English native speakers (SSLL), and Spanish native speakers from Mexico (SNS). I asked the students to write two argumentative/persuasive essays on the same topic: one in English and the other in Spanish. The text in Spanish was an essay on drug use among college students, whereas the English composition was a text about college education. Because the main motivation of this study was to examine the Spanish and English writing samples produced by the three different groups of students, I submitted their essays to a contrastive rhetorical analysis.[3] The comparisons of Spanish texts specifically analyze those produced by SHS in the United States, by SSLL in the United States, and by SNS in Mexico. Similarly, the comparisons of English texts analyze those produced by both SHS and SSLL in the United States.

With respect to the SHS, all of them ($n = 10$) were Mexican American descendants except one whose parents are from Colombia. All were the first generation of their families born in the United States, except one who was born in Mexico but came to the United States when he was 2 years old. All the SHS students were from the Chicago area and attended the University of Illinois at Urbana–Champaign, where they were enrolled in my Spanish heritage speakers class, which had a specific emphasis on writing. All the SHS students had learned Spanish at home. None had received formal education in Spanish before entering the university and attending my class.

The SSLL students ($n = 8$) also attended the University of Illinois. They were enrolled in my Spanish composition class, as part of their minor or major program in Spanish. All were White. They were born in the United States, where their families have lived for several generations. Furthermore, none of them had studied abroad in a Spanish-speaking country before enrolling in this course. The SNS were from Mexico ($n = 5$). They were college students from the Instituto Tecnológico de Monterrey in Mexico City, where they were attending a Spanish Composition class.[4]

The compositions I asked students to write were between 4 and 10 pages in length, yielding a total of 216 pages (a corpus of 49,428 words).[5] I analyzed a total of 41 essays (23 in Spanish and 18 in English) to determine whether the Spanish writing of the SHS used the same rhetorical strategies as the Spanish writing of the SSLL and the SNS, and whether the English writing of the SHS used the same rhetorical strategies as the English writing of the SSLL. Although all students wrote first, second, and final versions of their compositions, I decided to analyze only the first draft. The logic behind this decision was to evaluate the most representative sample of the rhetorical strategies that students use when they write, without having feedback from their peers or from the professor. I simply wanted to analyze their first attempt at composing a text in the two languages without including any suggestions or ideas that would modify the manner in which they express themselves and the rhetorical strategies they use when writing.

Once I had collected the writing samples, I found myself facing a tremendous dilemma. What model of rhetorical analysis, from the very few available,[6] was the most appropriate for examining the Spanish and English writing of these particular populations? What model would capture the richness and the wholeness of SHS Spanish and English written discourse that, at the same time, would account for the rhetorical differences displayed by their written discourse? Finally, after a detailed review of the few, varied rhetorical models available, and after testing various models of analysis in the pilot study, I decided to apply two models for examining persuasive student writing previously used by Connor and Lauer (1988): (a) the Toulmin Analysis of Informal Reasoning, which comprises three stages of rhetorical strategies (analysis of the claim, data, and the use of warrants); and (b) the Persuasive Appeals Analysis, which also includes three categories of persuasive appeals (rational, credibility, and affective). The application of these models guided my study and revealed important insights regarding the particular rhetorical features used by the SHS writers when composing in either Spanish or English.

Before a discussion of the major findings, it must be mentioned that the main goal of my study was not to illustrate "how poorly" or "how well" a specific group of students writes, but to identify specific rhetorical strategies in the writing of the different groups. All Spanish and English texts were thoroughly analyzed, with a focus on the specific components of these two rhetorical models.[7] Furthermore, the data obtained from this analysis were subjected to a statistical analysis of variance (ANOVA) to establish comparisons among the three groups of students and also between the two languages.[8]

What did I discover in my analysis of these two variables? What did the rhetorical and statistical analyses tell us specifically about the Spanish and English writing of the SHS? The results suggest that there are very important and relevant rhetorical differences in the ways that these three groups of students write. Most importantly, the findings show that SHS writers do not thoroughly follow the rhetorical patterns of either SSLL or SNS, but discover their own space within the confines of the writings of both SNS and SSLL, creating a unique mode of written expression. However, where do we find the main differences? And, why is SHS writing different from that of the other two groups?

WHAT DOES THE TOULMIN ANALYSIS OF INFORMAL REASONING TELL US ABOUT THE SHS WRITING?

The rhetorical analysis of the writing samples, according to the Toulmin Analysis of Informal Reasoning, suggests that the Spanish writing of SHS differs from that of both SSLL and SNS in all three of its components: claim, data and warrant. Likewise, the English texts of SHS writers are different from the English essays of SSLL writers for the claim and data components of this variable.

The *claim* is the thesis statement or the main assertion the writer wishes to expose throughout the argument. To be rated highly, it must be specific and explicitly stated, and it may include certain subclaims explicitly tied to the major claim. It also may include some feasible, original, and consistent solutions to the major claim as well. The *data* represent the support for the claim in the form of experience, facts, statistics, or occurrences. The data also must be specific and varied, and must relate to the claim for persuasive results. The final component, the *warrant,* is composed of the justifications or statements provided by the writer to make possible the bridge, or the link, between the data and the claim. The warrant "authorize[s] the claim down from the data" (Lunsford, 2002, p. 113). That is, a warrant "serves to validate the supportive relationship between the claim and data" (Crammond, 1998, p. 236). According to Toulmin (1958), warrants[9] are general justifications, certifying the overall soundness of all arguments. However, they may frequently be absent in an argument because they are implicitly understood by both the writer and the reader.

Regarding the claim category, SHS writers obtained a lower score than either SSLL or SNS writers for their Spanish essays, and also a lower score than SSLL writers for their English compositions. Some of the main differences that make the SHS writing distinct from that of the other two groups are that in some of the SHS Spanish and English compositions, the claim stated by the writers is not expressed in a specific and clear fashion. As stated, it is too general, offers no potential solutions, or offers solutions that are not consistent with the major claim. Moreover, in some cases, the reader does not know exactly what main points the writer wants to develop in the essay. An example of this aspect is illustrated in the following Spanish excerpt,[10] written by an SHS writer:

(1)

[El Alchohol para mí es la droga mas destructiva y (manipulate) legal en los Estados Unidos] **(A)** Claim

La familia tiene una gran responsabilidad de ensenar a sus hijos las ideas de la vida que aveces no se acuerdan que también lo que un adulto hace tiene impacto tremendo con los hijos ... (Here he includes a narration about a personal experience drinking alcohol.) **(B)**

... [El problema que teñimos en este tiempo es los padres no entienden o no pude ver que las costumbres y ideas que los padres hacen en el hogar siempre va afectar a los sus hijos no importa si es malo o bueno.] **(a1)** Subclaim

{El alcoholismo es un tipo de enfermedad que viene de la familia y aceptada por la sociedad.} **(a1)** Subclaim

[In my opinion, alcohol is the most destructive legal drug that is abused in the United States] **(A)** Claim

The family has such a great responsibility in teaching its children ideas on life that sometimes people forget that what

an adult does has a tremendous impact on children ... (Here he includes a narration About a personal experience drinking alcohol.) **(B)** ...

[The problem that we have at this time is that parents do not understand or cannot see that the habits and ideas that they have at home are always going to affect their children, whether they are good or bad.] **(a1)** Subclaim

{Alcohol abuse is a type of illness that comes from the family and is accepted by society.} **(a1)** Subclaim

Once the problem is specifically and explicitly stated (A), the writer includes some data (not shown here) based on his personal experience with alcohol in an attempt to support the claim. However, the writer offers no feasible solutions for the problem mentioned (B). Although the writer mentions that parents have the responsibility of being aware of how their actions may have a great influence on their children, he does not say what parents need to do specifically, or how they need to teach their children about problems with alcohol. In the conclusion, for example, the writer includes some ideas that could be perceived as an attempt at offering a solution (A1 and A2), but these are the only references to a potential resolution of the problem (A earlier).

(2)

[Nosotros como padres del futuro debemos entender nuestros hijos] **A1**

y [no perder comunicación porque solamente ellos son nuestro futuro y no deben perder oportunidades por nuestros ejemplos.] **A2**

El futuro depende de notros no de la sociedad.

[We, as future parents, must understand our children] **A1**

and [not lose our communication link with them because they alone are our future, and they should not lose out on opportunities due to our bad example....] **A2**

The future depends upon us, not on society.]

In this example, the writer does not exploit his ideas. They are mentioned, but not developed. According to the Toulmin rhetorical model, the writer should suggest exactly how parents could understand their children and what they could do to communicate with them. Thus, no feasible solution is offered for the major claim because it is not enough to just list the possibilities. The writer must explain them with specific examples that can strengthen the suggested solutions. This pattern was characteristic of many Spanish and English SHS texts.

What does the Toulmin analytical scheme show about the data component? What are the main rhetorical strategies that SHS writers use to support their claim? With respect to the data component, the analysis reveals that SHS and SNS writers tend to rely on personal experiences and on the "everyone knows" type of data to construct their essays. This strategy, however, is even greater in the case of SNS writers. That is, in almost all SHS and SNS essays, the writers do not include statistics, facts, or opinions from experts. Rather, the only data that appear in their text are based on personal experience. In contrast, SSLL writers use the data component significantly better than SHS and SNS writers when composing a Spanish text. In addition, the analysis of SHS and SSLL English writing indicates that SHS writers use the same rhetorical strategies in their Spanish texts. They build their essays primarily on the basis of personal experiences instead of including bibliographic sources to reinforce their ideas, suggestions, and statements. In contrast, SSLL writers, when composing in either Spanish or English, tend to include one reference after another, with little or no further explanation. They also tend to reproduce and repeat what others say, without including personal remarks or experiences. In fact, the lack of personal experience in the SSLL Spanish and English texts is one of the main characteristics revealed in this analysis. The following two examples—the one in English from an SHS writer and the other one in Spanish written by an SSLL writer—clearly illustrate the points discussed:

(3)

We have all heard these names a thousand times: Budweiser, Miller Genuine Draft, and Jose Cuervo. Every five minutes you can see a beer commercial while watching your favorite television show. **A**

You can also see alcohol advertisements while driving to work or flipping through a magazine. **A**

This is probably the biggest reason college drinking will never be stopped, alcohol and drinking are a major part of the American Society. **A**

They are also a major part of college life.... Another reason why college drinking cannot be stopped is because of the party atmosphere. Campuses are filled with thousands of students between the ages of eighteen and twenty-three. All are young, full of energy and like to party. **A**

(4)

Ritalin es un droga que muchos doctores prescriben a muchos jóvenes que sufren de "Attention deficit disorder." **Es un estimulante que aumenta el nivel de "dopamine" en la parte del cerebro que controla la atención y los impulsos. ... Según la Drug Enforcement Administration, la producción de Ritalin ha aumentado 500% en los cinco años pasados y las recetas para esta droga han aumentado 400% desde 1990–1995. ... Algunos efectos secundarios incluyen la incapacidad dormir, nerviosidad, fiebre, dolor del pecho, dolor de la cabeza, sarpullido, "weightloss", náusea, y vértigo.**

Ritalin is a drug that many doctors prescribe to young people who suffer from "attention deficit Disorder." **It is a stimulant that raises the level of dopamines in the part of the brain which controls the attention span and impulses.... According to the Drug Enforcement Agency, the production of Ritalin has increased 500% in the last five years and prescriptions for this drug have increased 400% since 1990–1995.... Some of its secondary effects are the inability to sleep, nervousness, fever, chest pain, headaches, skin irritation, weight loss, nausea, and vertigo.**

In the text written by an SHS writer (3), we see that the data are related and tied to the major claim. Yet, the data are mainly of the "everybody knows" type (A). According to norms for composition in the United States, although some personal experience is desirable, a writer cannot be persuasive if he or she relies only on this type of data. The writer needs to include some other kinds of data. In this specific essay, the writer includes only one reference on the first page, without specifying the source, to support his statements: "It is estimated that twenty-six percent of college students binge-drink one or two nights a week." The rest of the data included in the essay (eight pages in length) is based entirely upon personal experiences. On the contrary, in the Spanish text written by an SSLL writer (4), it can be seen how the writer incorporates one reference after another (in bold), with little reliance on personal experience or personal comments. Typically, SSLL writers carefully include one source after another, such as statistics, percentages, quotations, and the like, to construct their essays, but they do not comment on the information or analyze it. Thus, it appears that some SSLL writers do not reflect upon or do not elaborate on the references they include in their texts.

But how are warrants handled? How do SHS writers incorporate them into their Spanish and English essays? What are the main differences in comparison with SSLL and SNS writing? Warrants, as the supportive relation between claim and data, frequently may be absent in an argument when they are understood implicitly by both the writer and the reader (Crammond, 1998; Toulmin, 1958), or they are commonly taken for granted (Crammond, 1998). In fact, as Toulmin (1958) has observed, in an informal argument it is not always necessary to explicitly state a warrant. Therefore, in the following analysis of warrants, the readers should keep in mind two significant problems: the intrinsic difficulty in clearly identifying rhetorical elements that may be implicit, and the fact that the following examples reproduced are only excerpts whose essence, relation, and relevance in the whole text might be diminished since they are only partially reproduced.

As noted in the previous section, two main characteristics of SHS Spanish and English writing are that writers tend to make minimal use of data and that most of the data is either of the general knowledge sort or is based on personal experiences. These aspects affect the way that SHS writers establish the soundness of their argument. When composing in Spanish, SHS writers make less use of warrants than SSLL, but more than SNS. However, whereas the English texts of SHS and SSLL writers yield almost the same score for the use of warrants, they use them in notably different fashions. For example, because, as mentioned before, SHS writers rely more on a general knowledge type of data and personal knowledge than do SSLL writers, who rely more on reproducing what others say, the use of warrants is negatively affected in the case of both groups. That is, neither of these two strategies allows the writer to establish the connection between data and claim. For example, in the case of SSLL, writers present the data, but these are provided without an appropriate interpretation from their side. Their warrants, then, may not be fully reliable or trustworthy. Likewise, in the case of SHS writers, who tend to make minimal use of data or use data primarily of the "everybody knows" type or data based on personal experiences, writers do not have the opportunity to establish the bridge between data and claim. In other words, extensive use of warrants is understood as the situation in which the data provided not only are specific, but also are ample and relevant to the claim. Therefore, because there is the necessary background information (explanations, examples, and authorities), the warrants are reliable, relevant, and trustworthy for the topic discussed by the writer (Crammond, 1998). Another interesting aspect of the analysis is that SHS English texts obtained higher scores than SHS Spanish essays for the use of the warrants component.

The English texts of SHS writers receive better scores than their Spanish texts because the warrants expressed by SHS writers in their English essays have more support than in their Spanish compositions. Here it is evident, again, that the relations between data and warrant are very important elements in making an argument persuasive. In the following English text, taken from an SHS writer, the extensive, reliable, and relevant use of warrants is observed:

(5)

[In my personal experience of growing up in a inner city, I came to the conclusion that gangs are starting to take over our neighborhoods.] **A**

According to the National Institute of Justice in *Street Gang Crime in Chicago*, **"there are about 125 street gangs. And approximately 100,000 gang members active in the Chicagoland area" 1.1...**

[I know that there is a large amount of kids in my neighborhood who are involved in gang activities. I know of many individuals who join gangs because of economic problems in their living environment, lack of jobs, lack of self-esteem, and just because they want to belong. Many have turned to gangs and deviant behavior. **D**

[These gangs have taken the city of Chicago under siege and no one is immune from the street gangs and the harm they inflict. Unless something is done to stop a gang activity, our communities are going to be destroyed.] **C**

[Violence has become a way of life.] **B**

For example, according National Institute of Justice, **"Chicago recorded 129 gang-related murders in 1993, which was 13 more than the 116 gang murders occurring in 1992." 1.2**

Paul Almonte and Theresa Desmond in *Update: Street gangs,* stated that **"the rate of violent crime committed by youths has risen more than 25 percent since the early 1980s." 1.3**

In this example, the warrants explicitly stated (C underlined) allow the writer to make the bridge between claim (A and B) and data (in bold 1.1, 1.2, and 1.3) because the writer provides the appropriate and necessary information (examples, explanations, quotes from experts) to support his statements. That is, the writer strengthens the warrant by including both types of data: bibliographic support (bold 1.2 and 1.3) and personal experience (D in italics). In fact, this is an excellent example of how the writer has balanced both personal experience (D) with other types of data, such as statistics (1.1 and 1.2) and opinions from experts (1.3), to allow him to establish the link between claim and data. In this example, warrants not only are relevant for the topic, but also are extensive and trustworthy, allowing the writer to establish the legitimacy of the argument.

Although Toulmin's analytical scheme reveals very important insights on how SHS incorporate the claim, data, and warrant when composing in either Spanish or English, there are other rhetorical features that need to be taken into consideration to comprehend better the richness and fullness of their writing, for example, the use of persuasive appeals, whose results are presented in the following section.

HOW DO SHS USE PERSUASIVE APPEALS IN THEIR SPANISH AND ENGLISH ESSAYS?

As in the Toulmin analysis, the persuasive appeals analysis showed the Spanish writing of SHS writers to be different from that of both SSLL and SNS writers for all three components: rational, credibility, and affective. Likewise, the English writing of SHS writers is different from the English texts of SSLL writers for all three components of this rhetorical model. But what are the main differences and where do we specifically find them? What does the analysis of persuasive appeals tell us about the particular writing characteristics of the three groups of writers?

Rational appeals represent one of the most important and most effective means for logically supporting a written argument. Examples, precedents, testimonies, cause and effect, and analogies are some of the possible strategies that writers may use to make an argument convincing. Credibility appeals refer to the way that the writer establishes him- or herself as a credible entity. Writers, in general, can build credibility in different ways: by being knowledgeable about the topic at hand or by establishing a common ground with the audience. Finally, writers in general may supplement appeals to logic and reason with affective appeals intended to engage the emotional support of their readers. Some of the strategies the writer can use to have a powerful effect on readers involve the incorporation of detailed and careful descriptions, stories, and concrete or figurative language (i.e., figures of speech such as metaphors or similes).

With regard to the specific way that writers use rational appeals in their Spanish and English essays, although there is a tendency among the three groups toward a minimal use of rational appeals in the composition of an argumentative–persuasive text, the SHS writers in the current study used rational appeals more than either the SSLL or SNS writers. When writing in Spanish, the SHS writers incorporated more elements to help them construct rational appeals (e.g., analogies, testimonies, cause and effect, and examples) than the other two groups of writers. Likewise, when composing in English, the SHS writers used rational appeals more than the SSLL writers. Such is the case in the following excerpt written by an SHS writer:

(6)

Es cierto, los inhalantes son muy accesibles y económicos. **A la mano tengo tres artículos que si quisiera pudiera usar para drogarme. A mi alcanze tengo un corrector, un plumón, y un bote de espray que contiene aerosol que puedo usar para inhalar los vapores que emiten. A**

Muchos son de la opinión que los adolescentes usan drogas, inhalantes por lo fácil que son de conseguirlos para poder lidiar con sus problemas, quizas familaiares, amorosos, académicos, etc. Pero esto no es verdad. **[Por ejemplo, vamos a tomar el caso de Jennifer Jones. Jenniffer falleció hace dos años a consecuencia de andar inhalando freón, un gas usado en los aires acondicionados. Jennifer no tenía ningún clase de problemas en casa. Ella era una estudiantes de honor con un futuro muy prometedor.] B**

[Otro caso similar al de jennifer es el de Freddy Bustaque, otro joven sin nigún tipo de **problemas y un excelente estudiante que le encantaban las computadoras. Este chico fue encontrado muerto en su casa por su mamá. Junto a su cadaver encontraron un bote de desodorante que había usado para drogarse.] C**

It is true, inhalants are very accessible and cheap. **At hand, I have three different products that I could use to get stoned. Within reach I have some white-out, a magic marker, and an aerosol spray can that I could use to inhale the vapors that they emit. A**

Many are of the opinion that adolescents use drugs, inhalants, due to the ease in which one can acquire them to get rid of their problems, maybe family, romantic, academically-oriented, etc. But this is not the truth. **[For example, let's take the case of Jennifer Jones. Jennifer died two years ago due to the inhalation of freon, a gas used in air conditioners. Jennifer had no problems at all at home. She was an honor student with a promising future.] B**

[Another case similar to Jennifer's is that of Freddy Bustaque, another young person with no problems who was an excellent student who loved computers. This young man was found dead at home by his mother. Next to his cadaver was found a deodorant can that he had used to get high.] C

In this excerpt, the writer includes several rational appeals, such as examples and testimonies (in bold). That is, the writer incorporates her own example (A) and two more examples as testimonies (B and C) to reinforce and strengthen her statements, and to make her argument more convincing. It must be stressed that in many of the Spanish and English texts by SSLL writers, examples or testimonies are the only type of rational appeals commonly used. However, when this type of appeal appears, it is incorporated mainly into either the short introduction or into the bibliographic references included in the essays, as in the following example:

(7)

Even **[a cursory survey of the available literature reveals that the majority of educators view technology as a powerful and most beneficial educational resource.] A**

[Instructors cite numerous advantages to using technology with their students; these modern instructional media both add a new dimension to the school curricula and provide more effective ways of teaching other educational objectives.] B

Included among the former category is **[the power computers brings to access large quantities of information previously unattainable.] C**

In this sample, the writer makes use of several rational appeals, such as particular examples (A, B, and C, in bold). However, these three examples are based on the bibliographic references included in the essay. The writer could have incorporated other testimonies, such as her own reflections, or opinions from experts, teachers, and students involved in the use of technology in the classroom.

How do SHS writers specifically construct credibility when writing? What are the main rhetorical strategies they use to portray themselves as credible writers? The findings show that SHS writers make more use of credibility appeals than either SSLL or SNS writers when writing in Spanish. In their English production, however, SHS writers make less use of these appeals than SSLL writers. The analysis also shows that the three groups of writers use this rhetorical strategy in different ways. Whereas SSLL writers rely more on bibliographic references as the main means for constructing their credibility, both SHS and SNS writers rely more on personal experiences or general knowledge to demonstrate that they are conversant about the topic being discussed, and to establish credibility and gain the trust of their readers. This characteristic is observed in the following fragments:

(8)

[Drinking and bars are just as much part of college life as classes and studying. For example, at the University of Illinois you can find at least four bars within a four block radius. Karns, C.O. Daniel's, Cochranes and Joes are places where college students spend a lot of their weekends....] Educating college students about drinking and the consequences associated with it would be a waste of time and money. **A**

Incoming freshmen would not take an alcohol education class seriously. All information would go in one ear and out the other. **Most students drank socially before coming to college and already have their minds made up about alcohol. The education would be too little, too late. By the time people are eighteen years old they have already seen every beer commercial and advertisement with a pretty girl in the fast car hugging a muscular guy, who just to happens to be drinking a beer.**

(9)

To make a comparison, **[students in Japan attend school an average of 243 days a year, students in the United Kingdom attend school an average of 192 days, while students in the USA attend school an average of 180 days a year.] A**

[Statistically, by the time an American student has reached the twelfth grade, German counterparts will have spent 4 more years in school, a

large difference. In science tests given to high school seniors, students in the United Kingdom scored a 69.5%, students in Japan scored a 51.9%, and American students were left in the dust with a score of 37.7%.] B

This shows that the American school systems need to be analyzed and restructured to compete with other academically powerful countries. **[Also, in a 1995 study, year-round students outperformed their counterparts by 84 %.] C**

[Socorro Independent School District in El Paso, Texas, switched to a year-round school program because the district's enrollment doubled. In 5 years they eliminated the need to build four additional schools and therefore saved taxpayers almost $30 million.] D

Although the SHS writer (8) is not an authority on this topic, he combines several items of general knowledge (in bold), and personal experience (A, in italics) in a very organized fashion. This aspect allows the writer to build credibility based upon his personal experiences. However, because there is a lack of bibliographic support to reinforce the opinions and statements expressed in the essay, the writer does not make the argument more convincing and trustworthy. In essay 9, written by an SSLL writer, we encounter the opposite situation. Although the writer seems to be knowledgeable about the topic at hand because of the amount of information included (A, B, C, and D, in bold), this strategy is not enough to build credibility, because although information is a very important aspect of making an argument credible and of gaining the trust of the readers, it is not sufficient, nor is it the only way to do so. The SSLL text, in contrast to the text written by the SHS writer, does not include any personal experience or personal comments to improve credibility or to convince the reader that he or she is an authority on the issues treated throughout the essay.

Furthermore, the Spanish and English texts of the SSLL writer seem to be more impersonal than the texts by the SHS writer. It seems that SSLL writers are more detached from the problems they expose in their essays because they do not show the same kind of involvement as SHS and SNS writers when building their credibility appeals. For example, most SSLL writers do not address their readers directly, identify themselves with the problem discussed in the argument, or express or share their personal experiences with their readers. Only in some Spanish and English SHS and SNS texts do the writers express some type of awareness of their readers and their values, as in the following example that shows an SHS writer addressing his readers specifically and directly (in bold):

(10)

[Cheers to all the college students out there drinking and having a good time. **A**

Do what you want *because deep down inside* **you know** *no one can control you.*] [**Enjoy college**, *it may be the best time of your lives, but* **know your** *limits and* **be careful** *when drinking.* **Think** *about your decisions and* **consider** *the consequences,* **only you will have to face** *them.]* **You have got look out for yourself** *because no one else will. The university can not* **tell you** *what to do or watch over you all time.* **B**

[*If you are going to drink it is your choice.* **Judge wisely** *because* **you will have** *to live with the consequences.*] **C**

In this case, the writer not only demonstrates that he knows his audience by expressing his concerns about their welfare (A, B, and C, in italics), but he also addresses his readers directly several times (in bold) throughout this paragraph in particular and throughout the entire essay in general. Similar examples were found in the texts written by SNS writers. However, none of the SSLL writers addressed their readers directly throughout the essay. These results on how SHS writers construct their credibility appeals are paralleled by the results on the use of affective appeals, discussed in the next section.

What main strategies do the three groups of writers use to engage the emotional support of their readers? What are the affective appeals they use when writing? Although there is a tendency among the three groups of writers to make minimal use of these appeals, or at least to develop them minimally, SHS writers make more use of affective appeals than either SSLL or SNS writers when writing in Spanish. To stir readers' emotions, SHS writers include in their Spanish compositions detailed and careful descriptions, detailed stories, concrete or charged language, and the like. In addition, SHS writers make more use of affective appeals when writing in English than in Spanish. In fact, when the English texts of SHS and SSLL writers are analyzed, the findings show that SHS writers include significantly more affective appeals than SSLL writers. With respect to both the Spanish and English texts of SSLL writers, the use of affective appeals is minimal and limited exclusively to the introductory part of the essay, the short narration that all writers include at the beginning of their essay as a warm-up element. In contrast, the

Spanish and English texts of SHS writers exhibit rhetorical strategies that attempt to evoke readers' emotions throughout the entire essay. Such is the case in the following example in which the SHS writer clearly intends to stir his readers' emotions:

(11)

Ahi sangre todo alrededor de mí, mama, y es casi toda mia. Oigo al medico decir, mama, que morire en poco tiempo. **B**

Sólo quiero que sapes, mama, lo juro que no tome. Eran los otros, mama, los otros no pensaron. El probablemente estaba allí en la misma fiesta que yo estaba. La unica diferencia, creo, él tomó y yo morire. Por que toman la gente, mama, cuando puede costar una vida? <u>Estoy sintiendo fuertes dolores ahorita,</u> **A**

dolores como una navaja. El muchacho que me pego esta caminando, mama, y no creo que es justo. <u>Estoy acostado aqui, muriendo, y todo lo que hace es mirar.</u> **A**

Di le a mi hermano que no llore, mama. Di le a papá que sea fuerte, **y cuando vaya al cielo, mama, pon le Mami's hijo en mi tumba.** Alguien le vierra dicho a él, mama, que no tomara y manajara. Si le vierran dicho, mama, yo estubiera vivo. <u>Mi respiro se esta cortando, mama, me estoy asustando. Por favor, no llores por mi, mama. Cuando te necesito, todavia estas ahi.</u> **A**

Sólo tengo una ultima pregunta, mama, antes de que diga adios. Yo no tome y maneja, mama. Porque me estoy muriendo? **B**

There is blood all around me, around mama, and it is almost all mine. I hear the doctor say, mama, that I will die very quickly. **B**

I only want you to know, mama, I swear that I did not drink. It was the other guys, mama, the others didn't think. He was probably at the same party as me. The only difference is, I think, that he drank and I'm going to die. Why do people drink, mama, when it can cost them their life? <u>I'm feeling a lot of pain now,</u> **A**

pains like as if the blade of a knife were cutting me open. The kid who got me is going to walk, mama, and I don't think that that is fair. <u>I'm sitting here dying and all you do is watch.</u> **A**

Tell my brother to not cry, mama. Tell papa to be strong, **and when I go to heaven, mama, have them write mami's son on my tombstone.** Someone should have told him to not drink and drive, mama. If they would have told him, mama, I would be still alive. <u>My breathing is getting short, mama, I'm afraid. Please, don't cry for me mama. When I need you, you are still there.</u> *A*

I only have one last question, mama, before saying good-bye. I didn't drink and drive, mama. Why am I dying? **B**

In this text, the SHS writer uses detailed descriptions of feelings (A) (underlined) and weaves a carefully narrated story (the whole paragraph), through which he recreates a specific scene (B, in italics). In addition, the writer also uses figures of speech such as similes and metaphors (in bold), for example, "dolores como una navaja" or "cuando me vaya al cielo," to help the writer draw a detailed and vivid mental picture of what occurred.

One of the most significant differences between the Spanish and English writing of SHS writers is that they include more charged language—concrete words intended to provoke emotions (B, in bold)—when writing in Spanish than when writing in English. They also use quoted speech to enliven the story, as illustrated in the following example:

(12)

Nos salimos yo, mi hermano Mario y Jose. Empezamos a fumarnos uno de los cigarrillos y que crees que pasa, apenas que acabamos de fumarnos el cigarillo mi mama se asoma de mi ventana. 'Que **chingados estan fumando,** horale para dentro, **paresen pendejos?** Que no saben que fumando cigaros los va matar? No aprendieron a su tío Miguel que se acaba de morir de cancer por andar fumando cigaros?' Nos dijo que si queríamos andar fumando, que mejor fumaramos cigarrillos de marijuana endeves que cigaros legales porque los cigaros legales hacen mas mal para el cuerpo que los cigarrillos de marijuana.

We went out, my brother Mario, Jose, and I. We started to smoke one of the cigarettes and what do you think happens but that, just as we were finishing the cigarette my mother pops her head out of the window. "**What the hell are you smoking,** get in here, **are you stupid or what?** Don't you know that smoking kills? You didn't learn anything from your Uncle Miguel who just died of cancer because he smoked cigarettes?" She told us that if we wanted to keep on smoking, that we should smoke marijuana, not cigarettes, because cigarettes are worse for the body than marijuana.

Actually, in contrast to the SHS texts, there is only one example, from all the texts I analyzed, in which the use of charged language was explicitly used by an SSLL writer. It is important to mention however, that although the student who included this example of charged language in her English essay is a native English speaker, she is a bilingual person who also speaks Farsi at home.

CONCLUSION

What can we glean from this study about the rhetorical strategies that SHS writers use when composing an argumentative–persuasive essay? How can it help us understand the writing of SHS students such as Luis? This study suggests that both the Spanish and the English writings of SHS writers have unique characteristics that may be attributable to a process of cultural and rhetorical transculturation.[11] That is, they do not thoroughly follow the patterns of either SSLL or SNS writers, but find their own pathway to expression, creating their own rhetorical space somewhere between the writings of both SNS and SSLL writers. The findings show that SHS writers nourish their writing of both Spanish and English by using rhetorical strategies that correspond to both of these languages, reflecting the cultural borderland in which they live, where elements of North American and Latino cultures meld together into a unique syncretic composite. Their written texts in these two languages, like Luis' writing, thus reflect their own reality of living—and writing—between these two distinct linguistic and cultural worlds.

The application of the two rhetorical models used in the current study— the Toulmin Analysis and the Persuasive Appeals Analysis—suggests that the Spanish and English writings of SHS writers display unique characteristics, showing innovative modes of expression in these two languages. These two models of rhetorical analysis have allowed us not only to identify the main differences among the three groups of writers and between the Spanish and the English languages, but also, and most important, to comprehend better the writing of SHS writers. From the Toulmin Analysis, in particular, we have been able to identify very significant rhetorical differences among the writings of the three groups of writers. However, it was the Persuasive Appeals Analysis that allowed us to capture the richness and to observe deeply the wholeness of SHS writing in both languages. These two models of analysis have mutually complemented and broadened the findings yielded by each, allowing us to understand better the complexity of SHS Spanish and English writing. Yet, what are the overall patterns that SHS writers follow when writing an argumentative–persuasive essay, as compared with the other two groups of writers? What are the strengths that Spanish and English SHS writing display in contrast to SSLL and SNS written texts?

According to the scheme of the Toulmin Analysis of Informal Reasoning, the most important findings with regard to SHS Spanish and English writings show the following contrasts to the findings for the writings of the other two groups:

- SHS writers have the tendency, in both languages, to support their thesis statements by relying more on personal experiences and on the "everyone knows" type of data to build their essays than on statistics, facts, or opinions from experts. However, the analysis also indicates that this tendency is even greater when writers are composing in Spanish. SHS writers do not follow the pattern of SSLL writers who tend, in both languages, to include one reference after another, or who simply repeat or rephrase what other people say. In this specific aspect, SHS writers seem to be closer to the writing characteristics of SNS writers, who tend to rely, even more than SHS writers, on personal experiences and general knowledge as the only rhetorical strategies to construct their argumentative–persuasive essays.

The Persuasive Appeals Analysis indicates not only that the three groups of writers use these rhetorical strategies in different fashions, but also that, overall, SHS writers perform better than the other two groups in terms of the including persuasive appeals in their essays. These results show the strengths of their Spanish and English writing. The main differences, according to this model, are the following:

- SHS incorporate more analogies, testimonies, and examples to construct their rational appeals than the other two groups. Moreover, the analysis also indicates that SHS writers incorporate their rational appeals throughout their essays in both languages, whereas SSLL writers tend to include them either in the introduction or in the bibliographic references and quotations they incorporate in the essay.
- SHS writers tend to demonstrate that they are conversant in the topic under consideration, in both languages, by the inclusion of personal

experiences or general knowledge as the only rhetorical strategy for building credibility and for gaining the trust of their readers.

- SHS writers demonstrate that they are engaged with the problems they expose in their essays by addressing their readers directly, by identifying themselves with the problem discussed in the argument, and/or by expressing or sharing their personal experiences with their readers.
- SHS writers include more affective appeals than the other two groups in their Spanish and English compositions. Detailed and careful descriptions, detailed stories, and concrete or charged language are some of the rhetorical strategies that SHS writers use in their texts to stir readers' emotions.

The results yielded by the rhetorical analysis show us that SHS students like Luis represent a very unique group of students, different from both SSLL and SNS students, with distinct and specific needs. One implication of the current study, then, is the confirmation that these students need specific courses designed to polish and refine their already-existing Spanish language skills. The SHS students need courses with a greater emphasis on reading and writing in which they can practice these skills to make them feel comfortable about their writing abilities. They also need courses in which they learn, little by little, to manage written academic discourse, including the use of facts and bibliographic references. Spanish composition teachers and researchers, however, should also recognize and value the fact that SHS students bring into the classroom with them a different set of linguistic and cultural profiles that enriches and diversifies the learning environment. Only by adopting this perspective will we be able to enhance our comprehension of the rhetorical strategies that this group of students uses when composing in either English or Spanish.

It is important to note that, along with important results, there also are some limitations to this study. First, although I analyzed 216 pages, including compositions from 4 to 10 pages in length, the number of participants in each group was relatively small. Future research with more participants is highly needed. The second limitation relates to the instrument of analysis, for which several aspects must be taken into consideration. Some researchers (Kubota, 1997; Silva, Leki, & Carson, 1997) have warned of the danger that the discourses of modernization and Westernization represent when instructors are teaching and analyzing writing. However, in the particular case of the current study, it is necessary to recognize that, unfortunately, very few studies in contrastive rhetoric have focused on the analysis of argumentative–persuasive essays, and none of them have focused on the Spanish language. Therefore, researchers interested in this field, like myself, have to face this situation and draw the information from the few studies available, adjusting them to their specific needs, to provide more insights to support and encourage future research.

In the specific case of this study, selecting an instrument of analysis that included the rhetorical features used in both the Spanish and English languages was most difficult. Although, to my knowledge, this is the first attempt to analyze the Spanish and English writing of SHS, SSLL, and SNS writers, applying the two models proposed in this research—the Toulmin Analysis of Informal Reasoning and the Persuasive Appeals Analysis—the rhetorical analysis has provided important insights into the way in which SHS writers write in Spanish and English. However, continued research into rhetorical and linguistic strategies used for this type of writing, as well as other modes of writing, is greatly needed for a better comprehension of the Spanish and English writing of SHS students such as Luis. Likewise, the results of future analyses will cast further necessary light on the important linkage between written expression and identity, a relevant point we must consider when dealing with marginal—and marginalized—communities whose voices are beginning to be heard at an ever-increasing rate in the United States, as in the case of Luis, whose writings are an integral piece of this study.

REFERENCES

Ashcroft, B., Griffiths, G., & Tiffin, H. (2000). *Post-colonial studies: The key concepts*. London, New York: Routledge.

Connor, U. (1996). *Contrastive rhetoric: Cross-cultural aspects of second-language writing*. Cambridge, England: Cambridge University Press.

Connor, U., & Lauer, J. (1988). Cross-cultural variation in persuasive student writing. In A. Purves (Ed.), *Writing across languages and cultures: Issues in contrastive rhetoric* (pp.138–159). Newbury Park, CA: Sage.

Crammond, J. (1998). The uses and complexity of argument structures in expert and student persuasive writing. *Written Communication, 15*(2), 230–268.

Hidalgo, M. (1993). The teaching of Spanish to bilingual Spanish speakers: A "problem" of inequality. In B. Merino, H. Trueba, & F. Samaniego (Eds.), *Language and culture in learning: Teaching Spanish to native speakers* (pp. 82–93). Washington, DC: The Falmer Press.

Kubota, R. (1997). A reevaluation of the uniqueness of Japanese written discourse. *Written Communication, 14*(4), 460–480.

Lunsford, K. (2002). Contextualizing Toulmin's model in the writing classroom. *Written Communication, 19*(1), 109–174.

Merino, B., & Samaniego, F. (1993). Language acquisition theory and classroom practices in the teaching of Spanish to the native Spanish speaker. In B. Merino, H. Trueba, & F. Samaniego (Eds.), *Language and culture in learning: Teaching Spanish to native speakers* (pp.115–123). Washington, DC: The Falmer Press.

Silva, T., Leki, I., & Carson, J. (1997). Broadening the perspective of mainstream composition studies. *Written Communication, 14*(3), 398–428.

Spicer-Escalante, M. (2002). *Spanish heritage speakers' Spanish and English writings: Contrastive rhetorical and linguistic analyses.* Unpublished doctoral dissertation, University of Illinois at Urbana-Champaign.

Teschner, R. (1981). Spanish for native speakers: Evaluating twenty-five Chicano compositions in a first-year course. In G. Valdés, A. G., Lozano, & R. García-Moya (Eds.), *Teaching Spanish to the Hispanic bilingual: Issues, aims, and methods.* New York: Teachers College Press.

Therrien, M., & Ramírez, R. (2000). *The Hispanic population in the United States: March 2000,* Current Population Reports, U.S. Census Bureau: Washington, DC, 20–535.

Toulmin, S. (1958). *The uses of argument.* Cambridge, England: Cambridge University Press.

U.S. Bureau of the Census. (2001). *Statistical abstract of the United States.* Washington, DC: U.S. Government Printing Office.

The Toulmin Analysis of Informal Reasoning
Reproduced by permission from Connor and Lauer (1988, p. 145)

Claim

1   No specific problem stated/and or no consistent point of view. May have one subclaim. No solution offered, or if offered, nonfeasible, unoriginal, and inconsistent with claim.
2   Specific, explicitly stated problem. Somewhat consistent point of view. Relevant to the task. Has two or more subclaims that have been developed. Solution offered with some feasibility with major claims.
3   Specific, explicitly stated problem with consistent point of view. Several well-developed subclaims, explicitly tied to the major claims. Highly relevant to the task. Solution offered that is feasible, original, and consistent with major claim.

Data

1   Minimal use of data. Data of the "everyone knows" type with little reliance on personal experience or authority. Not directly related to major claims.
2   Some use of data with reliance on personal experience or authority. Some variety in use of data. Data generally related to major claim.
3   Extensive use of specific, well-developed data of a variety of types. Data explicitly connected to major claim.

Warrant

1   Minimal use of warrants. Warrants only minimally reliable and relevant to the case. Warrants may include logical fallacies.
2   Some use of warrants. Although warrants allow the writer to make the bridge between data and claim, some distortion and informal fallacies are evident.
3   Extensive use of warrants. Reliable and trustworthy allowing rather than accepting the bridge from data to claim. Slightly relevant. Evidence of some backing.

The Persuasive Appeals Analysis
Reproduced by permission from Connor and Lauer (1988, p. 147)

Rational

0   No use of rational appeal.*
1   Use of some rational appeals,* minimally developed or use of some inappropriate (in terms of major point) rational appeals.
2   Use of single rational appeal* or a series of rational appeals* with at least two points of development.
3   Exceptionally well-developed and appropriate single extended rational appeals* or coherent set of rational appeals.*

*Rational appeals were categorized as (quasi-logical, realistic structure, example, analogy).

Credibility

0   No use of credibility appeal.
1   No writer credibility but some awareness of audience's values.
or Some writer credibility (other than general knowledge) but no awareness of audience's values.
2   Some writer credibility (other than general knowledge) and some awareness of audience's values.
3   Strong writer credibility (personal experience) and sensitivity to audience's values (specific audience for the solution).

Affective

0   No use of affective appeal.
1   Minimal use of concreteness or charged language.
2   Adequate use of picture, charged language, or metaphor to evoke emotion.
3   Strong use of vivid picture, charged language, or metaphor to evoke emotion.

Mean Results From the Toulmin Analysis of Informal Reasoning for SHS Spanish Writing Compared With the Findings for SSLL and SNS Spanish Writing

	SSLL (n = 8) (%)	SHS (n = 10) (%)	SNS (n = 5) (%)
Claim	83.33	73.33	80.00
Data	66.67	53.33	33.33
Warrant	58.33	50.00	33.33

n = total number of texts analyzed in each group.

Mean Results From the Toulmin Analysis of Informal Reasoning for SHS English Writing Compared With the Findings for SSLL English Writing

	SHS (n = 10) (%)	SSLL (n = 8) (%)
Claim	73.33	91.67
Data	60.00	66.67
Warrant	60.00	62.00

n = total number of texts analyzed in each group.

Mean Results From the Persuasive Appeals Analysis for SHS Spanish Writing Compared With the Findings for SSLL and SNS Spanish Writing

	SSLL (n = 8) (%)	SHS (n = 10) (%)	SNS (n = 5) (%)
Rational	37.50	56.67	46.67
Credibility	45.83	53.33	40.00
Affective	38.39	50.00	33.33

n = total number of texts analyzed in each group.

Mean Results From the Persuasive Appeals Analysis for SHS English Writing Compared With the Findings for SSLL English Writing

	SHS (n = 10) (%)	SSLL (n = 8) (%)
Rational	53.33	45.83
Credibility	60.00	70.83
Affective	60.00	25.00

n = total number of texts analyzed in each group.

ENDNOTES

1. Heritage language speakers have been described as individuals who are raised in homes wherein a non-English language is solely or also spoken along with English, who speak or merely understand the heritage language, who are to some degree bilingual in English and their heritage language. The Hispanic population has already become the nation's largest minority group, with a population of 35.3 million persons, representing 13% of the entire population of this country (U.S. Census Bureau, 2001). That is, one in eight people in the United States is of Hispanic origin (Therrien and Ramírez, 2000).

2. Although the grammar and the spelling of the Spanish texts of SHS writers are very important aspects, their analysis is beyond the scope of this contribution. Moreover, they need to be identified and analyzed carefully because of their richness and variety.

3. Contrastive rhetoric is an area of research in second language acquisition that intends to identify differences in written texts "encountered by second language writers and, by referring to the rhetorical strategies of the first language, attempts to explain them" (Connor, 1996, p. 5).

4. This group was chosen because the Tecnológico de Monterrey is the only university-level institution in Mexico at which all students are required to take a Spanish composition course as part of the general education requirements. Moreover, according to the current curriculum, students receive specific instruction on how to write an argumentative–persuasive essay.

5. The total number of words in Spanish is 24,948 and the total in English is 24,480.

6. Little research has been conducted to examine the argumentative–persuasive discourse (Connor & Lauer, 1988).

7. See Appendix A for the complete description of the rhetorical variables.

8. The mean results of the statistical analysis are summarized in Appendix B. For a complete discussion of the statistical analysis, see Spicer-Escalante (2002).

9. For a discussion about the warrant component see Crammond (1998), Lunsford (2002), Spicer-Escalante (2002), and Toulmin (1958).

10. The grammar and the spelling of the reproduced examples correspond exactly to the original texts written by the different writers.

11. This term refers to the reciprocal influences of modes of representation and cultural practices of various kinds. It describes how "subordinated or marginal groups select and invent from materials transmitted to them by a dominant or metropolitan culture" (Ashcroft, Griffiths, & Tiffin, 2000, p. 233).

PART

IV

Within Community Spaces

Photograph by Janise Hurtig.

9

Resisting Assimilation: Mexican Immigrant Mothers Writing Together[1]

Janise Hurtig

University of Illinois at Chicago

Personal interpretations of past time—the stories that people tell themselves in order to explain how they got to the place they currently inhabit—are often in deep and ambivalent conflict with the official interpretive devices of a culture.

(Carolyn Kay Steedman, 1986, p. 6)

Myths of assimilation—from early 20th century myths of the melting pot (incorporation) to more recent myths of multiculturalism (pluralism)— are among the official interpretive devices of contemporary U.S. culture.[2] Like other comparable devices, these myths inscribe imaginary paths upon a dominant social landscape that promise the follower of those paths a visible and meaningful place within the landscape, while justifying the exclusion of those not willing (or able) to follow the prescribed paths. Myths of assimilation have immigrants as their objects, and the paths these myths inscribe are paved with the promises of opportunity, education, prosperity, security and a recognized ethnic identity for immigrants and their children.

In both its spatial and moral dimensions, the mythology of assimilation is thoroughly modern. Its unilinear, neofunctionalist plot converts the process of immigration into adaptation (Rouse, 1992, p. 25) or ethnic incorporation, and its meritocratic ethic offers "a universal promise of social mobility based on individual motivation and effort in a society in which there [are] no class barriers" (Schiller, Basch, & Blanc-Szanton, 1992, p. 16). Moreover, it does so in culturally and geographically bipolar terms: Immigrants are meant to "steadily shift their focus of attention and the locus of their principal social ties from one community to another" (Rouse, 1992, p. 26). The mythology of assimilation is also androcentric, inasmuch as it is constructed from the imagined perspective of a geographically mobile and socioeconomically upwardly mobile male worker and head of household. Myths of assimilation have men as their protagonists. Women are portrayed as passive recipients of money sent back home or of new opportunities, material comforts, and identities in the host society (Brettell, 2003; Mahler, 2003; Pessar, 1986, 2003).

In "The Storyteller," Walter Benjamin (1969) proposed that "it is the nature of every real story to contain, openly or covertly, something useful" (p. 86). The storyteller, then, is a person "who has counsel for his readers" (p. 86). It is with counsel that ordinary people have responded to the myths of their times, and it is precisely this ability to give counsel that enables the storyteller to confront and resist the force of those myths. But the use of stories to resist myths and give counsel depends on the recognition, by the storyteller and her listener or reader, of the value of common experience, because it is from that experience that the storyteller draws her moral and proffers her advice.[3] In this chapter I look at how a group of Mexican immigrant women have responded to, resisted, and counseled against the mythology of assimilation through the collective work of telling, writing, discussing, and publishing stories from their experiences.

For the past 2 years I have taught an adult writing workshop to Mexican immigrant women at Telpochcalli Elementary School, a small school located in a predominantly Mexican, working poor neighborhood on Chicago's southwest side. The program, called Parents Write their Worlds, offers parents and other neighborhood residents—people who do not usually think of themselves as writers—the opportunity to write and share stories based in their experiences, draw on their work to examine their lives, and develop the art of writing (Adams & Hurtig, 2002). Since I began the program at Telpochcalli School, more than 30 women—all of them mothers or grandmothers between the ages of 25 and 55 years—have participated in the workshops, although at most meetings there usually are between five and eight women in attendance. The group meets weekly during the school year to read and discuss their work and help each other develop pieces that eventually appear in the magazine *Real Conditions*.

While all the participants write in Spanish (a few speak a little English; one speaks with fluency) their stories are published in both Spanish and English. Since I began the writing program at Telpochcalli we have published four magazines, representing the work of 22 different writers. Copies of each magazine have been distributed free to the writers, their families and friends, and to the school's students, teachers, and staff. The magazines also make their way into and well beyond the writers' neighborhood to other schools, communities, and countries.

The women who have attended the writing program come from different regions of Mexico, some from small villages or *ranchos,* others from small or large cities. Although the women grew up under differing socio-economic conditions and have a range of educational backgrounds, they all came to this country in search of a better life for themselves and their families: "to obtain a better quality of life than that which we had in our country," they wrote collectively for the introduction to the third magazine.[4] Like many of their neighbors, some of the women in the writing group endured tremendous danger and humiliation to come to the United States without legal documentation, squeezing into trucks, crossing rivers and deserts, confronting immigration officers. Others came easily and legitimately by plane, car, or bus. Some women came eagerly, joining their husbands or other family members after a long separation. Others came reluctantly, especially those who left family behind. Whereas most came accompanied by husbands or other family, or with the intention of joining their families already in Chicago, a few women came alone.

Several writers were already mothers when they came to Chicago. Some brought their Mexican-born children with them, and have told stories laced with regret about how they risked their own and their children's lives to make the dangerous trek across the border. Others have described the excruciatingly painful decision to leave their children in Mexico and then return for them later. Most of the women also have given birth to children since their arrival in this country. Regardless of the conditions of their arrival, their family networks now stretch across two countries, and their migration north has caused the painful attenuation of many formative ties. "We are all Mexican mothers looking for a better life for ourselves and for our children," wrote Rita,[5] a mother whose children attend a nearby school. "However, at the same time we are sacrificing the support of our families in Mexico."

Each woman who has participated in the writing group has told unique stories of migration, relocation, and family formation. These stories have resonated within the cavernous classroom where we work each week, sitting around a long table in the middle of the room, children's books and games in one corner, coffee and snacks in another, blackboards along two walls and long windows on the other. The uniqueness of each woman's experiences and insights, as well as the threads of commonality they encounter across their differences, have spawned hours of discussion. Those discussions have led the women to tell and write more stories and to rethink the old stories and their significance.

For the women in the writing program, the reduction of the transnational complexity of their lives to a bipolar, unidirectional model of immigration and settlement as ethnic incorporation is only one of the ways in which the mythology of assimilation denies the expression of their experiences. Although the mythology of assimilation may romanticize the "ethnic enclave" as a transitional haven for immigrants on their way into the melting pot, or as a site of identity production in a multicultural society, it also depicts the enclave, the ghetto, the barrio as a marginal, dangerous and socioeconomically limiting place from which immigrants should move up and out. In this way, the mythology of assimilation troubles the relationship between immigrants and their neighborhoods. Another, particularly contemporary, facet of this mythology is the conversion of an ethic of hard work into an ethic of consumption or, as the women in the writing group refer to it, *"materialismo."* The notion that providing for one's children is measured in terms of what one can purchase for them is a topic the workshop participants have confronted in writings and discussions that revolve around decisions about whether they should seek paid work outside the home or not.

Many of the gender ideologies implied by the mythology of assimilation are particularly troubling to the women with whom I work in the writing program. They question the assumption that upward mobility should buy women their "freedom" from housework and home life, as though the home, and by implication motherhood, were imprisoning. They debate the presumption that a lack of formal education or literacy skills is related to, or diagnostic of, inadequate parenting skills. And they challenge the idealization of the (middle-class) nuclear family, in which the value of extended family ties is diminished and the marital relationship is elevated as primary. Although the women in the writing program are critical of many facets of the contemporary "American dream," they draw inspiration from other facets of that same dream in expressing their critique of *machismo* and the limitations placed on them by husbands, by other family members, or more indirectly by the gender ideologies they carry over from their homelands and that are among the cultural norms sustained by a "viable binational social structure" (Rodríguez 2003, p. 82).

The women who have participated in the writing project live in a Spanish-speaking community that forms part of a transnational migratory circuit and social space[6] through which they sustain meaningful communicative, affective, and material ties to their families in Mexico. They contribute their volunteer labor to improving a neighborhood in which they are invested, or in which their children attend a school that celebrates the history, arts, and culture of Mexico. They are women whose primary social role and personal commitment is that of motherhood and whose deepest hopes are both to return to Mexico and to see their children prosper in Chicago. Thus, for these women, the interpretations they have of their past lives, the stories they tell about their past and present, and the relation between the two often are in deep and ambivalent conflict with the mythology of assimilation.

In *Landscape for a Good Woman,* Carolyn Steedman (1986) wrote of her British, working-class mother's struggles to use stories to make sense of her life when those stories were in conflict with the dominant myths of the society in which she lived. That mythology silenced Steedman's mother so that she kept her stories secret, imparting them to her daughter as stories meant to teach Steedman "the terrible unfairness of things" (p. 6). Because her mother kept her stories secret, she was unable to use them to resist the exclusionary myths of her times or transcend the longing they produced in her. Steedman, by contrast, was able to tell a story that responded to and resisted the culture of longing passed on by her mother. She did so, I propose, by writing, and more specifically, by writing critically, historicizing both her mother's stories and her own in relation to the political and cultural landscapes of the times. But Steedman did not only write her story, she also published it for a wider audience. Unlike her mother, who kept her stories secret, Steedman made hers public. It is (at least in part) for these reasons that Steedman was able to accomplish what she set out to do through her writing: to step into the landscape from which she was excluded and to see herself in it (p. 24).

In an essay entitled "Speaking in Tongues," Chicana poet Gloria Anzaldúa (1981) similarly asserted the power and value of writing as a way of telling one's story in one's own terms. "I write," said Anzaldúa, "to record what others erase when I speak, to rewrite the stories others have miswritten about me, about you" (p. 169). Reflecting rhetorically on her compulsion to write, Anzaldúa also intimated the relation between writing one's own stories and creating a coherent landscape for one's world: "By writing, I put order in the world, give it a handle so I can grasp it" (p. 169).

Anzaldúa's essay, which carried the subtitle "A Letter to 3rd World Women Writers," aimed not only to inspire her *compañeras* to write but also, implicitly, to publish: to put their stories in print. This was a significant act. Anne Ruggles Gere (1997) discussed the gendered power of the printed text in her study of U.S. women's reading and writing clubs at the turn of the 20th century, noting that "[t]he transformative power of literacy was particularly apparent when clubswomen chose to represent themselves and their activities in print" (p. 29). Similarly, for the women who participated in the writing project, producing stories that would be read, not only by people they knew, but also by an imagined audience that existed beyond the scope of their social world, had tremendous bearing on how they chose to represent their experiences in their writing, as well as how they came to understand and articulate the value and purpose of their writing.

Although Anzaldúa tended to depict her writing process as an intimately individual, personally tumultuous, and solitary endeavor, I question the romantic implication that creative and critical writing can be produced individually. As Gere (1997) noted, "The story of reading and writing does not begin or end with solitary performers" (p. 37). Certainly in the Parents Write their Worlds workshops, the women's social, oral activities of telling, discussing, praising, and challenging each other's stories are as critical as the literate activities of writing and reading one's stories (Brandt, 1990). Writing against the ideology of racist patriarchy that locates the creative act in the solitary individual, Audre Lorde (1984) spoke to the creative and critical power of interdependency and difference: "Interdependency between women," she noted, "is the way to a freedom which allows the *I* to *be*, not in order to be used, but in order to be creative" (p. 111). In other words, it is through interdependency that one comes to recognize oneself as a subject of history. Moreover, the source of this creativity is located in difference: "Difference must be … seen as a fund of necessary polarities between which our creativity can spark like a dialectic.… Only within that interdependency of different strengths, acknowledged and equal, can the power to seek new ways of being in the world generate" (Lorde, 1984, p. 111).

In discussions about the experience of writing, many workshop participants identified the collective work of the group as the source of mutual support, creative inspiration, and critical understanding. One of the mothers wrote about how "sharing our common struggles gives us the strength to accomplish some of the dreams that have been tucked away, perhaps sleeping somewhere," whereas others have commented about the uniqueness of each writer's childhood experiences, or the variety of village traditions represented by the group. This dialectic of commonality and difference is what generates the creative spark to which Audre Lorde refers. Dolores Nava reflected on the relation between support and creativity in a piece she wrote and published about her experience in the writing workshop, entitled "The Experience of Writing":

> Having written and read in a group, it leaves me with the sensation of having tightened even more our existing bonds of friendship, the respect with which I was listened to.... I respect them, I appreciate them, and I also thank them for having shared something about themselves with the group through their writings.... I really enjoy expressing myself in new ways through writing. Thank you, friends, for listening.

In the process of writing, reflecting, and telling new stories, the women in the workshop respond critically and collectively to the mythology of assimilation, begin to rewrite the stories others have miswritten about them, "put order in the world" in their own terms, and use their stories to offer counsel to others that challenges the mythology of assimilation. In this sense, the literate and, more generally, the cultural work of this group constitutes acts of resistance.

In the remainder of the chapter I consider several related facets of these women's resistance as they rewrote the landscapes of their past and present lives. In the first place, I look at how they contested the bipolar, bicultural dimensions of the mythology or ideology of assimilation by writing stories that begin to narrate meaningful, if conflicted and critical, relations between their past in Mexico and their present in Chicago. I also consider how the women mediated the spatial, temporal, and cultural relation of Mexico and Chicago in terms of their social roles and identities as mothers, implicitly contesting the androcentrism of the assimilation mythology. Finally, I look at how they used their stories and the magazine as cultural artifacts to "give counsel." By drawing critically on the moral and social norms from their past and present experiences, they lent meaning and purpose to their present lives and gave advice to their children, their peers, and their community.

Before turning to the writings, however, I want to locate the stories in relation to two contexts that are particularly relevant to understanding how the women come to use their writing as a form of resistance. These are the writing workshop and the elementary school in which the workshop takes place.

MOTHERS BECOMING WRITERS

Who am I, a poor Chicanita from the sticks, to think I could write.

(Gloria Anzaldúa, 1981).

"Many people, especially women, do not see themselves as legitimate subjects of *history,*" commented the literacy educator and researcher Jane Mace (1995). "They do not believe that they are either 'relevant' or 'interesting,' let alone important to anyone else's understanding of the times in which they lived. In the same way, many people (again, especially women) do not see themselves as worthy to be *writers,* in the published sense" (p. 109; emphasis in original). These three perceptions—that one is an object, not a subject of history; that one's experiences and insights are not valued; and that one is not worthy of being a published writer—all are intimately related. (They are also, I hasten to add, pertinent to all social groups silenced by ideologies of linguistic legitimacy, not just to women.) They can be understood as the effects of a modern social and communicative landscape in which the experience of ordinary people is devalued (Benjamin, 1969), literate communication is valued over oral communication, and the voices of ordinary people are excluded from public conversations circulated and legitimized by print media. This ideological landscape reinforces the marginalization of certain groups of people, such as women, immigrants, and people who live in poverty. It is the work of literacy and community publishing, wrote Mace (1995), to challenge these ideas.

The Parents Write Their Worlds program similarly challenges these ideas, by providing a forum for creative expression in which participants write and share stories based in their experiences, draw on their writings to examine their lives, and develop the art of writing. The writing workshop method is inspired by the Freirian method for adult literacy education, in which dialogue based in participants' experience is the source of generative themes for writing, reading and reflection (Freire, 1971, pp. 85–118). In the writing workshops, we focus on personal narrative, or creative nonfiction writing, in which participants respond to prompts that encourage them to write concrete, detailed stories based in their experiences. The writing prompts for each session usually emerge from the group's discussion of the previous week's writings. In this way, the creative work of the participants is the primary content of the sessions, and their reflections guide the thematic direction the writing takes.

As is common among adults who begin to write about their lives for the first time, most of the women who have come to the writing workshop initially expressed reticence about writing. Some said they did not write well enough. They claimed they had not had enough formal education to prepare them for the creative task of writing, that the kind of education they had received had not emphasized writing, that their punctuation and spelling were terrible, or their handwriting illegible, or that too many years had passed since they had gone to school and they had simply forgotten how to write. (By this, they meant not that they had lost the technical skill of writing, but that they believed could no longer write a coherent narrative account.) Many women also claimed at the outset that they did not have anything meaningful to write about, or that their experiences were not interesting enough to write down or share with the group.

Most participants are initially astonished by the group's response to their writing, because many of the stories they write are drawn from events in their lives they had either forgotten or had "never bothered to tell anyone before." I remember the comment of one participant, a woman in her midthirties who had been raised by her mother and grandmother in conditions of extreme poverty and was therefore not permitted to attend school after the first grade. It was her second session, and we had read a short piece she had written the week before, entitled "A Special Place." In her story she described a garden in her village where she and her friends played house, too poor to have toys, making do with what they found in nature. Because she read haltingly, she asked to go last. As with each story that had come before, her story prompted a cascade of comments: about how one could find happiness as a child in Mexico without material things, about how nature was all around you in Mexico but nowhere to be found in Chicago, about the sense of freedom and safety one felt there, a feeling they wished their children could have in their Chicago neighborhood. The woman sat silently and attentively through the discussion. As we collected our papers and began to put on our coats, she turned to me and commented, "Who would have thought that such a simple story would produce so much talk (*plática*)?"

As participants read their stories to the group, as they receive praise and suggestions for their work, and as they listen to the extensive discussion prompted by their stories, they begin to identify the value of their experience and their capacity to write. María G., the grandmother of a Telpochcalli student and a *ranchera* with little formal education, described this recognition in a piece she wrote about the experience of writing with the group:

For me, writing is a new experience. I have felt very comfortable with this group of *compañeras*. I like to share my experiences with them, since we have a lot in common.... I never would have imagined that I could write or that someone would be interested in what I write, but now I realize that this is not so. We all have stories to tell. We all have something interesting to write, and we can all become great writers.

Twice each year the writers have selected writings for publication, which appear in *Real Conditions* in Spanish and English. The value of their stories and thus their experiences grow as they circulate in the magazines and the women receive praise and appreciation from their families and friends. Not only have the magazines made their way into the community through local meetings, forums, or workshops; they also appear on the book shelves in most of the school's classrooms, and several teachers have incorporated the magazines into curriculum units. Teachers in the lower grades have used the stories primarily to teach reading and writing, and one teacher had the students write a response to the author of their favorite story. In one case, the upper grade students used the magazines, and even interviewed some of the writers, for a research report on the topic of "Chicago's immigrant communities." Often examples of class projects that use the magazines are displayed on the school's stairwell wall for all to see.

Periodically, the writers have had the opportunity to read selections of their writing in public forums. Some public readings have taken place as part of school-related events, such as an eighth-grade graduation fundraiser or end-of-year arts and culture festival. The writers also have given public readings at forums around the city at which their stories or the writing project itself has particular relevance. These have included a public hearing, parent involvement conferences, community forums, and a meeting of community and university partners. Often after the release of a magazine or a public reading, the group has shared stories about the enthusiasm with which particular people—daughters, husbands, friends—read or listened to the writers' stories. The women tell and listen to these stories with an enthusiasm bordering on astonishment, as though each demonstration of interest in or praise for their work is an antidote to the daily practices and social forces that diminish them. Recognizing the personal strength they gain from the group, some writers have described the workshop as therapeutic, while others have said it has helped them become "leaders" or "teachers." One mother told the group that writing and sharing her stories gave her the strength to carry on.

known as *"las escritoras"* ("the writers") and have taken on the role of the organization's scribes. They were recruited to write TCEP's mission statement, they are often asked to write and read testimonials for public forums, and a subgroup of writers has formed TCEP's Research and Evaluation Committee.

Philosophically, structurally, and practically, Telpochcalli School and the TCEP create a rare institutional space that supports and sustains the transnational, bicultural reality of the students and families it serves, and that recognizes parents as thinkers, educators, and community leaders. For the women in the writing workshop, who talk often and write occasionally about Telpochcalli, the school is a haven in which they know that their language, culture, and values are respected. Rebeca Nieto, one of the workshop participants whose two oldest daughters attend the school, described it in this way:

> Telpochcalli is a school that is completely bilingual in English and in Spanish. The students are very proud to study here because in this school one breathes a familial atmosphere. This is because the principal and the teachers are very friendly with the students and the parents, since they try to integrate an appreciation for our families, our community, our culture, and the world.

REWRITING THE HOMELAND, RECONFIGURING THE BARRIO

> Migration is a statement of an individual's wordview, and is, therefore, an extremely cultural event.
>
> (Tony Fielding, 1992).

Personal narrative, or creative nonfiction writing—the kind of writing we do in the Parents Write Their Worlds workshops—inevitably involves participants in the work of reminiscence on experiences from their past, reflection on their current lives, and expression of their desires and dreams for the future. In *Landscape for a Good Woman,* Steedman (1988) emphasized the storyteller's interpretive use of her past in order to explain her present life. Phillida Salmon (1992), by comparison, drew on reminiscence work she had done with elderly people to propose a different interpretive relationship between the present and past in storytelling. She suggested that "from the vantage point of their telling, earlier events are seen as leading up to later ones, and the current end of the story in some sense governs what is to be made of its earlier phases" (p. 219). For

Salmon, in other words, it is in the storyteller's interpretation of her present life that she gives meaning to her past. I suggest that Salmon and Steedman are each describing one facet of a dialectic: a process of mutual interpretation of past and present through which the storyteller imparts a sense of continuity to her life.

For people whose lives are not explained by official interpretive devices, telling stories that bring past and present together is one way they can give coherence and meaning to their own lives and, through this biographic coherence, to "put order in the world." For the Mexican immigrant women in the writing group, the distance between their past experiences and present lives is marked by ruptures of time, space and culture. The cultural work of mending these ruptures through storytelling is a gradual, collective, and critical process that has led the women to begin weaving together their past experiences in Mexico and their present lives in Chicago.

Since the writing program began, the participants have written alternately about experiences and people from their childhood and youth in Mexico, and their present lives in Chicago. The group's early writings maintain a consistent distinction between these two places that is at once spatial, temporal, and moral. The early stories about Mexico are nostalgic reminiscences of places and people located far away and in the writers' past, and the narrative is contained within Mexico. Stories about Chicago, while similarly restricted to that place, tend to address the challenges of settlement and the struggles of living in a poor inner city neighborhood. Rarely has a writer located stories about positive moments or pleasant places in Chicago, even when the writing prompt left the location open. In this section, I look at how the women have begun to bring these two places to bear on each other, and the ways in which that mutual interpretation has changed their representations of each place.

"Recordar es volver a vivir" ("To remember is to relive [the past]"). I have heard this refrain many times from women during workshop discussions as they read and reflected on stories about their childhood, youth, or young adult life in Mexico. Although they often have said this as an appreciative reflection upon their own or another writer's emotional response to the work of reminiscence, the stories the Telpochcalli mothers write and discuss in the workshop about their experiences as children, youth, and young adults in Mexico are not written versions of stories they tell about themselves on a regular basis. To the contrary, workshop participants frequently comment that these stories lead them to recall or "relive" moments from their past that they never talk or even think about. In other

words, these stories, drawn from childhood and youthful memories, are based on experiences to which the writers had not previously attributed any social value. This is one of the reasons the group work of reminiscence through storytelling is transformative.

Recently, a long-time workshop participant warned a newcomer: "Writing in this group makes you think about moments in your life you had completely forgotten about. And then another moment like that pops into your memory, and you realize how important that time was for you and you want to write that story too." This sense of the value of their childhood experiences comes not simply from writing them down, but from the sympathetic responses they receive as they read their stories to the group. Once these stories appear in print, they acquire additional value, in particular when the women read their pieces to their children. During workshop sessions, the writers frequently describe their children's enthusiastic responses to the stories and the curiosity about their past the stories provoke. "Ever since I began reading my children these stories about my childhood," commented one woman, "they are always asking me to tell them more stories about life in Mexico."

In their early writings about Mexico, participants might address the role an older family member has played in their life, describe a place that carried fond memories or made an impact on them in some way, or recount a village tradition or family custom that had value to them. Unlike Chicago, Mexico was never the locus of strife, or more precisely, strife was never the driving theme of the story. If anything, the women's early stories about Mexico provided a means of redeeming the poverty they suffered. For instance, several childhood stories describe the great sacrifices the writer's mother or grandmother made to buy her a modest gift, such as the paper doll María Pineda received from her mother for the Day of the Magi, or the cloth doll Rebeca Nieto's grandmother made for her. Other stories recount the hard work they and their siblings did as children to help out in the home, work that often kept them from play or from school. Yet the emphasis of these stories is never on their own suffering or deprivation, but rather on the way in which the family came together in mutual support, or the way in which the writer found solace or happiness in a special place or a humble toy. "Those gifts were so valuable," wrote María Pineda, "like the treasure of the Titanic."

The writers' early stories about Chicago, in contrast, usually are critical responses to daily struggles they, or other immigrants, faced in the city: a writer's struggle during her first months in Chicago to keep a factory job in the face of linguistic barriers, verbal abuse, and the deadening routine; the struggle of an undocumented worker's daily effort to travel to his far-away job; the conflicting desire for and resistance to learning English; or the dilemma about whether they, as mothers raising their children in conditions of poverty, should work outside the home or stay home to raise their children. Unlike the stories based on childhood memories, in these stories the women address issues that are frequent topics of conversation at the school, at TCEP meetings, and in the community. That the women have written more assertively and critically about these issues since the workshop began may be attributable in part to the public currency and legitimacy the issues command, both in local conversation and in the local and national media.

Nonetheless, like the early stories the women wrote based on their childhood experiences in Mexico, in nearly all the early writings about settlement and life in the city, the authors contained their discussion to Chicago or the United States. This is the case whether they were writing about how they came to the decision to stay at home rather than work outside the house, about their dreams for their neighborhood, or about an arduous journey north and the pain, fear, and humiliation they experienced crossing the border. It is even the case that in these exceptional stories, the authors provide a positive depiction of their life in Chicago, as in Teresa Elen Dávila's story about the church she attends in her neighborhood, a place that "feels so much like another world I don't ever want to leave," or María Luisa Tellez' story "My Kitchen," in which she describes the warm, familial scene in her "simple but spacious" kitchen, the place where she spends most of her day and where the family unites at the end of the day: "We talk, we laugh, and we have a lot of fun. It is our favorite place." The spatial and temporal separation between Mexico and Chicago represented in these early stories and the moral and even aesthetic distinctions between the two places that reinforce that separation seem to express what Roger Rouse (1992) called a "cultural bifocality": "a capacity to see the world alternately through quite different kinds of lenses" (p. 41). In this sense the women's early stories also seem to acquiesce to the spatial, temporal, and cultural bipolarity of the mythology of assimilation.

The initial sharing of written work can be very threatening (Fitzpatrick, 1995), and it is possible that the women's early writings reflect a version of their world they were comfortable sharing with the group and, in the case of the published writings, with an imagined readership. In contrast to the writings, however, the group discussions that followed the reading of these early stories rarely reiterated the radical spatial, temporal, or moral distinctions represented in the written stories. For instance, a story about a favorite place to play near the *rancho* prompted comments about the lack of safe spaces available to their children in the inner city neighborhood; another woman's story about the family's regular outings to help her father sow or harvest their crops led to a conversation that moved from the bucolic landscape of their native towns to their present efforts to keep the family united, and to a discussion of how working together was as important as relaxing together. Similarly, the stories about coveted dolls or amulets they had received as children spawned lengthy discussion about the easy availability of material goods in the United States, even for poor people like themselves, and about the challenges of teaching their children to appreciate the few things they had.

These discussions did more than prompt the participants to use memories of Mexico as the moral compass by which to judge life in Chicago. They also led the writers to share stories about more trying aspects of life in Mexico: experiences of poverty, family strife, or personal loss that they were reluctant to include in their written work. This process of writing stories about their past, and the subsequent discussion about the significance of their experiences has served not only to give value to the women's pasts, but also to provide the critical and creative spark through which the women have come to reflect and write differently about their lives—to "see beyond what one sees physically," as Rebeca Nieto put it in a piece entitled "To Write."

I want to signal two ways in which the women's writing has changed. First, their stories increasingly contain both Mexico and Chicago in their frame. Some stories have revolved around the comparison of some aspect of their childhood in Mexico with a comparable aspect of their children's lives in Chicago. Claudia Romo has compared the celebration of May festivals in her native town to the ways they are celebrated in Little Village. María Pineda has offered direct counsel to her children about how to deal with unfair assessments in the classroom by telling a story about her experience of an injustice during her years in secondary school. In more recent stories, the writers have punctuated descriptions of a memorable outing or family activity—in each case the story contained implicit counsel—with a comment about how they have tried to bring the lessons they learned from that person to bear on the ways they live their lives in Chicago or raise their own children. "Now that I am an adult and married I always remember [my mother's] advice and lessons," wrote Rebeca Nieto. Leticia Bravo similarly ended a story about her trip to the market with her grandmother by noting: "Now I tell my children what I learned from my parents and my grandparents. I tell them how important it is that the whole family stay united, and above all to respect all people."

Second, this juxtaposing of Mexico and Chicago has led the women to write about their pasts from a more critical perspective. They write with more ambivalence and less nostalgia about the poverty they suffered, and they write more openly about family strife. Over time, the women have begun to draw on their childhood experiences in Mexico, not only to provide the moral basis from which to judge U.S. culture, but also to justify their migration north and to illuminate those qualities of life that they lacked or longed for as children in Mexico, but have been able to create for their children in Chicago. María Pineda has written about the sacrifices she and her husband made to buy a computer for their daughters, comparing their ability to do so with her mother's inability to provide her with the typewriter she needed for school. Guadalupe Lopez has written candidly about her troubled childhood experience, in which her two parents were so busy working that they became oblivious to the fact that her brothers were getting into serious trouble. In a conversation about the story as it went to print, Guadalupe noted that "people may think I am disrespectful by writing these things about my parents. It's not that they didn't love us. But I want parents here to know what the consequences might be if they put work first and forget to look after their children." Guadalupe's story is one of many showing how the women have resisted the proletarianization of their labor, especially when it has threatened their ability to be good mothers, according to their own values of motherhood. This is an important theme I return to later in the chapter.

Another example is Hermila Taboras' story "In the Kitchen." "When my children all arrive from school," the story begins, "they run right to the kitchen. They say to me, some speaking in Spanish and others in English, 'Mom, what is there to eat'?" Hermila then describes a delightful scene in which each of her children recounts their day as they sit to eat. "This is something very important for me," Hermila continues, "because I would have liked to do the same with my parents. But unfortunately there was not this kind of communication between us because when they weren't working, they were doing other things." Hermila ends her story by noting that it is because of her own experience growing up that she tries to "help my children whenever and in whatever way I can." It bears noting that Hermila, a woman who came to the program in its second year, wrote this story for her third workshop session. Because the value of the women's experiences and stories and their legitimacy as writers are sustained through the ongoing work of the group and made material by the magazine, the writers' collective confidence, creativity, and conviction continue to be passed on as new participants join the program and others move on.

The writers' work of mediating their past and present also has contributed to their critical rewriting of the neighborhood and their life in Chicago. Telpochcalli School, the site of the writing workshop and the school that most of the participants' children attend, is located in Little Village. Little Village is a predominantly Mexican, working poor neighborhood that, along with the contiguous neighborhood of Pilsen, forms Chicago's largest, most concentrated, and most segregated "Mexicano" community (Guerra ,1998, p. 24).[9] Nearly half the residents immediately surrounding Telpochcalli are immigrants to the United States, and the majority speak Spanish as their primary language.

From the perspective of community organizers, social service providers, and urban researchers, Little Village looks like many inner city neighborhoods. Residents live in a historic port of entry plagued in recent decades by processes of urban restructuring in which factories and other blue collar businesses have closed or been displaced, while gentrification nibbles at the neighborhood's heels. Current residents of Little Village face high rates of poverty, gang and drug-related violence, and limited access to living wage jobs, social services, recreational facilities, higher education or legal status for their families, all of which "makes Little Village residents some of the least advantaged people in the country" (Telpochcalli Community Education Project, 2003).

Meanwhile, from the perspective of social researchers interested in new patterns of global migration, Little Village is a vibrant community with a distinctly transnational commercial, cultural, religious, and recreational life. Researchers commonly refer to two qualities in particular that characterize the neighborhood as a transnational community. The first is the frequency, rapidity, and ease with which family members, material goods, and cultural products circulate between Mexico and the Pilsen/Little Village community, such that migration itself is formative of the cultural and social life of the community (Schiller, Basch, & Blanc-Szanton, 1992; Hurtig, 2000, p. 34). The second is the notion that Pilsen/Little Village is not merely the port of entry for migrants determined to settle in the host country, as assimilationist models of immigration would have it. Rather, it is incorporated culturally, socially, and economically into a larger spatially dispersed, transmigrant

culture (Hurtig, 2000, p. 32; Rouse, 1991). Nestor Rodríguez (2003) suggested that in immigrant settlement communities such as Little Village,
which he characterizes as "binational," intragroup relations between new
immigrants and long-term residents develop, such that for first-generation
immigrants, "incorporation into the mainstream or into established ethnic
groups of English-speaking Latinos becomes optional in the presence of a
highly viable binational social structure" (p. 83).

Each of these depictions of the immigrant neighborhood—as inner city
barrio and as transnational community—responds critically to certain aspects of the mythology of assimilation. For the women in the writing program, putting order in their world has involved writing stories about their
neighborhood that draw upon and partially reconcile these two perspectives, but that do so in their own terms, particularly as mothers. In a story
entitled "Nuestro barrio" ("Our Neighborhood"), María Pineda, a mother
who moved out of Little Village because of its plights but continued to
bring her children to Telpochcalli, gave a sense of how the residents of Little Village participate in and draw upon the construction of *Mexicanidad* to
respond to the plights and contradictions of their neighborhood, including
racial tensions with the Black community up the street, the vibrance of a
lively commercial district that belies the neighborhood's chronic poverty,
and an abundance of spirited children eager to play after school but
whisked home and away from the omnipresent street threats of gangs,
drugs, and violence:

> People live in a state of anxiety, but we live like this, not because we like it,
> but out of necessity. The Little Village neighborhood is very active. We feel
> identified with each other. Although there are few murals, it seems pictur-
> esque. On 26th Street there is always activity. On weekends, it is full of cars
> and people. Some come from other places and states. They come to shop or
> simply cruise on the street, showing off their cars and pickups. Others, the
> young ones, watch the girls. 26th Street is identified by the arch, many stores,
> the September 16th Day[10] parade, restaurants, and other events. That is our
> neighborhood, very Mexican. We are united with Cermak Street. Even if they
> are different streets, it is the same; we are all Mexican.

Certainly, the partial social autonomy of the neighborhood, as well as the
viability and legitimacy of Mexican culture within the neighborhood produced by this transnational context, lends credibility to the women's goals
as writers, and supports their narrative juxtaposing of Mexican and U.S. culture and social life. At the same time, the neighborhood's *Mexicanidad* op-

erates in tension with the assimilationist mythology of the dominant society, a mythology that continues to relegate neighborhoods such as Pilsen/Little Village to the margins of its social landscape. Rebeca Nieto, a writer who has participated in the writing workshop since its inception, responded to this marginalization in a story entitled *"¡El valor de los mexicanos!"* ("The Value of Mexicans!"). This story, which she published in the fourth magazine, has many of the characteristics I identify as indicative of the women's conscious resistance to assimilationist models through their writing.

Unlike Rebeca's earlier stories—reminiscences of her childhood and family life in Mexico or positive reflections on experiences she and her children have had at Telpochcalli—she began this story by comparing locally recreated Mexican national festivals to "the way it is done in Mexico." She then related the performance of these festivals to the festivals of her native village, recounting an experience she had as girl when she played the drum in the parades. Having created a strong and positive link between her Mexican childhood and her adult life in Chicago in the story's first paragraph, Rebeca then made a dramatic shift: "But sometimes in this country we are discriminated against for being Mexican," she wrote. Drawing on her own experience, she continued: "On one occasion I heard the security guards that maintain order at the parade comment among themselves, saying, 'These Mexicans are so scandalous; why don't they go back to their own country?'"

Rebeca's response to the denegration of Mexicans and Mexican culture was proud and redemptive: "They [the guards] don't realize that we Mexicans are full of life, with a great desire to improve ourselves and with the dreams that we wish to convert into reality." She then defended her people in a way that integrated the values of her people that mark their difference and those that mark their conformity with the mainstream: "Not only do we dress in brilliant colors and play contagious music," she contended, "inside of us one finds the seeds of work and effort to improve ourselves and move ahead. Some work and others study in order to be able to reach our dreams and make a better life for ourselves and our children, always struggling so that our values will be recognized."

In the last sentence of her story, Rebeca identified several dimensions of her and the other writers' daily lives that operate in tension and even conflict with each other, and which they work to reconcile in their writing. These include work, education, their own self-improvement, their children's futures, and the values from their past that they struggle to maintain and live by. Whereas the women's daily efforts to address these issues are perennial themes for group writing and discussion, the one topic that leads them to confront the mythology of assimilation most directly is whether to work outside the home or not.

This theme has prompted endless stories: some about friends, neighbors, or relatives in which both parents worked and the children grew up neglected, troubled, and in trouble; others about the pressures of materialism in this country and their efforts to resist those pressures and put the care of their children first. Often stories about their children's well-being, education, and safety have lead directly to discussions about the relative merits of working outside the house or staying home to raise and watch over the kids. For 2 years, the writing group's many participants have been unanimous in their position that the material comforts additional income might bring to their households were not worth the risk of their children "losing their paths" if not cared for and supervised by their mothers.

This is not to say that each woman in the group has come to this decision in the same way, or with the same long-term intentions for her life. Whereas some of the women are intrinsically uninterested in paid work and consider motherhood to be their "vocation," others have chosen not to look for paid work as long as they have children still living at home. Still other women have explored the option of combining informal service work with the care of their own children, or that of earning money by caring for a neighbor's children in the home.

What I have found most compelling about the women's stories on and discussions of this theme is the way that they resist the mythology of assimilation as they struggle to reconcile the value of family integrity they draw from their past and the personal pleasure and sense of fulfillment they derive from mothering, the hopes and dreams they have for themselves and their children, and the dangers and limitations they face as a result of their current socioeconomic condition. Given these women's critical understanding of their situation and their options, one would be hard pressed to draw the conclusion, as some researchers have suggested, that these immigrant women's decision not to work outside the home is a capitulation to traditional Mexican patriarchal family arrangements.[11] More likely, it is both a reasoned response to the real conditions of their lives and a form of resistance to the modern capitalist patriarchal arrangements and values they encounter in the United States.

MOTHERS AS WRITERS

As the many stories I have cited or described thus far may have made clear already, the primary social position and personal perspective from which the Telpochcalli mothers write is that of motherhood. The writers identify themselves as mothers to their readers. They care about being writers in the eyes of their children, and they tell many (although not all) of their stories for their children. This is not to say that they write "children's stories," but rather, as they state in the introduction to the third magazine, that they write their stories so their children "will know where they come from and what their roots are" and so their traditions will be read, not only by their children but by their grandchildren as well.

There are two points about this social positioning I highlight here. The first is that, as the stories I described in the previous section illustrate, the women mediate their two worlds—their past and their present—as mothers. In nearly every writing in which Mexico and Chicago are juxtaposed, the tension, contrast, or continuity between the two places is mediated by the writer's role as mother. It is thus as mothers that they struggle to reconcile the values of their native land and the opportunities they associate with the place they currently call home.

In a story entitled *"El clima de Chicago"* ("Chicago Weather"), María Luisa Tellez conveyed the visceral impact of her move to Chicago through a contrast between the climates of Chicago and her native Mexico. "When I came to Chicago," she wrote, "I was struck to see such a sad, gray city, the trees without leaves and the wind so cold it chills you to the bones. The climate is very extreme, whether in winter or summer." In Mexico, by comparison, "the climate is pleasant all year round. The trees are always green and they don't lose their leaves. One rarely sees gray and sad days. Of course there are rainy days, but what I love is how it rains for a while and then a radiant sun comes out."

In some ways the sensibility of María Luisa's story sounds conventionally assimilationist. For her, as harsh, sad, lonely, or uncomfortable as the transition to a new place, new climate, and new way of life may be, one adapts. "[As] time passes, María wrote, "one gets used to it. Today I can say I like Chicago." What strikes me about her story, however, is the ending: "Now the rainy and sad days are brightened by my children, with their mischief and innocence." In the end, it is her children who compensate for the climatic and, one can imagine, cultural losses María Luisa has suffered by making the journey to this country.

For other women in the writing program, writing about settlement is cultural work laden with ambivalence. Rebeca Nieto conveyed this ambivalence in her story *"Una triste realidad"* ("A Sad Reality"). After rationalizing the difficulties of migration in terms of the desire to make a better life for one's children, she described the difficulties of starting a new life in a country that "is like a time machine [where] people get sick from working so much." Rebeca concluded with the comment: "I think if there were more jobs and less poverty in our country, many of us would not be here."

The second point to make about the writers' social positioning as mothers is that it is the most common point of reference from which they use their stories to give counsel. It is as mothers that they assess the lessons learned as children and bring them to bear upon their current lives and daily decisions about how to raise their children. It is as mothers that they have found value in the activities of reading and writing, which they call upon their readers to "instill in our children." It is as mothers that they question the intrinsic value of paid work if it takes time away from raising and nurturing their children, and it is as mothers that they are committed to maintaining the language, traditions, and customs of their homeland.

Finally, it is as mothers that the writers articulate their dreams for a better community. We read this in Leticia Bravo's story *"La fuente"* ("The Fountain"), in which she demystified the picturesque image of a neighborhood fountain and park by signaling how rare such places are in the neighborhood, and by expressing the need for more places "where our children are safer, places where they can practice their sports and recreate." In *"Un sueño para mi barrio"* ("A Dream for My Neighborhood"), Guadalupe Lopez described a safe, clean, cooperative neighborhood in which mothers work together to raise and educate the neighborhood's children. Guadalupe's dream was not simply for her own children, but for the neighborhood as a community, and the role of mothering it envisioned was not confined to the nuclear family, but was collective and communal.

Motherhood is not, in other words, an intrinsically conservative social position from which to write. Rather, in responding to the androcentric, patriarchal mythology of assimilation, it is a position of critique, of resistance, a position that calls for the rewriting of that mythology. As a social role, identity, and experience, motherhood requires definition over and against the prevailing myths of both Mexican and U.S. societies. Thus, at the same time the women write as mothers, they inscribe themselves upon a landscape of immigrant life according to their own terms for motherhood.

Moreover, by drawing on their experiences of mothering, but also of being mothered, and by narrating their stories from their affective position as mothers, the women's writing becomes an intimate, interpersonal interpretive practice. Like the collective, literate work of clubswomen Anne Gere (1997) described in her book *Intimate Practices,* this intimacy infuses the writers' "continual textual negotiations with special power" because it gives the writers "the capacity to imagine new possibilities for themselves, to change their desires" (p. 53). In this way we can understand the writers' literate creation of an alternative landscape of immigrant life and their self-positioning on that landscape as immigrant mothers as mutually constituting acts of resistance.

CONCLUSION

In *The Politics of Education,* Paolo Freire (1984) wrote that "only a literacy that associates the learning of reading and writing with a creative act will exercise the critical comprehension of that experience, and without any illusion of triggering liberation, it will nevertheless contribute to its process" (p. 17). Over the past 2 years, the Mexican immigrant women who have participated in the Parents Write Their Worlds program have begun to exercise a critical comprehension of their experiences as immigrant mothers, writing stories challenging dominant interpretations of the immigrant experience that fail to account for their experiences, and replacing these interpretations with their own. Although I agree with Freire that these women's social, creative, and critical activity will not necessarily trigger liberation, I have argued that their work of writing, reading, discussing, and publishing their stories constitutes a form of resistance and thus contributes to the process of liberation. In the early months of the writing workshop, the writers enacted their resistance indirectly through their written representation of alternative worlds and values, but over time their resistance has become more direct, explicit, extensive, and self-conscious. This is evidenced by their willingness to rewrite previous, nostalgic versions of life in Mexico in more critical terms, by their clear articulation of the magazine's purpose, and by their inclination to give counsel to their readers in increasingly direct ways, albeit always building the moral of their stories upon their own experiences.

Through the support of the group and through the individual and collective positions from which they write their stories, the women also "work hard to sustain compelling images of alternative possibilities" (Rouse, p. 41) for their present lives and their children's future. By drawing critically on the moral and social norms from both their past and present experiences to give counsel to their children and their peers, the writers effectively and creatively challenge the moral assumptions and implications of the mythology of assimilation and begin to create an alternative synthesis, and thus an alternative landscape for future action.

Carolyn Steedman (1986) began *Landscape for a Good Woman* by noting that her mother shaped her childhood "by the stories she carried from her own, and from an earlier family history" (p. 8). To what extent these women's acts of resistance will shape the stories their second-generation children tell and write in response to the myths of assimilation they had contended with on a daily basis is a question that calls for more stories and more writing.

REFERENCES

Adams, H., & Hurtig, J. (2002). Creative acts, critical insights: Adult writing workshops in two Chicago neighborhoods. In E. Auerbach (Ed.), *Community partnerships* (pp. 147–158). Alexandria, VA: TESOL.

Anzaldúa, G. (1981). Speaking in tongues: A letter to 3rd world women writers. In C. Moraga & G. Anzaldúa (Eds.), *This bridge called my back: Writings by radical women of color*. New York: Kitchen Table: Women of Color Press.

Ayers, W., Klonsky, M., &. Lyon, G. H. (Eds.). (2000.) *A simple justice: The challenge of small schools*. New York: Teachers College Press.

Benjamin, W. (1969). *Illuminations*. New York: Shocken Books.

Brandt, D. (1990). *Literacy as involvement: The acts of writers, readers, and texts*. Carbondale: Southern Illinois University Press.

Brettell, C. (2003). *Anthropology and migration: Essays on transnationalism, ethnicity, and identity*. Walnut Creek, CA: Altamira Press.

Farr, M. (forthcoming). *Rancheros in Chicagoacán: Ways of speaking and identity in a Mexican transnational community*. Austin: University of Texas Press.

Fielding, T. (1992). Migration and culture. In T. Champion & T. Fielding (Eds.), *Migration processes and patterns* (pp. 201–212). London: Belhaven Press.

Fitzpatrick, S. (1995). Sailing out from safe harbours: Writing for publishing in adult basic education. In J. Mace (Ed.), *Literacy, language and community publishing: Essays in adult education* (pp. 11–22). Clevedon, Avon: Multilingual Matters Ltd.

Friere, P. (1971). *Pedagogy of the oppressed*. New York: Herder and Herder.

Friere, P. (1985). *The politics of education: Culture, power and liberation*. South Hadley, MA: Bergin & Garvey.

Gere, A. R. (1997). *Intimate practices: Literacy and cultural work in U.S. women's clubs: 1880–1920*. Urbana and Chicago: University of Illinois Press.

Guerra, J. C. (1998). *Close to home: Oral and literate practices in a transnational mexicano community*. New York: Teachers College Press.

Gutmann, M., Matos-Rodríguez, F. V., Stephen, L., & Zavella, P. (Eds.). (2003). Malden, MA: Blackwell.

Hollinger, D. (1995). *Postethnic America: Beyond multiculturalism*. New York: Basic Books.

Hurtig, J. (2000). Hispanic immigrant churches and the construction of ethnicity. In L. W. Livezey (Ed.), *Public religion and urban transformation: Faith in the city* (pp. 29–56). Albany, NY: New York University Press.

Lorde, A. (1984). *Sister outsider*. Trumansburg, NY: The Crossing Press.

Lyon, G. H. (2000). When *jamás* is enough: Creating a school for a community (A conversation with Tamara Witzl). In W. Ayers, M. Klonsky, & G. H. Lyon (Eds.), *A simple justice: The challenge of small schools* (pp. 125–136). New York: Teachers College Press.

Mace, J. (1995). Reminiscence as literacy: Intersections and creative moments. In J. Mace (Ed.), *Literacy, language and community publishing: Essays in adult education* (pp. 23–35). Clevedon, Avon: Multilingual Matters Ltd.

Mahler, S. J. (2003). "Engendering transnational migration: A case study of Salvadorans." In P. Hondagneu-Sotelo (Ed.), *Gender and U.S. immigration: Contemporary trends* (pp. 287–316). Berkeley: University of California Press.

Massey, D., Alarcón, R., Durand, J., & González, H. (1987). *Return to Aztlán: The social process of international migration from western Mexico*. Berkeley: University of California Press.

Omi, M., & Winant, H. (1994). *Racial formation in the United States: From the 1960s to the 1990s*. New York: Routledge.

Pessar, P. (1986). The role of gender in Dominican settlement in the United States. In J. Nash & H. Safa (Eds.), *Women and change in Latin America* (pp. 273–294). South Hadley, MA: Bergin and Garvey.

Pessar, P. (2003). Engendering migration studies: The case of new immigrants to the United States. In P. Hondagneu-Sotelo (Ed.), *Gender and U.S. immigration: Contemporary trends* (pp. 20–24). Berkeley: University of California Press.

Rodríguez, N. (2003). The real "new world order": The globalization of racial and ethnic relations in the late 20th century. In M. Gutmann, F. V. Matos-Rodríguez, L. Stephen, & P. Zavella (Eds.), *Perspectives on Las Américas: A reader in culture, history and representation* (pp. 81–85). Malden, MA: Blackwell.

Rouse, R. (1991). Mexican migration and the social space of postmodernism. *Diaspora 1*(1), 8–23.

Rouse, R. (1992). Making sense of settlement: Class transformation, cultural struggle, and transnationalism among Mexican migrants in the United States: Towards a transnational perspective on migration. In N. Glick Schiller, L. Basch, & C. Blanc-Szanton (Eds.), Towards a transnational perspective on migration. *Annals of the New York Academy of Sciences, 645*, 25–52.

Salmon, P. (1992). Old age and storytelling. In K. Kimberley, M. Meek, & J. Miller (Eds.), *New readings: Contributions to an understanding of literacy* (pp. 216–223). London: A & C Black.

Schiller, N. G., Basch, L., & Blanc-Szanton, C. (1992). *Towards a transnational perspective on migration* (vol. 645, pp. 1–24). New York: Annals of the New York Academy of Sciences.

Steedman, C. K. (1986). *Landscape for a good woman: A story of two lives*. New Brunswick, NJ: Rutgers University Press.

Telpochcalli Community Education Project. (2003). "Proposal to the Chicago Community Trust."

ENDNOTES

1. Special thanks to the women in the Parents Write their Worlds group, to the staff at Telpochcalli School, and to Hal Adams for his insight and support through many versions of this chapter. Thanks also to Elsa Auerbach, Bill Ayers, Lesley Bartlett, Marcia Farr, Anita Hurtig, Janet Isserlis, Victor Ortiz, and Bianca Wilson for comments and conversations that have informed this chapter. My work at Telpochcalli has been supported by a Spencer Foundation Small Grant and a University of Illinois at Chicago Great Cities Institute Faculty Scholarship.

2. On the mythologies of assimilation, pluralism, and multiculturalism see Hollinger (1995), Omi and Winant (1994), several chapters in Schiller, Basch, and Blanc-Szanton (1992), and several chapters in Guttman et al. (2003).

3. This passage is my own synthesis and paraphrasing of several passages in Benjamin's (1969) inspiring essay. Benjamin describes how the fairy tale in particular, and not stories in general, responds to the need for counsel created by the myth (p. 102).

4. For the sake of readability, I have included only the English translations of the women's writings, as they appeared in the magazines.

5. At the request of the writers, I have used their actual names and not pseudonyms, despite the conventions of academic ethics, when quoting from their published work. In all other cases I have used pseudonyms.

6. On the concept of immigrant neighborhoods as points along a transmigratory circuit, see Massey, et al. (1987), and Rouse (1991, 1992). For descriptions of Chicago's Mexican community of Pilsen/Little Village as a transnational migratory space or transnational neighborhood see Guerra (2000), Hurtig (2000), and Farr (forthcoming).

7. I place the term "small school" in quotes to signal Telpochcalli's philosophical affinity with the small schools movement, and its concrete relationship to the Small Schools Workshop at the University of Illinois at Chicago (Ayers, Klonsky, & Lyon, 2000). The Small Schools Workshop had a central role in the school's initial planning and development phase in the mid-1990s, and continues to provide technical and structural support to the school.

8. Nahuatl, an indigenous language spoken in central Mexico, was the lingua franca of the Aztecs.

9. Guerra uses the term "Mexicano" to refer to people of Mexican origin born in Mexico or their U.S.-born children who self-identify as Mexicano/Mexicana, in distinction to the term "Chicano" which refers to people of Mexican origin born in the United States. In some contexts, these labels have a political valence. When the women in the writing group, all of whom were born in Mexico, refer

to themselves as *madres mexicanas*, they do so descriptively and not for any political connotation the term may hold.
10. September 16th is Mexican Independence Day.
11. This perspective has a long history in research on women and immigration. For recent discussions of this perspective see Pessar (2003) and Mahler (2003). Here I am not arguing against these researchers' analysis per se, but rather suggesting that it does not apply to the women in the writing program.

Photograph by Ana Colomb.

10

Readings With Mexican Immigrant Mothers: Expanding Our Horizons by Expanding Theirs

Ana Ubilluz Colomb
University of Illinois at Chicago

Words visit us,
without announcing themselves,
visit our heart whispering
visit our minds demanding
an idea and then,
they peel it, destroying it.

Morpheus struggles to shield us.
Pretending innocence
Still, the English words blast
the remote corners of our lunacy
and our native intimacy.

Erratic, improper, devious
So unreliable,
many times
so utterly limiting,
they empty us

Rhythmical, sharp and quick,
Cadential, slow and sensual,

At times piercing
at times holding us,

visiting you, me, and them,
they both limit us,
and sustain us.

(Ana Ubilluz Colomb 2002)

I am my language. .... I will overcome the tradition of silence. (Anzaldúa, 1987)

FAILING ENGLISH AS A SECOND LANGUAGE (ESL) 1992

Twenty Mexican women are looking at me trying to understand what I am try-ing to say. Across the big room, Margarita, the other ESL instructor at a Pilsen[1] elementary school, is instructing her ESL students (Mexican immigrant moth-ers of school children) about the craft of making a fruit salad including back-ground knowledge about the juicy produce, quantities, and culinary vocabulary. She had the perfect ingredients for an eventful and unforgettable class, and then, just across the aisle, I could savor my failing class. Everyone in Margarita's class is up from their desks, laughingly pronouncing the foreign words: "cut," "peel," "tablespoon," "bowl," and on and on.

My class is about thermometers. A week before, after one of our twice-a-week ESL classes, Inés, one of the mothers, and I had talked about home remedies. Our conversation, of course, as it is for many people who share a common first language, was in the language into which we had been born, Spanish. But then I had smeared the conversation with my questioning:

Inés:	*Híjole, que tenía de fiebre el muchachito, que llamo a mi cuñada, le dimos Tilenol me parece y ya se le pasó al rato. Pero qué susto nos pegamos.*
Ana:	*Y ¿cuánto tenía de fiebre?*
Inés:	*Y ¿yo que sé? Sólo que volaba.*
Ana:	*¿No tenía termómetro, Inés?*
Inés:	*Y así lo tuviera, para ponérmelo en la oreja o algo, porque yo ni cómo agarrarlo.*

Inés:	Damn it, that boy had so much fever that I called my sister-in-law and we gave him Tylenol I think, and it went away. But what a scare we had.
Ana:	And, how much fever did he have?
Inés:	And, how do I know that? Only that he was flying ["high" fever].
Ana:	Didn't you have a thermometer?
Inés:	Even if I had it, [I would have had] to stick it in my ear or something, because I don't even know how to hold it.

Inés is always worried about her oldest son who has many health problems. I would help her situation in my next class, I thought, by teaching her and the other mothers to read thermometers. I bought some cheap ones at the dollar store, created a vocabulary and questions sheet, and I helped my students, women from rural Mexico who averaged three grades of formal education, with their English and their motherhood anxieties.

The thermometers are hard to read. The degrees are marked only on the 96.8 and the 101 red lines. All of a sudden everyone develops myopia, and nobody has reading glasses to count tiny little lines to get the readings. We have to forego the decimals, and the English.

"¿Es mucha la diferencia entre 99° y 100°, como 99° es una fiebre chiquita, 100 es fiebre moribunda?"
"No, antes de 100° es lo que nosotros llamamos calentura."
"Entonces ¿ para qué ponen esa flechita allí?"
"Para que se empiece a preocupar señora."

"Is there a big difference between 99° and 100°, like 99° is a small fever and 100 a dying fever?"
"No, before 100 is what we call *calentura* [feverish]."
"Then, why do they put that arrow there?"
"So you can begin to worry, *señora*."

Not long after, Inés and everyone are eating Margarita's class's luscious, ripe fruits, perfect ingredients to make an American fruit salad, with whipped cream and all. I look over to the other side of the room. The sterile thermometers are turning cold.

Now, years later, I realize that good intentions and much excitement were not enough. I still failed my ESL class. There is no more dramatic illustration of this than my attitude toward the teaching of English to Mexican mothers with low-level literacy. First was my training and my insistence that adult ESL classes should be held in English only, no matter what reading materials were involved. Second, rather than perceiving the possibility that the mothers needed to talk about critical issues such as health or clinics, I perceived Ines' lack of knowledge about a thermometer as a possible threat to the health of her family. An innocuous topic became the source of difficulty for the mothers.

TWO YEARS LATER: A LETTER[2] TO ANA FROM CARMEN, 1994

Two years after this ESL class, I became the literacy trainer for Inés, Carmen, Rosa, and 11 other women in the second part of the literacy program that

still provided ESL classes. After 2 years of participating in the literacy training, I received this letter, which from that day on guided my literacy training:

Estimada Ana:

*este año, para mi, quisiera poder aprender más, porque ha medida qué
aprendo algo nuevo me entusiasma mas ... quisiera poder aprender todo lo
que usted nos quisiera enseñar. Para así poder enseñar a otros padres lo que
he aprendido quizás poder lograr lo que una maestra buena logra*

Y así poder ayudar a mis hijos también.

Carmen

Dear Ana:

this year for me I would like to be able to learn more, because to the extent
that I learn something new makes me more enthusiastic.... I would like to
learn everything that you might want to teach us. In that way teach other parents what I have learned perhaps achieving what a good teacher achieves

And in that way also help my children.

Carmen

Carmen, like most of the other mothers in the literacy training program,
had been demanding for months that their roles within the program
change. They wanted more for themselves. Although the family literacy
program had been offering them ESL classes twice a week, and literacy
classes twice a month, at the heart of the program was the expectation
that the mothers learn, and then perform, certain sanctioned literacy behaviors or tasks at home with their children. Their concern for their roles as
trainers began to surface, as Carmen pointed out in her letter. Their concern had become intense.

For more than a year now, the mothers had complained about the limitations of the program for meeting their own learning needs, as well as for
their teaching of others. Their perception that the family literacy program
would be beneficial for their children's education had catapulted them to
participate, but as their experiences in the program matured, they began
to find faults with the literacy program that they once endorsed. They
wanted to improve it by creating better "training" workshops in which they
could learn how better to instruct their peers: other Mexican mothers in
the neighborhood. They craved to open up other venues for developing a
new type of literacy program, one that included their literacy needs and
their personal and social needs as women.

During our time together, we had spent countless hours discussing pertinent issues about their life conditions: *conversaciones de la grandísima ... vida*, talks about the mother ... life, I said once. This had been so valuable to them, so basically essential that they wanted more of this for themselves, and just as important, more for the mothers they trained, and more to give to their children. Such offerings, they believed, would allow them and the others to find more ways to support their children that went beyond just instilling in them "proper U.S. literacy behaviors."

Research tells us that many times literacy classes are boring and irrelevant to the interests and needs of the participants, and that given the intensity of the lives the participants lead, attending loses "meaning" quickly (Schmelkes & Kalman, 1996; Zuñiga, 1999). Related research in literacy programs states that when women have any opportunity to further their literacy knowledge, they often opt to not enter, and drop out of the program right after they begin to attend (Stromquist, 1997; van der Westen, 1994).

The attrition for this family literacy program mirrored these national trends. Yet, this group of trainers was different because, unlike those in many programs, they had an added sense of responsibility for training other mothers in the ways of U.S. literacy. During our meetings, many had learned that their opinions were needed, were welcomed, and were guiding the way I instructed. They provided these by suggestions, lived examples, questions, and at times, pleading letters. Therefore, in retrospect, because the mothers had established close relationships with each other and with me, it was neither peculiar that mothers in the training group sought something "different," perhaps something more meaningful, nor strange that I received Carmen's letter pleading her case before the beginning of our third year.

Thus, this chapter tells us the story of mothers who chose to stay in a family program, but only after they sought change and "custody" for their own learning.

READING AND THE ABSENCE OF BOOKS

Ideas on how to bridge the gap between the mothers' own educational experiences and the educational experiences they were hoping to receive were many: workshops on how to speak publicly, how to use different methods to teach others, and how to become a family literacy paraprofessional; and classes for such subjects as mathematics and reading and writing. Yet, our decision to read novels began with Rosa and Inés' conversation. I remember exactly the moment that everything started to change:

> *Rosa:* *Los niños son el reflejo de uno, de uno mismo. Y a veces decimos, de donde salió este monstruo? Como podemos motivar a los monstruos, sino nosotras no somos mejor(es).*
>
> *Inés:* *Yo ni leo siquiera, hago mis tareas para dar las clases de los viernes o para venir aquí, pero no leo. No tengo libros siquiera uno para releer[lo].*

> Rosa: Children are our reflection, our own. And sometimes we say, where do these monsters [children] come from? How can we motivate the monsters, if we [feminine we] are not any better.
>
> Ines: I do not even read, I do my homework for the Friday classes or to come here, but I do not read. I do not even have one [book] to re-read.

The absence of books in their homes intensified the crucial concern that separated their children's reading practices from their own. The only books the families had at home were those of their children: small children's books in Spanish borrowed from the library or bought at the school and the literacy program's book fairs, or older children's English schoolbooks from school and the library. Some mothers read with their small children, but many just heard the children read, for they wanted to make sure their children read well and read in Spanish. Older children, who already could read in English, were encouraged to read on their own, and there were very few questions or conversations about their readings. The mothers' struggles as family literacy givers were being undermined because their personal practices were disconnected from their children's readings in the English language.

> *Sabia leer.*
>
> *Fue el descubrimiento más grande de su vida. Sabia leer. Era poseedor del antídoto contra el ponzoñoso veneno de la vejez. Sabia leer. Pero no tenía que leer* (Sepúlveda, 1989, p. 62).

> He could read!
>
> It was most the important discovery of his whole life. He could read. He possessed the antidote to the deadly poison of old age. He could read. But he had nothing to read. (Sepulveda, 1993, p. 52[3])

This is the beginning of the reading life of Antonio José Bolívar in *The old Man Who Read Romance Novels*. At the age of "too many," perhaps 70 years and some, Antonio picks up a newspaper in the remote town of El Idilio, in the Ecuadorian jungle, and discovers he can read. Slowly "spelling out each syllable, whispering it as if with relish" (p. 26), he decides that the news articles about Congress and legislature are just too boring. He spends the "whole rainy season brooding on his unhappy plight as a frustrated reader" (p. 55).

This also was the end of a long rainy season for the Mexican mothers, who for years had not one book at home, not one for themselves. Most of the literacy materials in their homes, (some newspaper clippings such as obituaries and coupons from the Spanish newspaper (a free paper) and English newspapers (bought only for specific purposes such as that); a very little correspondence from their parents in Mexico, in Spanish of course (they confessed that with the lower international telephone rates, they were writing and reading letters less than ever before); monthly school calendars and the upper portions of school letters (the signed lower portions of which had already been sent to school), were accumulated in a box or a drawer because the use of magnets on the refrigerator to hold notes and notices of important events must be an American habit. Some of the elementary school correspondence was written in both languages, but if it was not, they asked other mothers at the school patio, or any of the Spanish-speaking secretaries and principals, or their children's teachers or teacher aides to translate. Letters or information flyers from the local high school, however, were written in Spanish, so the high school children translated these for their mothers. Many times I observed the way the children read the school correspondence to their mothers. They first read it to themselves, then "summarized" the information for their mothers. The mothers then questioned them for details: when, what time, where, why. The children complied patiently, but did not or could not translate verbatim when their mothers requested it.

As an ESL teacher and later as their literacy coordinator, I was asked many times after class to translate (only orally) some of the obituaries from the newspaper, but mostly I translated official letters from the Immigration and Naturalization Service (INS), the school, the local clinic, the Social Security Office, and the like. Sometimes, they told me, they asked several people to translate letters or newspaper clippings just to make sure that there were no mistakes. It was their way to check for consistency in the information they had received from other people, including immigration lawyers. For confirmation and consistency, they asked people they trusted such as family members and school staff.

Then there were the catalogs of home merchandise. These were extremely popular among members of this group. Catalogs were a way of earning a little extra money. They offered products to each other and flipped through pages insatiably wanting home decorations, jewelry, and children and women's clothing. The most popular were the jewelry catalogs because the children wore gold chains with a cross or a *Virgen de Guadalupe* medal around their necks, or both, and many wore gold bracelets engraved with their names on the top and their birthdays on the reverse. I understood all that jewelry buying because my mother had done the same for my brothers and me, and I had done the same for my own children. The catalogs for gold merchandise were in Spanish, but Susana had the best catalog company. It was an American company from Mead, Colorado, that gave the "sales person" monetary incentives, free shipping, or discounts on their own purchases once they had reached their goals. In this group, we all got Susana's sales discount. She had a monopoly on the gold commerce. The percentages of these discounts were negotiated at the literacy table.

Rosa: *Pero la semana pasada me ofreció 35% de descuento, y ahora me ofrece sólo 20%. Pero, Susana, ya me está sacando hasta las medias.*

Susana: *Este mes no he tenido muchas ventas, algo tengo que ganar, ¿no?*

Rosa: But last week you offered me a 25% discount, and now you offer me only 15%. But, Susana, you are taking even my socks away.

Susana: This month I did not make many sales. I have to earn something, right?

Besides offering the opportunity to figure out percentages and refine their salesmanship, these dabbles in home entrepreneurship gave them the knowledge to record sales and orders and to fill out forms in Spanish. Reading a book—a novel, a story, a poem—did not represent practicality to them in the way that catalogs did, nor did it correlate with the kind of literacy they perceived themselves as needing to conduct their lives in the United States, or for that matter, the lives they had lived in Mexico. Most of them had held jobs in factories and in small restaurants and had felt no need for more schooling for those jobs. Overall, their literacy skills allowed them to engage in the reading and writing tasks necessary for the contexts of their lives.

Also, because of their low-level English and because the family literacy program was focused only on their children's schools, they ... we ... never suggested a novel or a relevant story for the mothers to read in their ESL classes or to take home. Every now and then perhaps we read a children's book. That the group decided to read books and to write a journal seemed extraordinary to me because for years we had been so adult literacy-dry. Although their talk was already a privileged and welcomed space within the group, the program's message about the importance of children's reading and writing had not influenced their own roles as literacy facilitators, and they did not see themselves as individual readers and writers. At many levels, in fact, the program treated them as nonreaders and nonwriters. The family literacy program view was "divorced" from the importance the mothers were beginning to give to their own literacy, and this led them to request "custody" of a larger, broader, and different part of the family literacy process.

THE BOOKS

Al ver los textos de geometría se preguntaba si verdaderamente valía la pena saber leer ... los libros de historia le parecieron corolario de mentiras. ¿Cómo era posible que esos señoritos pálidos, con guantes hasta los codos y apretados calzones de funámbulo, fueran capaces de ganar batallas? Luego de revisar toda la biblioteca, encontró aquello que realmente deseaba. El Rosario, de Florence Barclay, contenía amor, amor por todas partes. Los personajes sufrían y mezclaban la dicha con los padecimientos de una manera tan bella, que la lupa se le empañaba de lágrimas. La maestra, no del todo, conforme con sus preferencias de lector, le permitió llevarse el libro, y con el regreso a El Idilio para leerlo una y cien veces frente a la ventana. (Sepúlveda, 1989, pp. 70–71)

Skimming through the geometry textbooks, [Antonio Jose] wondered if it was really worth knowing how to read.... History books seemed to him a string of lies. How could those pale-faced playboys, with gloves up to their elbows and skin-tight breeches like a tightrope walker's, have been capable of winning battles? After working through almost the whole library, he found what he was really after. *Rosary* by Florence Barclay contained love, love everywhere. The characters suffered and mingled love and pain so beautifully that his magnifying glass was awash with tears. The school mistress, who didn't entirely share his tastes, allowed him to take the book back with him to El Idilio, and there he read and reread it a hundred times. (Sepulveda, 1993, pp. 60–61)

Now we were on our third book. At the beginning of that year, I brought to the Rudy Lozano Library, where we now met, short novels and books of short stories books that I had already read and liked. I introduced the books one by one, and then they suggested which books they wanted me to copy. We began with the award-winning Mexican writer and journalist Elena Poniatowska's *Dear Diego,* fictional love letters that exiled Russian painter Angelina Beloff might have sent Mexican painter Diego Rivera after their 10-year love affair. As the only single mother of the group, Inés had pushed strongly for Poniatowska's love letters, sighing love noises, oooh's and ahhh's, trying to convince the group of her needs to fantasize about love. Oh, how upset we all became when Diego left Quiela (her nickname) pregnant in postwar Paris, not returning when their child died, and never claiming her back. Ah, but such a relish we felt when we read all those passionate and sad words in Spanish, feeling good about learning life lessons from a surviving starving woman.

Carmen had been captivated by Adela Irigoyen's (1994) foreword to her historical novel *El Ocaso del Quinto Sol,* The Dusk of the Fifth Sun: "The facts that are told are based on an indisputable reality, [selected from a] history that lavishes the simple truth we possess: surgical scalpel that wounds to cure!" (p.7). Only Carmen and I finished reading the book. To read through Irigoyen's ironic twists and raw commentaries, the reader needed historical background about the Spanish conquest of the Aztecs, and the latter had names that the women could pronounce a hundred times better than I could, but they could not read them as easily as I visually could. After three installments of the copied book, and against Carmen's frown (she was almost finished), I began giving them installments of the *The Old Man Who Read Romance Novels.*

There was no question about the methodological decision to read about Quiela or Antonio José and about others in Spanish, for it was the language that addressed the needs of the mothers in the group. In the broadest sense, reading in Spanish became a focused reexamination of their lives—cultural values and attitudes and power relationships, but our conversations as a group in many ways had already been doing that. During the ESL classes, the mothers had not been able to match their abilities to express complicated and abstract matters. By looking directly at the strength of these mothers—who turned toward reading in Spanish when they decided to confront their need to be better, *para ser mejores,* in their different literacy roles—it was important to see how their interaction with the readings provided them with a tool for deeper understanding of the struggles in which they were engaged as they began to make connections to different worlds and words. In a way, the readings became validations of what they were or had become. It also is important to point out that for them, reading was not part of individual or separate quests, but part of a shared condition—their own socioeconomic and political circumstances—that affirmed them, particularly when change moved them into the realms of hope.

In the following sections, I present some fragments of Rosa's, Carmen's, and Inés' responses to two readings, a novel and an academic paper, to show how these women revealed themselves in relation to others, particularly the Americans and their own children. Their responses also show their motivation to continue their readings on a path to change the context of their literacy roles and those of their children.

FINDING 15 COPIES OF THE BOOKS

NOTICE: I, the undersigned, confess the following: During those days as "trainer of trainers," I committed some crimes for which I do not think I feel much remorse even now. If someone is willing to confess to some delinquency, there is some merit to their talking, so the undersigned hopes for some understanding about the contexts of the crimes. The books we read over a period of three school years, not many really, all were photocopied. The undersigned had some accomplices that shall remain nameless until her dying days. (He gave me the reams of paper. Another "he" made the copies. The undersigned supplied the original books.) As attenuating circumstances, the following are presented as evidence: They were all short books, 150 pages at the most; nobody will foot the bill, not the program, not me, and not the women because no one had the money; all was done for nonprofit purposes; the undersigned, the accomplices, and beneficiaries were believed to be doing their best; St. Ephrem the Syrian (303–373) said: "Let books be your dining table, And you shall be full of delights, Let them be your mattress And you shall sleep restful nights.[4] So, in the absence of books, they the undersigned made books so the whole group could have delight, rest, and ... literacy.

The undersigned,

Ana

READING TO EXPRESS: *NO VENIMOS A ROBARLE A NADIE.* WE DO NOT COME TO STEAL FROM ANYONE.

Rosa read slowly and out loud just as when she reads alone. Her voice lost control, at times half laughing, anticipating some of the words she was about to read. Her laughter was contagious because it was unusual to hear it. At times, when she encountered long names or words and could not read them fast enough, the other mothers who read better, or I, volunteered the word in chorus. Then Rosa would read again, starting from two or three words before to make sense of the phrase. In general, her readings of the paragraphs took time.

Sin pedir permiso entraron a la choza, y uno de ellos, luego de reír a destajo, insistió en comprar el retrato que lo mostraba junto a Dolores Encarnación del Santísimo Estupiñán Otavalo. El gringo se atrevió a descolgar el retrato y lo metió en su mochila, dejándole a cambio un puñado de billetes encima de la mesa.

Le costó sobreponerse a la bronca y sacar el habla.

"Dígale al hijo de puta que, como no deje el retrato donde estaba, le meto dos cartuchos de la escopeta y le vuelo los huevos. Y conste que siempre la tengo cargada."

El gordo ... arguyó que los recuerdos eran sagrados en esas tierras, que no lo tomara a mal, que los ecuatorianos, y especialmente él, apreciaban mucho a los norteamericanos, y que si se trataba de llevarse buenos recuerdos él mismo se encargaría de proporcionárselos. (Sepúlveda, 1989, p. 87)

Without waiting to be invited, they walked into his hut, and one of them, after going into fits of laughter, insisted on buying the portrait photograph of him with Dolores Encarnación del Santísimo Sacramentón Estupiñan Otavalo [the old man's late wife]. The gringo had the nerve to unhook the picture and put it in his backpack, leaving in exchange a wad of notes.

With difficulty the old man managed to control his fury, and to speak out:

"Tell that [son of a bitch] that if he doesn't put the picture back where it was, I'll pump two rounds into him and blow his balls off. And tell him my gun is always loaded." The fat man ... explained that family mementos were sacred in these parts; Ecuadorians in general, and himself in particular, really like Americans, and if they wanted some nice souvenirs to take away, he personally would make sure they got him. (Sepulveda, 1993, pp. 77–78)

Rosa: *¿Habrá gente así, usted cree? Ni respeto ni ... porque quieras ... era una choza, y el viejo estaba ahí dentro, ¿eh?*

Inés: *No tuvo respeto el gringo por nada ni naidies. Ni los animales se salvaron siquiera. Así serán, pos, los americanos en [otros] países, todo para ellos. Toma p'acá, por allá, todo de ellos.*

Rosa: *Y tú qué, ¿envidiosa de qué todo lo tienen ellos?*

Inés: *Sí, quiero tener más, yo quiero mis cositas, sí, pero el gringo quería hasta con todo, hasta la foto de la dijunta, y después la piel de los jaguares, con todo lo que no era suyo, pero ¿para qué? Eso, eso [pregunto].*

Carmen: *Para enseñar a los demás. ¿Para qué compra uno recuerditos? ¿Para acordarse uno de lo que vio o para enseñar a los demás?*

Rosa: *Recuerdos sólo [los que tenemos] en la cabeza ... esas son cosas, objetos que quería del viejo sólo por tener.*

Inés: *Pero separado de eso, o mejor dicho, parejo, parejo con eso, era que su mamá del gringo mero que no le había enseñado a respetar a los vecinos.*

Rosa: Do you believe there are people like that? Neither respect nor ... because you just want to ... it was a hut and the old man was in there, yes?

Ines: The gringo had respect for nothing and for no one. Not even the animals were spared. That's way the Americans probably are, well, in [other] countries, everything for them. Take from here, from there, everything for them.

Rosa: And you say that because you are envious of everything they have?

Ines: Yes, I want to have more, I want my own things, but the gringo wanted everything, the picture of the dead, the ocelots' furs, everything that was not his, but, what for? That is it, that is it [that I am asking].

Carmen: To show the others. Why do you buy souvenirs? To remind oneself of what one saw or to show the others?

Rosa: Memories [same word as souvenirs] are only the ones in our heads ... those are only things, objects that [the gringo] wanted only to own.

Ines: Besides that, or better said, par, par with that, it was the mother of the gringo that surely had not taught him to respect neighbors.

Everyone laughed.

Carmen: *Ese no es problema de la mamá, Inés. Ya está recargando la culpa a las pobrecitas mamás de todos los gringos. Es un problema de la sociedad, más bien americana, todo lo quieren pero no para compartir, sólo para enseñar. A ver si el viejo Antonio José iba a la casa del gringo y le quitaba [la foto] ...*

Rosa: *No, no, ese viejo era un latino y no hacía eso, nosotros no hacíamos eso. Oigame bien Carmen, mire como el viejo era con los indigenas esos ...*

Inés: *Los shuar [nativos en la selva Ecuatoriana], ¿no?*

Rosa: *El al lado de la selva, y los shuar en la selva. Ellos allá, el más aquí, y cada uno con su pedazo.*

Carmen: *Nadie quita a nadie.*

Rosa: *Así tiene que ser ... estamos aquí y no queremos cambiarlos ni que nos cambien, allá ellos con sus problemas, nosotras también los tenemos ... pero si que sepan que no venimos a robar a nadie.*

Carmen: That is not his mom's problem, Ines. You are charging blame to all the poor mothers of all the gringos. It is a societal problem, better said, American, they want everything but not to share, just to show. Let's see if old Antonio Jose had gone to the house of the gringo and snatched [the picture] ...

Rosa: No, no, the old man was a Latino and would not have done that, we would not have done that. Listen to me well, Carmen, look how the old man was with those indigenous ...

Ines: The Shuar ... [natives from the Ecuadorian jungle].

Rosa: He [was] besides the jungle, and the Shuar in the jungle. They [were] there, he [was] closer, and everyone with their piece.

Carmen: No one takes away from anyone.

Rosa: That is the way it has to be ... we are here and we do not want to change them nor do we want to be changed; let them have their own problems, we also have them ... but they have to know that we did not have to rob anyone.

Rosa had chosen the paragraph. It was customary that, at the beginning of our discussions, everyone was invited to share, *compartir*, an excerpt of the book, and, explain why she had chosen it. By providing a context to respond to, the mothers were challenged to connect the text to any background knowledge or experience they had had or to discuss an issue that was relevant to their interests. Because in the past years the group had acquired a sense of connectedness—by recognizing mutual experiences and feeling individually responsible for the well-being of the group—the transformation into a community of readers also came with a sense of safety and comfort in which to express and critique the book and each other's opinions.

Rosa was incredulous about anyone taking someone's possessions in such a way, but when Carmen and Inés began to relate the paragraph in terms of their own lives—whether they would do that or not—it helped

Rosa stimulate her thoughts about her own values. They had tapped into familiar historical and cultural notions of colonization represented here by the verbal attacks against the gringo who went into the hut, and later against all the gringos. That these attacks, except those against the gringos' mothers, remained unchallenged in the classroom, was nothing new. Often conversations about the differences in cultural behaviors between the gringos or *americanos* and themselves or between the mothers' criticisms and their ways of thinking had more to do with their vital need for affirmation and recognition of the historical and cultural space they held themselves than their desire to inflict irreverent words about the habits and values of the *americanos*. The historical and cultural idea of feeling colonized existed, and it framed the discussion, but the attacks had more to do with resisting, opposing, and claiming a position within a hut, or a neighborhood, in terms of their rights to belong.

Comparing the position of the old man in his hut to *estamos aquí,* we are here, Rosa built an argument of collective proportions when she said *nosotras*, feminine we, are here, and we have come robbing no one of "their space." We are here and this is our space. These expressions of collective solidarity are understood only if seen as expressions of cultural strength and defiant voice. Understandably, when bringing these vernacular affirmations and demands for space, the women's voices were charged because they understood the larger political framework of a society that excluded them and others and wanted to deny them their space.

Reading from Sepulveda's words about the colonization of the jungle by White men and gringos seen through the actions of Antonio Jose, the old man, helped them to ground the way they thought about themselves and their condition. The literature seemed to give them license to express and make meaning of their attempts to surmount their colonized condition within the group by collectively building onto the social, political, and educational spaces within the family literacy program, and out of it.

READING TO FORGET

Unlike Rosa, when Carmen read her words, they flowed smoothly. She pronounced the hard letters harder that any Mexican I had heard before. After she finished her long guttural *jotas,* j's, as when she read, for example, JJJosé, I always thought she was ready to spit something. She read with such emphasis that some of us preferred to look at her while she read rather than follow along in the book as we needed to do with others. Because Spanish sound–letter correspondences are quite regular, it is not a hard language to read. Carmen read four long pages in Spanish. These are paraphrases of what she read.

> Antonio José had been living in the jungle and befriended the Shuar [Ecuadorian natives]. One day, five White men had dynamited the dam forming the fishes' spawning ground, killing at the same time some Shuar, among them, the old man's best friend Nushiño. One of the White men escaped towards the other shore. Before dying, Nushiño tells the old man: "I can't go in peace, my brother. Until his head hangs from a stake I'll wander like a sad, blind parrot, bumping into the trees. Help me, my brother." Antonio José armed himself with a blowpipe and he swam across the river. He missed his target and got hold of the White man's gun, shooting him in the stomach. He dragged him by his feet to the other side. When the Shuar saw the White man, they began to cry for Nushiño. How could they shrink that head, when in life it had been frozen in an [expression] of fear and pain? Antonio José Bolivar had disgraced himself, and was thereby responsible for his friend's eternal misery. Still weeping, they gave him their best canoe, they embraced him, gave him supplies, and told him that from that moment he was no longer welcome. He could pass through the Shuar encampments, but would not have the right to linger.

Carmen: *Venimos a leer un libro lleno de problemas también, pero lo extraño es que uno lo lee. Pasó este hombre toda su vida con miles de penurias. Llega uno a ese punto de que pasa uno por tanta cosa a diario, diario, diario, que mejor uno busca su escape como Antonio José buscaba su escape en novelas, novelas de amor. Pero eran días y meses lo que duraba en leer algo, porque le gustaba releer y releer aquello y aprendérselo. Era su escape para olvidarse de lo que lo rodeaba. A veces uno necesita este tipo de libros para olvidarnos de lo que nos rodea a nosotros. ¿No les parece extraño, él y nosotras?*

Inés: *Leer es un relajador, más en la noche cuando uno piensa en todos los problemas que hay. Así en la cama, se mete uno en la lectura y ya se olvida uno de todo. Nomás me fijaba en lo desgraciado que era el viejo.*

Rosa: *No se va [usted] a complicar más porque está leyendo algo así. Lo mejor [que le puede pasar] es que se va a comparar con lo que está leyendo y encuentra alguna solución. Cualquier cosa que estemos leyendo está bien.*

Carmen: *Pero vuelvo a preguntar, ¿no les parece raro?*

Carmen: We came to read a book full of problems too, but the strange thing is that we are reading it. This man spent all his life with thousands of miseries. It comes to the point that one goes through so many things daily, daily, daily, that it is better to find an escape like Antonio Jose was looking for in his novels, love novels. But it would be days and months that he would spend in reading something, because he liked to reread and reread this and learn it. It was his escape to forget about everything that surrounded him. Sometimes one needs this type of books to forget about what it is that surrounded us. Don't you find it strange, him and us?

Ines: To read is a relaxer, even more at night when one thinks in all the problems that there are. Like this in bed, one gets into the reading and already one forgets about everything. I was only paying attention to how miserable that old man was.

Rosa: [You] do not have to make it harder for you to read something like this. The best [thing that could happen] is that you are going to compare what you are reading and try to find a solution. Everything we are reading is fine.

Carmen: But I ask again, isn't it strange?

Inside the library where we met, among thousands of books, it was not difficult for me, and at times for them, to forget the urban social landscape that surrounded us. The familiar faces and the feelings of care, safety, and control over their space, time, and effort they experienced together here differed from their experience in the outside world, a poor neighborhood where streets tended to be dirty, polluted with drug dealers, gangs, and hard-core crimes. Yet, the book had brought all these factors together and contributed to Carmen's critical words about their own daily existence. What triggered them? Troublesome enough, it was death and isolation, both words related to an old man and his friend, and themselves.

The added irony, the strange thing, according to Carmen, was that their reading mirrored the old man's readings. They were reading mostly to forget about their own lives when she encountered an old man reading to forget. Although Rosa and Inés did not follow or understand the strange coincidence that Carmen saw in her reading, they both agreed that reading was about forgetting themselves, about resting their minds from their daily burdens, and perhaps, about finding who, between those pages, could be more miserable than they were. *A diario, a diario, a diario*, daily, daily, daily, and then at night, going to bed, thinking about all the problems they had, they turned to reading in our group, not to further complicate their lives, but perhaps to find some solace from their problems. They read, not to escape the routine or tedium of their lives as many might suspect, but to find moments of hope and peace amid the turmoil of their lives, to forget about oneself in someone else's living.

During our time together, the women constantly talked about their hard lives, and we knew how depressed some of them were at times. Carmen told the group:

"Por lo referente a mi, sí, tengo miedo o nervios casi todos los días. Aunque eso me hace sentir viva, es un reto nuevo que vencer día a día. Si estuviéramos seguras de cada día, empezaríamos a morir un poco cada día porque tendríamos la seguridad del mañana, y cómo no la tenemos ..."

"When it refers to me, yes, I am afraid or nervous almost every day. Although that is what make me feel alive, it is a new challenge to defeat day by day. If we were sure of each day, we would begin to die a little each day because we would have the security of tomorrow, and since we don't have it ..."

When Carmen explained further to the group that living was about not being certain of the world, the group began to point out their uncertainties and worries.

Rosa: *La verdad es que yo me siento muy, muy, mal de no dominar el inglés a cómo se necesita. Siento la necesidad de estudiar alguito, alguito. Pos la vida con un miserable sueldo es muy difícil, y pa' que trabaje y gane sólo pa' pagarle a una cuidadora ... Miren, yo nunca trabajé, nunca, pero ahora sí lo voy a necesitar, ya mis niños están más grandes. Yo quiero superarme más, pero no se cómo, no sé ... pienso y repienso y no le doy una ...*

Inés: *Yo me voy a morir de vieja, pero seguiré tratando. Esta vida es una chingada, ya, ya lo sabemos, todas acá lo sabemos, pero ¿qué le vamos a hacer, ahogarnos todas con todos los hijos así como en las noticias? Hay que seguirle, seguirle ... así se nos parta el alma y el corazón ... ¿ajá?*

Rosa: The truth is that I feel very, very, badly for not controlling English as it is needed. I feel the need to study a little something, a little something. Because life with a miserable salary is very difficult, and why work and earn only to pay a caregiver. Look, I never worked, never, but now I am going to need to, now my children are older. I want to better myself, but I do not know how, I don't know ... I think and rethink, and I do not find one [way] ...

Inés: I am going to die being an old woman, but I will continue trying. This life is a fucking [thing], already, already we know it, all here know it, but ¿what are we going to do, drown all of us with all of the children as [we saw it] in the news? One must continue, continue ... even if it breaks our soul and heart ... Yes?

Here, the women showed how concerned they were about their quandaries, saying how hard it would be to realize their dreams: to be better at English, to obtain a worthwhile job, and even to improve their daily lives. The women also felt exhausted at times, because the combination of their responsibilities at home and the hours they spent doing childcare for others' children, and doing other odd jobs (mostly at subminimum wages) were neverending. Their wanting to read books had been something I had not expected, but as their world was changing by giving them more responsibility for their own literacy and that of their children, their dedication to read and the seriousness of their discussions was remarkable. They came to our meetings prepared with their no-cover, one-sided copies of the books, and that had been beyond my wretched expectations. During their conversations, the women presented themselves as aware of their life conditions by contrasting the hard lives they lived with the ways they dreamed of living them, and at least during their readings, they had hoped to forget about their lives, for others lived harder.

Yet these book discussions also had moments of laughter. At times, our laughter seemed neverending, minutes at a time. Any silly punch line or someone telling a joke that came to mind would take us on a tangent, or several of them. Other times, laughter occurred because the mothers made fun of their lives as compared with the lives of others, including me. Once when I told them I had been driving like a maniac to finish all my errands before coming to the library, although they did not tease me directly, they "commented" with one another how they had sped in their roller blades through the neighborhood, pushing people on the sidewalks to get to the laundrymat with their baskets on their heads, their children in their arms, and their folded clothes, while reading the whole time with one eye and watching the children with the other. The mothers had already constructed a consensus about their shared experiences, so it was not hard for them to poke fun at themselves, and at others who had it easier and still complained. Anyone from the outside, most likely, could have understood their sense of humor, their ironies, and their self-deprecating tirades. I did. Yet, I could not joke like they did about the reality of their lives. Responding to their readings and conversing with them was about their reality and their hardships. I was not one of them.

This particular afternoon, the women communicatively had constructed a reading community in many ways: maintaining their talk around the same topic, feeling dismayed at their daily conditions, recommending not to emphasize extra sorrows, and approaching reading as escapism.

A YEAR LATER: READING THAT DISTURBS

Over that year, we read one more book, Puerto Rican writer Magali Garcia Ramis' *La Familia de todos Nosotros* (1979) (The Family of All of Us) and a compilation of famous poems by Latin American poets from several poetry books I owned. It was during the month of October of the last reading year, 1996, that one day I decided to introduce a short academic essay, "Bilingual Classroom Studies and Community Analysis: Some Recent Trends," to the mothers because its author, Luis Moll (1992) was coming to visit the university. One of his stops was at the Rudy Lozano library in Pilsen where the family literacy group met, and where the 15 trainers were making lunch for him and other guests.

Neither the mothers nor I had met Luis Moll before, but I was quite aware of his work with Mexican families in Tucson, Arizona. His study advocated teachers' learning "funds of knowledge" from their own students' households as a viable method for bridging the gap between school and community. I wanted the mothers to know about someone who was validating Mexican households, personal and cultural knowledge, and in many ways, Mexican lives. Never before had I translated a research paper for them. Until then, I was feeling good about what the readings had brought to the literacy group. My history with my failed ESL classes was a thing of the past. The connections the mothers had with each other, with me, and with the reading word had spilled over into my teaching. I was captivated by my own thoughts that drawing from their experiences and their readings, the mothers were able to create stories that acknowledged their voices, their dreams, and their struggles, and by doing so in their own language, they were able to confront them and move them beyond the boundaries of silence. So, that day, inspired by the haughtiness of my position, I read aloud Luis Moll's (1992) first paragraph:

> *La mayoría de niños que asisten a clases bilingües en los Estados Unidos son estudiantes de la clase trabajadora. Aunque raramente la literatura se refiere a ello, este hecho tiene grandes implicaciones para las metas y para la clase de instrucción en esas aulas. Comparado con la educación [schooling] de niños de familias de ingresos más altos, la instrucción para estudiantes de la clase trabajadora, sea en aulas bilingües o monolingües, se puede caracterizar como de rutina, de repetición y práctica, e intelectualmente limitada, con énfasis en un bajo nivel de lectura, escritura y habilidades para hacer cálculos.*

Most children attending bilingual classes in the United States are working-class students. Although rarely addressed in the literature, this fact has major implications for the goals and nature of instruction in these classrooms. In comparison with the schooling of peers from higher income families, instruction for working-class students, be it in bilingual or monolingual classrooms, can be characterized as a rote drill and practice, and intellectually limited, with an emphasis on low-level literacy and computational skills. (p. 20)

That was the last paragraph we would read together that afternoon. We could not go on because its impact did not go away. How do I sum up what happened that afternoon to all of us, separately? The far from perfect reality of urban bilingual education and education in general for Latinos struck the hearts and minds of these women, and that personal upheaval regarding their children's schooling had wounded the safety net in which they had been reading. I had presented them with "unsafe" material that in no way corresponded to their reading expectations. This reading turned out to be an unsafe place where their children were imperiled. Nobody had ever told them that their children were receiving a type of "watered-down" education, and nowhere had they ever read that middle-class children were receiving a higher level of education. I was there with the bleeding "words-as-powerful-as-the-sword" article as a witness of a crime committed against their children: the marginalization of their schooling.

Carmen: *¿Qué dice ese Ricardo Moll? A ver Ana, explíqueme usted, porque lo que yo estoy entendiendo no me ha gustado nadita, nadita.*

Ana: *Luis, su nombre es Luis. ¿Qué entendió usted de todo ésto?*

Carmen: *¡Qué este hombre está loco! La educación es la educación, los libros son todos igualitos para todos los niños de, por ejemplo ... tercer grado, en todas partes ... en este país. Pero ¿de qué está hablando éste?*

Inés: *¿Qué quiere decir literatura? Yo creí que eso era novelas, cuentos, eso.*

Ana: *Se refiere a estudios que se han hecho acerca de algo. La literatura son todos los estudios acerca de la educación bilingüe o de otra cosa. Aquí dice que en todos los estudios, en la literatura, no se habla de que la mayoría de niños en clases bilingües son de la clase trabajadora.*

Carmen: *Eso no es lo importante. Dice que si se compara con otros niños la educación es limitada, en otras palabras, es mala. Niños ricos, de dinero.*

Ana: *Bueno, mala no dice, sino que es inferior. Y Carmen no necesariamente tienen que ser ricos, sino los que no son de la clase trabajadora.*

Rosa: *Ay, Ana, si es inferior no estará requete-mala, pero está mal porque no es igual*
           para todos.

Carmen: What is this Richard saying? Let's see, Ana, you explain this to me, because what I
           understand I am not liking at all, at all.

Ana: Luis, his name is Luis. What is your understanding of all this?

Carmen: That this man is crazy! Education is education wherever [you are]; all the books
           are the same for all children of, for example … third grade, everywhere … in this
           country. But, what is he talking about?

Ines: What does literature mean? I thought they were novels, stories, and that.

Ana: It refers to studies that are made about something. Literature is all the studies
           about bilingual education or something else. Here it says that all the studies, the lit-
           erature, do not talk about the fact that most children in bilingual classes belong to
           the working class.

Carmen: But that is not the important part. It says that if compared with other children, their
           education is limited, in other words, it's bad. Rich children with money.

Ana: It doesn't say bad; it says it is inferior. And Carmen, they do not necessarily have to
           be rich, just not from the working class.

Rosa: Ay, Ana, but if it is inferior, it might not be [really, really] bad, but it is bad because it
           is not the same for all.

How could I have been so blind to a simple truth: After years of being in
a family literacy program, the mothers did not know that the issue of bilingual education was much larger than whether it would take the children
a longer or shorter time to learn English. Before that afternoon, when
talking about bilingual education, I had tried to dispel myths about the relation between the ease and speed with which children learn, orally, a
second language and the optimal time to begin second-language instruction, about the relation between oral communication skills and academic language skills, and also about cultural and individual differences
in language learning styles. Even after countless hours of our conversations, other "experts," school principals and teachers, Chicago public
schools, and a national agenda that prescribes "regular" school as soon
as possible would easily sway the mothers' opinions about their children's language education. The majority of the mothers in this group
talked about other mothers they knew who, *no se dan cuenta que están
haciendo* (they did not realize what they were doing) when they registered them for "regular" school.

The latter group considered it an honor when their young children were
asked to start or transition early into the "regular" program. They would

promptly sign the papers. The younger the child entered the "regular," the prouder the mother was. Their children might never go through what she herself was going through she thought. They would learn English.... They would make it. A few knew that when their children were transitioned from a bilingual classroom to a "regular" classroom, their academic achievement the following year would decline, and that the range of the difference would depend on how considerable the drop was, how long it would last, and whether the child would fully recover from the change.

Virtually every child who starts school before the age of 12 years in this country becomes fluent and literate in English (National Center for Education Statistics, 2001), but the issues are larger than just English. Nevertheless, they are trampled into that issue alone: will our children be literate in Spanish, thus bilingual. However, even if they are literate only in English, will their education help them gain social, political, and economic status, and whose responsibility is it to make sure this happens? But, one day, in one reading instance, the poor and the poor Latino children, bilingual students or not, were slipped into the same category *requete-mala*, really, really bad.

There we were, looking on the table in front of us at Moll's essay, the reading that disturbed them, concerning the condition of minority students and Latino families. I sat deep in my chair, and they sat on the edge of their seats, as we allowed the emotional moment to build a totally different understanding than the one they had had seconds ago, *que no les estaba gustando nadita, nadita*, that they were not liking at all, at all, and the significance of its relevance for their children's future, for themselves, and their future within the literacy program. This awkward moment was the first time the mothers had read about the greater challenges that come with being either poor or Mexican in an American school.

EXPANDING THEIR HORIZONS BY EXPANDING OURS

Carmen: *No hay peor sordo que el no quiere oír.*

Ana: *Um, yo sé ésa así: No hay peor ciego que el no quiere ver.*

Rosa: *Pior que ciegas y sordas porque nosotros leemos para saber y total, no sabemos nada.*

Carmen: There is no worse deaf [person] than the one who does not want to hear.

Ana: Hum, I know that one this way: There is no worse blind [person] than the one who does not want to see.

Rosa: Worse than [those who are] blind and deaf for we read to know and after all, we know nothing.

To be aware, *darse cuenta*, to realize the world we live in, *darse cuenta de la sociedad en que se vive*, to remake the world, one's world, *rehacer el mundo, el mundo de uno*, all seemed to happen one afternoon, but then it had started long before. It had happened when the existing notion about the schooling of their children had fallen upon their competing notion that it was *requete mala* (really, really bad), and the notions had battled, and they had negotiated, and they had contested, and then they had settled, *a regañadientes*, reluctantly. Reluctantly, they had learned about the situation, and also had blamed themselves for not knowing that they needed to blame someone else.

Their talk about being deaf and blind was poignant. Through harsh words, the women were confronting their disgust for the educational world to which they had entrusted their children, and for the trust they had put on themselves. Rosa had always been tough, and many times other women had tried to soften her meanings with more delicate words. Not that day. Rosa's toughness was meant to represent the furious understanding of the sad situation. They were reading to know, Rosa had said, *estaban leyendo para saber*. Why didn't they?

The urgency of their voices upon reading Luis Moll's *Bilingual Classroom Studies and Community Analysis* signified a profound edge, a margin in which they located themselves and their children's schooling as a place of contradiction: a place that held dreams and hopes, but also estrangement and alienation. The reading had brought them to an uncertain ground, one that resisted the reality of the place where they now stood. Yet theirs was a difficult, but necessary, place to stand. First, Carmen, intellectually and intuitively, had understood the meaning of "low-level" literacy and "intellectually limited" in their children's schooling. Then, Rosa had articulated that the importance of their readings and their presence in the family literacy program had not brought them the crucial awareness about the reality of the schooling of Latinos. Both women had seemingly endangered and undermined the two structures. But in coming to terms with the realities of these structures, the mothers had created a new conflictive role that would give them a stronger need to be included, not avoided, in their efforts to read and learn more about their situation, and that of their families, in this country.

The mothers spent the rest of the time together that afternoon questioning me about the schooling of Latinos in the United States, in Pilsen, and in some specific schools. The translated article lay alone on top of the table. Later, I left the library exhausted, and as I was walking toward my car, I broke down into tears. Why had those issues not come out before? Why had I not brought them forth? Good intentions and much excitement had not been enough. I felt I had failed again, several years later. An innocuous topic had become the source of difficulty for the mothers, and I ... again had not had a clue. Carmen, on behalf of all the mothers, had written me to ask me to be better so she could be better for other mothers and for her children.

When Luis Moll came to the library, they asked him to compare the education of the Latinos in the United States with the education of Latin Americans in their countries. Luis Moll talked about poverty being an equal opportunist here and there, but that his experiences were based on his studies of Latinos in the United States. He could not have known what the mothers wanted to know: whether their decision to give their children better opportunities in the United States had been the correct one.

They never asked me that question. I am glad because I did not have an answer for them.

SEVERAL MONTHS LATER: THE END OF THE PROGRAM FOR TRAINERS

Rosa:	*Aquí le traje una ensalada de fruta, Ana. Coma, coma.*
Ana:	*Ay, que rico, Rosa, gracias.*
Rosa:	*Ahí le puse bastante chili y limón.*
Ana:	*¿Chili y limón a la fruta?*
Rosa:	*¿Usted que le pone a la fruta?*
Ana:	*Si está agria, le pongo algo de canela y azúcar.*
Rosa:	*Coma, coma, después me va a dar las gracias por enseñarle a comer como Dios manda.*

Rosa:	Here I brought some fruit salad, Ana. Eat, eat.
Ana:	Ay, how delicious, Rosa, thanks.
Rosa:	There I put a lot of hot peppers and lemon.
Ana:	Hot peppers and lemon to fruit?
Rosa:	What do you put on?
Ana:	If it is sour, I put cinnamon and sugar.
Rosa:	Eat, eat, afterwards you are going to thank me for teaching you how to eat like God has ordered.

It was 3:00 on a sunny afternoon. We had been painting a large canvas with all the Latin American flags for our final presentation. It would be the last day for the trainers in the program. The ESL teachers would teach the literacy classes to the mothers. I often wondered whether they would be like me. Would they have a clue? The trainers' program was dismantled because it had been too costly. That day, however, we had realized that the canvas was too big, but that we had to finish. Most of the mothers had already left because it was time to pick up the children from school. The mothers who lived close by had gone home to eat something with their children and had come back with them to help us finish the painting. We needed to finish, and I was starving. Rosa came back with some food for me. I ate the first piece. From then on, I could not stop eating the luscious, ripe fruits with hot peppers, lemon, and bittersweet, the perfect ingredients of a Mexican fruit salad. That was our last day together at the library. As they walked me to my car, helping me carry the painting supplies and the flag, I remembered our reading:

> *Sin dejar de llorar, le entregaron la mejor canoa. Sin dejar de llorar lo abrazaron, le entregaron provisiones, y le dijeron que desde ese momento no era más bienvenido. Podría pasar por los caseríos Shuar, pero no tenia derecho a detenerse.* (Sepúlveda, 1989, p. 57)

> Still weeping, they gave him their best canoe; they embraced him, gave him supplies, and told him that from that moment he was no longer welcomed. He could pass through the Shuar encampments, but would not have the right to linger. (Sepulveda, 1993, p. 47)

REFERENCES

Anzaldúa, G. (1987). *Borderlands/la frontera: The new mestiza.* San Francisco: Aunt Lute Books.

Irigoyen, A. (1994). *El ocaso del quinto sol.* México, DF: Anaya Editores.

Moll, L. C. (1992). Bilingual classroom studies and community analysis. *Educational Researcher, 21*(2), 20–24.

National Center for Education Statistics. (2001). *English literacy and language minorities in the U.S.* (Report No. 2001-464).Washington, DC: U.S. Department of Education, Office of Educational Research and Improvement.

Poniatowska, E. (1978). *Querido Diego, te abraza quiela.* México, DF: Era Editores.

Ramis, M. G. (1976). *La familia de nosotros.* Rio Piedras, Puerto Rico: Editiorial Cultural.

Schmelkes, S., & Kalman, J. (1996). *La educación de adultos: Estado del arte: hacia una estrategia alfabetizadora para México.* México, DF: Instituto Nacional de Educación de Adultos.

Sepúlveda, L. (1989). *Un viejo que leía novelas de amor.* Barcelona: TusQuets Editores.

Sepulveda, L. (1993). *The old man who read love stories*. New York : Harcourt Brace .

Stromquist, N. P. (1997). *Literacy for citizenship: Gender and grassroots dynamics in Brazil*. Albany, NY: SUNY Press.

van der Westen, M. (1994). Literacy education and gender: The vase of Honduras. In L. Verhoeven (Ed.). *Functional literacy* (pp. 000–000). Philadelphia: John Benjamins.

Zuñiga, M. (1999). Towards a pedagogy of education programmes for grassroots women. In I. Jung & L. King (Eds.), *Gender, innovation and education in Latin America*. UNESCO: Institute of Education, Hamburg, Germany.

ENDNOTES

1. Pilsen is a predominantly Mexican community in Chicago.

2. I reproduce Carmen's words and sentences just as she wrote them.

3. I have used the Spanish and English versions, thus, the difference in page numbers.

4. Quoted in Bar Hebraues' *Ethicon*.

Writing and reading during Catechism class in family home on Saturday morning.
Photographs by Marcia Farr.

11

Literacy and Religion: Reading, Writing, and Gender Among Mexican Women in Chicago[1]

Marcia Farr

Ohio State University

Literacy has been linked often with religion, that is, with what have been called "world" religions or "ethical" religions (Goody, 1986). In contrast to religion in traditional societies, world religions generally show a missionary impulse (Parrinder, 1971). In traditional societies, religion is local and so interwoven with other aspects of the society that it is particular to that society and thus restricted to the people of that society. World religions, in contrast, travel over time and space, advocating what they deem to be a universal set of beliefs. Incorporating people into these religions usually involves literacy, especially for the three world religions that emerged from the Middle East: Judaism, Christianity, and Islam.

These three religions, like other world religions, rely on written traditions, rather than solely oral ones, but they also focus on a single book that is held sacred. Thus they often are referred to as religions of the book. Conversion to and membership in these religions involves literacy abilities. Christian missionary efforts, for example, include devising alphabets for languages that have no writing system, teaching the new literacy, and translating the Christian Bible into the newly written language. Rapid literacy development has occurred in some countries (particularly Protestant countries) because of religious pressures. Mass literacy was achieved rather quickly in Sweden, for example, as the result of a campaign promoted by the Church Law of 1686:

> This reading campaign was forced through almost completely without the aid of proper schools. The responsibility for teaching children to read was ultimately placed on the parents. The social pressure was enormous. Everybody in the household and in the village gathered once a year to take examinations in reading and knowledge of the Bible. The adult who failed these examinations was excluded from both communion and marriage. (Johansson, 1981, p. 152)

Practicing the religions of the book also frequently involves literacy abilities. Reading often supplements memorized prayers and is used in a variety of ways to enrich the religious experience, both during and outside religious services. Members may use writing as well for organizing activities within the congregation, for producing pamphlets urging others to convert (Markelis, personal communication, 1994), or for composing prayers to be used in services or in other religious meetings.

Thus religion has promoted literacy, and literacy has promoted religion. To be more precise, specific religions have promoted specific literacies and, conversely, specific literacies have promoted specific religions. For example, Christianity has promoted and has been promoted by literacies based on the Roman alphabet, and Islam has promoted and has been promoted by literacies based on the Arabic writing system. Yet although literacy has become virtually inseparable from religion (i.e., world religions) in modern times, the oral traditions that sustained preliterate religions have not disappeared, even in the religions of the book. Much of the practice of these literacy-based religions centrally involves oral processes and traditions. Some oral performances are based on written materials (e.g., in the Christian church service, the reading aloud of the gospel), but other oral performances are strictly oral (e.g., in Quaker services, the spontaneous sharing of thoughts aloud). Moreover, congregations vary culturally in the extent to which oral and literate traditions are valorized.

Moss (2003), for example, studied three middle-class African American congregations that highly valued spontaneity and orality in the performed sermons of their ministers, but that differed in the extent to which the ministers (all highly educated) used literacy in preparing their sermons beforehand. One minister (called a "nonmanuscript" minister) thought about his sermon only for several days beforehand, expecting to be inspired by the word of God during the service, which he unfailingly was. A second minister prepared sketchy notes for his sermon beforehand and delivered a sermon also inspired by the word of God. The third minister (called a "manuscript" minister) actually wrote out his entire sermon verbatim several days before performing it. His performance, however, was equally inspired by the word of God, and it was replete with the skillful use of oral features (e.g., repetition, parallelism, and personal testimony). Whether written beforehand or not, the sermons of all three ministers were considered excellent by the members of their congregations, and two of the ministers (the "manuscript" and the "nonmanuscript" ministers) were widely known regionally in religious and political circles. In addition, the "manuscript" minister had appeared on the local PBS television station in a documentary that included his sermons. All three ministers, then, met the culturally based expectations of their congregations in performing (seemingly) spontaneous, orally skilled sermons, whether or not literacy was used in their preparation.

Such valorizing of orality, which, of course, is not limited to African American congregations, can be seen as symbolic of the religious "spirit." In this view, literacy symbolizes the "letter," whereas orality symbolizes the "spirit." Thus, although literacy has been intricately connected to religion for many centuries, some practitioners still greatly appreciate St. Paul's comment in the Christian New Testament that his second epistle to the Corinthians was "written not with ink, but with the spirit of the living God, ... for the letter killeth but the spirit giveth life." The history of Christianity details many conflicts between the "letter" and the "spirit" of the law. The tension underlying these conflicts, in fact, has generated not only dissension, but also subsequent differentiation into separate sects.

Conflicts between the letter and the spirit, however, although in impetus representative of literacy and orality, actually have drawn on these two channels of language in more complex ways. The complexity is related to a conflict inherent in the way literacy is used in missionary Christianity. As the religion and its written traditions are proselytized, knowledge that was previously available only to the literate clergy is democratized among church members:

> This [is] manifest in the missionaries' proclamation that God has offered a way to salvation for all, that the divine message is written down in the Bible which contains the truth—final, complete and available to everybody. But such a position also entails a democratizing element that inevitably

challenges any clerical meritocracy that tries to establish itself as the cus-
todian of the truth and supervise a correct interpretation of the scripture.
(Probst, 1993, p. 213)

With increasing literacy and religious knowledge, then, church members
realize that they can study the Bible themselves, and that they therefore are
authorized (literally, they can become "authors") to challenge church leaders. Therefore, the tension between the letter and the spirit, or what is in part
a tension between literacy and orality, has a political dimension as well.
Throughout history, literacy has been associated with authority and power.
Within the domain of the church, the authority of literate clergy has been
vested in their ability to read and interpret the scriptures (literally the written
doctrine) that define the standards according to which people are expected
to live. Rebellions against this authority and power have emphasized spiritual renewal and the simple faith of ordinary people, as opposed to the
"empty book learning" of the more highly literate church leaders (Peel,
1968), and yet they also have claimed authority via literacy for rebel leaders
as well. That is, although based on a "return" to oral traditions and spirit,
such rebellions also have used literacy for their own purposes.

One example of this can be seen in the Aladura movement among the
Yoruba in western Nigeria during the first decades of the 20th century
(Probst, 1993). Missionaries to this area promoted both Christianity and
literacy, with the result that a large number of indigenous Yoruba acquired enough literacy to fill an expanding number of clerical positions in
British colonial government agencies. Apparently, the Yoruba quickly associated the power of writing with the political and economic superiority
of Christianity (and Islam as well), but eventually were disappointed to
realize that the power of literacy did not give them full access to all the
power held by the colonialists.

One particular convert to Christianity, who was educated in mission
schools, Joseph Oshitelu, formed the Aladura sect (aladura in Yoruba
means "one who prays") that broke away from the missionary church.
Oshitelu claimed his authority as a prophet was based on visions that
came to him in a dream. These visions, significantly, included a new writing system similar in appearance to Arabic. The authority of such prophets
historically has relied on their ability to interpret the "unwritten words of
God" that were revealed to them in visions (Probst, 1993, p. 213). To the
traditionally oral culture of the Yoruba, such prophets had great appeal.
Oshitelu, however, did not rely only on such a valorizing of oral traditions

and spirit, but claimed the authority of writing as well by transcribing his visions of the new script into massive notebooks. Thus the new sect (now the Church of the Lord) was syncretic in that it combined old traditions with new, literacy with orality, the letter with the spirit.

Syncretism, of course, refers to the process in which elements from different cultures are combined into a new system. Mexican Catholicism, for example, is said to be highly syncretic, having combined elements from indigenous Mexican cultures with Spanish Catholicism. In Mexico, however, some of the indigenous cultures were literate (e.g., both Mayans and Aztecs), unlike the Yoruba in the case just described. The Spaniards clearly enhanced their colonization of indigenous Mexicans, and certainly gained more converts to Catholicism, by allowing the blending of Indian and Spanish elements into a new culture and religion. The Catholicism that resulted from this blending incorporated oral traditions from both cultures (e.g., Indian ceremonial dates celebrated with Christian symbols), but attempted to destroy completely the literate traditions of the Indians. Clerics burned more than 400,000 manuscripts, believing that the written words would be too powerful in supporting the religious beliefs of the Aztecs (Vigil, 1984). Some book burning also occurred among Europeans who were competing for their version of Christianity, primarily Catholics against Protestants.

Thus the old literacy was destroyed and a new literacy put in its place. Many Spanish priests learned the indigenous languages of Mexico and worked to convert people solely in their native languages, both orally and with books written in indigenous languages with the Spanish alphabet. Many clerics taught the liturgy and catechism in native Mexican languages to further understanding of the doctrine. Acceptance of Christianity was further hastened by the Church's sanctioning of the vision seen by a recent convert, Juan Diego, who "reported that he had seen the embodiment of the Virgin Mary in a saintly, brown-skinned apparition" at a holy site formerly dedicated to the Aztec goddess Tonantzin (Vigil, 1984). Thus the Patron Saint of Mexico, the Virgin of Guadalupe, was established. The Virgin is a central symbol of the syncretic nature of Mexican Catholicism, and many churches in Chicago that serve Mexican congregations now include a shrine to the Virgin of Guadalupe.

With this background, we can see that Mexican Catholicism combines indigenous elements with Spanish ones, and that it combines as well the letter and the spirit, literacy and orality. In what follows, I discuss oral and literate religious practices within a transnational social network of Mexican families based primarily in Chicago. I focus in particular on one woman, the eldest of the first generation to migrate to Chicago from their rural village in Michoacán. This woman, here called Doña C., is active in the Charismatic Renovation, a movement within Catholicism that involves much literacy activity yet also valorizes the spirit as expressed through orality.

LITERACY AND ORALITY WITHIN ONE SOCIAL NETWORK OF MEXICAN FAMILIES IN CHICAGO

For more than a decade I was a participant observer in the transnational lives of this social network of Mexican families in Chicago and in their village-of-origin (a *rancho*) in the state of Michoacán, Mexico. People from this and other *ranchos* in the region are small landowners with at least some livestock, and they have used money earned in Chicago to, among other things, buy more land on which to plant avocadoes back in their *rancho*. The first network members to migrate to Chicago came to work in railroad construction, which still is one of the primary occupations of the men, 40 years ago. During that time, more family members came to Chicago, first men, then wives and children, then single women. Many of them now own houses in Chicago, in the neighborhoods of Pilsen, Little Village, and, more recently, further south in McKinley Park, Marquette Park, Back of the Yards, and Gage Park. Many also own houses back in the *rancho* in Mexico, and travel by various people between the *rancho* and Chicago is very frequent.

This tightly knit network of families lives, works, and socializes together. It could be said, especially with regard to the adults, that they form the fabric of each other's lives. Such close ties are characteristic of many immigrant groups, but they are particularly important for Mexicans because of their system of *compadrazgo* (literally coparenting) in which each child has three sets of godparents, and because of the importance to them of *la familia,* which is the extended, not the immediate, nuclear family. Such networks sustain members physically, economically, and emotionally.

The research I conducted was ethnographic. Thus I gathered data through participant observation over the long term, and I attempted to understand meaning from the point of view of various family members. My focus in this research was on the uses of language in context, not abstracted from the settings, participants, or sociocultural processes with which they co-occur. These types of understandings, of course, require the careful nurturing of human relationships, and I have been very fortunate, as an outsider, to have been accepted and included so regularly in network activities.

One aspect of this research has included the description of literacy practices among the adults in these families across the domains of their lives. These literacy practices involve both reading and writing, in both Spanish and English, in a variety of contexts. I have described these practices in five domains: the church, the state and law, commerce, family and home, and education (Farr, 1994a, 1994b). The religious domain is unique among the five in that it is the only domain in which Spanish rather than English literacy predominates, and it is the only domain in which primarily text-level literacy occurs (e.g., the reading of books and magazines rather than institutional forms).

The women in these families generally are more involved with the church than the men, and some of the women read religious materials more than anything else. *Rancheros* (small property owners) from Michoacán, like those from other western Mexican states, are regarded as conservative and intensely Catholic, and these families fit well within these perceptions. During the revolution of 1910, in fact, *rancheros* in western Mexican states supported the *cristero* movement that fought against the revolutionaries, whom they saw as anti-Christ and who were attempting to close some churches (Jacobs, 1982; Meyer, 1976). The churches did not remain closed, and Catholicism is a central part of these families' lives, both in the *rancho* and in Chicago. Catechism (*doctrina*) was held in one family's home on Saturday mornings, and religious holidays are celebrated within homes as well. Around Christmas in particular, families host *Posada* visits by other church members, and they organize home ceremonies in which the infant Jesus is laid to rest in a manger (*el asentamiento*), and in which he is taken up again and put away for another year (*el levantamiento*). All these activities involve literacy, always in Spanish.

One woman in particular (Doña C.) is regarded as the most religious person in the network. Like the others, she was a practicing Catholic in Mexico and after moving to Chicago. Her religious activity increased dramatically, however, when she joined the Catholic Charismatic Renovation in Chicago. Along with being the most religious person in the network, she is correspondingly the most active reader and writer among the adult women. She says that at first she was reluctant to join this group, feeling that it was not really Catholic, although it met in a Catholic church:[2]

No fue fácil a mí entrar en la Renovación. Porque yo siempre he sido católica y, y siempre este—yo no he querido nunca cambiar. Pero tampoco quería, quería oir—tenía miedo. No tenía principio, no estaba preparada. Y no quería que nadie me hablara de otras sectas. Tal vez, inconscientemente por ese miedo, verdad, de que no sabía responder, no sabía—no, no tenía preparación. Pero una amiga mía me empezó a, a decir que, que por qué no iba al círculo de oración. Pero yo le decía, "Esto es diferente esto no, no es católico, esto será—quién sabe qué religión será." Aunque me tenía esa duda de que estaba en la iglesia católica—

[It] was not easy for me to enter the Renovation because I have always been Catholic and, and always um—I have never wanted to change. But I also didn't want, want to hear—I was scared. I didn't have the foundation, I wasn't prepared.[3] And I didn't want anyone to tell me about other sects. Perhaps, unconsciously because of that fear, right, of not knowing how to respond, I didn't know—I wasn't prepared. But a friend of mine started asking me why I didn't go to the prayer circle. But I would tell her, "This is different, this isn't, isn't Catholic, this is—who knows what religion it is." Even though I had that doubt that it was [held] in a Catholic church.

Later, however, when events in Doña C.'s domestic life were causing her almost unbearable stress, she consented to go to a prayer meeting in a friend's home. From then on, she was impressed with the power of the Holy Spirit to heal and the sense of community that this entailed:

Eso es lo bonito de nuestra religión, que nuestro Señor no, no hace—no actúa El solo sino nos—nos necesita a nosotros. Nos necesita no para El sino para nosotros mismos. Por ejemplo, El no viene a perdonar los pecados por una confesión directamente y tú te confiesas directamente con El, pero usa sus sacerdotes para que tú te confieses y ellos te perdonen. Entonces así nos va usando, usa nuestras manos para reemplazar las de El y ponerlas en los enfermos. Eso es lo bonito y eso es lo que uno—lo llena decir "Soy un instrumento del Señor." Pero con humildad tiene que pedir uno esto.

That is the beauty of our religion, that our Lord doesn't—he doesn't act alone but rather—he needs us. He needs us not for him, but rather for ourselves. For example, he doesn't come to forgive sins because of a direct confession, and you confess directly to him, but he uses his priests so that you can confess and they forgive you. So then, that is how he uses us, he uses our hands to replace his and place them on the sick. That is the beauty and that is what one—what fills one to say "I am an instrument of the Lord." But one has to ask for this humbly.

This movement is reminiscent of Protestant fundamentalist sects because of its Pentecostal character, especially in its stress on communicating directly with God through the scriptures rather than solely through intermediaries in the church. This emphasis contrasts with that of the traditional Catholic Church, in which only the clergy were highly literate, and in which priests interpreted scripture for the laity. Catholic Charismatics, like members of similar Protestant movements, believe one can interpret the authority of the Bible oneself: One can read and comprehend it oneself. Moreover, one can appeal, through prayer, directly to God to be filled with the Holy Spirit. In Catholicism, of course, the church also is vested with authority, and Doña C. has commented about this hierarchy and how it provides a person with someone to turn to for help. She has reflected on the fact that although some priests are very understanding of this movement, others are not, dismissing it as "crazy." She seems, then, to have struck a delicate balance between respecting the church hierarchy as authoritative and claiming that authority for herself through her reading and reflection. In addition to the reading of scripture and a variety of other published religious books, she writes prayers in advance of her weekly prayer circle that often take the form of letters addressed to God, Jesus, or the Holy Spirit (Guerra & Farr, 2002).

Literacy, in fact, seems to have been an important part of her experience from childhood on. Although she attended school only until the third grade (higher grades were not available in the *rancho* at that time), she liked to read as a child. She says:

> *Desde niña me gustó mucho leer. Yo cogía cualquier periódico, cualquier pedazo de papel que trajera letras, yo lo leía. Yo leía revistas de amor, leía cual—revistas baratas. Todo lo que—todo lo que caía a mis manos, como te dije, yo lo leía. Pero hubo una revista que a mí me impactó. Se llama* Selecciones. *Porque esas* Selecciones *traen mucha enseñanza. Ya no era la, la novelita de amor que, que tiene el mismo desenlace, la misma porquería. Sino ya venía algo más, más fuerte, más, más—una enseñanza mejor.*

Since I was a child I really liked to read. I would pick up any newspaper, any piece of paper that had letters, I would read. I would read romance magazines, I read what—inexpensive magazines. Everything that—everything that fell into my hands, as I told you, I would read. But there was a magazine that made an impact on me. It's called *Selections*. Because those *Selections* have a lot of teachings [in them]. It was no longer the, the same little romance novel that, that had the same climax, the same garbage. But rather there was something more, something stronger, more, more—a better teaching.

A significant literacy event in her childhood also involved her mother's leadership. As she explains it:

> *Este, nosotros todo el tiempo fuimos, este, católicos, verdad. Y entonces cuando yo era niña, mi mamá me llevaba a misa y la misa era en Latín. Entonces no se sabía nada lo que la—solamente la persona que sabía Latín sabía lo [que] estaba diciendo el padre, verdad. La demás gente no. Pero mi Mamá fue una persona muy precavida; fue una persona con mucha sabiduría. Ella compró un misal en, en Español. Entonces toda la gente estaba en misa, pero mi Mamá y yo estábamos leyendo. Entonces ... o sea, desde entonces ya—sabíamos lo que decía la misa.*

> Um, we were always, um, Catholics, right. So when I was a girl, my mother would take me to mass and mass was in Latin. So nothing was known about what the—only the people who knew Latin knew what the priest was saying, right. The rest of the people didn't. But my mother was a very prudent person; she was a person with much wisdom. She bought a missal book in, in Spanish. So then, all the people were [listening] in mass, but my mother and I were reading. So then ... that is, since then, we knew what was being said in mass.

In retrospect, this could be seen as laying the foundation for Doña C.'s later joining of the Charismatic Renovation. Her mother had taken the first step to understanding the scripture, here the mass, for herself and for her young daughter. That act of assertion left its imprint on Doña C. It was replicated later when her family was the first to buy a Bible when they became available for 25 pesos.

Currently, her uses of reading and writing, although almost entirely religious, strike some interesting parallels with academic literacy. She believes that *la literatura te enseña* (literature teaches you) and that *hay libros que te llenan* (there are books that fill you). There are times, she says, "*Que me meto en un libro y no quiero dejarlo*" ("that I get into a book and don't want to leave it"), particularly when it enables her to feel as though she is "*caminando con El en ese momento. Estás viviendo en El, estás, te—parece que tú estás viviendo en ese tiempo en que, en que El vino*" (walking with him [Jesus] at that moment. You are living in him, you are, you—it seems as if you are living in that time in which, in which he came). Doña C. clearly distinguishes between books according to how well they are written, recognizing those that are *bien narrado* (well narrated), that pull the reader into them, make the writing as alive as the life one is living now. She maintains that some of the Bible even is not *bien narrado* because some parts really are simply written versions of what some people experienced. Some of the writers were actually quite *rústicos* (rustic) and perhaps uneducated:

> *Cada uno fue formando, según se les vino a la, a la mente, a la cabeza, dejar escrito lo que ellos vieron, testigos de lo que ellos fueron testigos. Pero no con una—ellos no se preocuparon de que el mundo fuera a pensar—por ejemplo, no, no, este, no pusieron su niñez de Cristo, no la pusieron.*

> Each of them went forming, according to what came to, to mind, into their head, leaving written accounts of what they saw, witnesses of what they witnessed. But not with a—they didn't worry that the world would wonder—for example, they didn't um, they didn't write down Christ's childhood, they didn't write about it.

Thus Doña C. distinguishes between writing crafted for the reader and that which is simply a written account of experience. This parallels the value network members place on well-crafted oral language that is artfully articulated for audience appeal (Farr, 1993). Such interweaving of orality and literacy belies the dichotomy suggested by some scholars.

Doña C.'s understanding of the writing of the Bible also suggests an awareness of the "historicity" of the text, an awareness that also is evident in her comments about the languages and dialects in which various versions of the Bible were written. This sense of a different time and place in which the text was created also is emphasized when she asserts that "*la Biblia se puede leer fácilmente pero no se puede entender fácilmente*" (the Bible can be read easily, but it can't be understood easily), and that the Bible is not to be taken literally. Moreover, it indicates a certain sophistication about literature.

Commenting on how expensive one of her books was (50,000 [old] pesos in Mexico), Doña C. stresses that such books are well worth it when one likes them. This particular book, she says, "*tiene mucho de ... política*" (it has a lot of politics), "*la política en la que se desenvolvió Cristo en aquellos tiempos*" (the politics in which Christ was involved in those times), including information about the laws and how they were interpreted, and how they were used to imprison and crucify Jesus. This interest in politics indicates that Doña C.'s religious reading is not simply a noncritical, passive process. In fact, she applies what she learns from her books to current politics as well. (In the following transcription, accents on four verbs follow Doña C.'s own rural dialect usage rather than standard Spanish; these are marked with asterisks.) Discussing the story of Moses, Doña C. says:

El, él era hebreo, y los egipcios no querían la raza hebrea porque los hebreos estaban multiplicándose rápidamente. Tenían miedo que les quitaran el, el poder. Es lo mismo que en Estados Unidos está pasando. Si uno analiza las cosas, es lo mismo. Estados Unidos tiene miedo que los hispanos gánemos* este país, destrúyamos* su, su, su raza. Porque la raza de, de, del mero mero es an—anglosajón, es poca. Pero este país está—está mezclado con muchas razas. Y la que más ha crecido, la raza morena y la raza hispana. Entonces, ellos tienen miedo que nosotros al—a lo largo de la historia, quite—los destrónemos*, los los quítemos* del poder. ¿Me entiendes? Eso mismo tenía—ese mismo—esa misma historia pasó en Egipto.

He, he was Hebrew, and the Egyptians didn't like the Hebrew race because the Hebrews were growing rapidly. They were afraid that [the Hebrews] would take the, the power away from them. It's the same thing that is going on in the United States. If one analyzes things, it is the same thing. The United States is scared that we Hispanics will win this country, destroying their, their, their race. Because the race of the, of the, of the true Anglo-Saxon is few. But this country is, is mixed with many races. And the ones that have grown most are the Black and the Hispanic races. So then, they are afraid that we, in the long run of history, we dethrone them, we take power away from them. Do you understand me? That was the same thing—that very thing—that same story happened in Egypt.

Thus Doña C. uses what in academia is called "critical thinking": Drawing on historical sources, she analyzes a contemporary political situation through analogy. Although people certainly exercise such critical thinking with and without literacy, it seems that for Doña C., her activities within the Charismatic Renovation have stimulated both her literacy and her analytic thinking.

In addition to emphasizing literacy, however, the Charismatic Renovation emphasizes the personal experiencing of spirituality and community, contexts in which orality is highly valued. Doña C. refers to the precolonial and pre-Christian religions of Mexico as highly spiritual, claiming that Mexicans are more open to spirituality than some other people. She also has referred to the writings of the Spanish Saint, Teresa de Avila, who is considered to be one of Catholicism's great experts on spirituality and mysticism. Prayer meetings and other religious classes she attends emphasize self-expression. This focus on orality is particularly evident when someone "speaks in tongues."

Pagels (1979) associated the spiritualism of the gnostics with feminism, and women in these families also connect women with spiritualism, in ways that are compatible with the traditional Mexican view of woman as the spiritual center of the family. As a gender role, this sometimes requires suffering and sacrifice on the part of the mother, but it also includes clear authority and power within the domestic and religious domains. In the Charismatic Renovation, spiritualism is associated directly with power. Through prayer, one asks to be filled by the Holy Spirit to bring peace to one's soul and to empower one to heal others through the laying on of hands. This power is deemed to be so forceful that it is sometimes frightening, but it is also deemed to be effective. In Doña C.'s words:

Pero hay un, un momento que viene un descanso en el espíritu.... En nuestras reuniones, en nuestras ora—círculo de oración, sucede, pero mucha gente no las comprende. O sea el—cuando te ponen las manos y tú estas en el posición, el Espíritu Santo viene y te descansa. Como que toma todo tu, tu, tu ser. Y lo transforma en, en, en paz.

But there is a, a moment when a rest comes to the soul.... In our reunions, in our pra—prayer circle, it happens, but many people don't understand it. In other words the—when they place the hands on you and you are in the position, the Holy Spirit comes and lets you rest. As if it takes all your, your, your being. And it transforms it into, into, into peace.

Thus the power of the Holy Spirit is used for healing, and the charismatics, filled with this power, heal others in the community. To Doña C., the beauty of her religion is the communal nature of this healing, that she herself can be an instrument of God's work. Rather than relying only on the church hierarchy, she herself can fully participate in such transformative, powerful processes.

With such power democratized within the church, with the ability to communicate with God and the Holy Spirit directly, there should be less need for the saints to intercede on one's behalf with God the Father. Nevertheless, Doña C. insists on inserting the Virgin of Guadalupe into the readings she prepares for church meetings. According to her,

Por ejemplo, se está diciendo que en la renovación se habla muy poco de la santísima Virgen.... Y la gente se, se, se siente mal porque uno de católico ama mucho la santísima Virgen, verdad. Y no la quiere dejar uno hacer a un lado. Aunque en verdad, la santísima Virgen fue la esclava del Señor, fue—ella en su, en su ser, siempre estuvo como oculta, como, como no ocupando un primer lugar. Ella siempre estuvo en un, en un segundo plano. Pero ella es muy importante en, en nuestra iglesia, es importantísima. Entonces yo trato de sacar, casi siempre, siempre, las lecturas, las prédicas que yo llevo, yo siempre trato de meter a la santísima Virgen. Para para que no nomás sea, por—todo se habla del Espíritu Santo, de nuestro padre Dios, de, de del señor Jesucristo, que es la divina providencia, pero hay que tener también, de la santísima Virgen. Entonces yo busqué en otra—en otra vez que me tocó llevar la prédica, busqué en el, el, el—el adiós de de Jesús con su madre. ¡Ay, es una cosa hermosa, cuando Cristo se fue a despedir de la santísima Virgen!

For example, there is talk that in the renovation there is little talk about the Virgin Saint.... So the people feel bad because, being Catholic, one loves the Virgin Saint very much, right. And one doesn't want to let her be put to the side. Even if in reality, the Virgin Saint was the Lord's slave, she was—in her, in her being, she was always hidden, like, like, not occupying first place. She was always in the, in the background. But she is very important in, in our church, very important. So then I try to bring into, almost always, always, the readings, in the talks that I give, I always try to bring in the Virgin Saint. So that it isn't only—everything is always said about the Holy Spirit, and God our father, and, the Lord, Jesus Christ, who is the divine providence, but we must also have the Virgin Saint. So then I looked in other—the other time that it was my turn to preach, I looked for the—for the farewell between Jesus and his mother. Oh it is such a beautiful thing when Christ went to bid farewell to the Virgin Saint!

The apparent paradox of insisting on including the Virgin, although not needing her for intercession between oneself and God, is resolved if we interpret Doña C.'s insistence on the Virgin as a symbol of a powerful woman and mother. For Mexican Catholics generally, the Virgin is *importantísima* (extremely important), but for women in particular, she may be even more important. Doña C. refers to the Virgin as being *en un segundo plano* (in the background), even as an *esclava* (slave), as if *la santísima Virgen estaba en el—en la cocina cocinando con las señoras, ¿verdad?* (the saintly Virgin was in the—in the kitchen cooking with the other women, right?). These phrases echo comments she has made about the secondary position of women in contemporary society. In these comments, she has been critical of discrimination against women in the assumption held by many that boys, not girls, should be educated. Her concerns reflect the daily life she lives, which often is burdened by tensions and conflict inherent in a patriarchal system.

Doña C., like the other women in the network, is of very strong character. She continues in the renovation despite opposition to it from many, although by no means all, members of her extended *familia*. For her, the sense of empowerment that comes with these activities allows her to resist and often transcend very oppressive situations. She describes one such situation:

> *Cuando yo estoy este, eh, leyendo para mí, yo casi siempre estoy [leyendo] en voz bajita. O sin, sin hablar, con la pura mente. O sea hay veces que yo me concentró en la lectura. [Mi marido] está oyendo la televisión—hay veces que a él le gusta tanto ver ese programa de "Porcel." Antes yo peleaba mucho con él porque ese programa es un programa sucio. Es un programa que a mí no me gusta. Entonces yo cojo mis libros y yo me recuesto allí donde estoy y yo me meto en mi lectura y nada me interesa de lo demás. Pero es para mí, sí. Pero cuando hay oportunidad de de de leerle a alguien una—algo, se la leo, se las explico más o menos. Y en la iglesia seguido me pongo a—me ponen a leer los salmos, a leer las primeras lecturas, la última lectura, y así. Por eso, sí leo en público, [y] leo también para mí. Así.*

When I am, um, reading for me, I am almost always reading with a low voice, or without, without speaking, only with my mind. In other words there are times when I concentrate on the reading. My husband is watching the television—there are times when he likes so much to watch that program of "Porcel." I used to fight a lot with him because that program is very dirty. It is a program that I do not like. So then I pick up my books and I lie down right where I am and I get into my reading and none of the other stuff interests me. But it is for me, yes. And when there is the opportunity to read someone a—something, I read it, I more or less explain it to that person. And in church I—they often have me read the psalms, the first reading, the last reading, and so on. So I do read in public, [and] I also read for me. Like that.

Doña C. thus uses both the letter and the spirit, both literacy and orality, to gain the power to overcome the considerable difficulties with which she contends in her daily life. Although the culture in which she was raised highly values oral traditions and the skillful use of oral language, literacy is equally important to Doña C. and the other women who read religious materials. By immersing herself in her religious readings at difficult moments, Doña C. is able to assert control over her own life and over her own space. She did not, after all, leave the room in which her husband was watching TV, ceding the space to him. She stood her ground. She read her books and was filled with a sense of power that enabled her to transcend the limits imposed on her by a system that assigns women such as her secondary status.

What we cannot yet know is whether such a sense of empowerment allows only survival—a coping with the status quo—or whether it leads to more profound change, either within Doña C.'s own life or more broadly within the extended *familia* and larger community. The indications across the network of families, however, and especially across the generations in the families, are that gender roles are changing dramatically, both here and in Mexico. More women are limiting the number of children they bear, and others are avoiding marriage either entirely or until they find someone with whom they can have what they view as a more equitable relationship than has existed for many of their mothers and grandmothers. I argue, however, that the acts of assertion I have discussed (Doña C.'s mother buying the missal book; Doña C. asserting herself through literacy, religion, and spiritualism), inasmuch as they are observed and noted or learned about later through discussion, contribute significantly to the gender role changes that many, although not all, of the younger women are making. These acts of assertion, then, are small yet significant steps that clearly can lead to wider social change.

REFERENCES

Farr, M. (1993). Essayist literacy and other verbal performances, *Written Communication, 10*(1), 4–38.

Farr, M. (1994a). Biliteracy in the home: Practices among *mexicano* families in Chicago. In D. Spener (Ed.), *Adult biliteracy in the United States* (pp. 89–110). McHenry, IL and Washington, DC: Delta Systems and Center for Applied Linguistics.

Farr, M. (1994b). *En los dos idiomas*: Literacy practices among *mexicano* families in Chicago. In Beverly Moss (Ed.), *Literacy across communities* (pp. 9–47). Cresskill, NJ: Hampton Press.

Goody, J. (1986). *The logic of writing and the organization of society*. Cambridge, England: Cambridge University Press.

Guerra, J., & Farr, M. (2002). Writing on the margins: The spiritual and autobiographical discourse of *mexicanas* in Chicago, *School's out! Bridging out-of-school literacies with classroom practice* (pp. 96–123). New York: Teachers College Press.

Jacobs, I. (1982). Ranchero *revolt: The Mexican revolution in* Guerrero. Austin: University of Texas Press.

Johansson, E. (1981). The history of literacy in Sweden. In H. Graff (Ed.), *Literacy and social development in the west: A reader* (pp. 151–182). Cambridge: Cambridge University Press.

Meyer, J. (1976). *The Cristero rebellion: The Mexican people between church and state, 1926–1929*. Cambridge: Cambridge University Press.

Moss, B. (2003). *A community text arises: A literate text and a literacy tradition in African American churches*. Cresskill, NJ: Hampton Press.

Pagels, E. (1979). *The gnostic gospels*. New York: Random House.

Parrinder, G. (Ed.). (1971). *World religions: From ancient history to the present*. New York: Facts on File Publications.

Peel, J. D. Y. (1968). *Aladura: A religious movement among the Yoruba*. Oxford: Oxford University Press.

Probst, P. (1993). The letter and the spirit: Literacy and religious authority in the history of the Aladura movement in Western Nigeria. In B. Street (Ed.), *Cross-cultural approaches to literacy* (pp. 198–219). Cambridge, England: Cambridge University Press.

Vigil, J. (1984). *From Indians to Chicanos: The dynamics of Mexican American culture*. Prospect Heights, IL: Waveland Press.

ENDNOTES

1. This chapter is a revised version of Farr, M. (2000). Literacy and religion: Reading, writing, and gender among Mexican women in Chicago. In P. Griffin, J. K. Peyton, W. Wolfram, & R. Fasold (Eds.), *Language in action: New studies of language in society* (pp. 139–154). Cresskill, NJ: Hampton Press,.

2. Doña C.'s words in this chapter were tape-recorded by me and a friend/member of the social network, Beatriz Leonor Navarro. Doña C.'s original Spanish is in italics; an English translation follows (Mayra Nava, an undergraduate at the University of Illinois at Chicago who worked as my Research Assistant, transcribed the tapes and did a rough first translation, which I revised). The excerpts are from a 3-hour conversation in which I said very little. Doña C. took control of the "interview" immediately after I turned the tape-recorder on, leading us all in a prayer to begin our session. She determined all topics of conversation, seizing the opportunity, perhaps, to persuade us of the rightness of her choices, or even to convince us to join the movement. Virtually all the discourse on the tape is hers.

3. The word *preparada* (prepared) in Mexico often refers to having been schooled and thus "prepared" for (modern) society. Doña C. may be using it here partly in that sense: she didn't have the formal education to know how to deal with this new experience. She also may intend another, related meaning: She wasn't *spiritually* prepared to deal with this new experience. I thank Elías Dominguez Barajas for raising this latter point.

Photograph by Richard Gelb.

CHAPTER

12

The Magic of Verbal Art: Juanita's Santería Initiation[1]

Richard G. Gelb

Benito Juarez Community Academy, Chicago

It was Friday, July 7, 1995, and Juanita Figueroa and I were sitting at the kitchen table in the back room of her *botánica*,[2] which was where we always met to discuss Santería. It was almost 6 p.m., the time Juanita closed the store. Through the years I had come to know this table as Juanita's workbench, for on any given day, at any time, she would be using it for grating coconuts, chopping fruits, sorting large bags of herbs into smaller retail bags, threading a variety of colored beads to make necklaces, painting religious statues, or sewing clothes. Juanita had taught me about the magical significance of these items, and I was now ready to learn how to conduct divination and exorcism rituals.

Juanita, a Puerto Rican woman slightly taller than 5 feet and matronly in appearance, was in her early 60s. She was wearing her typical work clothes, which consisted of a white blouse and a matching white skirt. We were alone, and the purpose of our meeting was for me to have one of my first "classes" on how to perform seashell divination,[3] which is an essential aspect of a *santero's* spiritual obligations. Before we had a chance to get started, I casually mentioned that in response to my inquiry, I had received a letter from Juanita's *madrina*[4] in the religion. We talked for a while about her, and then I asked Juanita if she could tell me again about how they had met. I tape-recorded Juanita's dramatic response, but before I present my transcription of Juanita's performance, I first must explain where the *botánica* is located and how I came to be there, then provide the theoretical background to support my claim that verbal art should be regarded as oral literature.[5]

NORTH AVENUE

The *Botánica Yemayá* is located in Chicago's Humboldt Park community, on North Avenue, a street that runs east and west, connecting Lake Michigan with the suburbs. A clear distinction can be made regarding the varying degrees of economic vitality of the neighborhoods along this route, from which the *botánica* predominantly draws its clientele. For example, a distinguishing characteristic of both the urban, gentrified, Lincoln Park, and the affluent suburb, Oak Park, which form Chicago's eastern and western boundaries, respectively, on this street is that the emphasis of the retail stores is on selling products "new" to their customers. The emphasis in the neighborhoods where family incomes are low, in contrast, tends to be on products that are "used" or "repaired." To appreciate more fully Juanita's role as a healer in her community, and its significance in relation to her performance, I provide a brief description of North Avenue.

To begin with, *santeros* believe that the goddess *Yemayá,* who rules the oceans and lakes, resides in Lake Michigan. As one continues west, through Lincoln Park, where affluent people of predominantly European ethnic backgrounds reside (Chicago Fact Book Consortium, 1995), and the recently gentrified West Town, the economic landscape begins to change.

The difference between selling "new" and "used" becomes obvious near Ashland Avenue. This is the place where security gates first begin to appear in front of display windows, where the Logan Square neighborhood begins, which is located to the northeast of Humboldt Park. It has the largest Puerto Rican population in the city, a large Mexican American community, as well as Cubans and Hispanics from Central and South America (Chicago Fact Book Consortium, 1995). Here the advertising first begins to appear sporadically in Spanish, and the stores begin to advertise used and repaired items. Near Western Avenue, there is a small grocery store that has a Puerto Rican flag painted on it. This signals the unofficial entry into the Puerto Rican community.

Originating on the way from Oak Pak, to the west of Humboldt Park, beginning at Austin Boulevard, is the predominantly African American Austin community. The security gates that protect the store windows silently announce the border between Oak Park and Chicago. Here are boarded-up stores, and, unlike the more affluent communities, churches are now housed in storefronts. Just past Laramie, on the south side of the street, there is a Catholic Church, whose sign in front advertises that on Sunday there are separate masses in English and Spanish.

Just before you get to Hamlin Avenue is the Puerto Rican Civic Society, with the star and bars of the Puerto Rican flag painted on it. Near the west end of Humboldt Park, on the south side of the street, is the *Botánica Yemayá*. Juanita, the proprietress of the *Botánica Yemayá*, has seen many entrepreneurs, including businesses, churches, and *botánicas*, come and go since she first opened for business in 1971.

LITERACY AND MAGIC

I also arrived at the *Botánica Yemayá* from two directions. My personal journey began with a youthful interest in storytelling that led to my becoming a teacher, and subsequently to the attainment of a doctorate degree in English. My passion for literature, which initially fueled my pursuit of advanced degrees, however, was surpassed by my interest in literacy, specifically, in how individuals use literacy outside of school settings. I also maintained a lifelong interest in the practice of ceremonial magic. My two diverse interests, literacy and magic, converged in my dissertation, which revealed literacy practices within the Santería religious community at the *Botánica Yemayá*. One finding of my study was how literacy and orality are interrelated, and because of this, I argue that they should not be discussed as skills that can be abstracted from each other or their contexts. In this chapter I provide my transcription of Juánita's verbal performance, then my analysis, which demonstrates how she used literary techniques and verbal art, to produce a work of oral literature.

I first met Juánita in January 1990, when I walked into the *botánica* while conducting research for a course I was taking. My subsequent visits produced the paper for the course, and I continued to stop by to see Juanita. We had struck an immediate rapport, and my admiration for her led me to ask her to become my *madrina* in the religion. She performed the introductory ceremonies of *Los Collares* and *Los Guerreros*[6] on April 16, 1990, at which time I became a Santería initiate. My initiation as a *santero* occurred April 24, 1994. As a *santero* trainee and Juanita's godchild, Juanita's traditional role included teaching me the art of divination. That was the reason I was meeting with Juanita on that late afternoon in July.

VERBAL ART

How does verbal art differ from any other form of communication? Bauman (1984) emphasized that verbal art is not "deviant from normal language" and that language is "multifunctional" (p. 17). Although elements of performance occur in ordinary conversations, a variety of features distinguish a verbal performance from other forms of oral communication. First of all, a performance begins when an individual assumes the responsibility to convey information to an audience (Bauman, 1977/1984, p. 11; Hymes, 1981, p. 84). Second, a performance is framed by using verbal and nonverbal means to indicate, among other things, when a performance begins and ends (Bateson, 1955/1972, p. 188; Goffman, 1974). A third characteristic involves stylistic features, such as an increase in the use of figurative language and parallelism (Bauman, 1977/1984, pp. 17–20; Jakobson, 1960, pp. 356, 358). Finally, verbal performances emerge out of the interaction between a context, art form, audience, and performer (Bauman, 1977/1984, pp. 37–38; Hymes, 1981, p. 86). This communication is facilitated by the use of "contextualization cues," which work to signal interpretive information to the audience (Gumperz, 1982, pp. 131–132). Juanita's report and performance of the events surrounding her Santería initiation demonstrate the similarities and differences between these two forms of communication.

Juanita received the *asiento*[7] initiation in 1979. She had alluded to me about the events surrounding her own initiation on November 12, 1994. At the time, it had been just more than 6 months since my own *asiento,* and during our discussion, Juanita began to reminisce about the events surrounding hers. She related details that I recorded in my field notes, but it had not been a performance, although certain elements of a performance were contained in it. Instead, she reported a series of highlights that were now meaningful to me because we had shared a similar experience. Hymes (1981) made the distinction between a report and a performance by classifying genres of oral language into the following categories: interpretable, reportable, and repeatable. According to Hymes' system, a report can be interpreted and repeated. A performance, on the other hand, is not repeatable because the performer, audience, and context will not be exactly the same (Hymes, 1981, pp. 84–85). Juanita's performance was therefore explicitly designed for me, based on our long acquaintance, and our co-membership in the religion, and she may have remembered that she had told me some of these details previously.

JUANITA'S PERFORMANCE

Now, let me return to my opening scene. We were sitting at Juanita's kitchen table, and I had just asked Juanita to tell me about how she had met her *madrina*. My tape-recorder was between us on the table. For a few moments, Juanita fell into contemplative silence, and then, with only my own brief responses, nonstop, she performed the following story.

Preface[8]

(Throughout the performance, Juanita's lime green Puerto Rican parrot rhythmically squawked.)

```
 1  R:   How did you meet her? Because, how, was she going [to
 2  J:                                          [How
 3       did I meet her? {interrupts}
 4  R:           Chicago? Or what]
 5  J:                            [No, No, No, No, [No. {waving her hand}
 6  R:                                             [Okay, this should be a good
 7       story. {chuckling}
```

Scene 1

```
 8  J:   {clearing throat—3-second pause}
 9            In 19 ... .. 78 ... ... I was real sick.
10  R:          Right.
11  J:   I went to the hospital, I have, I spend about .. 35 days in hospital. I
12       have a surgery ... . When I get out of there ... the doctor, you know I have
13       surgeries every year, every year, every year. And .. one time a doctor told
14       me, "Juanita, ... I open you, but everything was okay; I close you because
15       there is nothing to be done."
16            I said, "Why you make the hole; you know, why you cut me?"
17            "I cut you because you were so sick, but everything is okay. I'm
18       going to be honest with you; I don't need customers. I've been in a ... . a
19       doctor for 40 some years; I'm gonna retire; I don't need new customers.
20       You better find some help, .. not in the medicine, because .. you come here
21       every, every year for surgeries, and we open you, and is nothing wrong with
22       you. So, I don't know."
```

Scene 2

```
23            I said, "He's the doctor, and he told me to find some, another way to
24       get cured."
```

25   So, I uh, I come home. And I feel weak and I can hardly walk. I was
26   open, and they told me that I have to have another surgery in two more
27   weeks.
28   And when I, when I was in the hospital, was a big lady ... .. about
29   1:30 in the morning. With a scarf, a long dress with ruffle in the back. A
30   hu : ge woman. And she told me, ... "If you want to get out of here, ...
31   drink a glass of water, an extra glass of water, and drink it in the morning,
32   and, and at noon ... three times a day. And you got to get out of here; if you
33   stay here, you don't get out of here."
34   And I say, .. "I don't care." {indifferent tone}
35   And she told me , "And after YOU, it's going to be YOURS." {warning and scold-
      ing tone}
36   And I told her, "WHY? Why they have to go through what I'm
37   going through? They don't do nothin'. WHY? WHY?" I get ..
38   And she say, "All you have to do is give up, and do what we want
39   you to do."
40   And I say, "HOW?"
41   She say, uh "Come over here." {gently}
42   So I get up, .. my, my body wasn't there, but I get up from the bed, ..
43   and I stood by her. I was real, like a little, very small. And she go like that
44   in the front of me, {waving her hand slowly from left to right} and I saw ...
45   like a hill. I was standing on the hill, and a lot of people were coming to me.
46   And then she told me, "All of those people need your help."
47   And I look at her and I said, "How I'm gonna help them?"
48   She say, "You just .. say 'yes'; I be there."

Scene 3

49   Next morning, .. I said, "That was not a nurse. She was not dressed
50   as a nurse. .. Who is she? .. Aaah, she told me about drinking water, I don't
51   gonna drink nothin'." ... And I was fighting with myself, with the vision I
52 R: Mmhm. {softly}
53 J: have. ... {clearing her throat} BUT, I ask for water. .. I bless my water, because
54   my fever was so sky-high. Nothing put my fever down. .. And the the
55   surgery that I have was infected; it was bleeding.
56   So, uh, at lunch-time, I blessed the water, and I drink the glass of
57   water. And I say, "Yemayá," what she told me to say, {explanatory tone}
58   "Yemayá."

Scene 4

59   Three days later, I get out of hospital. My fever go, disappear. So I

60 was here, I can hardly walk. And a lady, Black lady, she's a teacher; she

61 come here.[9] She's not a *santera*; she's nothin'. Just a teacher from school.

62 And, she told me, "JUANITA, WHY DON'T YOU GO .. TO A *SANTERA*?"

63   I said, "Oh, *matasano!*[10] Did you believe in that shit?"

64   She say, "THERE'S SOMETHING WRONG WITH YOU. IF THE

65 DOCTOR CAN'T FIND WHAT'S WRONG WITH YOU, YOU'RE

66 GONNA DIE."

67   I said, "Everybody die. You only die once."

68   She say, "GO TO THIS LADY."

69   Aaah, I took a piece of paper, and hang it. .. Couple more days, she

70 come over.

71   "DID YOU WENT TO THAT LADY?"

72   I say, "No."

73   I said, "DID YOU GO TO THAT LADY?"

74   She say, "No, I never went to that lady."[11]

75   I said, "Why you want me to go?"

76   She said, "BECAUSE YOU NEED HER."

77   "I don't!"

Scene 5

78   I went to her house, walking from here to .. to Central Park. I can

79 can hardly walk; took me about half an hour. When I get there, I ring the

80 bell; nobody answered. I sit on the steps. That was three o'clock. I sit there

81 to five o'clock. Five o'clock, I ring the bell again.

82   And she was watching me from inside the house. And say, "THAT

83 LADY, SHE STILL THERE; I NOT PLANNING TO SEE ANYBODY

84 TODAY, BUT SHE STILL THERE. AND I GOT TO GO OUT, AND

85 SHE'S OVER THERE, AND I DON'T NEED THIS."

86   And, I told her, "Lady, you don't know me; I don't know you either.

87 I'm not a bad person. I'm here because somebody told me to come over

88 here. And, I think I need your help. If you could help .. you don't have to,

89 but, let's see what you can do about it."

90 Then she threw the shell, and the shells say, "that the hole in the

91 ground is open, waiting for my body." And I have to pay 5,000-

92 some dollars, plus the clothes, plus the *soperas*,[12] so some things that I

93   don't understand, myself.

94   And then she told me, "I WANT TO TALK TO YOUR HUSBAND."

Scene 6

95   When my husband come from work, I said, "This lady told me to for

96   you to go to talk to her. THESE PEOPLE, THEM CUBAN PEOPLE,

97   THEY JUST CARE FOR MONEY, THEY JUST WANT TO ROB YOUR

98   MONEY. SO, DON'T GIVE HER NO MONEY. JUST LISTEN WHAT

99   SHE HAVE TO TELL YOU."

100   So she told him, if I stay the way I am, I am going to die .. not too

101   long.

Scene 7

102   And .. he come home, he say, "You know a lot of things that she told

103   me, I think is true. And, I give her 3,000 dollars."

104   I said, "WHAT? WHAT YOU DO? TOLD ME WHAT YOU DO,

105   WHAT YOU DO?" {anxious tone}

106   He say, "I don't going to live long, to take care of your kids;

107   somebody has to be alive. We cannot leave, we cannot both LEAVE, leaving

108   them alone. They still need you."

109   I look at him and I said, "I'm going to go see that lady; I'm going to

110   ask for the money back."

Scene 8

111   So I went to her, and she take a measurement, and she take a

112   measurement. ... I said, "You know I don't come to measurement; I come to

113   get the money he give you."

114   She said, "He give me the money; I'm not going to give it to you. If

115   you don't want to make the *Ocha*,[13] fine; I got the *Ocha* made, and I'm

116   healthy; I'm okay. You're the one who need it. If you want it done; if you

117   want to live a couple more years, get that DONE; if you don't want to, I

118   don't going to give you the money. The same way you come; the same way

119   you can leave!"

Scene 9

120   I went home and I told my husband, I said {softly and calmly},

121   "Honey, you know somethin' what you do? You give her that money. But

122   I got that in my mind: If I die, they gonna spend about 5,000 dollars

123   to bury me. {clearing her throat} If I get the *Ocha* made, that don't happen. ..

124   Maybe she's right. .. Maybe I need the *Ocha* made, but I don't know what's
125   that."

Scene 10

126   So she say, "I'm leaving next month. You need this list of this stuff!"
127   I went and I buy clothes, but, very sexy, you know.
128   {clearing her throat} She say, "Not any of those shit that you buy is
129   good."
130   I say, "Why don't you told me the first time. You know what I need;
131   I don't. You know what you're going to do to me; I don't know. So why you
132   don't told me, the first time, how I need to buy the stuff. Maybe I can make
133   the skirt."
134   I was TOUGH with her. (aside)
135   So, she say, ... "If you want to make the *Ocha*, you can make the
136   *Ocha*. If you don't want the *Ocha* be made, you can go HOME!"
137   I want that lady—Oh, I feel like kill her. (aside)

Scene 11

138   And another time she told me, uh, ... "We're going to, you're not
139   going to have no hair, because we got to cut, take off your hair out."
140   I said, "Listen lady, you're not going to do everything that you feel
141   like you do with me. I'm an old person; I'm 40 years old; you don't have
142   to tell me what to do."
143   She say, "If you want to live a little, couple more years, you do what
144   I say; otherwise, you can LEAVE!"
145   That old lady, she kicked me out of her house. And I come back; I
146   don't know why I'm doing that.
147   "So you be ready everything for next month. We leave the 5th, the
148   5th, August 5th."

Scene 12

149   I get what I need, and we go over there. .. She want to go ..
150   driving. ... My, my surgery was open, too many hours. I said, "I cannot go!"
151   I said, "If I can't go, you cannot.
152   "Well if you don't want to go driving, in a car with us, you pay for
153   for the ticket, and we all fly there." {sarcastic tone}
154   I look like I punch her, you know. (aside)
155   I said, "Yes, *madrina*, but I got ..THIS open {pointing to her
156   abdomen.}, **and it still hurt me. I can't hardly walk.**"

157   "Say, well, ... be ready to 5 o'clock, Friday .. Tuesday, we got to be

158   there by Friday."

159   "Okay."

Scene 13

160   And I come home and I was so mad, I say, "I never do what others

161   told me to do, and now I'm just like a, I feel like a little Chihuahua,

162   following this lady. And, this lady took my money; she told me she don't

163   going to give my money back; I don't know what the hell she is going to do

164   with me. And you agree with her. Are you my husband, or my enemy?"

165   He was just laughing and he say {swaggering tone}, "Do what she

166   say. You're going to lose the money. Don't worry about it; we make more."

167 R: {laughs}

Scene 14

168   So, when I get there, the following, that, that, for that week, that

169   Friday, they took the other lady to the river; her and her son.

170 R: This was in, uh, Miami?

171 J: In Miami.

172   And I was watching, you know, watching every move they do,

173   watching everything they do. When I saw all those animals, and all those

174   things, I said, "Uh uh, they don't gonna catch me." And after she finished

175   with the ceremony and everything, .. and *Itá*[14] and all that, I told her, "I

176   want to talk to you. .. That Teresa told me, that I'm going to sell my soul;

177   that I don't going to belong to God anymore; that I .. be in the quick, soft

178   sand, and .. you don't ever told me that. What you going to do to me?

179   What's going to happen? I don't want to lose my soul. I'm Catholic. And,

180   I want you to explain. Otherwise, I leave."

181   She say, "Well, If you want to leave, you can leave. You don't going

182   to get the money back; you don't get the *Ocha* either. You can go HOME!"

183   But it was in the country, no car, and I need somebody to take me to

184   the airport. .. I don't have no cash with me, but I got my credit card.

185   And ... then she talked to me. ... ... like a person; and we have a long

186   talk. And she say, "You know something, you are a very spoiled person.

187   You want everything your way. You're used to do what you please, and

188   I'm the same way. You don't take no shit from nobody; I don't have to take

189   no shit from nobody either. So, let's be like humans, okay? Let's talk like

190   humans." So, she said, "It's for your own good. You don't understand what

191   you get into; it's something new for you. But I don't do anything to HURT

192   you, that I don't do for my, my daughter. I want you to live. I want you to
193   be well. I want to CLOSE the hole in the ground that you have open."
194   I just listened to her. And that night I was thinking: "Maybe she's
195   right, maybe she's wrong; MAYBE SHE'S RIGHT, AND MAYBE SHE'S
196   WRONG." ... It was hard.

Scene 15

197   So following Friday, that was MY turn. They took me to the river ..
198   cars passing by .. and they give me the bath. I was so ashamed. ... That dirty
199   water, with this open {pointing to her stomach} ... "I'M GONNA DIE! I'm
200   gonna get infected or ..." {voice trails off}.
201   When I come home, you know I can hardly walk. I'm very picky to
202   eat. I don't eat because I see things there were not too clean ... So, uh, I said,
203   "YOU KNOW I CANNOT SLEEP ON THE FLOOR; IT'S CEMENT!"
204   They only give me, a, a towel, and the *wisiera*[15] . ... I saw they did that to
205   the other girl, but I thought I gonna be {laughing} different.
206 R: (laughs—4-second pause)
207 J: "Ay : : !" {sighs} They gave me the pigeon in[16] my head; they give
208   me the *rogación de cabeza*,[17] and I was messy and have to stay with that. But
209   I fall asleep; I sleep like a log.

Scene 16

210   Next day, .. she took all of my medicine, and she took it away from
211   me. ... "From today, you don't going to take no more medicine. That's it."
212   I said, "I need my penicillin. I need .. for this still, you know,
213   bleeding."
214   She said, "You don't need THAT."
215   I said, "Oh my God."
216   Next morning,[18] no coffee, no nothin'. .. I was starving—I was tired—
217   I was DYING. So they start the ceremony. And I was sorry for the animal.
218   I was so sorry for them. And, .. when they start, you know, taking my, .. at
219   the beginning, when they start taking my, my hair out, my hair,[19] I just ... go
220   away. ... And whatever happened, I don't feel nothin'. When I come back, I
221   don't want to come back, they already have my *trono;*[20] they sit me there;
222   that is when the *matanza*[21] start. ... But I feel very calm. ...I feel happy
223   inside because when they were singing and all doing all my ceremony on my
224   head:
225   I went to a place where there was a lot of Black people;
226   they played tambores,[22] and I was dancing, and I was

227   dancing, and I was so happy. .

228   When they wake me up, to come back; I don't want to come back, I want to

229   stay there. The party was good, so when they start the *matanza* and

230   everything, I was tired. When they gave me the soup to drink, I drink it

231   because I was starving. They don't give me nothing during the day.

232   That night, I lay down on that cement; I sleep. ... My .. things don't

233   bother me.

Scene 17

234   Next morning, that water they give me, yucky {facial expression of

235   displeasure}, .. okay. Second day, the same story, fine, I keep it inside. But,

236   ... after *Itá*,[23] .. the room was on the first floor. I can see the moon at

237   nighttime, through the window. And one night I saw the same lady I saw in

238   the hospital. She was smiling like this: {smiling, and slowly nodding her head
         approvingly.}.

239 R: Oh, and nodding her head. Right.

240 J: And I say, "Oh she's here; she's with me."

241   .. And next day I was so happy, I saw her again. You know?

242 R: Mmhhm.

243 J: And I said, "I got a FATHER, I want to see MY father.

244   And they told me, I got, Oggún is my father, but I DON'T KNOW

245   HIM."

Scene 18

246   About, couple days later, in the same window, I saw naked man,

247   with little pants, a *machete* in her hand, in his hand, black, and he go:

248   {slowly nodding her head in approval.}.

249 R: He's nodding too.

250 J: And I tell my *madrina*, "Did you know I saw two people?"

251   She say, "Who do you see?"

252   "A fat lady, that I saw her in the hospital, in Chicago, before I know

253   you. That was not YOU, but she's big like YOU. [{chuckles}

254 R: [{laughing}

255 J: And a tall man, ... but he's not too black, and his hair is kind of red because

256   the sun."

257   And she smiled at me and say, "That's Oggún."

Scene 19

258   "And .. I get so sick, the third day; the fifth day, I can't hold nothing

259   in my stomach. Diarrhea. It hurt me so bad. She don't give me no

260   medicine; and, I stop eating. I drink the water in the morning; I stop eating.

261   And I told her to give me a little cornflour, with lemon and water."

262   She say, "No." ... .

263   "Okay, don't give me nothin'."

Scene 20

264   Next, following day I don't drink, just drink the water they give me

265   in the morning, and I don't eat nothing else."

266   Then she told me, "What you say that you want?"

267   I said, "Cornflour, lemon, and water. That take what I have in my,

268   my stomach."

269   So they give it to me.

Scene 21

270   The following day I was better. So by Friday when I get out, feel

271   weak, .. but I was okay. My "cut" was getting better. And I get used to that

272   cement. ... So, .. I learned to respect her.

273   .. And I want her to be like a friend, but she was so hard, that no

274   matter how hard you tried to please her, she was very cold.

Scene 22

275   So I say, "Well, .. now I got that thing done, but my husband, he

276   don't know what I'm getting into. He thought I'm going to be so nice, so

277   sweet, that no matter what he do, everything going to be alright, because I'm

278   a *santo*.[24] And when I start coming complaining, and I was stronger .."

279   He say, "They changed you. You not the same. Before you was a

280   son of a gun, mom, but now you no *santo*; you *diablo*.[25] {both laughing—

281   8-second pause}

282   I don't want those things in my house."

283   And I took all my *soperas*, and I moved upstairs. I don't have no

284   furniture, everything I leave it over there. I put a, a mattress on the floor,

285   and I sleep there. I sleep there for about, o ::: h 14–15 years, up

286   there.

Scene 23

287   Then after that, 6 months later he die. The hole that was open for

288   me, ... cover with him.

289 R: Mmhm.

290 J: **Because everything go to him and my brother. My brother die; he die; and,**
291   **another one, I don't remember who, die. So, all those people die, for me to**
292   **live.**
293 R: Mmhhm.

Coda[26]

294 J: So from then, .. I learn to love Yemayá because I see the many changes
295   in my life. And no matter how hard or how tight in money, I be always to solve
296   my problems. Little by little, NOT A LOT, but step by step I making to go by.

Juanita's full performance ended in line 296, signaled by her shift to the present tense, and her evaluative comments. At this point she shifted the topic to that of her children, and although she continued to talk about other subjects connected to the initiation, they were related to the present, and not directly connected to her story.

ETHNOPOETICS

The significance of storytelling as a cultural resource has been enhanced by work in the field of ethnopoetics (Hymes, 1981; Tedlock, 1983). This work provides methods for both transcribing and interpreting oral narratives. More recently, researchers such as Richard Bauman (1986), Charles Briggs (1988), Deborah Tannen (1989), and Marcia Farr (1994, 2000) have shown by illustrations that these poetic techniques are also manifested in conversational settings. The field of ethnopoetics provides a structure by which Juanita's performance can be described and discussed.

Before I analyze the literary qualities of Juanita's performance, I need to explain why I believe she told me the story of her initiation at this time. According to Jerome Bruner (1990), people construct autobiographies with a definite purpose in mind: "It is an account given by a narrator in the here and now about a protagonist bearing his name who existed in the there and then, the story terminating in the present when the protagonist fuses with the narrator (p. 121). I believe Juanita's purpose for first reporting her narrative to me in November of 1994, and later performing it in July 1995 was to justify her work as a healer. It also provided her with the spiritual credentials, so to speak, not only to perform her work, but also to be my teacher. The purpose of my visit had been to interview Juanita, so she could teach me to perform divination., but Juanita took control of the interview. Briggs (1986) discussed problems inherent when researchers conduct interviews, one of which is "the fieldworker's failure to discern a shift in genre," which can result in "interpretive errors" and missed opportunities (p. 47). Not only did I become immediately aware of this shift, but I was also fortunate to have turned on my tape-recorder.

Juanita did not alter the facts of her narrative in her performance in July 1995, but she enhanced her story through the use of magical realism and poetic devices to dramatically portray and expand the plot, which distinguishes the report of her initiation into Santería from that of her verbal performance. This was not a planned communicative event, but a spontaneous performance that emerged from the context.

Bauman (1977/1984) defines the "emergent quality" of a performance as "the interplay between communicative resources, individual competence, and the goals of the participants within the context of particular situations" (p. 38). The situation for both the report and the performance was similar, for they both took place in Juanita's kitchen, which made the time of year irrelevant. The time of day, however, may have been a factor. The time of the reported version was in the morning, before Juanita began her work. Her performance for me, then, may simply have been one more in a long series of performances. My comments communicating with her *madrina* acted as a catalyst for her story. My personal involvement with her narrative's antagonist stimulated Juanita to respond by adopting the role of storyteller that she uses in seashell divination.

The most obvious difference between Juanita's two versions of her story is with regard to length. The reported version lasted approximately 5 minutes, and with a few exceptions, it was delivered in a monologue, by which I mean with few interruptions. What was exceptional was when Juanita's insertion of dialogue between her characters into the story. This demonstrates that there is not a clear dichotomy between a report and a performance. Yet there is nonetheless a clear difference between Juanita's reported and performed versions, in both length and the extent of her use of poetic devices.

The performance version lasted 23 minutes. I believe this is significant, because published examples of verbal art (Bauman, 1986; Briggs, 1988; Tannen, 1989) involve smaller amounts of text or focus on conversations. The advantage of a longer text is that Juanita had more opportunity to demonstrate her ability to use literary techniques. Although literary techniques were contained in both versions, the performance placed greater emphasis on the following: syntactic and thematic parallelism, repetition, constructed dialogue/reported speech, metanarration, and imagery. I demonstrate how the use of these stylistic features expanded the plot and worked to create my involvement in her story.

The performance begins when I interpret Juanita's contextualization cues.[27] According to John Gumperz (1982), these are signaling devices that elicit a predictable response from the listener (pp. 131–132). The performance is framed when Juanita repeats the word "no" five times, while simultaneously waving her hand, motioning me to be quiet, to get my attention. This dramatic display serves to silence me, and Juanita may have used this time to collect her thoughts. She also may have used the pauses at the beginning of the scene to control the pace and timing of her narrative to build suspense.

What prompted me to realize that Juanita was preparing to tell a story when she did not provide any explicit cues? First of all, it was signaled by her interrupting me, which is something she rarely does, for her job demands that she not only be a good storyteller, but also a good listener. Second, when she paused to adopt a serious demeanor, I quickly recognized her semitrance-like state as a nonverbal context cue, which normally would follow her ritual tossing of the cowrie shells. Therefore, our shared cultural knowledge of Santería divination prepared me to adopt the role of audience/client, whereas Juanita was consciously making the transition to her role as performer/diviner, although the traditional setting provided by the ritual of reading the cowrie shells was absent.

William Labov (1972) used the following framework to describe the structure of a narrative: orientation, complicating action, evaluation, resolution, and coda (p. 369). The length of Juanita's narrative and the fact that it takes place in many settings and with several characters requires, like an epic poem, orientation to take place in each scene.

Juanita begins her story by situating her characters in a hospital setting. The character of the doctor immediately inserts a dramatic sense of urgency into the plot that creates audience involvement. The characters of the doctor and Juanita, as well as that of the others, all are developed solely through Juanita's use of dialogue, for she does not provide much in the way of a physical description of them.

Juanita indicates the seriousness of her medical condition by embedding in her narrative a form of repetition that Bauman (1986) labeled "redundant, paraphrastic parallel constructions," which are syntactic phrases used to expand the plot (p. 97). For example, after my response to her introductory statement, Juanita states, "I went to the hospital … spend about .. 35 days in hospital." She uses this device again when her character states, "Why you make the hole; why did you cut me?" These redundant phrases intensify the dire nature of Juanita's situation, as does her repetition of "every year." She uses this device throughout her performance.

The function of the use of reported speech, according to Bauman and Briggs (1990), is to enable "performers to increase stylistic and ideological heterogeneity by drawing on multiple speech events, voices, and points of view" (p. 70). Deborah Tannen (1989) warned, however, that the use of the term "reported speech" is misleading because one cannot "speak another's words and have them remain primarily the other's words" (p. 101). Tannen (1989) found the term "constructed dialogue" to be more accurate because "it is constructed just as surely as is the dialogue in drama or fiction" (pp. 109–110). Juanita's use of constructed dialogue is one of the strategies she employs to create involvement in her performance and to express her attitudes toward the speaker she is "quoting."

Juanita uses a brief soliloquy as a metanarrational device to open scene 2, which took place in her hospital room. Labov (1972) explained that the evaluation aspect of narrative can occur at any time, and it can appear in several forms (pp. 370–375). Juanita's soliloquy is an example of embedding her evaluation of the situation in her character's dialogue.

The hospital vision acts as the catalyst for the plot and builds the rising action. The character Juanita is at a physical and spiritual crossroads, and the dialogue with the Goddess Yemayá provides her the motivation to link her mental and physical resources for the purpose of regaining her health. Yemayá gives Juanita an ultimatum: She will be allowed to live and raise her family, but only if she submits to the authority of the Goddess and is willing to dedicate her life to helping others.

Juanita makes extensive use of constructed dialogue in this scene, as well as "syntactic parallelism" (Bauman, 1986, pp. 96–97), which are essentially phrase or clause structures that parallel earlier phrases. The parallel elements include the following phrases and their variations: "And I say," "And I told her," "And she told me," and "And she say." Another repeated phrase is "get out of here," which builds the sense of urgency of Yemayá's warning. According to Tannen (1989), repetition "facilitates the production of more language, more fluently," and "enables a speaker to produce fluent speech while formulating what to say next" (p. 48). These techniques provide a lively, natural tempo to the characters' conversational exchange.

Juanita contrasts the image of the "huge" figure of Yemayá, with that of her own "very small" nonphysical "body" on the "hill," as the two of them are watching the people coming to Juanita for help. This distinguishes

Juanita's waking-vision of Yemayá, which is so real that Juanita believes the vision could possibly have been a nurse, from what Juanita believes to be an omen that predicted her future. Juanita also uses nonverbal gestural imagery in this section to enhance the audience's involvement. When she waves her hand to indicate the large number of people moving toward her, she also is metaphorically involving me in the scene as I join Juanita as a spectator, viewing the scene that she, as Yemayá, has created.

In scene 3, once again, the settings are the same: It is the day after the vision, and Juanita is alone in the hospital. At this point in the story the conflict is primarily internal, within Juanita herself, and it is revealed through metanarration, what Bauman (1986) defined as "those devices that index or comment on the narrative itself" (p. 98). Juanita's frequent metanarrative tool is the "aside," which Labov (1972) considered a form of "external evaluation." For example, when Juanita refuses to drink the "water," she states: "And I was fighting with myself." Juanita grudgingly follows Yemayá's directives, and she soon is medically stable enough to leave the hospital.

In scene 4 the character of the teacher is introduced. She provides the connection between the character of Juanita and the "lady," who serves the dual role of Juanita's antagonist and spiritual adviser. The setting in this scene is unclear, yet it is irrelevant, for constructed dialogue gives this character her identity.

Juanita represents the teacher by speaking louder (indicated by all capitals) in the constructed dialogue throughout this section. Again, Juanita uses syntactic parallelism to accentuate the urgency the teacher feels for her friend to receive help. The teacher asks Juanita twice about going to the "lady," and Juanita tells her "no" twice. Once again, Juanita does not have faith in what others tell her to do. She writes down what her teacher-friend tells her, but the teacher senses that Juanita does not intend to follow through on her advice. The teacher is not dissuaded by this action, and continues to dialogically force the issue.

The unnamed "lady" is introduced in scene 5. The first indication of her character as the antagonist is foreshadowed in her attempt to avoid Juanita. Juanita, who is literally sick and tired, has no choice but to remain on the lady's front steps, until, finally, the woman acknowledges Juanita's presence. Juanita uses constructed dialogue to reveal what the woman is thinking, and she represents the woman's voice by speaking louder. The woman "threw the shells" to divine Juanita's future and uses metonymy in the form of "the hole" to foretell Juanita's impending death. Providing only sparse details because they were confusing to her, Juanita relates the woman's plan to save her, which involves the expenditure of "5,000-some dollars." Juanita does not reveal her own reaction, but a negative response can be surmised, because the woman asks to speak with Juanita's husband.

The husband is introduced in scene 6, but he is not given any lines to speak. He only listens. The character Juanita also speaks more loudly to emphasize her agitated emotional state. The word "money" is repeated in these lines three times in the space of 14 words to demonstrate her concern. Juanita's husband apparently follows his wife's directive to speak to the woman, for this section ends with the repetition of the woman's initial prognosis.

Scene 7 opens with the husband's return from his talk with the woman. Juanita is astonished when he reveals that he gave the woman 3,000 dollars, after she had specifically told him not to give the woman any money. Juanita repeats the word "what" four times in the space of 10 words to demonstrate her anxiety. The husband's tone in this constructed dialogue is calm, and his cavalier response provides a counterpoint to Juanita's emotional reaction. The husband then reveals his reasoning, which includes that he is worried about his own health, and the ultimate purpose for giving the woman the money was out of concern for Juanita's children.

In scene 8 Juanita again uses constructed dialogue to reveal the authoritarian nature of the woman who is referred to only as "lady." The woman's temperament is foreshadowed in the scene in which she tries to avoid talking to Juanita, and she now adopts an indifferent attitude: Juanita can "make the Ocha" or "leave," but she will not get her money returned. The woman's response to Juanita's desire to retrieve her money is developed by the use of syntactic parallelism. The woman's initial statement is always juxtaposed with a response to it. For example, "He give me the money" establishes the situation and "I'm not going to give it to you" refers to the woman's position on the matter. This pattern is repeated throughout the woman's response.

Juanita returns home in scene 9. She wants to argue with her husband about what he had done, but she changes her mind in midsentence, revealing the reasoning she followed to support her decision in her aside. Syntactic parallelism is used again when the woman rejects the clothing Juanita purchased. Juanita's repetition of "you know" and "I don't" reveals her frustration. The scene opens with her interacting with her husband, but it closes with her aside that reveals that she too considers the ceremony a last resort. The confrontation between Juanita and the lady continues in scenes 10 to 12. Juanita uses asides to reveal her feelings of anger.

The submissive exterior that Juanita displays to *madrina* disappears when she returns home to her husband in scene 13. Her husband's action of giving *madrina* the money has set in motion Juanita's current troubles. He is not going through the anxiety over the uncertainty of the initiation, and he is not involved in the power struggle that Juanita is experiencing. Juanita uses the simile of the Chihuahua to emphasize her point symbolically. The husband is given only three short lines, but his constructed dialogue provides comic relief, for Juanita depicts him in a swaggering manner.

The climax of Juanita's narrative occurs when the group arrives in Miami in scene 14. Watching the events that she did not understand finally caused Juanita to confront her fears and talk to *madrina* about them. Initially, *madrina* still is authoritarian and dispassionate, but Juanita's sincerity finally causes her to soften. *Madrina* reveals to Juanita that she believes they have similar temperaments, and that Juanita will not be harmed, but rather, her life will be saved. Juanita is reassured, but she is not completely convinced that she is taking the best course of action. Juanita uses repetition to add emphasis, which appears in *madrina's* constructed dialogue at the climax of the story. *Madrina* repeats "you" and then "I" in this section to establish the idea that they are similar personalities who share the same goals.

The ceremony begins on a Friday. Juanita narrates the ceremonial events almost exclusively as images, which I know, from firsthand knowledge, is how they are experienced. She interjects humor into the story when she explains that although the other girl slept on the floor, Juanita did not believe that she would also sleep there. Juanita's chuckling cues my own laughter.

The second day of the ceremony begins with *madrina* having returned to her former authoritarian role, for without any prior discussion, she throws away Juanita's medications. This was of such significance that Juanita forgot to mention that the events occurred the "next morning," until the following paragraph. She refers to images and events in a nonsequential manner. The only coherent segment is her dream. Juanita embeds in her narration the repetitive phrases "I was starving—I was tired—I was DYING." Her use of hyperbole adds emphasis to her description of her state of exhaustion. She also repeats the personal pronoun "I" frequently throughout this section, for although the ceremony involves a group of *santeros,* Juanita's focus is internal. In her dream she repeats the phrase "I was dancing" to give the audience an enhanced sense of her experience in her vision. The scene closes with Juanita indicating that the physical healing had begun with her phrase, "My things don't bother me."

The second day to which Juanita refers actually is the fourth day of the ceremony because that is the day of *itá*. At night, the hospital vision of Yemayá returns, and Juanita pantomimes her actions. The sequence of days becomes unclear at this point because the images take precedence over the concept of time. Section 17 concludes with Juanita requesting of Yemayá to be able to see Oggún, her spiritual father.

The next night Oggún appears in a vision. Once again, Juanita uses the nonverbal nodding of her head to precipitate my involvement. I acknowledge Juanita's silent action by stating what she is doing. Juanita is excited about her visions, and she shares them with *madrina*. When Juanita relates to *madrina* the visitation by Oggún, *Madrina* begins smiling.

The battle of wills begins again, however, in sections 19 and 20, which span the next 2 days. The "water" that Juanita refers to in line 281 is called *omiero*.²⁸ As the *omiero* begins to take effect, Juanita stops eating. She then goes on a hunger strike, and this time it is *madrina* who gives in to Juanita's request.

In section 21 the 7-day *asiento* comes to an end, and Juanita reflects on her experience. The immediate results are that she feels that she is improving physically and that she has learned to respect *madrina*. Juanita explains that she had hoped that they could become friends, but *madrina's* nature was "hard" and "cold."

The conclusion of the story occurs when Juanita returns home. Her husband is surprised that the ceremony made her stronger physically and emotionally. This creates another battle of wills, when her husband demands that she remove her ritual objects. Juanita uses her husband's dialogue to interrupt her after she says "stronger," which emphasizes that her strength actually is the reason for the husband's surprised negative reaction. The husband's metaphoric response, comparing Juanita to the devil, causes us both to laugh, but it is juxtaposed with a serious consequence, because rather than fight, Juanita moves with her belongings to another floor in their home.

Scene 23 is the resolution. Her husband's concern about his own mortality was justified, for in "6 months" he dies. Juanita once again uses metonymy as redundant parallelism, when she refers to her husband's death and subsequent burial. The word "die" is repeated five times, which completes the theme that is first presented in the opening scene. Two other people also die, and Juanita believes that "death" took them instead of her.

Juanita concludes her performance with the coda. Labov (1972) explained that this narrative device connects the time between the conclusion of the story and the present (p. 365). She uses it to briefly point out what this experience has meant to her.

CONCLUSION

In literary terms, Juanita's story fits the classic pattern of the universal hero quest, which Joseph Campbell (1949/1968) delineated in *The Hero With a Thousand Faces*. Juanita is called to her adventure by her chain of repeated illnesses, and the "herald" who arrived to summon her to "mark the dawn of religious illumination" was the goddess Yemayá (p. 51). Michael Taussig (1987) explained that illness often acts as "the call" for folk healers:

> Folk healers and shamans embark on their careers as a way of healing themselves. The resolution of their illness is to become a healer, and their pursuit of this calling is a more or less persistent battle with the forces of illness that lie within them as much as in their patients. It is as if serious illness were a sign of powers awakening and unfolding a new path for them to follow. (p. 447)

The healer is not necessarily alone on this journey.

Campbell (1949/1968) explained that "supernatural aid" is the next phase in the heroic cycle: "The helpful crone and fairy godmother are a familiar feature of European fairy lore. In Christian saints' legends, the role is commonly played by the virgin" (p. 71). Juanita's helpers included the woman who instigated Juanita's search for spiritual counseling and her own husband. *Madrina* acted as her spiritual guide in the initiation process. Juanita next crosses "the first threshold" (Campbell, 1949/1968, p. 77), which is her trip to Miami, her venture into the unknown world of Santería.

The climax of Juanita's story is her ceremonial "death," which Campbell (1949/1968) interprets as "instead of passing outward, beyond the confines of the visible world, the hero goes inward, to be born again" (p. 91). For Juanita, this involved the river baptism, the ritual head shaving, and the animal sacrifice. During the climax of the initiation, Campbell explained, "The hero moves through a dream landscape of curiously fluid, ambiguous forms, where he must survive a series of trials" (p. 97). Instead, in this phase, Juanita experienced dancing and peace in a waking dream, and afterward her actions were given the approval of the deities Yemayá and Oggún.

In the last phase of the journey the hero returns with the "life-transmuting trophy" for "renewing the community" (Campbell, 1968, p. 193). Juanita was transformed into a more confident and independent person.

Her physical health was restored, and as was prophesied in her dream, the members of her community have been coming to her ever since to seek her aid in their own healing.

The manner in which Juanita related her story also is important in cognitive terms. She chose the strategy of constructing her narrative in a dialogic format, which serves to heighten the sense of drama. In so doing, she increased the degree of involvement of the audience in her action. Tannen (1989) described the act of constructing dialogue as "active" and "creative," because it "expresses the relationship not between the quoted party and the topic of talk, but rather the quoting party and the audience to whom the quotation is delivered" (p. 109). Therefore, Juanita constructed her dialogue specifically for me, her audience, in regard to a particular context. This was, in part, because of our shared *asiento* experience. Another reason could have been my purpose for visiting her on that day, which was to learn divination. Juanita's narrative was an example of her relating a story to a client as part of her interpreting the pattern of the cowrie shells in the divination communicative event. In effect, she was teaching me the magic of divination through her verbal art.

On a metacognitive level, Juanita's parable demonstrates the importance of divination to determine the nature of a problem, as well as its use in finding a solution. It also establishes her own "spiritual calling," and her quest to come to terms with her faith. On the surface, the conflict appears to be between herself and her godmother, but closer inspection reveals that it is about her internal struggle, which pits her self-reliance against the trust she needs to establish with other people. She will need this in her role as a healer. The ceremony transforms her. It integrates her personality, which allows her to become completely confident in her actions. However, her confidence also has the ramification of putting a strain on her marriage.

On a literal level, her husband's prophecy came true, for she needed to restore her health so she could take care of her children. Also, she needed spiritual stamina so she could help others and simultaneously support her family.

Bauman (1986), whose work includes the study of West Texas oral narratives, explained that "ethnocentric and elitist biases ... privilege the classics of western written literature over oral and vernacular literature" which is considered to be "simple, formless, lacking in artistic quality and complexity ..." (p. 7). This study demonstrates that the oral literature produced in verbal performances, when analyzed from an ethnographic perspective and in terms of ethnopoetics, reveals the creativity of the performer. Juanita's performance of her autobiographic narrative is an example of the techniques she uses as a diviner to create audience involvement. The magic she performs is as much about the artistic manipulation of language, as it is divination and exorcism.

REFERENCES

Bateson, G. (1955/1972). *A theory of play and fantasy. Steps to an ecology of mind: Collected essays in anthropology, psychiatry, evolution, and epistemology.* New York: Ballantine.

Bauman, R. (1977/1984). *Verbal art as performance.* Prospect Heights, IL: Waveland.

Bauman, R. (1986). *Story, performance and event: Contextual studies of oral narrative.* Cambridge, England: Cambridge University Press.

Bauman, R., & Briggs, C. L. (1990). Poetics and performance as critical perspectives on language and social life. *Annual Review of Anthropology 19,* 59–88.

Briggs, C. L. (1986). *Learning how to ask: A sociolinguistic appraisal of the role of the interview in social science research.* Cambridge, England: Cambridge University Press.

Briggs, C. L. (1988). *Competence in performance: The creativity of tradition in* mexicano *verbal art.* Philadelphia: Pennsylvania University Press.

Bruner, J. (1990). *Acts of meaning.* Cambridge, MA: Harvard University Press.

Campbell, J. (1949/1968). *The hero with a thousand faces* (2nd ed.). Princeton: Princeton University Press.

Chicago Fact Book Consortium. (1995). *Local community fact book: Chicago metropolitan area, 1990.* Chicago: Academy Chicago Publishers.

Duranti, A. (1997). *Linguistic anthropology.* Cambridge, England: Cambridge University Press.

Farr, M. (1994). *Enchando relajo:* Verbal art and gender among *mexicanos* in Chicago. In *Cultural performances: Proceedings of the Berkeley Women and Language Conference.* Berkeley, CA: University of California Department of Linguistics.

Farr, M. (2000). *"¡A mi no me manda nadie!:* Individualism and identity in Mexican *ranchero* speech." *Pragmatics 10*(1), 61–85.

Goffman, E. (1974). *Frame analysis: An essay on the organization of experience.* New York: Harper and Row.

González-Wippler, M. (1994). *Santería: The religion* (2nd ed.). St. Paul, MN: Llewellyn.

Gumperz, J. J. (1982). *Discourse strategies.* Cambridge, England: Cambridge University Press.

Hymes, D. (1974). *Foundations in sociolinguistics: An ethnographic approach.* Philadelphia: University of Pennsylvania Press.

Hymes, D. (1981). *"In vain I tried to tell you": Essays in Native American ethnopoetics.* Philadelphia: University of Pennsylvania Press.

Jakobson, R. (1960). "Closing statement: Linguistics and poetics." In T. Sebeok (Ed.), *Style in language* (pp. 350–377). Cambridge, MA: MIT Press.

Labov, W. (1972). *Language in the inner city: Studies in Black English vernacular.* Philadelphia: University of Pennsylvania Press.

Tannen, D. (1989). *Talking voices: Repetition, dialogue, and imagery in conversational discourse.* Cambridge, England: Cambridge University Press.

Taussig, M. (1987). *Shamanism, colonialism, and the wild man.* Chicago: University of Chicago Press.
Tedlock, D. (1983). *The spoken word and the art of interpretation.* Philadelphia: Pennsylvania University Press.

APPENDIX A

Transcription Conventions Key

Bold typeface	Performance
CAPITAL letters	Emphasis/louder than surrounding speech
Colon (:)	Vowel lengthening
Curly braces { }	Nonverbal sounds and paralinguistic features
Parentheses ( )	my commentary
Bracket [	Overlap
Brackets [	No pause
]	
Italics	Spanish and/or Yoruba
Comic Sans font	Juanita's dream sequence during her *asiento*

Pauses

Comma (,)	1 second
Period (.)	End of sentence, 2 seconds
Two periods (..)	2 Seconds
Ellipsis (...)	3 Seconds

ENDNOTES

1. Santería is a religion that originated in West Africa, in the country now known as Nigeria. It was transported to Cuba via the slave trade, where it became syncretized with Catholicism (Gonzalez-Wippler, 1994, pp. 1–3). Today it exists in many areas of the United States, including Chicago.
2. Juanita asked me to use her real name. A *botánica* is a store that sells religious paraphernalia, most of which is used in the practice of the Santería religion. People patronize *botánicas* for the purpose of transacting business that involves the magic of invoking some form of spiritual assistance to help them in solving their

problems. Customers purchase products to develop personal rituals and spells, or they may request a consultation with a professional spiritual intermediary, a *santero* (priest), to aid them in eliciting some type of change in their lives. In any case, people do not go to a *botánica* when everything in their lives is in order, but rather, when, metaphorically speaking, something is broken and it needs to be repaired, or when someone is sick and needs to be healed.

3. Santería divination (*Dillogún*) is based on the manipulation of 16 cowrie shells. There are 256 possible *odu* (number patterns). There are many stories attached to each *odu*.

4. Godmother.

5. The theoretical framework I used to conduct my study was the ethnography of communication (Hymes, 1974), and I utilized the participant observation technique as part of my methodology to identify communicative events.

6. The Necklaces and The Warriors: Elegguá, Oggún, & Osun.

7. A*siento* literally means a "seat." This refers to the initiation ceremony a person undergoes to become a *santero*, which includes the initiate being possessed or "mounted" by a saint (deity). The ceremony lasts 7 days.

8. I used Tedlock (1983) and Tannen (1989) for transcription conventions, and Bauman (1986) for the utilization of a number system to highlight narrative variation and for segmenting the versions into scenes. Refer to Appendix A: Transcription Conventions Key.

9. Juanita has a very light complexion.

10. Killer.

11. Lines 73–74 are literally what were said on the transcript, but Juanita may have misspoken. It was clear to me as a listener that Juanita had reversed the pronouns, for the teacher–friend was trying to convince Juanita to seek help from the *santera*.

12. Soup tureens that are especially designated to hold ritual objects.

13. *Ocha* is a Hispanicized Yoruba term for *orisha* (saint). "Making the *Ocha*" and "making the saint" are synonymous; they both refer to the *asiento* ceremony.

14. The fourth day of the ceremony, when the initiate is given a "life" reading with the shells. It includes, among other things, what the initiate is supposed to do, as well as what should be avoided. My *Itá* lasted seven hours, but they can last much longer.

15. A straw mat used in ceremonies.

16. She is referring to the sacrifice of a pigeon "to" her head. This occurs at the beginning of the ceremony.

17. This is a cleansing ritual.

18. This is the second day of the ceremony.

19. She is making reference to the ritual shaving of her head.

20. Throne.
21. Animal sacrifice.
22. Drums.
23. This is the fourth day of the ceremony.
24. Saint.
25. Devil.
26. I did not bold the coda because Juanita uses it as a transitional device to link her performance with the present.
27. Alessandro Duranti (1997) would consider my limited dialogue with Juanita a form of co-authoring (p. 316). Considering the extent to which Juanita's words make up the text of this article, it also is very much a collaborative effort.
28. *Omiero* is a liquid made by *santeros,* who ritually combine water, traditional plants, and prayer as part of the *asiento* ceremony. The *omiero* is used to cleanse the body, both internally and externally, as well as ritual objects.

Photograph by Jeanne Herrick.

13

What It Means to Speak the Same Language: An Ethnolinguistic Study of Workplace Communication

Jeanne Weiland Herrick

Northwestern University

One need only look around any Chicago workplace—bank, store, factory, hospital, government or business office—to see evidence pointing to the changing face of the Chicago workforce. The faces of Chicago employees are becoming older, more female, and more likely to be of color than they were 50, 20, even 10 years ago. If one listens to the casual conversations that take place daily in these same workplaces, one also is likely to hear, not just more accents, but also languages other than English, especially Spanish.

These changes in Chicago's workplaces reflect those taking place in workplaces throughout the nation: The U.S. workforce is becoming more and more diverse. In addition, since the 1970s, more and more workplaces are or have converted to self-directed work teams or management by teams, making it more crucial than ever that those from different linguistic backgrounds, including those who speak different national languages, find ways to communicate successfully with one another every day.

The question that drove this ethnolinguistic study asked: Just what is happening in Chicago's workplaces as employees, especially Spanish-speaking Latino employees, must communicate across linguistic boundaries? My initial supposition was that those who speak the same national language have an easier time communicating and, therefore, working with each other. My purpose was to identify specific incidences and sources of communication breakdowns across linguistic boundaries, to discover the sources of the communication problems and develop strategies that would help those working with diversifying workforces find ways to facilitate successful, effective communication that would not leave those whose first language is not English clinging to the bottom of the economic ladder.

After 6 months of participant observation at a plastics factory in the greater Chicago area and an analysis that involves more than 100 hours of audiotape interactions and meetings there, I identified very few miscommunications. My question then became "Why is this so?" After further research and analyses, including more than 70 interviews, I concluded that the role of factors other than sharing the same national language have been underconsidered and underanalyzed in the examination of workplace communication.

This article aims to illuminate some of these factors, both social and dialectic, and to explore how they affect what it means to speak the same language. In the investigated workplace, I learned that nonlinguistic variables, particularly social connections and social cohesion, can sometimes be more significant in facilitating communication than sharing the same mother tongue, and that sharing the same mother tongue does not necessarily mean speaking the same language. This, then, is a presentation of that study and its findings.

BACKGROUND

In the late 1980s, in preparation for the new century, the U.S. Department of Labor commissioned the Hudson Institute, a private, nonprofit research organization, to identify and document labor trends. Its report, *Workforce 2000,* predicted that the American workforce would become increasingly female, non-White, nonnative born, and older (U.S. Department of Labor, 1988). All totaled, the Hudson Report predicted that women, non-Whites, and immigrants would account for roughly 83% of the new additions to the workforce by the year 2000, whereas these groups had comprised only 50% of new entrants to the American workforce in the 1980s (United States Department of Labor, 1988).

The U.S. 2000 Census confirmed these predictions. According to this census, 12.5% of those residing in the United States identified themselves as Latino, regardless of race (Grieco & Cassidy, 2001, p. 3). From 1990 to 2000, the U.S. Latino population increased by 13 million, or a whopping 58% (p. 78). This high rate of increase is attributed to both high birth rates and immigration. In 2000, Latinos accounted for almost as many employees in the United States as African Americans, with Latinos representing 10.9% and African Americans 11.3 % of the total workforce (U.S. Labor Bureau of Labor Statistics, Table 10, Employed Persons by Occupation, Race, Hispanic or Latino Ethnicity, and Sex). In the state of Illinois and the metropolitan Chicago area, approximately 25% of those employed are Latino (Illinois Department of Labor, p. 13).

Furthermore, according to the Hudson Institute, the largest percentage of new entrants to the U.S. workforce will be immigrants, especially Latino immigrants.[1] Non-Hispanic Whites in the workforce declined from 80% to 76% in the 1980s, and *Workforce 2020,* the Hudson Institute 1998 update of its report, predicts that this trend will to continue, with non-Hispanic Whites accounting for only 64.3% of the workforce by the year 2020 (Judy & D'Amico, 1997). Hispanics, who accounted for only 9% of the population in 1990, are expected nearly to double by 2020, reaching 16% of the population, thus replacing African Americans as the largest minority group in the United States. In fact, Latinos replaced African Americans as the largest minority ahead of schedule in July 2003 (El Nasser, 2003, p. A1). Moreover, the Hudson Institute's report points out that these increases in the Hispanic population will be disproportionately higher in geographic areas such as California and the Southwest and in cities, such as Chicago, where historically there have been larger Hispanic populations.

Chicago's Latino community leaders, policymakers, and politicians alike eagerly awaited the results of the 2000 Census. Recognizing the problems of underreporting that occurred during the 1990 Census (Elias-Olivares & Farr, 1991) and resolving to ensure a more accurate count for purposes of political representation as well as federal, state, and local grants, community leaders and Latino politicians made a concerted effort with the 2000 Census to allay the fears and dispel the confusion of Latino residents.

The growth of the Hispanic population and the anticipated increased accuracy in reporting is expected to show a decided increase in the number of Hispanics who live and work in Chicago and its surrounding area. The early data in from the 2000 census indicate that Chicago's Hispanic population increased by an amazing 38% from 1990 to 2000. One of every four Chicagoans is now Hispanic (Arndorfer, 2001, p.15). Over the past twenty year, the number of manufacturing jobs held by Hispanics has doubled with Hispanics now accounting for 40% of the manufacturing workforce in Chicago and its suburbs (p. 15). In response to these changes in their workforce, many manufacturers are hiring more and more bilingual supervisors and increasing the education and training programs they offer their Hispanic employees (p. 17).

Some areas of Chicago have experienced an even more amazing increase in Latinos. For example, in Chicago's Brighton Park neighborhood, which has been traditionally Polish, the Hispanic population increased from 37.4% in 1990 to 76.6% in 2000. Said Donald McNeeley, President of Chicago Tube, a manufacturer in Brighton Park, as "employees attrition out, there's a very high probability that their jobs will be filled by Hispanics" (Arndorfer, 2001, p. 17).

One of the cities in the Chicago metropolitan area that historically has had a large Latino population is Aurora, one of Chicago's collar counties, Kane County. Aurora has historically been a port of entry for many Latinos, especially those emigrating from Mexico. In both Chicago and Aurora, Mexicans are by far the largest nationality of all the Latino groups, just as they are throughout the United States. For example, in Chicago and its suburbs, the 2000 Census showed 530.4 thousand Mexicans lived in Chicago, with 255.9 thousand in suburban Cook County as compared with the next largest Latino group, Puerto Ricans, who account for only 113 thousand Chicago residents and 17.3 thousand in suburban Cook County (Northeastern Illinois Planning Commission, 14000, p. 1; Northeastern Illinois Planning Commission 031, p. 1). Latinos accounted for 26% of the total population of Chicago alone. Mexicans comprised 18.3% of the city's population, whereas Puerto Ricans and other Latinos represented 3.9% each. What is more significant for the purposes of this study is the finding that 23.3% of Chicago residents speak Spanish at home, and more than half of these report that they speak English "less than very well" (Table DP-2, Chicago, 2002, pp. 1–2).

The same pattern holds true for Aurora, where Mexicans greatly outnumber every other Latino group. In the city of Aurora, Latinos comprise an even larger segment of the population (32.6%) than in Chicago. Once again, most of these Latinos are Mexicans, almost 90%, or 39,351 of the total 46,557 Latinos. Again, the language separation between Latinos and their neighbors is even greater than in Chicago. Almost 35% (34.7 %) of Aurora residents reported that they speak Spanish at home, and almost 30% (29.7 %) admitted that they speak English "less than very well" (Table DP2: Aurora, 1-2).

Most Mexican immigrants come to escape the fate of almost certain poverty in their homeland. Indeed, the opportunity for a better-paying job represents one of the principal reasons why most Mexicans come to the United States, whether they come as undocumented illegal or documented legal aliens, to stay or to return. As ethnographer Ralph Cintron (1997), who has done extensive ethnolinguistic research among Latinos in Aurora, says,

> [If]there were still jobs to be had—if not in Angelstown [Aurora] itself then nearby—and even if they were low paying, they still offered more wages than could be had in Mexico or Puerto Rico. In all my interviews, I have yet to find someone who would choose the wages of their native home to the wages found in Angelstown [Aurora] or the Chicago area. (Cintron, 1997, p. 47).

Therefore, the increase in Latino population in Chicago and the Chicago metropolitan area most likely will mean an increase in the number and percentage of Chicago workers who are Latino, especially Mexican. The most recent information available from the State of Illinois indicates that in 1996 an estimated 406,348 Latinos were employed in the Chicago Metropolitan Statistical Area (url www.lmi.ides.state.il.us). Thus, there is an ongoing and pressing need to better understand what happens when Latinos try to communicate with others in the workplace, including their efforts to communication among themselves.

Cultural Diversity Programs

The recognition of the diversification of the U.S. workforce has led many corporations and businesses to institute what they term "cultural diversity programs." Initial efforts to ease the transition from a supposed culturally homogeneous to a multicultural work environment operated under the rubrics of "managing diversity" or "valuing diversity" (Lynch, 1997, p. 9). Just as the Hudson Institute had speculated, Workforce 2000 gave these efforts new impetus and a sense of urgency. As Frederick R. Lynch (1997), a critic of cultural diversity efforts, reported in *The Diversity Machine: The Drive to Change the "White Male Workplace,"* in response to a growing business' concern, a whole new industry was spawned: cultural diversity training. By 1995, a survey of top Fortune 50 companies showed that 70% of these companies had their own in-house diversity management programs in place, and of the remaining 30%, 8% were in the process of developing such programs, whereas another 8% had scattered programs that targeted specific cultural diversity issues, such as sexual harassment. The October

2000 issue of *Training,* the corporate training industry's premier publication, reported that 60% of all organizations surveyed provided some sort of diversity training (Anonymous, 2000, p. 60).

However, this training is almost exclusively focused on large-scale, culture-wide patterns of behavior, with little or no attention paid to actual communication taking place in work sites. Furthermore, most cultural diversity programs are premised upon two unspoken, and relatively unexamined, assumptions. First, people who share the same language, especially if it is their first language, will be more likely to understand and communicate successfully with one another. Second, the differences that separate and distinguish cultural groups are more significant than any similarities between or among them. This study challenges and refines these assumptions to say—not necessarily and not always. Sometimes variables other than language and national or ethnic origin enable communication across differences, whereas at other times, knowing the same language is not tantamount to understanding. Social factors can play a disruptive role in the ability of those who speak the same language to communicate and work together.

METHODS

The Research Site

Solare Plastics Corporation,[2] a small, injection-molding plastics manufacturer in the far western suburbs of metropolitan Chicago, employs between 400 and 700 people, depending on the season. The direct workforce, those who actually operate the molding machines and assemble the components into finished products, then package and ship them, is 98% Latino—predominantly Mexican—whereas the majority of the nonproduction support staff is of European American descent, by a couple of generations.

Solare, a family-owned corporation, was spun off from the parent company, Specialty Plastics, owned by Solare owner's father, Guiseppe Colisemo. Guiseppe began Specialty in 1953, purchasing a plastics extruder, which he set up and operated in the back of his brother's butcher shop in the west-side Italian neighborhood on Chicago's Taylor Street. His big break came with the Hula Hoop craze of the 1950s. Specialty was one of five manufacturers in the United States attempting to meet the explosive demand for the "Hoop." With the profits from this venture, Specialty Plastics moved to the suburbs and into the injection-molding plastics business, primarily making plastics component parts, which they supplied to larger manufacturers, such as Sears.

In the mid-1970s, Guiseppe's son, Peter, began to experiment with proprietary products, those owned by the corporation under a trademark or patent and sold to retailers. Hoping to catch the wave of another craze, the horticultural interest in houseplants, Specialty began to produce its own line of plastic flowerpots. From this experience, Peter learned about selling to mass merchants such as WalMart and Sears. In the 1980s, Specialty began to produce extruded plastic lawn edging and molded plastic reels to store garden hoses. These products were so well received that by 1984 Peter purchased a 250,000 square foot building in another suburb of Chicago near Aurora, moved 13 molding machines and eight extruders there, and started Solare Plastics Corporation on January 1, 1985.

It was not long after Solare implemented a Quality Leadership Program, moving the organization from the older managerial paradigm of a hierarchical organization to the new, more horizontal, organization of management by teams, that Peter Colisemo recognized the crucial need for a workplace literacy program and classes offering English as a second language (ESL) for Solare's largely Mexican direct workforce. Everyone at Solare, including Peter Colisemo himself, was tested to determine the educational level of his or her math and verbal skills. These tests revealed considerable disparity. Whereas the nonunion employees, most of whom worked in the front office, had a mean reading score of 11.1 and a mean math score of 10.0, the union employees, who worked at the lowest levels in production, had a mean reading score of 3.2 and a mean math score of 3.0. However, the test scores for each category, union and nonunion, were not broken down according to ethnicity or first language. Furthermore, the university that administered the reading and math tests to the union workers conducted these tests in English, making no allowances for lack of or low competency with English. Working with this same local university, Solare obtained both federal and state grants to fund their ESL and workplace literacy programs. These programs have been so successful that in 1995, the Illinois Secretary of State's office, which oversees workplace literacy, selected Solare for the keynote address at the annual Illinois Literacy Council Conference.

Data-Gathering Methods

From August 1, 1995 to January 1, 1996, I spent approximately 36 hours per week, from 6 a.m. to 6 p.m., 3 days per week at Solare. This allowed me to encounter and interact with employees on all three shifts: first shift (7 a.m. to 3 p.m.), second shift (3 p.m. to 11 p.m.) and night shift (11 p.m. to 7 a.m.). Although the production plant operated around the clock, 7 days per week, I limited almost all my time at Solare to the weekdays, because this was the time when management was most comfortable with my visits. Although I wanted to work on the line, union and liability concerns limited my access.

DATA

I facilitated my acceptance into the Solare culture by acting as a scribe and consultant to six teams set up to improve Solare's inventory control. Because so many of the direct workforce was Spanish speaking, more than half of whom spoke little or no English, the need to translate work procedures into Spanish was evident. I worked with a team of four Mexicans gathered from the 6 a.m. ESL class to translate the procedures as written by the inventory control teams. These meetings were audiotaped, and later transcribed and translated.

Intraethnic Confusion

The following excerpt is a transcript derived from one of these Translation Team meetings. At this meeting, three employees—Theresa, Eduardo, and Miguel—are dictating their translations of a procedure to Roberto, who is using my laptop computer and transcribing what they dictate, with his own "editions and corrections." Two of these employees, Theresa and Eduardo, work together daily in the molding department. Although Miguel is the only member of the translation team who works in the extrusion department, he is well known by both Theresa and Eduardo because he has been at Solare for a long time, has been active in the union, and has served as a translator for many of the other Mexicans at Solare. Roberto not only works in a different department than the other three, maintenance; he also works third shift, whereas Eduardo, Theresa, and Miguel all work first shift. Their only contact with Roberto is during the 6 a.m. ESL class, where he is often the class clown, bantering with Miguel in particular. All of these employees were born and raised in Mexico, immigrating to the United States as teenagers or older. Theresa and Eduardo attended school in the United States, middle and high school and community college, respectively. Although Roberto and Miguel have not attended school in the United States, both graduated with professional degrees in accounting from universities in Mexico. (See Appendix A for transcription conventions.)

0016	Eduardo:	*Poner el porta etiquetas en la esquina derecha del gaylord* (Put the label pouch on the right corner of the gaylord [technical term]).
0017	Roberto:	[repeating] *Poner el porta etiquetas en la parte derecha del gaylord* (Put the label pouch on the right corner of the gaylord).
0018	Theresa:	*Va arriba* (It goes up there).
0019	Miguel:	*Poner el porta etiquetas* (Put the label pouch).
0020	Eduardo:	*Parte superior no es lo mismo* (Upper side is not the same).
0021	Jeanne:	Just pick one and move on.
0022	Roberto:	If you are new in this country, you asked what is the gaylord?
0023	Jeanne:	Upper is *"superior or alta?"*
0024	Miguel:	*Poner en el frente del gaylord en la parte superior* (Put on the front of the gaylord on the upper side).
0025	Roberto:	*Tomar el peso del gaylord vacío que se va usar para poner el scrap en cada máquina, **ésto es lo que no me gusta*** (Take the weight of the empty gaylord that will be used to put the scrap in each machine, **this is what I don't like**).
0026		*Poner porta etiquetas en las esquina superior derecha del gaylord esquina superior derecha del gaylord* (Put the label pouch in upper right corner of the gaylord upper right corner of the gaylord).
0027	Eduardo:	*No estas especificando si es derecha o izquierda* (You are not specifying if it is right or left).
0028	Jeanne:	You are going back to step l?
0029	Roberto:	*Poner el porta etiquetas en la esquina superior derecha del gaylord.* (Put the label pouch in the upper right side of the gaylord).
0030	Jeanne:	*Paso 2* (Step 2).
	Eduardo:	*Tomar el gaylord vacío pesado* (Take the empty gaylord weighed).
0031	Theresa:	*Tomar el peso del gaylord vacío* (Take the weight of the empty gaylord).
0032	Roberto:	*Toma el peso del gaylord vacío* ([You] take the weight of the empty gaylord).
0033	Theresa:	// *Tomar* **take** //
	Eduardo:	// *Tomar* **take** //
	Miguel:	// *Tomar* **take** //
	Roberto:	*Toma el peso* "([You] take the weight").
0034	Eduardo:	*TOMAR* **(TAKE)**/
	Jeanne:	The gaylord will be next to the machine
0035	Roberto:	I'm changing this. Take the gaylord empty to the machine

0036	Jeanne:	The empty gaylord that you already weighed?

0037 Roberto: *Tome el gaylord anterior y póngalo junto a la máquina, y preguntar por el sitio correcto* ([You] take the previous gaylord and put it in next to the machine, and ask for the correct place).

0038 Eduardo: **NO, OLVIDALO**

NO, FORGET IT [exasperated]

No le pusiste el gaylord pesado (You didn't put the weighed gaylord).

0039 Roberto: Mention it before the gaylord

Eduardo: *Especifíca bien* (specified well).

0040 Miguel: *Tome el peso del gaylord vacío* ([You] take the weight of the empty gaylord).

Theresa: *Ya está pesado* (It's already weighed).

0041 Eduardo: *Ya está pesado* (It's already weighed).

Roberto: *Tome el gaylord descarado se dice descarado, ésto significa que ya tomaste el peso* ([You] take the *descarado* gaylord. "Descarado" means you already weighed the gaylord).

0042 Jeanne: You are saying that was already explained in the first step?

0043 Eduardo: *Tomar el gaylord vacío (*Take the empty gaylord).

0044 Roberto: [interrupting]

Tomar el gaylord. Tome el gaylord descarado (Take the gaylord. [You] take the descarado gaylord. (3.0) Miguel said to take the weight).

0045 Eduardo: *Tomar es el verbo* ("Take" is the verb).

Miguel: *Pesado* (Weighed).

0046 Eduardo: *Llevar el gaylord ya pesado a la máquina* (Take the already-weighed gaylord to the machine).

0047 Roberto: *Déjame decir el paso, (interrumpiendo) para que me entiendas, necesitas seguir una secuencia sino no sabes*

// (Let me say the step (interrupting) so you can understand me, you need to follow a sequence if not, you do not know) //

0048 Eduardo: *No, no estamos hablando del pasado* (No, we are not talking about the past).

0049 Roberto: You are not speaking about different gaylords, just one. "Take the gaylord before mentioned," I put that

Eduardo: (angrily)// **No te enredes tanto** // // **(Don't confuse yourself so much).** //

0050 "Take the gaylord"

Roberto: [interrupting]

Déjame hablar

"Paso uno—Tome el peso de gaylord vacío que se va usar para poner el scrap en cada máquina. Poner el porta etiqueta en la esquina superior derecha del gaylord."

0051   *"Toma el gaylord anterior y póngalo junto a la máquina en el lugar asignado. **MUY SENCILLO** !! [very excited]. Para que te hace bolas, anterior no creo que nadie tenga problema."*

            (Let me talk).

            "Step one—Take the weighed gaylord to use to put the scrap at the machine. Put the label pouch on the upper right corner of the gaylord"

       "Take the previous gaylord and put it at the assigned place at the press. **VERY SIMPLE** !! [very excited]. Why are you getting all messed up? Before, I don't think anyone had a problem".

0052   Miguel: *En el primero. Cada gaylord está en cada máquina* (At first, every gaylord is at each machine)

0053   Roberto: *Si, pero en su lugar asignado.* (Yes, but in the assigned place).

          Put the gaylord in the machine

          Está muy sencillo (It is very simple).

0054   Eduardo: [very loudly]

          ***VAS ENREDAR A LA GENTE MAS, ESPECIFICA MAS. TE CONFUNDES TU MAS.* (YOU'RE GOING TO CONFUSE THE PEOPLE, BE SPECIFIC. YOU GET MORE CONFUSED).**

0055   Roberto: *"Paso 1—Tome el peso de gaylord vacío que usar para poner el scrap en coda máquina. Poner el porta etiqueta en la esquina superior derecha del gaylord"* ("Step 1—Take the weighed gaylord to use to put the scrap at the machine. Put the Label pouch on the upper right corner of the gaylord").

0056   *Paso 2—Tome el gaylord anterior y póngalo junto a la máquina en el lugar asignado. No hay confusión"* "Step 2—Take the previous gaylord and put it at the assigned place at the press. There is no confusion").

0057   Theresa: *Vamos a traducir lo que está aquí, no añadir* (Let's translate what we have here, not add)

       Miguel: *Tome el gaylord indicado* (Take the assigned gaylord)

0058   Roberto: [interrupting]

          // Vamos a traducirlo lo mejor que se pueda //// (Let's translate the best we can). //

[Jeanne leaves the room at this point]

0059   Roberto: *Yo siento que es así, con el mismo gaylord va a terminar* (I feel that is the way, with the same gaylord is going to finish)

          [All talking at the same time]

0060   Eduardo: *// Es más sencillo, vas a confundir a ia gente, no todos te van entender* //

          // (It is more simple; you're going to confuse the people. Not everyone is going to understand you. //

Roberto:	*// Muy fácil //*
	// (Very easy) //
Miguel:	*// Ponga el gaylord descarado en la máquina indicada.//*
	// (Put the <u>*descarado*</u> gaylord at the assigned press.) //
0061 Roberto:	*Aquí dice, más claro que el agua* (That is what it says, more clear than water).
0062 Theresa:	<u>*Descarado*</u> *no es la palabra correcta* (<u>Descarado</u> is not the correct word).
0063 Roberto:	**¿COMO NO? (WHY NOT?)**
0064 Theresa:	**DESTARADA**, *todo el mundo sabe esa palabra.* (**<u>DESTARADA,</u>** everybody knows that word).
Eduardo:	*// NO //*
	// NO //
Roberto:	*//NO //*
	//NO //
0065 Theresa:	*Usen una palabra sencilla. Estamos diciendo lo mismo.*
	(Use a simple word. We are saying the same thing.)
0066 Miguel:	*Llevar el gaylord ya pesado a la máquina* (Take the already-weighed gaylord to the machine).
0067 Theresa:	*Más claro el agua* (More clear the water)
0068 Roberto:	*Mejor use mencionado*
	(Better use the word <u>*mencionado*</u> [mentioned]).

[All speaking at the same time]

0069 Eduardo:	*//Es lo mismo que pongas anteriormente que gaylord//*
	//It is the same previous gaylord. //
Roberto:	*// ¿COMO? ¿COMO? No entiend. Muy confundida. //*
	// **HOW? HOW?** I don't understand. I'm confused. //
Miguel:	// Llevar el gaylord ya pesado a la máquina //
	// (Take the already weighed gaylord to the press.) //
Theresa:	// Tres estamos de acuerdo, uno desacuerdo. //
	// (Three of us agree, one doesn't.) //
0070 Roberto:	*"Lleva el gaylord vacío ya pesado a la máquina"* ("Take the empty gaylord already weighed to the press").
0071 Miguel:	*"A la máquina indicada"* ("To the assigned press").
0072 Roberto:	*¿Cual indicada?* (Which assigned?)
0073 Theresa:	*Si Eduardo tiene que llevar un gaylord a la máquina uno, él ya sabe que es la uno.* (If Eduardo has to take a gaylord to Press 1, he knows that it is 1).
0074 Eduardo:	*A la máquina, nomás* (Just to the press).

[At this point, Jeanne reenters the room]

Interethnic Understanding

The discord, misunderstanding, and confusion of the previous excerpt contrasts the following excerpt from a meeting of the Production Planning Team. Unlike the Translation Team, which is called together and meets only to serve a specific need, limited in time and duration, this standing team meets every day at 7 a.m. and then again at 1 p.m. The function of this team is to coordinate plans for production with the orders for products. After laying out the work plans for the day at the morning meeting, the team meets again at 1 p.m. to see how the production goals are being met. If the production and assembly of ordered products is ahead or behind schedule, adjustments can be made. Also, if changes in orders have been made during the morning, to accommodate a rush order coming in, for example, adjustments can also be made. A tentative production schedule for the next day is also negotiated and set at the afternoon meeting.

The members of this team are chosen because of their function within the organization, so the same people attend each of these meetings. Consequently, these employees get together twice a day, every day and have done so for years. The production scheduler, Doug Kramer, chairs the meeting. Doug is a White, middle-class European American, about 30 years of age and married, with two young sons. Olga, a middle-aged Romanian woman, gathers and compiles the order information, having already computed the orders that need to be filled for the next couple of days before coming to the meeting. Scott Thompson, another production planner who handles the computing of planning schedules, also attends, representing the front office. Scott, a White, 31-year-old, middle-class European American, grew up in Harvey, Illinois. During the course of my participant observation at Solare, Scott and his wife Karen had their first child, a daughter Michelle. Michelle was born after a problematic pregnancy for Karen and the death of Karen's mother.

As the Manager of Extrusion, Assembly, and Hose Reels, 40-year-old Sean Monahan is the highest-ranking member of this team. The oldest of nine children in an Irish family, Sean is married to a Latina he met at another workplace. Sean and his wife have a 10-year-old son, Kevin, who is the center of Sean's life. His wife has four children from an earlier marriage whom Sean helped to raise, one of whom works in the Purchasing Department at Solare. Sean often gives support, financial and other, to his wife's extended family.

From Production, Juan Guzman, the supervisor of the Hose Reel Department, is a middle-aged *Mexicano* who has worked at Solare for most of the 15 years he has lived in the United States. Juan graduated from college in Mexico and had his own business there. He hopes someday to have a Mexican import–export business and has tried to convince Solare to allow him to set up a Mexican sales territory for their products. So far, he has been unsuccessful. He is married, with four children—a pair of teenagers born and raised in Mexico and two younger children born to the same wife after she and the older children followed Juan and immigrated to the United States some 8 years after he did. He often helps other Mexican employees by translating for them or by taking them to a local attorney when they need legal help.

Hermosa, a 53-year-old Puerto Rican woman who manages the Small Assembly Department, reports directly to Sean Monahan, as does Juan Guzman. Hermosa was born in Puerto Rico but raised in the United States, the youngest of six children. Because she is bilingual, Hermosa often is asked to translate at meetings for Mexicans who have no or limited English ability. She does so willingly and capably, although her Puerto Rican dialect often creates confusion and sometimes she is baffled by the Mexican varieties of Spanish she is asked to translate.

Never married, Hermosa lives with a female partner. She spends her leisure time fishing and enjoying her home computer. Although there has been some speculation that Hermosa is a lesbian, I never heard any gossip or derisive remarks made about her possible sexual orientation. She has worked at Solare almost since the day it first opened its doors. She is well known, well respected, and well loved. Although a lesbian lifestyle would be a violation of the traditional Solare values for appropriate female behavior, no one at Solare seems to care whether Hermosa is a lesbian or not.

This team has two other regular members, both *Mexicanos* from Production. Felix, Hermosa's assistant, 30 years of age, married, with an 8-year-old-daughter, attended school in Mexico. He has limited but improving English skills, and is learning to read books in English. In an interview, he said, "I think education is the key to reach the goals."

The other *Mexicano*, Carlos, married, with a young daughter, is one of Juan's assistants in the Hose Reel Department. Carlos, who also is 30 years of age, has the least formal education of all. He came to the United States to work in the fields of Florida farms. Most of the English he knows, he learned at Solare. He was on Solare's first team that designed a class on safety for all production employees. For the team's formal presentation of its report to top management, he memorized his portion of the presentation in English. This is when he really began to learn and became encouraged to learn English, although he still is reluctant to speak it. I have, however, frequently observed him assist other Latinos whose English skills are more limited than his own.

Each of these production meetings is centered around filling out and updating a preprinted daily production schedule form. Each of the meetings I observed began the same way for me. Carlos would smile at me, and nod his head. When I was lost during the meetings, which was most of the time, particularly at the beginning of my participant observation, he would slyly point out on the form where the team was, then smile and nod again.

After the first 6 months of my on-site observations, this team agreed to continue tape-recording some of their meetings for me, in my absence. This excerpt is a transcript derived from one of those meetings. At the Friday afternoon meeting when this except was audiotaped, the production for the upcoming weekend was being planned.

0001	Doug:	Senor [indicating that Carlos is to begin reading his report]
0002		CWs? Run CWs? (pause) Run out the label?
	Sean:	// Is that what you want, Carlos?//
		Yeaa? Is that okay? [pause] Any other changes?
Doug:		//Make sure [inaudible] //
0003		How about HRCs?
0004	Hermosa:	Let's start
	Sean:	//Let's get a quick number of people—aaaaa—You can do that
0005		in here. Quantity of people. 27 people in Hose Reels, 33 50 on [inaudible]
0006		[Inaudible mumbles]
0007	Hermosa:	No, Gornita's party's next week.
	Doug:	// Yea.//
	Hermosa:	Oh, the Christmas party
0008	Sean:	Have a good vacation [to Juan]
	Juan:	Thank you.
	Sean:	Don't go to Vegas.
0009	Hermosa:	We'll get together after this meeting real fast. Okay?
	Sean:	That sounds very good to me.
0010		Carlos pass one to ... Let uh ... Did you give one to Felix? If you guys want to
		change that [pause] Give one to Hermosa and Juan.
0011		Hermosa, this is something Carlos asked for. It's the same sheet we use
		every day.

0012		But we turned it and tried to fill it all in to give you more room for part numbers
0013		and stuff.
	Hermosa:	//Okay.//
	Sean:	Anyone want to change it let me know but the guys will start using it as they get it.
0014	Scott:	//You want to put lockers and space? // [Scott is asking Olga]
0015	Doug:	Well. Why don't we get small Sunday out of the way. It's gonna be a challenge.
	Scott:	That's why you wanted me here today.
0016		[paper rustling as people get organized]
	Sean:	Need to do a good job with the weekend. Make sure everybody
0017		[pause] Give 'em backups and stuff like that.
0018		[more paper rustling]
0019	Sean:	finish my lunch [softly]
0020–36		*[Carlos reads the number of each product (hose reels) to be assembled over the weekend, while the other members of the team ask for clarification, make adjustments, and write down the figures Carlos reports.]*
0037	Carlos:	0-four-0-sixteen
0038	Hermosa:	The -O-Four-Six-O- what?
	Carlos:	Sixteen
0039	Sean:	I thought he said that just fine.
	Doug:	//Yea, he did.//
0040	Sean:	Why did you say "0-four-six-what"? He said "four-sixteen," and he did it real good.
	Doug:	// He did it real good.//
		[laughter]
0041	Hermosa:	We just haven't been running that.
	Doug:	// We're going to be running that again tonight.//
	Sean:	//We liked it so much //
0042		first time we came back for more. It's like these Oreo cookies.
	Hermosa:	//Okay// [pause] // How many for tonight?//
		[faint laughter]
	Doug:	3 thousand
0043–86		*[Carlos continues to report, until Felix takes the floor to deliver his report at 0063.]*
0087	Felix:	To morning wanted 28 or two pieces. [to Hermosa] you remember this morning you talk to me about these lockers.
0088	Hermosa:	Yaaaah [pause] Two pieces?
	Felix:	Yah
0089	Felix:	

		To morning … aaa … wanted one skid and [pause] and you had [pause] naw.
	Olga:	//Are there any finished to //
0090	Hermosa:	Ya. They had already. I had these people working over here.
	Olga:	//Well, Fox called and
0091		want two pieces to ship, if possible today, and we have one hundred ninety-six generic.
0092		We don't have to do new, just put the labels in and let 'em go.
	Hermosa:	//All right//
		I'll make an announcement to do that. Two of 'em?
0093	Olga:	Mmm. Two.
	Hermosa:	Okay.
	Olga:	Okay.
0094	Hermosa:	Twenty-four fifty-four?
	Olga:	//A-huh.//
	Hermosa:	And that's the tigers.
0095	Olga:	No. Padres.
	Hermosa:	//Padres?//
	Olga:	There are no padres. Pirates.
0096	Hermosa:	[Chuckling] What am I [pause] Pirates.
	Olga:	//Pee rats.//
	Scott:	// Pie rats? [pause] Pee rats.//
0097	Olga:	Pirates?
	Doug:	Pee rats?
	Juan:	Piratas Piratas
	Hermosa:	What the hell are Pee
0098		Piratas Piratas del amor.
	Juan:	Piratas.
	Olga:	That how you say it in Spanish?
0099	Sean:	What that mean? [general chuckling]
	Olga:	[laughing] //It something bad if they laughing.// [laughs]
	Hermosa:	//Pirates of love, ain't it?//
0100	Olga:	Look at them how they get red. [laughs]
	Juan:	Piratas is the guy who stoles love from somebody.
	Sean:	Ooh. Okay.
0100	Olga:	Oh. Okay. Now I know why you say piratas.
	Hermosa:	//There's a song like that except celesta?//
0101	Juan:	Celestile?
0102	Doug:	So you guys know what you are doing this weekend. Kit vayer [technical term]?

0103	Hermosa:	No. Do you know what I'm doing? That's the question. Do you know?
	Doug:	//I think.//
0104	Sean:	So is the list for the kit vayer for the weekend valid then? Or what?
	Doug:	//Ya.//
0105		[Olga quietly is having a side conversation.]
	Sean:	There's a separate meeting going on. Hold on.
	Doug:	[laughs]
0106		That should be plenty. Eighty-six hundred a week. More than the schedule.
0107	Sean:	Who's in charge here?
	Doug:	//Who? From// a Romanian? I don't think so.
0108		[General laughter, especially Olga]
	Sean:	Is everybody done over there?
	Olga:	[chuckling]//Okay.//
	Doug:	He said "Take control." I said, "From the Romanian? **I don't think so.**"
0109	Olga:	[laughing] You bad. "I don't think so."
		[general laughter]

INTERPRETATION OF THE DATA

These two excerpts from transcripts of meetings at Solare stand in sharp contrast to each other. In the first, the members of this team share the same first language, Spanish. Not only that, because they all were born and raised in Mexico, they all speak Mexican varieties of Spanish. In addition, they all work in production. No one on that team comes from the other side of "the Wall," the partition that separates management from production, the so-called blue collars from the white collars.

The second excerpt is from a meeting of a team that is very diverse. Linguistically, the members of this team speak three different national languages: English, Spanish, and Romanian. In addition, because one of the members, Hermosa, is a Puerto Rican raised in the United States, there are also dialectal differences. Her variety of Spanish is Puerto Rican, not Mexican, unlike the other native speakers of Spanish on the team. The members of this team also cut across departments, the organizational hierarchy, and come from both sides of "the Wall."

The relative homogeneity of the all Mexican translation team and the heterogeneity of the production planning team would lead to the expectation that there would be more instances of miscommunication evidenced in the second excerpt, and that these miscommunications could lead to misunderstandings and even team discord. The following analysis of these excerpts shows just the opposite, and offers an explanation why this is so.

Intraethnic Discord and Interethnic Harmony

As stated earlier, my reading of John Gumperz (1982a, 1982b), Deborah Tannen (1993) and other sociolinguists who do conversational analysis led me to anticipate finding and documenting multiple instances of interethnic miscommunication caused by the linguistic and cultural differences extant among Solare employees. I specifically selected the Production Planning Team as a likely site for such miscommunication because of the diversity among its members in national origin, race, ethnicity, gender, class, occupation, organizational position, education, training, citizenship, and language and language variety. After sitting in six of these meeting per week for 6 months, with almost no miscommunications or problems to document, I had to ask myself, "Why not?" What was going on here that offset these differences and enabled communication?

The answer I eventually came to understand is that these employees who have known and worked closely with each other for more than 4 years constitute a social network, and within the context of that network they are motivated and committed to find ways to overcome communicative problems. They use visuals such as the form.

Notice in line 0011, Sean mentions that the form has been changed to accommodate Carlos: "This is something Carlos asked for. It is the same form we use every day, but we turned it and filled it all in and to give us more room for part numbers and stuff." But Sean leaves the change open to the approval and the modifications of others. "Any one want to change it let me know, but the guys will start using that as soon as they get it" (lines 0012–0013).

When misunderstandings do occur, they are quickly repaired, and these miscommunications often become the material of playful banter and jokes. This is consistent with the findings of Richard Cameron and Jessica Williams who did a conversational analysis of interactions in a psychiatric unit of a major metropolitan hospital in the United States. The interactions they studied took place between two male patients, both of whom were native speakers of English, and a Thai female graduate nursing student for whom English was a second language. What Cameron and Williams discovered was that these communicants used a variety of communication strategies to repair conversational breaches to achieve their

communicative goals (Cameron & Williams, 1997, p. 45). When motivated, native and nonnative speakers will do whatever they need to, using
whatever they can, to achieve mutual understanding across linguistic barriers. The production planning team uses a variety of strategies, including,
but not limited to, using forms, writing down words and numbers, repeating, using their hands and facial expressions, and even using props to try to
communicate their meaning to those who do not understand. When a
communicative rupture is perceived, other members of the team, not just
those directly involved in the particular interaction, intervene to enable
communicative goals to be reached.

However, team members use their strategies sensitively. For example,
when Hermosa either does not understand or does not hear Carlos say 16,
both Doug and Sean help her out, and then Sean teases her and at the
same time makes a rhetorical move to let Carlos know his English was understandable. This is clearly a face-saving move by Sean on Carlos' behalf.

0039	Sean:	I thought he said that just fine.
0039	Doug:	Yea, he did.
0040	Sean:	Why did you say "0-4-6-1"? He said "4-16," and he did it real good.
	Doug:	He did it real good.
		[laughter]
0041	Hermosa:	We just haven't been running that.
	Doug:	We're going to be running that again tonight.
	Sean:	We liked it so much
0042		first time we came back for more. It's like these Oreo cookies.
	Hermosa:	Okay How many for tonight?
		[faint laughter]
	Doug:	
3000		

Business researcher Anne Donnellon (1996), after using sociolinguistic
methods to analyze the transcripts of team meetings, maintains that one
can determine whether a team has formed to become a genuine and effective team by what these analyses reveal. She claims that the discourse of
"real teams" is marked by an identification with the team indicated by plural
first person pronouns ("we," "us," "our") (pp. 40–41). Real team demonstrate their interdependence by being comfortable expressing their own
needs ("I need...") or a shared need of the team (see "we need to ...," e.g.,
line 0016). There is a low-power differential; no one speaker dominates the

conversation, and overlaps are cooperative rather than interruptive. Team members with organizational power, in this case Sean, Doug, and Scott, invite or allow others to change the topic, seek opinions, ask questions to get information, and allow themselves to be interrupted (0042).

Furthermore, according to Donnellon (1966), successful teams are socially close (p. 43). They are comfortable joking with and teasing each other (see 0038–0042; 0094–0109). They use colloquialisms and slang, leave out words, and express admiration for each other. They make requests without hedges (e.g. 0009; 0087–0093). One of the stories the Production Team often tells about itself and enjoys recounting is about Olga. One of the products Solare produces is a footlocker decorated with the decals of different sports teams. One day during a production meeting, Olga said they needed to produce 350 "cubes." They were all stumped. What was a "cube?" "You know," Olga kept repeating, "The 'cubes.' The 'cubes.' You all love them." Still they did not understand. Finally she said, "You know. The Chicago 'Cubes.'" With that, they all burst out laughing, realizing she meant the Chicago Cubs. To this day, the team still teases Olga about the "Chicago Cubes." But, as Olga revealed in a personal interview, her perception of her teammates' laughter was that of playful support, not mocking or derision.

Miscommunications such as these are not only quickly repaired; they also do not create problems. Katzenbach and Smith (1993), in *The Wisdom of Teams,* note that the characteristic that marks high-performing teams is their commitment to each other on a personal level.

> What sets apart high-performance teams … is the degree of commitment, particularly how deeply committed the members are to one another. Such commitments go well beyond civility and teamwork. Each genuinely helps the others to achieve both personal and professional goals. Furthermore, such commitments extend beyond company activities and even beyond the life of the team itself. (p. 65)

As I mentioned earlier, during the period of my fieldwork, Scott Thompson's wife had serious medical problems related to her pregnancy. During this time, every meeting began with different members of the team inquiring about her welfare. When her mother died, a woman they had never met, many of them traveled more than 40 miles to attend her wake. They all gave baby gifts to Scott, and genuinely shared in his joy at the healthy birth of a baby daughter. This is just one example of the caring I saw regularly exhibited among these team members, as well as among many of Solare's other employees.

I had expected that the Procedure Translation Team would have the greater harmony because of their shared language and ethnicity. However, this was the most openly rancorous team I observed during my fieldwork. If the rancor had ever been resolved and team had ever formally agreed upon working processes, I would have considered that this team was merely going through the "storming" stage, in which team members encounter and resolve conflicts to establish a workable consensus, as almost all teams do before they are able to perform effectively. However, this team never resolved their conflict and remained a site of verbal combat throughout the entire translation project.

During the course of our translation meetings, two points of view were taken up by these four. Roberto and Miguel argued that the words and phrases suggested by Theresa and Eduardo were "wrong," not the correct words. They argued that the words' meanings differed from the meanings intended by the teams who wrote the procedures. Theresa and Eduardo argued that the people "on the floor" would not be able to understand the words Roberto and Miguel were using, words that in their view were also incorrect. In this meeting, overlaps were not cooperative, but the results of frustration and even anger.

I struggled trying to determine just what the dividing line was that separated these two lines of argument. When Roberto and Miguel were out of the room, Theresa and Eduardo would tell me not to listen to them. "They don't know," Theresa would say. "They don't understand how the people talk." When Theresa and Eduardo were out of the room, Roberto and Miguel would tell me that they were "ignorant," "uneducated." "They don't know," Roberto would say. "Don't listen to them."

Besides the division between these two pairs based on education (Roberto and Miguel are both college graduates, whereas Theresa and Eduardo are not), they also are divided by their urban and rural backgrounds. Whereas Roberto is from the city of Guadalajara and Miguel is from Vera Cruz, both Theresa and Eduardo are from rural farming communities. Roberto once told me, "We have hillbillies in Mexico. *Rancheros.* They are ignorant, uneducated. It is not their fault. They are poor. They do not have the money for education." On the other hand, both Eduardo and Theresa claimed that Miguel and Roberto did not understand how most of the Mexicans on the floor talk. Because Roberto and Miguel work in departments (maintenance and extrusion) that isolate them from the majority of the hourly employees, they may not be as familiar as Eduardo and Theresa with both the terms used by the hourly employees and with the hourly workers themselves.

Two other social factors separated Roberto even more from the other three. Roberto had grown up in a wealthy, upper class family around Mexico City and Guadalajara. In an interview, he recounted to me how he was taunted as a child when his family placed him in a public school, bullied, and called a *rico* (a rich kid).

While doing further research in a *maquiladora* in Nogales, Mexico, I discovered another salient difference that further explains the animosity and reaction of the others to Roberto. There is a profound accent difference between *Chilangos* (Mexicans who live in and around Mexico City and in the southern states and cities surrounding that area) and *Nortenos* (Mexicans who live in the more northern states, especially along the border.

The dialectal difference also carries a social significance. *Chilangos* are perceived by others as "supposedly rude, and ill-tempered, and they think the street (and Mexico …) is theirs" (Vila, 2000, p. 40). In *Reinforcing Borders,* Pablo Villa (2000) observed that the appellation *Chilango* is not so much a regional reference as it is "an insulting nickname, that alludes to a small, slippery fish" (p. 23). By contrast, several of my interviewees from the central and southern states of Mexico characterized Nortenos as unsophisticated and inauthentic Mexicans because of the heavy U.S. influence on their lives and ways attributable to the close geographic proximity to the United States.

This lens of regional dialectal and social difference helps us understand further the discord and misunderstanding among these four Mexican employees. Their disagreements and arguments drove home to me just how much the variational differences within even the same national variety of Spanish can affect communication. Although Theresa and Eduardo work together (and sometimes bicker), they know each other and are basically respectful of each other's abilities. They are friends. Other than meeting in the ESL classes, Roberto and Miguel have no social contact with either each other or the other two. These four, although all Mexican immigrants, do not share a social network either at work or at home. Furthermore, their class difference in their country of origin, Mexico, has meant that there have been two different levels of education. Roberto and Miguel have had the opportunity to receive a more advanced education in Mexico, and thus are more likely to know the "correct" variety of standard Mexican Spanish. However, Theresa and Eduardo understand the varieties of Spanish uses by their coworkers on the shop floor, the language variety of "the people," as they refer to it, and they understand that any instructions or procedures must be written in this dialect if they are to be useful to the majority of Solare's employees, who also come from the lower classes in Mexico.

Implications

So what does this mean for cultural diversity programs in the workplace? If intragroup differences are addressed at all, the variations within cultural, ethnic, racial, and gender groups are minimized in favor of emphasizing differences between groups. Although most anthropologists no longer conceive of cultures as neatly bounded units, fixed in homogeneity of beliefs, values, and practices (Goode, 2001), the practitioners of workplace diversity programs, both those internal to organizations and those external who work with organizations as consultants, continue to speak and think of cultures as homogeneous groups, rooted in common and predictable behaviors and loyalties. In other words, they continue to work from an outdated model of cultural essentialism.

As Suzanne Oboler (1995) argues in *Ethnic Labels, Latino Lives: Identity and the Politics of (Re)Presentation in the United States* (1995), this tendency has been particularly true when it comes to Latinos in the United States, whose individual national identities have been conflated and confused by U.S. Census categories. Oboler (1995) points out that the imposition of a unifying label, such as Hispanic or Latino, obscures some very real differences, "cultural, social, ethnic, and racial" (p. 163) that divide members clustered under these homogenizing labels. Says Oboler (1995), "Latin American immigrants in the United States, like people everywhere, are a very complex group whose class and race values, differentiated gender experiences, national differences, and political convictions and beliefs may interfere again and again with construction of group solidarity among themselves" (p. 162). As anthropologist Judith Goode (2001) says, "cultural essentialism by invoking bounded cultures masks possibilities between for changing relationships" (p. 436). I argue that this one-sided emphasis on difference not only distorts how various social and cultural identities play out in the workplace, it also masks potential for constructing alliances and grounding agency across ethnic lines.

Most cultural diversity work done in workplaces discusses the replacement of the dominant Melting Pot metaphor from the earlier 20th century to describe the mixture of ethnic and racial diversity within the United States by metaphors such as "mosaic" or "salad bowl." All of these metaphors, however, deal with a national metaphor, not individual metaphors of identity.

I offer another metaphor for social and cultural identities, that of "kaleidoscopic identities." I argue that this concept of separate identity pieces or subject positions, motile and in constant flux, adjusts according to the specific situation or context in which the individual is temporarily involved. Therefore, differences and similarities are constantly under construction. At any one moment, however, these identities can be caught in a temporary and provisional relation, one that is always subject to change.

Furthermore, I suggest that identity overlaps among employees clear a space for building coalitions that can work to transform workplaces to make them more responsive to the work and life needs of all employees and their families. I contend that a more valid and useful understanding of cultural diversity in workplaces, as well as in other settings, must look at both the centripetal forces that draw people from different cultures and identities together and the centrifugal forces[3] that give rise to divergent identities and cultural memberships that can create problems and cause conflict. Likewise, we must attend to the centrifugal forces of differences in gender, age, immigration status, class, education, and race that differentiate groups and their interests within broad cultural categories, seeing members of cultural groups as situated in multiple, interacting subjectivities, rather than one single overriding one. Only then will we see them as individuals with agency, not passive types who can only be acted upon. Furthermore, we need to ground our macrolevel theorizing and abstractions about multiculturalism at work in more sustained studies investigating the microlevel, everyday practices of actual work sites. Only then will these theories, as compromised as they may be in this postmodern age, have any relevance at all.

REFERENCES

Anonymous. (2000). Industry report 2000: A comprehensive analysis of employer-sponsored training in the United States. *Training: The human side of resources, 37:10*. Minneapolis, MN: Bill Communications.

Arndorfer, J. B. (2001). Labor's changing accent. *Crain's Chicago Business, 1*, 15, 17.

Bakhtin, M. M. (1981). *The dialogic imagination: Four essays by M. M. Bakhtin.* (Translated by C. Emerson and M. Holquist). M. Holquist (Ed.). Austin: University of Texas Press.

Cameron, R., & Williams, J. (1997). Sentence to ten cents: A case study of relevance and communicative success in nonnative–native speaker interactions in a medical setting. *Applied Linguistic, 18*, 4.

Cintron, R. (1989). *The use of oral and written language in the homes of three Mexicano families*. Doctoral dissertation, University of Illinois at Chicago.

Cintron, R. (1997). *Angel's town:* Chero *ways, gang life, and rhetorics of the everyday*. Boston: Beacon.

Donnellon, A. (1996). *Team talk: The power of language in team dynamics*. Boston: Harvard Business School Press.

Elias-Olivares, L., & Farr, M. (1991). *Sociolinguistic analysis of Mexican American patterns of nonresponse to census questionnaires: Final report to the U.S. Census Bureau*. Chicago: University of Illinois at Chicago Press.

El Nasser, H. (2003, July 19). 39 million make Hispanics largest minority group. *USA Today*, pp. A1, A2.

Goode, J. (2001). Teaching against culturist essentialism. In I. Susser & T. C. Patterson (Eds.), *Cultural diversity in the United States: A critical reader* (pp. 434–456). Malden, MA: Blackwell.

Grieco, E. M., & Cassidy, R. C. (2001). *Overview of race and Hispanic origin: Census 2000 brief*. Retrieved July 15, 2004, from http://www.census.gov/prod/2001pubs/c2kbro1-1.pdf

Gumperz, J. (1982a). *Discourse strategies*. New York: Cambridge University Press.

Gumperz, J. (Ed.). (1982b) *Language and social identity*. Cambridge, England: Cambridge University Press.

Illinois Department of Labor. (2004). *The Illinois workforce: Identifying progress of women and minorities*. Retrieved July 15, 2004, from http://www.state.il.us/agency/idol/wm/2004/wmBOOK04.pdf

Judy, R. W., & D'Amico, C. (1997). *Workforce 2020: Work and workers in the 21st century*. Indianapolis, IN: Hudson Institute.

Katzenbach, J. R., & Smith, D. K. (1993). *The wisdom of teams: Creating high-performance organizations*. Boston: Harvard Business School Press.

Lynch, F. R. (1997). *The diversity machine: The drive to change the "white male workplace."* New York: The Free Press.

Northeastern Illinois Planning Commission. (n.d.,a). *Table DP-1. Profile of General Demographic Characteristics 2000: Chicago city, Illinois*. Retrieved July 15, 2004, from http://www.nipc.cog.il.us/GDP4-munis/gdp4_14000.pdf

Northeastern Illinois Planning Commission. (n.d.,b). *Table DP-1. Profile of General Demographic Characteristics 2000: Suburban Cook County*. Retrieved July 15, 2004, from http://www.nipc.cog/il/us/GDP4-counties/gdp4_subcook.pdf

Oboler, S. (1995). *Ethnic labels, Latino lives: Identity and the politics of (re)presentation in the United States*. Minneapolis, MN: University of Minnesota Press.

State of Illinois. (2002a). *Contrasting Illinois labor by gender, race, and ethnicity* [online]. Retrieved September 9, 2002, from www.state.il.us/agency/idol/BOOK02/Chpt502.htm

State of Illinois. (2002b). *Workforce availability information: Cook county*. Illinois Department of Employment Security [online]. Retrieved September 9, 2002, from www.ides.state.il.us

Tannen, D. (Ed.). (1993). *Framing in discourse*. New York: Oxford University Press.

U.S. Department of Commerce. (2001). *Overview of race and Hispanic origin*. United States Census 2000 [online]. Retrieved September 9, 2002, from www.census.gov/main/www/cen2000.html

U.S. Department of Labor. (1988). *Opportunity 2000: Creative affirmative action for a changing workforce*. Washington, DC: U.S. Government Printing Office.

Villa, P. (2000). *Reinforcing borders: Social categories, metaphors, and narrative identities on the U.S. Mexico frontier.* Austin, TX: University of Texas Press.

U.S. Department of Labor Bureau of Labor Statistics. (2001). *Table 10: Employed persons by occupation, race, Hispanic or Latino origin, and sex.* Retrieved July 15, 2004, from http://www.bls.gov/cps/cpsaat10.pdf

APPENDIX A

The following transcription markings were used for the dialogue in this chapter.

- Numbers correspond to counter numbers on the audiotape recorder.
- **Boldface** indicates loud.
- **BOLDFACE IN ALL CAPS** indicates yelling or shouting.
- // indicates an overlap //
- Horizontal placement of utterance indicates where a speaker begins.

ENDNOTES

1. Although the Hudson Institute's update of their study, *Workforce 2020,* published in 1998, emphasizes that their predictions apply only to new entrants to the workforce, not total entrants, as the report has frequently been misconstrued, it still maintains that there will be a slow but steady increase of minorities in the workforce.

2. To respect the confidentiality of all informants, pseudonyms were used for Solare Plastics, the name of its owner and the names of all who work there.

3. Russian language philosopher and literary critic Mikhail Bakhtin claims that all life is moved by two contending, but not opposing, centripetal forces that move to unify and stabilize and centripetal forces that move to disturb unity and differentiate. For Bakhtin, language was the primary and clearer site for observing this struggle. I believe Bakhtin's observation is a useful one to apply to the construction and deconstruction of individual identities and social coalitions.

Afterword

Ralph Cintron

University of Illinois at Chicago

Doesn't every land have its invisible double, its alien shadow that walks at our side the same way each of us walks accompanied by a second "I" we don't know?

—Carlos Fuentes, The Crystal Frontier, 1997, p. 250)

The chapters in this volume cover considerable intellectual space: Some are more sociolinguistic, others more rhetorical; some emphasize writing or literacy, still others orality. Of course, in some fashion or another, all address *performativity,* a term that I use loosely to describe how in daily life specific actions, including language actions, are conscious and unconscious projections—sent, watched, heard, overheard, and so on. (Think here of how gossip—a grand performance to be sure—entails another artful performance, that is, ceaseless, obsessive interpretation by immediate, and not so immediate, parties.)

I intend in this Afterword not to summarize or critique the chapters collected in this volume but rather to say something more about Latino/a Chicago and to speculate, informally, about the sorts of social forces and analytic predicaments that may be emerging and thus impacting the kind of research represented in this book.

I have been watching for some time the emergence of urban theory, the evolution, say, from Henri Lefebvre's (1999) *The Production of Space* to Michel de Certeau's (1988) *The Practice of Everyday Life* to David Harvey's (2000) *Spaces of Hope*. This research trajectory enters Latino Studies in the recent and excellent study of Los Angeles called *Latino Metropolis* by Valle and Torres (2000). Does this distinctly materialist or post-Marxist research tradition have any bearing for *Latino Language and Literacy in Ethnolinguistic Chicago* and, more generally, on similar sociolinguistic research? Take, for instance, Valle and Torres' claim, following the work of Sharon Zukin (1995), that large-scale economic shifts from manufacturing to service have made culture (the consumption of art, food, fashion, music, tourism) the principal business of cities. Consider how many major American cities have seen a recent growth in the number of upscale restaurants specializing in artistic meal presentations that are heavily dependent on Mexican migrant labor. Indeed, in a city like Chicago an INS sweep of just downtown restaurants would probably create a temporary financial crisis for the city. Does this potential threat not suggest silent agreements between the mayor's office, state and federal governments, the restaurant lobby, and undocumented immigrants?

My larger point is that the soaring numbers of Latinos in Chicago, as partially documented at the beginning of Herrick's chapter (chap. 13, this volume), are significantly connected to the service economy. This shift, which has been made abundantly clear by researchers at UIC's Center for Urban Economic Development,[1] represents the new flexible economy marked by low wages, temp work and day labor, just-in-time delivery and production, and limited benefits—to name just a few. In other words, the old economy on which immigration/migration used to depend has over several decades given way to a much riskier economy whose very instability seems suited to and profits from the insecurities of many transnational laborers.

Moreover, the traditional entry ports—which for Mexicans, the fastest growing group, have been Pilsen and Little Village—are giving way to a pattern of more scattered dispersal in both the city and many of the suburbs. In Chicago, for instance, a number of long-standing African American and Anglo political wards are becoming Latino, causing a serious scuffle over redistricting, and in Cicero, a suburb that borders Chicago, a major demographic reordering from "White" to Mexican/Mexican American has characterized the decade of the 1990s. Latinos, then, are at the forefront of spatial, labor, and political changes in greater Chicago. These dimensions are some of the material coordinates that create opportunities and constraints. Taking all of these elements together suggests, to me at least, that urban theory—most particularly the understanding of urban political economy in the context of accelerated globalization—should underpin much of the work of urban ethnographers who wish to study language use and/or rhetorical issues among communities resembling those in *Latino Language and Literacy in Ethnolinguistic Chicago.*

Another way to phrase my argument is to ask the following: how do symbolic dimensions (in this volume, oral and written language use) intersect with material conditions? To what extent is the symbolic inextricably tied to the material? Take the fact, as Ruben Martinez (2001) documents in *Crossing Over: A Mexican Family on the Migrant Trail* and the 2000 national census figures reinforce, that Mexican migration is no longer a *barrio* phenomenon but is also occurring in "Small Town USA." Are these new living and laboring spaces impacting language use and change in new ways? How might sociolinguistic or rhetorical research programs, along the somewhat descriptive lines of *Latino Language and Literacy in Ethnolinguistic Chicago,* adapt to these changes of space, labor, and political life? Was the Hymesian tradition sufficiently materialist to account for these changes? Can its more recent explicit articulation of the ideological be understood as late compensation? To state the obvious, a research program that begins with the supposition that symbolic life is enmeshed in material conditions repeats the Marxist/post-Marxist ideal that any analysis of the superstructure must occur alongside an analysis of the base. But what specifically does this mean for ethnographically grounded sociolinguistic and rhetorical research programs?

Two of Farr's chapters (chaps. 1 and 2, this volume) attempt to answer this question when they link *transnationalism* (a spatial and labor issue) to *hybridization* (a symbolic and cultural issue). This fusion, still mostly embryonic in other chapters of this volume, may be one of the more important future directions for work of this sort. One of the core goals in sociolinguistics from Hymes (1974) on has been delineating the "ways of speaking" of particular groups. But what happens when those groups become transnational, that is, exceedingly mobile and hybrid? It is likely that mobility and hybridity amplify the linguistic repertoire of a group. But how and to what extent? In one sense, pidgin and creole languages are the results of mobility and hybridity staying in place long enough to make a difference (as paradoxical as that might sound). In contrast, trans- nationalism is hybridity and mobility accelerated. That is, the movement of bodies and cultural experiences do not slow down enough to create the sort of stability necessary to enable the formation of pidgin and creole languages. What globalization is about—or so I am hypothesizing—is that language change moves glacially when compared to changes in cultural experiences under accelerated hybridity and mobility. For example, Farr's Mexican networks in the United States may cross borders frequently and thus find themselves back in Mexico for months or weeks at a time. At most these visits change the Spanish of their towns and *ranchos* only slightly; more importantly, the visits help to reinforce and conserve the Spanish the network members speak. In short, under transnationalism the discursive characteristics of *franqueza* remain fairly intact both *here* and *there*.

But we can ask another question: Does the speaking of *franqueza* have any material consequence? Delineating *franqueza's* material bases is precisely, I take it, what Farr is up to in *"A Mi No Me Manda Nadie.…"* Here she attempts to ground the speaking style of *franqueza* as part of a wide-ranging "liberal individualist ideology" that first emerged among lower ranking Spaniards who handled cattle on large haciendas and who were always on the colonizing frontier. Honor, self-reliance, and private property ownership constitute the iconography of the *ranchero* as memorialized in film, music, and folklore. Consider, for example, the *bandidos* and revolutionary figures of the late 19th and early 20th centuries and the *corridos* that were sung about them. Deeply attached to this iconography was classism and racism that denigrated the indigenous and the communitarian economics of the *ejido*. It is through such mechanisms that *rancheros* distinguished themselves from *los campesinos humildes*. Her argument, to which I am highly sympathetic, presumes that material circumstance actively shapes language use and vice versa. That is, a collective history and political economy shape collective desires and convictions, which in turn shape language use. In most sociolinguistic work, these presumptions are not forcefully argued, but the extent to which material conditions can be shown to animate language use strikes me as a bold research agenda that goes much further than noting, say, the dialectical markers of class stratification that marked some of the early work in sociolinguistics.

But how conclusive is this presumption? Is language use definitively wedded to particular material conditions or is it more free-floating? That is, do specific language uses ever fully align themselves to specific sets of material conditions? Strong arguments can be made for either position. For instance, we all judge the class status of members in our speech community by listening to accents and so on. Hence, we implicitly acknowledge that material conditions are linked consistently enough to accentual patterns and bodily gestures, and so we claim to recognize class standing by listening to and observing elements of symbolic life. Indeed, Bourdieu's (Bourdieu & Eagleton, 1999) understanding of *doxa* theorizes that very notion. In other words, material differences are partnered to distinctive discursive and gestural differences—and this is so because not all material conditions are available to everyone. Nevertheless, and despite this obsession of ranking ourselves and others, do we not also agree that the symbolic dimensions of life—*precisely because they are symbolic*—are less tied to the material? Consider, for instance, social conditions that become unstable and/or economically dynamic, and mobility (down or up) becomes the norm. Under these conditions, material life and symbolic life become less tethered to each other and our judgments less reliable.

More to the point, *franqueza* may be part of the linguistic repertoire of the *ranchero*, but, I presume, so are other styles and registers. Similarly, might not *franqueza*—or something that looks a lot like it—belong to other groups whose local histories and political economies differ sharply? If so, why? Would such similarities be due to linguistic exchanges? If such exchanges were geographically impossible, would the similarities be due to similar political economies or structures of history? Or what if no causal linkage is discernible—no linguistic exchange between groups, no shared political economy or history—what then? What I am suggesting is that sociolinguistic and/or rhetorical projects that calibrate the extent to which language use remains simultaneously fixed to and free of material conditions is important.

Let us be clear: It may be difficult to draw clean conclusions about the intersections of symbolic life and material life. Nevertheless, our analyses should not split the two, for material life is the deep context of any symbolic performance. (Take note that I am making a subtle distinction between material life being "causal" as opposed to "contextual." Causal connection may be, in the end, impossible to prove, but the idea of context, which, seemingly, is not held to as high a standard of proof, can still be heralded as forceful and important.) Understanding context, of course, is one of the specialties of sociolinguists and rhetoricians. They keenly observe relationships among speakers, audiences, and occasions. At deeper contextual layers, however, lie matters of hierarchy, desire for power or the management of those who desire power, and so on. But at still deeper layers—particularly for the essays in this volume, even if not always explicated—are patterns of wealth distribution, in short, of political economy. These patterns, though not causal and deterministic, are compelling and bring into being a transnational flow of labor and capital. These are some of the external structures, the deep context to be displayed along with the internal structures of linguistic performance. If the latter occurs without the former, language use becomes detached from its conditioning scenes; when external structures are detached from linguistic performance, they appear merely statistical, incapable of improvisation, individualization, and even transformation.

This last point takes me to still another: Farr's analyses of transnationalism as context for linguistic performance as well as Barajas' analyses of proverb use on both sides of the border point to something quite crucial. That is, the ethnographic fieldsite, that long enduring anthropological reality/trope, has shifted from a geographically conceived place to one that is more discursively conceived. A clearer way to say this is that increasingly as ethnographers chase down the language of their subjects they span geographies, whereas not so long ago geography contained language. Many of the chapters in this volume do not confront this necessity explicitly, but it is becoming unavoidable in the context of a research working group with which I am currently involved in Chicago. To take just one example, the life of the undocumented cannot be adequately understood if the ethnographer sticks only to her subjects as they move about in their private and public lives. Equal attention must be paid to those sites that determine policies regarding the undocumented. I am not talking here merely of examining laws that have been passed regarding the undocumented, but actual fieldwork in those sites where laws are being debated by legislators and lobbied for by, say, Project USA, an anti-immigration lobby group. So, even if one is not crossing nation/state borders but only crossing the borders that frame the many conditions of the undocumented (or whatever group the ethnographer is concentrating on) pursuing the circuitry of power, both those who maintain it and those who are at its mercy, has become increasingly important. Avoiding these sorts of multiply integrated fieldsites risks a sentimentalized vision of marginalized folks struggling within the limits of some sort of anonymous power. Such analyses offer exceedingly thin understandings of the logics and rhetorics of power itself, which means among other things that the paths toward social change become mysterious. Those who wield power, less we forget, make their own brand of common sense, their own rhetorically shaped logic, morality, necessity, and expediency. Ethnographers should want to know these intricacies and not just wear the cloak of social justice, pointing righteously to and decrying the machinations of power that make the marginalized come into being.

Let me reflect further on an issue that relates to claims in the prior paragraph. When talking of power, the term *structure* often summarizes the discussion. Its *natural* opposition is often termed *agency*. In short, structural forces are seen as impeding, determining, or shaping the agency of the marginalized—or, for that matter, all subjects, including you and me. Rather than following that line of reasoning, however, I prefer to articulate the entanglement of structure and agency. In one sense, there are no such things as structural forces, in so far as structures too are the visible performances of subjects (agents). That is, structural forces are the result of a kind of subjectivity that acquires objective shape through rhetorical means. Indeed, so-called structural forces are, at their moment of origin, subjective. They may begin as individually held, subjective motives, but in the process of becoming public laws, policies, and so on, they become collectivized. That is, they represent collective subjectivities and motives. From this line of reasoning, then, we can say that *objective structural forces* represent the rhetorics that emerge from collective subjectivities. Let me provide some clarity with an example: Heads of state around the world are facing problems with immigration. But how they define those problems and construct (or fail to construct) policies are the results of individual motives and the motives of different power blocks; assessments of local laws, histories, and political economies; and assessments of how other states are addressing similar problems. Whatever policies emerge, therefore, constitute that state's temporary immigration structure, which is saturated with motives (subjectivities) that are probably more obscure than clear, even to the actors themselves. The will of the state, then, which has so much power to impede, determine, or shape the subjectivities of people, reveals itself not so much as objective as rhetorically constituted and distinctly subjective in its origins. Similarly, agents, who are too often seen as shaped by or resistant to the dominant structures, are themselves rhetorically constituted. That is, they lack a specific identity that is somehow not in symbiosis with the structures themselves. Structures and agents, therefore, are not so much divided from each other as entangled inside each other.

And this brings us finally to the genius of ethnography, for ethnographies can lay bare the complexity of motives and subjectivities. In this volume, Del Valle (chap. 4), Cohen (chap. 7), Gelb (chap. 12), and especially Colomb (chap. 10) tell us much about the workings of subjectivity. Olmedo (chap. 5), Potowski (chap. 6), and Spicer-Escalante (chap. 8) seem to lean a bit more toward structural analyses—but I may be forcing this particular topos upon those chapters. At any rate, some attention might be placed on Hurtig's chapter (chap. 9) because it offers both a trenchant analysis of the structural as well as a compelling, even moving, depiction of subjectivities becoming increasingly analytic of their "entanglement" in structural forces. Notice, for instance, how she analyzes "parent involvement" programs and the ideology of "equality of opportunity" as "apparatuses" (a conscious use of Althusser, 1999, I presume). The former implies, among other things, that the lower achievement rates of poor children are due to parental deficiency, and the latter claims that education, which is available to all if they are willing to work hard, is the best route to socioeconomic advancement. The subjectivities of the poor willingly cooperate with these structural apparatuses. Indeed, as apparatuses become internalized ideologies, they begin to explain powerfully one's life and its "limitations." But these apparatuses and ideologies may not be able to survive scrutiny in the contexts of literacy classes where the poor themselves reflect on their experiences and those of others. Hurtig's point, then, is that a literacy that fosters rhetorical reconceptualization starts with symbolic change and ends with material change. Even modest material change is significant. And so, we are brought full circle to where this book began—the need, that is, to link symbolic life to material life, to consider linguistic performance as intimately tied to political economy. To my mind, *Latino Language and Literacy in Ethnolinguistic Chicago* has begun this important task.

REFERENCES

Althusser, L. (1999). Ideology and ideological state apparatuses (Notes towards an investigation). In S. Zizek (Ed.), *Mapping ideology* (pp. 100–139). London: Verso.

Bourdieu, P., & Eagleton, T. (1999). Doxa and common life: An interview. In S. Zizek (Ed.), *Mapping Ideology* (pp. 265–277). London: Verso.

de Certeau, M. (1988). *The Practice of Everyday Life* (S. Rendell, Trans.). Berkeley: University of California Press.

Fuentes, C. (1997). *The crystal frontier: A novel in nine stories* (A. MacAdam, Trans.). New York: Farrar, Straus, and Giroux.

Harvey, D. (2000). *Spaces of hope*. Berkeley: University of California Press.

Hymes, D. (1974). Ways of speaking. In R. Bauman & J. Sherzer (Eds.), Explorations in the ethnography of speaking (pp. 433–451). New York: Cambridge University Press.

Lefebvre, H. (1999). *The production of space* (D. Nicholson-Smith, Trans.). Oxford: Blackwell.

Martinez, R. (2001). *Crossing over: A Mexican family on the migrant trail*. New York: Metropolitan Books.

Valle, V., & Torres, R. (2000). *Latino metropolis*. Minneapolis: University of Minnesota Press.
Zukin, S. (1995). *The cultures of cities*. Cambridge, MA: Blackwell.

ENDNOTE

1. I am thinking of papers by Nina Martin ("Pushing Down Risk: The Precarious Relationship between Chicago's Low-Wage Labor Market and Social Institutions") and Marc Doussard ("After the Boom: Inequality in the Post-Industrial Chicago Economy"). Both are at the Center for Urban Economic Development at the University of Illinois at Chicago. I am also thinking of another paper by James Lewis and Rob Paral of the Institute for Metropolitan Affairs at Roosevelt University, "Illinois Industries and Their Use of Undocumented Workers: Indications from the Census." All papers were presented at the Conference on Chicago Research and Public Policy: The Changing Face of Metropolitan Chicago on May 13, 2004.

Author Index

Subject Index